CELEBRATE RICHMOND

type Lakeland Fell Terriers, black and tan, and, like many of her kind in those days, she had a very small white blaze on her chest. She was looser in coat than the modern Lakeland Fell, which sports an extremely tight wire-wool coat and a foursquare stance. Even the working terrier show ring does eventually change the look of a breed!

A LETHAL TEAM

All my school holidays were spent with my dog, sometimes in the company of another young friend and his Fell Terrier. I was even allowed to keep a ferret, named Weasel, which added scope to our adventures. Ferret and terrier were best friends, mouthing each other in pretend fights played out on the living room carpet. Outside we formed a lethal team, hunting rabbits and rats – the ferret going to ground and the terrier waiting at the exit hole. Most times, Patsy caught anything Weasel flushed out. Weasel had the annoying habit of turning back into a rabbit hole even if it was empty, but on my command Patsy would unceremoniously drag her out by the tail. Surprisingly, Weasel did not object too strongly to this undignified extraction. I would carry my ferret around in my shirt next to my skin, and I adored her as much as I did my terrier, until one night she was killed by a cat raiding her cage. Cats became the enemy for me and my terrier (although, of course, if cats and terriers are trained up together in a household, they can become friends). My disapproval of the free run given to cats was confirmed by observing the havoc they caused to the local bird population.

These were formative years with the first terrier I could really call mine, and I took for granted many of her skills. If she decided to head home (perhaps because my friends and I had started a game she was not involved in) she could find her way over a distance of several miles. She could seek me out even when I had left home on my bicycle – ignoring my parents' calls, she would streak off, nose to the ground, apparently on the track of the tyres, sometimes finding me playing football in the park, where her obsession with ball-chasing would then wreck our game. When hunting, I just needed to mention the name of the quarry of the day, be it rats, rabbits, mice, or whatever, and she could focus on that animal without distraction.

This inseparable partnership with my terrier lasted until I was sixteen, when I took up rock climbing and mountaineering, becoming totally consumed with the sport which has since influenced my entire life. I left school and went to work with the Forestry Commission, where the hard physical labour of felling trees would build up my fitness. I felt guilty that Patsy was now mostly restricted to sedate walks with my parents, but within a few months my little terrier was dead – another victim of the dreaded automobile. I was devastated; my only consolation was that most of her life had been spent doing what terriers love most: foraging freely in the wilds of the countryside. In the years that followed, my love for, and affinity with, terriers never left me, and I often longed for that unique companionship I had found with my terrier Patsy.

Eighteen years passed, during which time mountaineering had brought me to America. With a house in New Hampshire, I felt settled enough to keep a dog again. Jack Russells had a reputation for being intelligent and good workmanlike terriers, but although there were a few breeders in the USA, their prices seemed high. I waited, and when I was next in England I bought a puppy – a funny little bitch I named Meg, with an odd-shaped short tail, whose apparent pedigree came from the Fourbarrow Hunt. The person who bred her told me it was a 'self-docking' line!

When I later bred Meg to a normal-tailed Jack Russell, half the pups were indeed born with tails that developed naturally to a normal docked length. I quite believed the breeder when she told me that if I bred to another of her 'self-docking' type, the pups would all be born with short tails!

Meg was not what one would call a 'quality' Jack Russell. She had straight legs of medium length and propeller ears, but she had a nice friendly temperament and was a keen hunter, if uncontrollable and scatter-brained.

THE TRADITIONAL JACK RUSSELL

I started to research the breed, collecting all the modern books on working terriers, and then many old nineteenth-century books on the old Fox Terrier. Very soon I realised that the traditional Jack Russell was in fact the Fox Terrier pre-1900; i.e., before the show ring had taken over, increasing its size and length of head. The Reverend John Russell, for whom the breed was named, was one of the top working Fox Terrier breeders of the nineteenth century. However, at this time my interest in the breed was concentrated on temperament and working ability. Judging and showing terriers were still to come. To keep abreast of the goings-on amongst Russell enthusiasts, I joined clubs in both the UK and the USA. From the books, I picked up clues as to the whereabouts of terriermen and successful breeders in the UK. My holidays were spent travelling through Britain, visiting terrier shows and listening to the various opinions of the experienced (and often obsessive) owners – not that they always agreed with each other!

It was on one of these visits in the mid-

The Parson Jack Russell Terrier (right), and the short-legged Jack Russell, both bred in the UK.

Photo: Sheila Atter.

It is an education to watch Jack Russells interacting.

Photo: Sheila Atter.

1970s that I met Eddie Chapman. Eddie had but four terriers and worked as a terrierman for a Welsh hunt. At that time, his line of working terrier came predominantly from the Exmoor hunt. These dogs were smooth-coated, with deep chestnut markings, and stood around 12 inches (30 centimetres) at the shoulder. He took me out to demonstrate their ability with fox and badger (at that time, terrier work with badgers was not illegal in the UK). 'Impressive' was an understatement – these terriers were, without doubt, some of the finest workers in the country. Also impressive was their soft and friendly behaviour, not only with Eddie but with all others who handled them. I have always maintained that the best-behaved and friendliest terriers, both to people and to other dogs, come from the kennels of the best workers. Eddie bred only one or two litters a year, usually for his own use, and I was lucky enough to arrive on one of those occasions. He sold me Kelly, a truly wonderful terrier whose hunting ability and faithful temperament never faltered throughout the 17 years of her life. She retired to live with my son in Salt Lake City, Utah, far from her birthplace in the Welsh Valleys.

Kelly was the foundation of my successful

The overriding instinct of the Jack Russell – to dig!

Photo: Sheila Atter.

breeding stock of Russells, and over the years I got several other terriers from Chapman. Now, in turn, my interest in Jack Russells took over from climbing. All my energy and time was spent with my terriers as I slowly built up my kennel, mostly by breeding. The house I moved to at around this time had grounds of six acres giving onto open fields, woods and river banks, where the neighbouring farmer kindly allowed me and the pack to roam at will. I built a line of kennels, heated to combat the intense cold of the New Hampshire winters, while up to four of my favourite terriers lived in the house. The rest of my pack got occasional live-in privileges. It is very important to spread affection as evenly as possible to a large pack of terriers, otherwise jealousy can cause aggression problems.

I was very fortunate to have grounds bordering on open country, and every day I released my whole pack – a dozen or more dogs – and we set off en masse to rampage through the woods and fields, encountering all manner of wildlife. This might include groundhog (woodchuck), squirrel, raccoon, skunk, chipmunk, porcupine, beaver, and occasionally, fox. Once there was a brief encounter with an Eastern coyote. The whole pack would supplement their diet by feasting on field mice. Plucking porcupine quills from the terriers' mouths and faces with pliers was quite often one of the less pleasant outcomes of these 'quiet walks', as was washing them in tomato juice after a skunk had sprayed them. Sometimes the terriers would find a raccoon den (racoons often go to ground in the winter months in New Hampshire), and then I would be in for a long wait. Digging was out of the question, with the ground frozen hard as concrete. You could tell it was a raccoon rather than a groundhog or fox because the terriers eventually emerged with much of their head hair gone. When they got too close for comfort, the raccoon gave them

a haircut with its very dextrous front paws.

The Jack Russell's most common quarry in the eastern United States was groundhog – considered a great pest by farmers. Its habit of burrowing, often vertically, in the middle of fields posed a serious threat of broken legs to cattle and horses. Consequently my neighbouring farmer, who was also my vet, soon became a fan of my Russells.

PACK BEHAVIOUR
Having a large pack of Jack Russells and being able to walk them off-lead is an education in dog behaviour that very few people can experience. I feel sure the vast majority of so-called dog behaviour experts never observe really natural behaviour, and I have yet to read convincing explanations of some of the most common kinds of dog behaviour. Let me share some of my own observations, starting with socialisation. I never kennelled more than two dogs to a pen, and every day, when I released them, there would be a general hubbub of greeting, licking, cowering, chastising and so on. For a long time I considered this random, but with more careful day-to-day observation a pattern emerged, hard to see as it was worked through at great speed. To my surprise there was a general greeting system, with each terrier going to the next terrier in the same order each day, with variations in body language depending, I suppose, on status within the group or personal feelings between particular dogs. This behaviour among my Jack Russells followed exactly wolf-pack behaviour I had seen on television nature programmes. Licking and wide-open mouthing of each other's muzzles is one example of submissive, affectionate behaviour. Your dog may try it on you, and you will discover that when a wet tongue finds your nose, the more you push the dog away the more insistent he becomes, fearful his affection is being rejected. Of course, not

The telepathic qualities of the Jack Russell have been noted by many owners.

Photo: John Valentine.

all Russells are lickers – perhaps only the ones with strong pack tendencies or lenient owners!

Another behaviour pattern emerged when, on occasions, I had to leave my large pack of Russells under the care of someone else. All would go well for three or four days, then some members at the upper end of the pecking order, becoming restless, could get uncharacteristically snappy with one another. It is just possible they were planning a new pack leader in place of me. They would also get up to unusual feasts of bad behaviour. Once they decapitated a rather nasty-tempered goose that roamed my grounds. On another occasion, I returned to find that Badger had just eaten one of my large roosters, which had blithely flown into his pen. I have never ever seen a Russell with such an extended stomach, and could hardly believe it, as only a couple of feathers remained in evidence! A flock of about 30 hens had free run of the grounds and, apart from that one instance, my terriers never paid any attention to them.

HOWLING

Another activity owners often try to suppress is howling. Of course it annoys any neighbours within earshot, but I feel it has greater significance to dogs than we realise, and I am sure that it must be some sort of communication – even a complex language. My pack did not howl every day, but had periods of a few weeks when they howled each day, usually in the morning and/or evening. I thought of it then as a form of singing when they were in good spirits and had plenty to talk about! Much later, I returned to Britain with only a dog and a bitch. They slept in the kitchen, and would have a short howling session, usually when I had just gone to bed, but occasionally before I got up. Wondering if it could be significant, I recorded many of these sessions and noted that they were, strangely enough, always started by the bitch, lasted 20 to 35 seconds, and always employed a different pattern of yaps, howls and so on. After a couple of months, the regular howling stopped and thereafter, for some unknown reason, occurred much less often. A lone dog

15

howling makes a very different song from a pair or a group. I feel sure that howling communicates more than we realise, and this is one more example of our lack of understanding of animal behaviour.

TELEPATHY

Another remarkable attribute is the Russell's telepathic ability, which I think is beyond any doubt. My remaining Russell, Badger, has been my constant companion for his full 14 years. When my wife and I prepare to go out, he can always tell if he is coming with us. When he senses he is coming with us he exhibits great excitement, but if our business does not include him he remains in his chair with an expression as if to say "I am not at all pleased, and do not be away too long!" Similarly, I could never understand how my terriers always knew when they were a mile or two from home no matter how prolonged or distant our journey had been, and would start stretching in their boxes, preparing for the return.

TEMPERAMENT

Prospective owners of Jack Russells should realise that terriers, indeed all dogs, show just as many variations in temperament as humans. From the thousands of people we meet in our lives, few become close friends, and finding the right dog for you can be just as difficult. Many owners put up with a completely incompatible dog (the dog has no choice) and simply think this is the way all dogs of that breed behave. Of course, a breeder of Jack Russells will have access to a wide range of temperaments. Companionship was my main interest, breeding came second, and showing terriers last. Successful breeding is, I think, 50 per cent planning and 50 per cent luck. If luck did not play a part, every breeder would produce a Champion – there would be no losers!

BLENCATHRA

After much research and help from various British terriermen, I concluded that line breeding seemed to produce the most

There is enormous variety of temperament within a breed, but for most people, companionship, is the most important quality. Photo: John Valentine.

Blencathra Badger and his litter sister Blencathra Nettle.
Photo courtesy: Paul Ross.

The great Blencathra Badger, aged 14, pictured in the Lake District.   Photo: Paul Ross.

The Jack Russell is still highly prized as a working dog.   Photo: Sheila Atter.

consistent results in terms of type and conformation. I also managed to find several Fox Terrier books dating from the Reverend Russell's time, showing quite clearly the type of terrier he preferred. I based my ideas of type on photos and prints of two dogs. The first was Old Jock, a smooth-coated terrier that the Reverend Russell thought one of the best he had ever seen and had bred to several of his best bitches; the second was Carlisle Tack, a rough-coated terrier bred out of one of Russell's bitches.

My success at breeding came in 1984 when I put a rough dog, English-bred from successful working and show terriers, to a smooth bitch I had bred from Exmoor stock, a superb little working terrier named Dorset. She had a litter of eight pups of which I kept two – a dog and a bitch. The dog, Badger, had a coat that appeared similar to Old Jock's – a rich, smooth coat that never needed attention and a slightly rougher hair on the face. The bitch, Nettle, had a rough, broken coat. I adopted the kennel name of Blencathra from my local fox hunt in the

English Lake District. Blencathra Badger and Blencathra Nettle commenced an illustrious career that will be difficult for any future Jack Russells to match. While still in the USA, Badger won 90 first-place ribbons and 11 Best in Shows, and in 1986 was Champion of the Jack Russell Terrier Club of America National Show out of 400 entries, judged by the English judge Derek Hume. In 1987, he was Champion at the Jack Russell Terrier Breeders Association National Show. He also proved his working ability, earning three Field Hunting certificates to grey fox, red fox and ground hog. Badger sired 174 pups in the USA, including the famous TV star 'Wishbone', and later, 79 in the UK.

I returned to England with Badger and his sister Nettle, where they spent six long months in quarantine. When they recovered, both won many ribbons in British terrier hunt shows. Badger, for example, took second Best Dog in the famous Lowther show, judged by Eddie Chapman, and a fourth in the Dog class in the Great Yorkshire show, judged by David Jones. In 1990, the

The adaptable Jack Russell will take on all challenges that come his way.

Photo: Kim James, Badgerwood.

The breed has been propelled into superstar status with the American TV series 'Wishbone'. This is a portrayal of Romeo in 'Rosie, Oh, Rosie, Oh!'

The Jack Russell at his best: Full of life and burning with curiosity.

Photo: Sheila Atter.

Kennel Club of Great Britain recognised the breed and Badger became the first Jack Russell to win Best of Breed (Scottish KC May 1990) at a Kennel Club Championship show, which qualified him for the world-famous Crufts show. In 1991 he became the first Jack Russell to win BoB at Crufts, and his sister Nettle took third place in the Open Bitch class at the same show. Two of his British-born sons, Tithebarn Tally and Tithebarn Bracken, took first and second in the Postgraduate Dog class. At the time of writing, Badger is 14 years old and still in fit condition, walking the mountains of England and Scotland. His litter sister died at 11 years of age.

THE FUTURE
So, what of the future of this breed? It has become extremely popular, not only because of its great personality; the media have done much to promote it in TV advertisements and programmes. Many famous people own them – Charles, Prince of Wales, is one. While living in the USA, I founded the Jack Russell Terrier Breeders Association (now renamed the Jack Russell Terrier Association of America) to promote the original working type of Fox Terrier, as preferred by the

Reverend Russell, which these days is referred to in Britain as the Parson Jack Russell Terrier. Before I left the USA, we decided to try to work towards recognition of the breed by the American Kennel Club; this was accomplished in 1997. Recognition is, of course, now well established in Britain.

I like to think that whether we show, work or just have a Russell Terrier as our household pet, we all have, deep down, a great love for this animal. I would ask those of you who decide to go into breeding and showing to consider first if you can give all your terriers the lifestyle they deserve, and I beg you not to keep them permanently imprisoned in a run or used as breeding machines. Will you be able to give your terriers walks and exercise in a nice environment? No matter how well-fed and groomed, a Russell without access to fields and woodlands and all the scents of nature, is like making a fish live out of water. Finally, when a terrier's days of work or show are over, try to make sure that his services to you go well-rewarded with a happy retirement, preferably in a family environment. And yes, let him sleep on the bed!

2 THE PARSON'S TERRIER

John Russell was born at Dartmouth in Devon, England, on December 12, 1795. His father, also John and also a clergyman, was at that time Rector of Iddesleigh in North Devon. The family moved to Cornwall when the young John was just 14 months old, but eventually the boy returned to Devon to study – first at Plympton Grammar School, and then, when he was fourteen years old, at Blundell's School at Tiverton.

It was at Blundell's that the young John Russell was first able to indulge in his passion for hunting, and this was to be the first of many occasions when his enthusiasm for hounds and terriers would get him into trouble with the authorities. With the willing help of a fellow pupil, Robert Bovey, Russell gathered together a small scratch pack of Foxhounds, which were kennelled in a shed behind the local smithy. The little pack soon established a reputation for the quality of their sport, and it was inevitable that, before too long, news of their activities would reach the ears of the school's headmaster, Dr Richards, a man renowned for his strictness. The unfortunate Bovey was expelled, but Russell managed to wriggle out of such a severe punishment, and escaped with a beating, even though he was almost certainly the instigator of the activity. Despite the harshness of the regime at Blundell's, Russell

retained a great loyalty to his old school and was to return regularly to functions held there when he grew older.

OXFORD

In 1814 John Russell left his home county for the University at Oxford. By all accounts he was not a great academic, but he managed to secure a Scholarship to Exeter College which was worth £30 a year for four years and which helped to pay his fees. His family, although well established and very well connected in Devon society, were not rich, and throughout his long life lack of money was to be one of Russell's major problems.

For the first two years, at least, of his stay at Oxford he made little attempt to study but indulged to the full in the various sporting pursuits that the University had to offer. He was a tall, athletic young man and he soon became renowned for his prowess in both boxing and wrestling. However, it was hunting which took up most of his time, and which was to remain his passion, virtually to the exclusion of all else, throughout his long life. For someone as interested in the sport as Russell, Oxford was the ideal place to be at that time. Within easy reach of the town were some of the most famous packs of Foxhounds. The present Heythrop country, north-west of the town, was then hunted by the Duke of Beaufort, assisted by Philip

Mindlen Whiskey Fly: Bred by Anne Murray and Lesley Miller.
There are few breeds that have such a well-documented history as the Parson Jack Russell.

Payne as Huntsman and Will Long as whipper-in; to the north, now Bicester and Warden Hill country, Sir Thomas Mostyn had recently taken over from John Warde, regarded by many as the father of fox-hunting. To the south west was the Vale of White Horse Hunt. John Russell could hunt four or five days a week if funds allowed. When he was unable afford a day's hunting he would excuse himself on the grounds that he was prevented by doctor's orders. "I am suffering from tightness of the chest. It's the old complaint and my doctor won't let me hunt at any price." This tightness of the chest was to afflict him on many occasions throughout his life, as he was never to have an income which would support hunting on any sort of lavish scale.

It was in his final year as a student at Oxford that Russell was to acquire his first terrier, a bitch that was to ensure his name became known worldwide. She was called Trump. His friend and biographer, E. W. L. Davies, tells the story eloquently.

"At the end of May, when strolling round Magdalen meadow with Horace in hand, but Beckford in his head, he emerged from the classic shade of Addison's Walk, crossed the Cherwell in a punt, and passed over in the direction of Marston, hoping to devote an hour or two to study in the quiet meads of that hamlet, near the charming slopes of Elsfield, or in the deeper and more secluded haunts of Shotover Wood. Before he had reached Marston, a milkman met him with a terrier – such an animal as Russell had yet only seen in his dreams; he halted, as Actaeon might have done when he caught sight of Diana disporting in her bath; but unlike that ill-fated hunter, he never budged from the spot till he had won the prize and secured it for his own. She was called Trump, and became the progenitress of that famous race of terriers which, from that day to the present, have been associated with Russell's name at home and abroad."

It is interesting to speculate as to whether this was purely a chance meeting. Russell was certainly impetuous on many occasions, but

even at that young age (and especially bearing in mind his continual state of financial embarrassment), would he really have bought a terrier of totally unknown breeding on first sight? It is tempting to believe that he was well aware that the milkman would be in that vicinity – certainly the words 'a milkman met him with a terrier' could be taken to mean that the encounter was prearranged! More than fifty years later, Hugh Dalziel, a well-known Fox Terrier authority, tried to find out more about the milkman from Marston and his terriers. He discovered little, not even a name, but did ascertain that the man had a very good reputation for the type of terrier that he bred.

THE YOUNG CURATE

Russell was soon ordained and became Curate at George Nympton in Devon. His stipend was just £60 a year. The parish consisted of around 50 houses and 240 people. Soon afterwards he was persuaded to add the Curacy of the neighbouring parish of South Molton to his duties, although with no increase to his meagre income. Another 2,700 people came into his care. From the start he was a conscientious parish priest, but although he devoted much of his not inconsiderable energy to his flock, he always made time to indulge in his passion for hunting.

'Trump': The Rev. John Russell's first terrier.
Photo courtesy: Sheila Atter.

It was not long before he had gathered together the nucleus of another small pack of hounds. They were kennelled at the home of a parishioner, and for some time he attempted, without success, to hunt otter. Eventually he obtained a hound called Racer, drafted from another pack because he was mute. However, Racer had been entered to otter, and soon the pack were showing good sport. So marked was their success that the sporting journalist Nimrod wrote, in 1820, that the Parson had killed "...the almost incredible number of twenty-five otters in the last two summers, for which he should receive the thanks of the fish."

Hunting otter provided John Russell with sport in the summer, but fox hunting was still his main passion. He hunted frequently with the vicar of the neighbouring parish of Knowstone, the Reverend Jack Froude, whilst he remained at South Molton – a period of some six years. In 1826 he married Miss Penelope Bury, whose parents lived at Swimbridge, and who shared Russell's passion for hunting. The young couple soon moved to Iddesleigh, where John Russell became his father's curate. This was a much less demanding position, and with his wife's help and encouragement, it was not long before a new pack of hounds was gathered together, although the following season they were amalgamated with hounds owned by Arthur Harris. This pack was soon showing great sport over a vast country which stretched from Broadbury to Bodmin.

"With many great rivers between them; and a country abounding in wild open moors, fairly undulated, and holding a grand scent, over which a hound and a horse could travel at tip-top pace, while every passage of a run might be seen by the rider."

It was for this type of country that Parson Russell bred his terriers. The hounds had to

cover vast distances at great speed and the terriers were expected to have stamina and intelligence in plenty so that they could work out their best route to keep in touch with the pack and be on hand when they were needed. This type of terrain made enormous demands on his terriers. They trotted behind his horse to the Meet, ran with hounds all day, dealt with their fox when necessary, and then trotted home at the end of the day. Occasionally Russell would put a tired or injured terrier across his saddle as he hacked home at night. Davies' account gives an idea of the challenge that they faced.

"Russell's country is technically known as a hollow one; that is a country in which rocky fastnesses and earths, excavated by badgers, abound in every direction. Consequently, on every hunting day a terrier or two invariably accompanied him to the field; and certainly no general ever depended with more trust on the services of an aide-de-camp than he on those of his terriers. If in chase they could not always live with the pack, they still stuck to the line, and were sure to be there or thereabouts when they were wanted, if the hounds threw up for even a minute.

"I like them to throw their tongue freely when face to face with their enemy", said Russell one day, as he stood listening to his famous dog Tip, marking energetically in a long drain some six feet below the surface; "you know then where they are, and what they're about."

Entered early, and only at fox, Russell's terriers were as steady from riot as the staunchest of his hounds; so that, running together with them, and never passing over an earth without drawing it, they gave a fox, whether above ground or below it, but a poor chance of not being found, either by one or the other. A squeak from a terrier was the sure signal of a find, and

there was not a hound in the pack that would not fly to it, as eagerly as to Russell's horn, or his own wild and marvellous scream."

HIS OWN PARISH

After six years at Iddesleigh there was yet another change in the Russells' lifestyle, for in 1832 the living of the parish of Swimbridge and Landkey fell vacant. Patron of the living was the Dean of Exeter, who was Penelope Russell's cousin. With 1600 people in the two Parishes and a stipend of just £180 a year (from which the Curate at Landkey had to be paid), this was hardly a well-paid career move, but the prospect of having his own

Vicar of Swymbridge 1832/1880

Rev: John Russell.

The Rev. John Russell.

Photo courtesy: Sheila Atter.

Swimbridge Parish Church: A conscientious parish priest, John Russell served here for 45 years.

parish must have been enticing to John Russell, whilst his wife no doubt relished the idea of no longer living with her parents-in-law. In addition, the young couple were already well-known in the area. They had, after all, been married in the Parish Church, and Penelope's widowed mother still lived at nearby Dennington House.

John Russell and his wife moved to Tordown, high above the village, a long, low house with stables built on the opposite side of the road, and approached by a narrow lane climbing steeply up the hillside. For the first two years of his incumbency at Swimbridge, Russell kept no hounds, although there is every indication that he still kept his strain of terriers. However, in 1834 Harry Fellowes, Master of the Vine Hunt, arranged for six-and-a-half couple of his

hounds to be presented to the Parson. He was overjoyed.

"There they stood alone in my kennel – the greatest beauties my eye had ever rested on – looking up into my face so winningly, as much as to say, "Only give us a trial, and we'll not disappoint you", that I mentally determined to keep the lot and go to work again."

Soon the pack of Foxhounds were kennelled at Tordown, although in truth their keep was way beyond his means. However, Penelope Russell was aware of her husband's dilemma, and it was she who persuaded him to keep the hounds as he was always so miserable without them. Russell's pack remained in existence for 37 years, until 1871. The Parson soon developed an enviable reputation as a skilled breeder, and his hounds were of such quality that they were welcomed in any pack.

John Russell was to stay at Swimbridge for 45 years – virtually all his working life. He was very happy there and proved himself to be a conscientious and devoted parish priest. He was an enthusiastic fund-raiser, and energetically set about raising funds to build a new village school, amongst other projects.

Despite his fame in the hunting field, Russell was a hard working parish priest. His kindly nature and cheerful disposition made him very popular. His parishioners were devoted to him, and even when, on occasion, his hunting activities apparently interfered with parochial responsibilities, they backed him to the hilt. The Bishop was not always happy with the reports of the young clergyman, and matters came to a head when he heard that Russell had postponed a child's funeral in order to go hunting. However, the child's mother declined to make any complaint, so the matter was allowed to rest. His biographer, Davies (also his curate), says: "No man has been more venerated – nay

loved – by the poor than Mr Russell. And with good reason too, for none of them in distress ever appealed to him in vain."

His faith was a simple one, and he felt that religion was something that should be lived each day. His creed was to help those in trouble and to give kindness and charity to those less fortunate than himself. His favourite charity was the North Devon Infirmary, and at the age of 80 he rode through a tremendous thunderstorm to Barnstaple Church where, soaked to the skin, he preached an eloquent sermon appealing for funds for the Infirmary. The collection that day was a record. Russell was in great demand as a preacher, for his imposing stature, his sonorous voice and his impressive delivery brought him continual requests to appear in the pulpit, and if at all possible he always accepted.

He combined with his attributes an excellent sense of humour. On one occasion he visited Haccombe, where the recently

installed harmonium was making extraordinary noises. When the sound died away, Russell climbed into the pulpit and, with a broad smile, gave out his text: "For this relief, much thanks". He raised a great deal of money also for the restoration of his church at Swimbridge, and was to see the building of a new school in the village, endowed with money from his fund-raising efforts.

THE PARSON'S PASSION

If religion and his parish were Russell's life, his hounds and his terriers were his passion. That first terrier, the bitch called Trump, had been bought back in 1819 when he was a student at Oxford University. Although we have no knowledge of the breeding behind Trump, we do at least have a very clear picture of what she looked like. A painting, dated January 20 1820 (just eight months after Russell first bought her) was said by him to be a true likeness of the terrier. By 1878, this painting had come into the possession of the Prince of Wales – perhaps it was a gift from the Parson himself? Davies also gives a description of Trump, and again this was said to be an accurate description by her owner.

"In the first place the colour is white with just a patch of dark tan over each eye and ear, while a similar dot, no larger than a penny piece, marks the root of the tail. The coat, which is thick, close and a trifle wiry, is well calculated to protect the body from wet and cold, but has no affinity with the long, rough jacket of a Scotch Terrier. The legs are straight as arrows, the feet perfect; the loins and conformation of the whole frame indicative of hardihood and endurance; while the size and height of the animal may be compared to that of a vixen fox."

Parson Russell was to establish an enviable reputation for his terriers. Because they were

A typical working terrier of the 19th century.
Photo courtesy: Sheila Atter.

bred always with function in mind, the type stayed consistent. Fox hunting itself was changing, from a careful and deliberate puzzling-out of the scent left by the quarry into a desire for speed and a headlong dash across country. Only in the less fashionable areas such as the South West and the North of England did the old type of hunting continue. The North had its own breeds of terrier – the Lakeland and Border in particular – and it was only in the extreme South West that the white Fox Terrier retained its position. In 1872 the Reverend Thomas Pearce wrote:

"The breed would have died out, I am persuaded, but for the Rev. John Russell, of Dennington, near Barnstaple, North Devon, who has always declared them to be the best of good Terriers, and his opinion carries great weight."

Despite their old-fashioned appearance, Russell's terriers were always in demand and several went as foundation stock to kennels in other parts of the country. The Parson's kennel was modest, for he always had to watch costs, but he had an eye for quality. "Where shall you find any terrier strain, or for that matter any strain of dogs, so honoured and renowned as that of the Devonshire Parson?" asked a contemporary. Russell delighted in telling his visitors of the courage, and above all the intelligence of his terriers. One of the most famous was Tip, who hardly missed a day's hunting for several seasons and never appeared in the least tired, although he occasionally trotted fifteen or twenty miles during the day.

Although he was living in the depths of the Devon countryside, John Russell did not limit his breeding programme by using merely stud dogs that were living locally or were easily obtainable. Davies described Trump as "progenitress of that famous race of terriers" but there is no evidence as to which

dog or, indeed, dogs were used in the foundation of the dynasty. The county of Devon was known at that time for its own strain of white-bodied rough-coated terriers – indeed it is entirely likely that the young Russell was attracted to Trump in the first place because she was fairly similar to the terriers with which he was already familiar. Therefore it would seem entirely probable that she was first bred to a dog that was fairly similar in type to herself, although it has also been suggested that she was at some point mated to a rough-coated black and tan terrier. Later in life, the Parson was to use some of the most famous Fox Terriers of the day on his bitches. Form and function are inextricably linked in a working terrier. A terrier of correct conformation will always have the edge over a badly constructed dog simply because it can cover ground more economically and dig more efficiently. So it is not surprising that John Russell, to whom working ability was always paramount, should seek out the top show winners, although these were, in any case, from a purely working background. A case in point is that of Old Jock, one of the most famous Smooth Fox Terriers of all time. Rawdon Lee wrote of Jock that he was:

"said to be bred by Jack Morgan, who when the dog was pupped some time during 1859, was first whip to the Grove when Tom Day hunted them and Sir Richard Sutton was the Master. I have also heard it stated that Jock was born at Quorn Kennels.

Rawdon Lee stresses the fact that Jock's parents were "huntsman's terriers both of them we may be sure"although little is known of his sire, who was probably Captain Percy Williams' dog, also called Jock. His dam was Grove Pepper. Of her, Thomas Wootton said:

Fox Terrier types enjoyed enormous popularity for many years.

"Jock's dam, Grove Pepper, was left in the kennel by Will Merry the retiring huntsman. The bitch was given to me by Morgan; white in colour with a slight tan mark on her face, about 16lb. She was a wonder, with a hunting coat, and could go the pace and do the trick."

The Parson probably saw Pepper either when she was at the Grove or during her time with Thomas Wootton. Of her son, Jock, he himself wrote that he "never saw a sweeter animal than Jock, so perfect in shape, so much quality. He is as near perfection as we poor mortals are ever allowed to feast our eyes on." Rawdon Lee provides a very detailed description of him.

"In show form Old Jock was just about 18lb weight, standing a little high on his legs, which gave him an appearance of freedom in galloping. His colour was white, with a dun or mixed tan mark on one ear, and a black patch on the stern
at its root. He was not what one would at the present time (1893) call a 'varminty-looking' dog, i.e. one with an unusual appearance of go and fire and gameness in him – he was a little deficient in terrier character. His ribs were well sprung, and his shoulders and neck nicely placed. When in this condition he had the appearance of a rib short; but his hind quarters and loin were strong and in unison with the other parts of his formation. To some modern tastes he would appear a little loaded at the shoulders; his forelegs, feet and stoutness of bone were good, and his stifles strong and well turned. His ears were well placed, neither too large nor too small and he had a nice strong jaw. With increasing years he grew a little full in the cheeks. All round Jock was a symmetrical terrier...Jock, who is said to have run seasons with the Grove Hounds, had his tail cut, but the portion left on was longer than one usually sees at the present day."*

Several of the Parson's terriers were gifted

*Parson Jack Russell type:
Master Broom.*

Photo courtesy: Sheila Atter.

to his friends. In 1879 he sent two pups to Colonel John Anstruther Thompson, who had a remarkable career as Amateur Huntsman of several famous packs of Foxhounds, including the Atherstone, the Pytchley and the Bicester. The letter accompanying the pups was typical of Russell:

"I will send off the two terrier puppies by train to Charleston tomorrow morning and 'hope they will arrive fresh'. Take your choice of them and send on the other to Pat Carnegy with my best wishes to the missus and himself. Please put a few potatoes into the hamper and send it back – not that I want the hamper, but I do the potatoes."

Old Jock was sold for "more than his weight in silver", but John Russell was content with a few potatoes for his valuable puppies!

Another who owned the Parson's terriers was Thomas Henry Pearce who wrote, under the pseudonym Idstone. In *The Dog* (1872) he described Russell's type:

"The best breed are wire-haired. The peculiar texture does not interfere with the profile of the body, though there is a shaggey eyebrow and a pronounced moustache. The eyebrow is the great mark, giving the dog the look of a Bristol merchant. Mr Russell's have a keen jaw; narrow but strong; short, well-set limbs; a long back; small ears; and white is the prevailing colour; but one of the best looking and most serviceable bred by him, and belonging to Lord Poltimore's capital huntsman, Evans, was a pale tortoise shell, mixed with white and grey, a hard-coated, enduring dog, fit for any work, however hard, with a rough jacket, defiant of all weather and resolution (combined with sense enough) to serve him in all difficulties."

And also:

"The old sort was a blunt-headed dog; how Mr Russell has refined them I cannot tell, but refined they are, and easily educated, especially when in the hands of their breeder, whose power over Hound or Terrier has been equalled by few and surpassed by none.

White is the useful as well as the fashionable colour, but a coloured ear or head is not objectionable. The eye generally is small and black, the neck long, the shoulders deep, the form long and low; the tail, about as brushy as a

hound's is carried higher than that of a Terrier's in general. In other respects the points are those of a Foxhound as to body and legs."

It is of interest to note that Pearce assumed that his readers would be completely familiar with the conformation of a Foxhound. Phrases such as 'short limbs', 'long back'and 'the form long and low' are obviously not meant to be taken literally (or the terrier would be more the shape of a Dachshund!) but are used merely in comparison with the overall shape of the Foxhound and the shorter-backed, slightly longer-legged show Fox Terrier.

A RESPECTED OPINION
Probably the first terrier carrying Russell's own breeding to actually appear in the show ring was Pearce's own bitch Venture, shown in 1866 in a class for terriers 'of no definite breed'. The appearance of terriers like her in the show ring brought about a gradual

change of attitude amongst those who, until then, had regarded the Wire Fox Terrier as a very poor relation of the Smooth variety. Edward Ash attributed much of the credit for this change to Parson Russell:

"During the years 1872-80, wire-haired terriers appeared only in small numbers at the shows. The Jack Russell'strain, as they were popularly known, because of keenness and pluck, gradually put an end to the hard-dying prejudice, and brought the wire-haired into better favour. Not surprisingly indeed, for 'Jack Russells'were hard-bitten, hard-working, four-legged, small souls, whose company was a pleasure to all at every time."

John Russell's opinions were well respected in the West Country, and he became an enthusiastic supporter of the newly popular Agricultural and Dog Shows. In 1831 he had been a founder member of the Devon Agricultural Society, and in 1840, of the

Parson Jack Russell type: Oakley Topper.   *Photo courtesy: Sheila Atter.*

29

North Devon Agricultural Association. Societies based at North Molton, Swimbridge and Torrington all received his support. He exhibited both hounds and terriers and achieved a certain amount of success, even though he was an old man and his terriers were regarded as being of an old-fashioned type. He joined the Kennel Club in 1873, the year of its foundation, and remained a member until his death some ten years later. Eventually he was prevailed upon to judge his beloved terriers at the Crystal Palace in 1874 (when he was already nearly eighty). Later that same year he was to travel to Darlington and to Nottingham to judge Fox Terriers. He had certainly judged in the West Country prior to this. Charlie Littleworth, from Wembworthy in North Devon, wrote:

"A bitch I once owned, named Mustard....was by Whitemore's Trick out of Eggesford Fury, who was out of the Rev. J. Russell's Fuss, a most famous one as a worker. She was a hard-coated bitch, and eventually became the property of Mr Wootton, and was stolen from his father's place in Leicestershire. Mustard had taken prizes at the West of England shows, under the well-known and popular sportsman above mentioned, including first prize at Plymouth in 1873."

There is no record of his having judged again after 1874, but given his advancing years and the difficulties of travel at that time, it is perhaps not surprising. Russell's involvement with Agricultural Societies led to him being presented to the Prince of Wales (later King Edward VII) at Plymouth in 1865. His reputation as a hunting man brought him invitations to many of the great houses in the West Country, where he was made welcome. His fame spread farther afield, and in 1873 he spent a week in Norfolk where he again met the Prince. The Prince invited him to a ball at nearby Sandringham House. Russell danced until four in the morning (he was seventy-eight years old!) then caught the early morning train to London. The country Parson must have made an impression on the Prince and Princess, because Russell was invited to Sandringham for Christmas week. His simplicity of speech and manner must have endeared him to the Royal couple. Accustomed to the old-fashioned ways of Devon, he called the Princess 'My dear'– still today a Devonian form of speech – before remembering that his wife had cautioned him against such familiarity. On another occasion he enjoyed his helping of fish so much that, without being asked, sent his plate up for a second helping. The Prince asked him if he liked fish. "Yes, Sir"replied Russell. "I'm very fond of fish and I've sent up my plate a second time; and now I remember that's the very thing my wife charged me on leaving home not to do." After this, far from being offended, the Prince saw to it that Russell always got a second helping of fish.

However, time was taking its toll in Russell's circle. In August 1873 Will Rawle, who had been the Parson's kennelman for more than forty years, had died. It was a sad time for the old man, but worse was to come. Penelope Russell's poor health had prevented her from accompanying her husband on that first visit to Sandringham and she was to die on New Year's Day 1875. The couple had been married for nearly fifty years. Russell's financial state was even more desperate since he had made some unwise investments. Lord Poltimore, who had great respect for the Parson's work in the Church as well as meeting him socially in the hunting field, sought to help the old man out by offering him the living of Black Torrington, a parish still in Devon, but away from the Parson's beloved Exmoor. Russell was torn with doubt. He wrote to his old friend Davies, by now living in retirement in Bath:

"Tell me, my dear old friend, what shall I do about West Torrington? I cannot live on £200 a year which is all I shall have after I have paid a certain annuity for another three or four years. Black Torrington is a clear £500 a year and there is a good house, but then it is neither Tordown nor Exmoor; and by the time I am settled in there, I shall perhaps be called upon to leave it again for Swimbridge churchyard! What shall I do? How can I leave my own people, with whom I have lived in peace and happiness for half a century? It will be a bitter pill to swallow, if it must be taken; but it will be my poverty and not my will that will consent to it."

John Russell bowed to the inevitable and moved into the rectory at Black Torrington in July 1879. He had new stables built for his two hunters and those terriers which did not live in the house. Tragedy was to strike almost immediately, when the building and its occupants were destroyed by fire shortly afterwards. He was lonely and unhappy in his new home, and spent as much time as possible away from it. He continued to hunt with his old enthusiasm, but now was reliant on his friends to provide him with a mount, as his own horses were not replaced after the fire.

However, a smaller parish and freedom, at last, from financial worries meant that he was

John Russell Memorial Window, Swimbridge Parish Church.

Photo: Sheila Atter.

able to indulge his passion to the full. He had reluctantly parted with his foxhounds in 1871. The pack had been in existence for 37 years, and by careful breeding the Parson had produced hounds of great quality. When old age forced him to give them up they went to Henry Villebois, Master of the West Norfolk. Russell was entirely miserable without hounds, and soon a scratch pack of harriers was in residence. These remained until 1882,

Parson John Russell's grave, Swimbridge, Devon.

Photo: Sheila Atter.

when with great reluctance he finally parted with them, entrusting them to his old friend Arthur Harris on condition that "you give an especial account in Bailey's of my dear hounds."Despite his age he spent one November week in the Shires, first attending the Quorn's opening meet, where the hounds were hunted by Tom Firr. On the following day he was out with the Cottesmore, and on Wednesday it was the turn of the Belvoir. On Thursday Russell travelled from Leicester to Bath by train, and on Friday was out with the Beaufort hounds. He travelled home on Friday night, and after spending Saturday with Lord Portsmouth's pack was in his pulpit on Sunday!

In 1882 he again visited the Prince and Princess of Wales at Sandringham, but by the Autumn of that year the old man was beginning to fail. In January 1883 he paid a last visit to his beloved Exmoor, but the end was close. His many friends kept him in touch with the hunting season, and even confined to his bed his passion for the sport remained. Hearing faint 'view-halloas'coming from his bedroom one day, his housekeeper found him hunting a flea among his bedclothes!

John Russell died in his 88th year, on April 28 1883. The churchyard at Swimbridge was packed with more than a thousand people for his funeral. The interior of the church was filled. The Mayor and Town Clerk of Barnstaple, representatives of the North Devon Infirmary, members of the great county families, all came to say their last farewell to a man who was loved and respected throughout the West Country. As the coffin was lowered into the grave, little children, weeping as they filed past, dropped in bunches of wild flowers. Amongst the multitude of wreaths was one from the Prince

and Princess of Wales. Knowing how much John Russell loved the Devon countryside, they sent not a formal tribute but a wreath of cottage-garden flowers.

His obituary, published in the Kennel Gazette, spoke with respect of both the man and of his terriers.

"His journey through life may be looked upon as an odd sort of mixture between the old-fashioned parson, the country gentleman, and the courtier. In his parish he was the adviser and the friend of his flock, at cover-side or at the agricultural meeting he was hearty and well met with everyone, and in the hall of the palace he was polished and affable to a degree...whether in bringing together broken ties, or preaching a charity sermon, he had a way of his own of reaching the heart that few could equal and no one could surpass.

Mr Russell started his strain at Oxford when he was eighteen, so something like seventy years ago; he has his pedigrees that he could trace to from the time he started them. As the oldest Fox-terrier breeder in England Mr Russell's connection with the Kennel Club was an honour to that body."

He was a country clergyman who had worked amongst his parishioners for more than fifty years. He won great renown as an eloquent preacher, always willing to give his services to support good causes; a friend of a future King of England, who visited great houses and mixed with the famous, but a simple man whose religion was very real to him. Yet it is for none of these things that he is remembered today. He left as his permanent memorial the breed that bears his name. So long as there are men who love a game terrier, the name of Parson John Russell will never be forgotten.

3 THE JACK RUSSELL PUPPY

Purchasing a Jack Russell Terrier should be carried out with a great deal of care and planning. The popularity of any breed waxes and wanes with time; however, a puppy should be a commitment for the life of the dog. Keep in mind that Jack Russell Terriers, if well cared-for and loved, can live into their mid to late teens while maintaining a high level of energy and alertness. Because of this breed's zest for life, many an adult dog has been mistaken for an older puppy.

FINDING A BREEDER

Once you have decided that the Jack Russell Terrier is the breed of dog that will best suit your lifestyle, it is then very important to be a careful shopper. One of the best places to start is with your kennel club or national breed club. Through these organisations, you will be able to obtain a list of approved or

Taking on a puppy is a big commitment, and you must think carefully before making your final decision.

Photo: T.M. Strom.

registered breeders. Young puppies well cared-for, and left with their mothers until they are ready to go to their new homes, can be a delightful addition to your family. On the other hand, puppies that have poor care before and after their birth, or are separated from their dams too early, can have problems that last throughout their lifetime. Young puppies need to be raised in clean, caring conditions, with a good-quality diet in order to reach their full potential. Make sure the breeder that you purchase a puppy from has the dog's best interest at heart. If your circumstances change for any reason and you cannot keep your puppy, then a responsible breeder will be willing to take the dog back, or help you to re-home the dog. Responsible breeders will never sell puppies through a pet shop.

Some other alternatives to purchasing a Jack Russell Terrier puppy are to consider adopting a rescue dog or a dog that has been retired from a breeding programme. As this breed's popularity increases there are bound to be the backyard breeders who neither screen their buyers nor care where the dogs end up. Rescue dogs, with a bit of remedial training, love, and understanding, can often make excellent pets and companions. Some breeders will retire a dog from their breeding programme; many of these dogs, because they are older, are more settled, and can provide excellent companionship without quite the energy of the young puppy. Be aware that there will usually be a small fee for adoption with either of the above alternatives.

CHOOSING A PUPPY

MALE OR FEMALE
Over years of fielding inquiries on puppies, it is always interesting to me that people will have the preconceived notion that females are easier to raise than males. This simply is not

Female Jack Russells tend to bond closely with one member of the family.

Photo: Sheila Atter.

The male Jack Russell is easy-going and gets on equally well with all members of the family.

Photo: Sheila Atter.

Hopefully you will be able to see close relatives of the puppies, and this will give you some idea of how they will develop. *Photo: Kim James, Badgerwood.*

true. Actually, both sexes can make equally good pets. With the advent of modern surgical techniques, there is little risk involved in neutering or spaying your dog if it is going to be a pet. Males in this breed do mature quickly, and to have the least amount of 'marking' behaviour both indoors and out, they should be neutered at or just before six months of age.

If it is your desire to show and/or breed your dog, than spaying and neutering may not be an option, unless you are showing in non-conformation events. However, with the decision to show or breed comes a much higher level of responsibility which should be carefully considered. Females in this breed usually come into season twice yearly and will need close watching, along with having to plan more carefully a show schedule. It has been my experience that females are more moody before and after oestrus and they are generally not as co-operative, nor do they

show as well during their seasons. A male, for someone wishing to show, can be an advantage as they are rarely moody, and there are no seasons to work around; however, a mature male will need careful monitoring around other adult males.

Another frequent argument seems to be that females have a softer temperament than males. In this breed I have not found this to be true, indeed quite the opposite. Females will often bond more intensely with one member of the family, where males will generally bond equally with the entire family. For this reason it is my opinion that there is no better pet and companion than a neutered male.

The one area where the sex of the puppy can make a definite difference is in the case of a multiple-dog household. It is very difficult for a first-time or novice dog owner to run a pack of dogs effectively and safely. For that reason I do not recommend more than two

Jack Russells for any pet owner. Bitches tend not to get along consistently well with other bitches of their breed, especially in and around oestrus. However, Russell bitches do tend to get along well with females of a different breed, though even this type of arrangement should be carefully supervised. The same is true for males, as very few intact males will be able to live harmoniously in a household together, though neutering can be helpful. The optimum arrangement, if you want to have two dogs, is to have one of each sex. It is very rare to find a male and female that cannot live together happily.

Whatever your choice, male or female, be aware that often you will have to wait longer for a quality female pup, as some breeders will price their female puppies higher than a comparable male.

Often a prospective puppy buyer will concentrate more on the sex of a puppy, markings or coat type than on the puppy's personality and temperament. Keep in mind this puppy will be your constant companion and friend for his lifetime, so temperament, personality, and trainability should be the very first considerations for any new owner, whether for pet or show.

PET OR SHOW
Most people are usually quite clear about their decision between wanting a pet or a show dog, but many do not fully understand the disadvantages of buying from a pet shop, puppy mill, or backyard breeder. Many of the qualities that careful breeders will choose in their efforts to produce show dogs are also the same qualities you would hope to find in your pet. A Jack Russell Terrier bred for the show ring should be healthy, outgoing, stable in temperament, alert and intelligent. Keep in mind that not every puppy in a litter from two show-quality parents will necessarily grow into a show-quality individual. The pet puppy in a litter may fall short in some small way from being competitive in the show ring; however, most people may not even notice the fault without asking the breeder. The pet puppy has the same parents, the same excellent prenatal care, environment, socialisation and veterinary care as the one the breeder will later take into the show ring.

One of the first questions many breeders will ask someone inquiring about a puppy is whether they are interested in a dog for show, for breeding, or as a pet. A young puppy can have 'show potential' but not necessarily

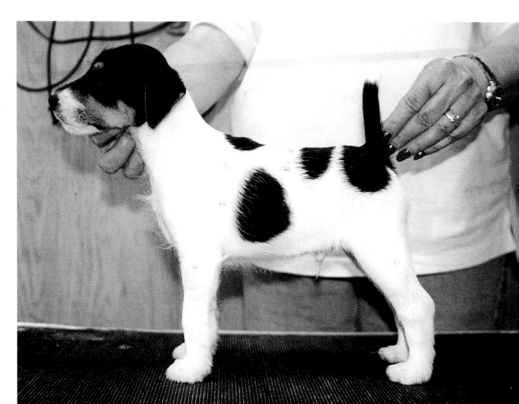

If you are planning to show your Jack Russell, the breeder will help you to assess conformation.

Photo courtesy: Mary Strom, Snow Wind.

Heythrop Blazer (left) is broken-coated; Hoelio Clarinda is smooth-coated.

Photo courtesy: Mary Strom, Snow Wind.

guaranteed show quality. Most experienced breeders will have a very good idea of the quality of a given puppy; however, if you are counting on your pup to be a successful show dog, then you may want to consider purchasing an older puppy or even a young adult. Many breeders who breed for show will keep the best puppies out of a litter, and then run them on to see if they will mature to expectation. These older puppies of around six or seven months of age are often a safer bet as show-quality dogs than the very young puppy.

COAT TYPES

Unlike many of the other terrier breeds, the Jack Russell comes in a wide variety of coat types, colours and markings. However, not all of the coat types, colours and markings found among Jack Russells are those that are correct or appropriate as defined by the Breed Standards.

It was probably best said in *A Memoir of the Reverend John Russell and his Out-of-Door-Life* by the Reverend E. W. L. Davies with the following description of the painting of Trump, the Reverend John Russell's ideal terrier: "The coat, which is thick, dense and a trifle wiry, is well calculated to protect the body from wet and cold, but has no affinity with the long rough jacket of a Scotch Terrier." For all the different coat types that one sees within a group of Jack Russell Terriers, the proper and preferred coat is the one that is described in the Breed Standard as "having a natural appearance: harsh, weatherproof, either broken or smooth." Coats that are soft in texture, curly or woolly are not only a disqualification under the Breed Standards, but they would not be suitable for a dog that has spent his day working in the fields, as the Parson's own terriers did many years ago.

Though none of the Breed Standards mention all three coat types as being acceptable, in reality the smooth, broken, and rough coats are all to be found within the breed. Alys Serrell, an early breeder of Jack Russell Terriers, who was given many of her terriers by the Parson himself, described her

ideal foundation dog, Redcap, as having "the very best coat that could be – short, hard, and dense – with plenty of undergrowth, and a thick skin". Her description is that of what a true smooth coat should be.

Mr Idstone, writing in *The Field* in 1865, gave an excellent description of the broken coat as being "rather long, very hard or harsh, and yet perfectly smooth". This I think would be the way most breeders would describe a true broken coat. A broken-coated dog will appear to be smooth from a distance, and only upon closer examination will you see the longer hair that lies flat against the body. A rough-coated dog will have still longer hair, a dense undercoat, and a scruffy face with more pronounced whiskering and eyebrows. The rough-coated Jack Russell should never have the same abundance of hair as our modern-day Wire Fox Terriers, nor should they require as much stripping or sculpting.

Because of the variety of coat types, and the way in which coat type is inherited, sometimes for even the most experienced breeder it can be difficult to ascertain exactly what a young pup's coat will be. The only guarantee within a litter of pups is when a breeder puts a smooth-coated female to a smooth-coated male, as that will result in an entire litter of smooth-coated pups. Coat type is determined by a polygenic factor, which means that it can be infinitely variable from smooth to rough within a single litter of pups. Many breeders have had the experience of selling a pup as a broken coat only to find six months later that they have really turned out to be rough or more heavily coated. The reverse can be true as well, when placing what they thought to be a smooth-coated pup only to find that as the pup matured, he developed a lightly broken coat. It would not be likely that a young pup which appeared to be smooth would mature to be rough-coated. So if you are particularly interested in a

smooth coat, it is probably best to find a breeder that specialises in that particular coat type.

The one common factor that can be found with all three coat types is the harsh feel and texture of the coat. This harshness should not be mistaken for a 'brillo' type of look, wave, or curl. The texture of the coat is the ingredient that makes these dogs so easy to care for. When a dog comes in muddy from the field or garden, they can be placed in their crate to dry and within an hour or so the dog may well come out with no apparent signs of the day's work or play. The mud and dirt literally fall off the dog because of the wiry texture and natural oils within the coat. So whatever coat an owner may prefer, all three should require little grooming for the pet owner, other than perhaps the normal brushing given when the dogs shed their winter coat in the spring.

MARKINGS
From a historical standpoint, we know that the Parson's ideal dog, as stated in his

Traditionally, markings are confined to the head and the root of the tail.

Photo courtesy: Mary Strom, Snow Wind.

memoirs, written by E. W. L. Davies, was Trump. Davies'description of Trump is as follows: "the colour is white with just a patch of dark tan over each eye and ear, while a similar dot, no larger than a penny piece, marks the root of the tail."

The Parson, because he was a gentleman who loved to hunt, preferred a dog that had less colour, rather than more; a white-bodied terrier in the field was easily spotted. We know from historical accounts of the day that others preferred their terriers to be white-bodied as well. One account, written by the Reverend Pearce (a.k.a. Idstone), described his terrier as "white with a blue black pair of ears, one black eye, and a black nose. A sort of smutty black extends from the nose halfway to the eyes, as though his nose had been smudged." The first Standard, written by Arthur Heinemann, states that the Jack Russell Terrier was to be "white, with acceptable tan, grey, or black at the head and root of the tail. Brindle and liver markings are objectionable." Both the British and American standards written thereafter mention that colour is "preferably confined to the head and root of the tail." The specific language and emphasis regarding where and how much colour a Parson Jack Russell Terrier should have is one of the main points that separate this breed from the Smooth and the Wire Fox Terrier of today.

Because the ancestry of this breed has its roots primarily with breeders interested in hunting and working pursuits for their dogs, it is not hard to understand how they may have bred more for working ability than emphasising colour. Because of the crossing-in of other solid-coloured terriers, such as the Lakeland, Fell, and Border Terriers, breeders of today will 'occasionally have puppies that are heavily marked. Generally these puppies are sold on as pets, as they do not then conform to the Breed Standard of being "predominantly white" . It has been my

experience over the years that in actuality pet owners are generally more attracted to those pups with more colour rather than less. For breeders it is definitely something to give careful thought to, as if all considerations are equal, such as temperament, excellent structure, and working ability, then a pup with a larger amount of colour could have a place in a limited breeding programme.

COLOURS

The acceptable colours for this breed are white combined with tan, black, brown, or lemon colouring. The only disqualification with regards to colour would be of brindle, which is a colour pattern that, in combination with darker hairs, gives the effect of stripes.

The tan colour can have a wide variation within it, as there are lighter and darker shades of tan. Tan can also have a reddish-brown appearance that some pet owners will mistakenly refer to as red and white, which is not listed as an acceptable colour. Lemon can also be mistaken for tan; however, lemon truly has a yellowish cast, and is a paler version of tan with less overall vibrancy. Tricolours can have variations as well; the most common tricolour would be that of predominantly black with points of brown, but it is just as correct for a tricolour to be predominantly brown with points of black.

Within certain breed lines of tricolour Jack Russell Terriers, there is a phenomenon where the deep black that the puppies are born with gradually fades away to more of a brown or tan with a sprinkling of black hairs, or to a lemon-colour with a sprinkling of black hairs. This is caused by the mode of colour inheritance. Usually if you study a young puppy carefully you will see the beginnings of this process, in that there will be a sprinkling of these lighter hairs underneath the darker ones. However, the best way to judge how your puppy's colour

Colour may be tan and white.
Photo: Will Hahn, Eastlake.

Tri-colour (tan, black and white)
is a striking combination.
Photo: Will Hahn, Eastlake.

will develop is to look carefully at the parents.

There can be many surprises with variables such as colour and markings in a given litter of pups. One of those surprises for breeders is the brown- or liver-nose puppy. Since this is a Breed Standard disqualification, puppies with brown or liver noses are normally sold as pets with spay/neuter contracts and limited registration. However, breeders need to be aware that the mode of inheritance for a brown-nose pup is recessive, which means that both parents have to be carriers of the gene for it to be dominant or visible in a litter of pups. For this reason, a mating which results in a brown-nose pup should not be repeated, and careful thought should be given to using any siblings of a brown-nose pup in a breeding programme, as those pups could then be carriers of this unacceptable colour.

TICKING AND PIGMENTATION

Ticking and pigmentation are other ingredients of colour and colour patterns that evoke many questions among breeders and pet owners alike. The definition of ticking is a group of coloured hairs against a white background, forming small spots or 'ticks'of colour. Ticking many times is not readily apparent at birth, although it can continue to develop from puppyhood until the dog is over a year of age. A pup then can actually look as if it will be white-bodied at a young age, and then gradually over the period of a year develop small patches of colour and patterning over the entire coat.

Pigmentation is similar to ticking in that it can expand and develop until a terrier is well over a year of age. Full pigmentation of the nose is regarded as desirable in terriers, which simply means that a dog that has pink spotting on its nose, or a nose that is not fully pigmented with black, is considered to have a fault, and under some Standards, this

Ticking may be discernible on the body coat.   *Photo courtesy: Earl and Nelsine Ellsworth.*

is a disqualification. Eye pigmentation, referring to the colour around the rim of a dog's eye, is often not fully apparent in the young puppy, but again it can gradually fill in by adulthood. Although it is certainly desirable to have full pigmentation around the eye, it is not considered essential in the Breed Standards. It is my personal opinion that full pigmentation or colour around the eye considerably enhances the overall expression of the dog and is therefore something that should be afforded a fair amount of attention in any breeding programme.

PREPARATION

Hopefully, because of your excellent planning and the careful advice from your breeder, you will have already purchased the basics that you will need for your puppy. It is quite common for breeders to provide a list of needs, such as food, type of crate, toys and vitamins that you should have on hand prior to your pup's arrival into his home. New

babies and new puppies have quite a lot in common; both need lots of attention as well as a predictable routine and schedule to feel truly at ease. If you work outside the home you may want to consider taking an extra day and adding that to your weekend or time off so as to have more time to establish that routine; after all, this new puppy is a long-term commitment, and a good start is important.

COLLECTING YOUR PUPPY

One of the best approaches is to pick your puppy up in the morning of the appointed day. This will give you the entire day to get to know your puppy and it provides the puppy with plenty of time to explore and feel comfortable in your house before bedtime.

A few essential items to take along when you pick up your puppy are a bath towel, plastic bags and a roll of paper towels. If your puppy has already been familiarised with a travel crate and/or is already crate-trained, then you can use the towel for him

*The big day arrives when your puppy
is ready to go to his new home.*

Photo: Sheila Atter.

to lie on inside the crate. If the puppy has not been crate-trained, then the best place for him to ride is on a towel in your lap, and in that case you will need to have someone else to drive. It is a good idea to bring along a collar for your puppy; some puppies are just harder to hold onto than others. Most puppies have a comfortable and uneventful ride home; however, there are a few that will become car-sick, so the items above can be very helpful to have at hand.

THE FIRST DAY

You will want to make that first day a rather quiet one. Puppy's first day home is not the time to invite all the neighbours and family over to meet him, nor is it the day to take him to the pet shop to pick out toys. Puppies and babies, when they become over-

stimulated and tired, have a hard time winding down, and it is quite normal for young puppies to take several naps within a day. Never wake a sleeping puppy; because of the speed with which puppies grow they truly need their rest. It is also important to have discussed this fact with your children ahead of puppy's arrival. You will want to make sure your puppy is aware of where all his basic needs are to be found, such as water, feeding dishes, crate and door to the outside.

Any introductions to other animals in the household should be done slowly and gradually, and if there are multiple animals, such as cats, birds, horses etc., then it is best done one at a time. I have found that most Jack Russell puppies do very well with other animals as long as they are raised with them from early puppyhood.

FEEDING

Keep in mind that abrupt changes can be stressful for a puppy, and one of the main signs of stress in a puppy is loss of appetite. It is not unusual for a new puppy to have little interest in food and sometimes water for the first 24 hours. If his loss of appetite continues for longer than this, then you should consult your breeder, and/or veterinarian. Besides food, water consumption is something to watch. Puppies have very sensitive noses and so therefore your water may smell and taste different from what he is used to, particularly if you live a distance away from his birthplace. One of the best ways to get a new puppy to drink the water is by adding a few drops of lemon juice to it. As the puppy gets used to your water you can gradually stop adding the lemon juice; however, many people that routinely travel with their dogs for showing or companionship will keep a bottle of lemon juice handy.

There are about as many brands and ways to feed your dog as there are breeds of dog;

Puppies are very sensitive to changes of diet, so it is best to stick to what the breeder has been feeding – at least in the initial stages.

Photo: Sheila Atter.

it can all be rather confusing. The best advice is your breeder's. Although there are situations where the food your breeder feeds may not be available, you will want to feed a high-quality food. Once you are standing in the pet aisle of any major supermarket or pet food store, the choice can be overwhelming. Below I have included the guidelines established by the American Pet Institute (API) on what to look for in a quality dog food.

- Stay away from foods that state the following on the dog food label: meat and bone meal, or meat by-products.
- Look for meat as the first ingredient, preferably turkey or lamb.
- Consider which grains are used in the product; rice is the most digestible of all grains used in pet foods.
- If corn is listed more than once in the first five ingredients, then try another product.
- API prefers foods that use natural preservatives, such as mixed tocopherols or vitamins C and E, rather than chemical

preservatives such as Ethoxyquin, BHT, or BHA.
- Check the expiration date for freshness.
- Open the bag and smell the food; if it smells rancid, then return it.
- When changing foods, mix one-third to two-thirds of the old food, and then increase the new food gradually every day to prevent gastrointestinal upset.
- Take note of your dog's stools; they should be firm, and have minimal odour.
- Take note of your dog's coat and weight, to ensure a new food suits its individual needs and does not cause major weight loss or gain.
- Store your dog food in a cool dry place in a sealed container.
- Stay away from 'trendy' foods that make unverifiable claims related to companion animal health.
- Always be sure that, in addition to proper nutrition, you supply your dog with fresh water at all times, and adequate exercise.

It will take a few days for your puppy to adapt to the household routine.

Photo: Sheila Atter.

Jack Russell puppies are very bright, lively and intelligent individuals. For this reason, if you fail to establish the house rules straight away, you may soon find that, in the absence of your rules, your puppy will make his own. This is why I always recommend crate training as a way of beginning to establish the rules, and to aid in the house-training process. No matter how much we love our dogs and assign them all sorts of human motives and emotions, they see the world in black and white – leader and follower. One of the best things you can do for your puppy in order to establish this relationship is to start with consistency in every aspect of his training.

HOUSE TRAINING

Young puppies need to be on a feeding schedule. Simply said: if you know when things go in, then you will know approximately when they will be eliminated. Most puppies in the 8 to 12 week age group are on a feeding schedule of twice a day – a meal first thing in the morning, and then another late in the afternoon – and this is ideal. Leave the food down for 20 minutes; most puppies will eat what they want in this period of time. Unless a puppy is ill, he will not intentionally starve himself.

Your puppy will need to go outside first thing in the morning, and once outside you should praise him for urinating and defecating in the spot you designate. Think up one particular set of words to use with your puppy, such as "hurry, go". You may be surprised that within a period of time, whenever you use that set of words, your puppy will eliminate on command. This can be very helpful if you plan to do a lot of travelling with your dog. Always take your puppy to the same area to eliminate. Dogs, because of certain scent signals, tend to eliminate in the same area repeatedly. Keep this specific area clean for sanitation reasons;

Whatever your choice in type of food, keep in mind that, if the food is very inexpensive, it is probably not made with quality ingredients. Sometimes the money you save in buying inexpensive food may later be spent at your vet's office trying to cure the myriad of health problems that a poor diet can cause. See Chapter 4 'Keeping your Jack Russell Fit' for more details.

SETTLING IN

It will take your puppy a few days to settle into your routine and household. These first few days should be spent concentrating on house training, crate training, and providing general structure for your puppy so that he will feel secure as quickly as possible in his new home.

House training should start as soon as your puppy arrives home. Photo: Sheila Atter.

dogs tend to seek new areas to defecate in once an area is badly soiled. Once your puppy has eliminated and come back inside, keep in mind that if he plays or runs hard in the house, it is wise to take him immediately back outside.

When you see your puppy start to make a mistake in the house you may often be several feet away, so toss something to startle him or shake a soda can with a few pennies inside to startle him. Gently pick him up while praising him for stopping, and then take him outside to his special area allowing him to eliminate again. When he does go outside, praise him again, give him a hug, and take him back inside.

Since dogs are so sensitive to scent, it is very important to be thoughtful about what types of products you use to clean up puppy's mistakes. Do not use ammonia; it is in urine, and instead of cleaning up the spot, you may actually be calling him back to it to use that spot again. Instead, use some type of odour-neutralising product to completely take the

smell away. Also check for toxicity with cleaning products; certain products that contain heavy amounts of pine oil can be harmful to young puppies. Young puppies should never be bedded on cedar shavings for the same reason, although they can be fine for adults.

In order to be really successful with house training, puppies need immediate feedback and careful watching. Out of sight is always trouble for a young puppy, and to learn properly that eliminating in the house is unacceptable they will need to be caught in the act. If you notice that your puppy has eliminated in the house, even if it is only a short while after the fact, it is best to just clean up the mess, and watch the pup more carefully. Disciplining after the deed is done is of no use, and could actually be harmful to further training. If you cannot watch your puppy, then he should be put in his crate for a short period of time.

CRATE TRAINING
Dogs in the wild generally live in dens. What a den offers to a dog is protection from the cold, heat and predators, as well as a sense of security and well-being. Domestic dogs also have a strong natural tendency to seek out a den, usually a small place to curl up in and get their backs up against something in order to feel safe and secure. A crate will provide a puppy's natural need for a den. Many a Jack Russell puppy will try and find his own den/crate, if one is not provided.

If your puppy is not familiar with a crate, then you will want to purchase one immediately. It is best to buy a crate that will suit your puppy as an adult so that you do not have to buy a larger one as your puppy matures. Dimensions should be approximately 17 to 18 inches (43 to 46 cms) high by 18 to 20 inches (46 to 51 cms) wide for this breed. If you will not be travelling with your puppy, then you may

A puppy will soon learn to regard his crate as a safe haven.

Photo: Sheila Atter.

consider having a wire crate, or purchasing both types of crates – one for home and one for travel. You should always provide soft, absorbent bedding and a chew toy in both types of crates.

Your breeder may have been able to start the crate-training process, but if not, then you will want to start very slowly. Leave the crate door open with a few toys inside for the puppy to play with, so that he can go in and out of the crate, without being confined. When first introducing your puppy to the crate, toss a treat into it to encourage the puppy to go inside, never force him in. Coax him with food, and reward him with praise. At first your puppy may grab the treat, and come right back out of the crate, which is very normal. Take it slowly, and keep encouraging him to go inside on his own.

If your puppy begins to look sleepy during the day, gently place him in the crate with the door open and see if he will at least catch a short nap. He should be put into the crate for very short periods of time at first, gradually increasing the time as he becomes accustomed to it. There will most likely be some yowling and screaming at first; however, stick with it and be firm. Tell the children in advance that, once a puppy has

gone to his crate to sleep, he should not be disturbed, as it is puppy's 'time out'. Keep in mind that no young puppy should be confined to a crate for more than a couple of hours at a time. As your puppy ages, the time he spends in a crate can be lengthened; however, even as an adult, the dog should not be confined to his crate for longer than eight hours.

Whenever you are unable to supervise your puppy he should be placed in his crate. It is certainly one of the best ways to prevent unwanted chewing, and your puppy should always have a selection of approved chew toys in his crate. The crate should be placed in an area where he can still see you, if possible, so perhaps in the kitchen during meals and in the bedroom at night. Puppies need to know that someone is there for them, so that if they whimper or cry, a family member will hear them and take them outside. For this reason, a wire crate in the house can have the advantage over a less open travel crate, particularly for a puppy that may be insecure.

Following a strict schedule when crate training is vital for your puppy's success, as this schedule will stay with him throughout his life. A puppy consistently left in his crate

for long periods of time, or with a very inconsistent schedule, loses hope that he will be taken out and may then see no advantage in waiting or holding his bowels and bladder until he is taken outside again. It is, however, very normal for a young puppy to occasionally make mistakes in his crate, and the mistake should simply be cleaned up with little fuss or attempt to discipline. Unless you catch him in the act, the discipline is wasted effort on your part.

When taking your puppy out of his crate, let him come out on his own and take him directly outside to eliminate. Praise him for doing so, and then take him into the house for a little playtime. Do not put him straight back into the crate. Part of his reward for holding his bladder in his crate and eliminating outside should be some quality interactive time with you.

By the time your puppy is six to eight months old, he will probably be able to hold his bladder and bowels for around eight hours. However, that is still a long period of time for a young puppy to be crated so if you work during the day, I recommend that someone come home at lunchtime to let the puppy out and give him some attention as well as time to relieve himself. If you cannot do it yourself, perhaps a friend or neighbour would be willing to let your puppy out once a day. If neither of these is an option, try leaving the puppy in a metal exercise pen with newspapers in one corner and his crate in the other. Remember that the Jack Russell can easily become bored and then look for things to do; unfortunately their entertainment choices may be destructive ones. Be observant: if your puppy is a climber, you will need a top for the metal exercise pen.

Most puppies by around six to eight months of age can begin being left unattended in the house for short periods of time. This should be done very gradually, leaving the dog alone for five minutes at first, and then praising for good behaviour when you return. The time your puppy is left alone should be increased, based on consistent good behaviour. If your puppy does any unapproved chewing or has any accidents while you are gone, go back to the crate, and try again in a couple of weeks. A puppy or dog should never be punished for accidents or chewing done in your absence. The dog will never understand why he is being punished, and this will only increase his anxiety the next time he is left alone.

Crate training has been proven to be one of the most successful ways to housebreak a puppy. Dogs that are crate-trained will tend to have fewer behavioural problems and are more secure and confident, easier to obedience train; they also may stay calmer and more settled when they need to be boarded. It is always a good idea to use a

The safest way to transport your dog is in a crate.

Photo: Sheila Atter.

crate to transport your puppy to and from your vet's, particularly after any surgical procedure, such as spaying or neutering. Many puppies are still quite wobbly from anaesthesia after a surgery, so the crate is excellent protection for them.

CAR TRAVEL

Taking your puppy with you in the car can be an important part of the total socialisation process. Puppies riding loose in the car can be an accident waiting to happen; any sudden stops or turns can send them flying about the car. The safest way to transport your puppy is in a crate. Never use a wire crate to transport your puppy. If you were to have an accident, a wire crate could become a death trap, for if there is a substantial impact, the wire, because it is welded, has a tendency to break apart and the sharp metal edges will face inwards towards your very frightened puppy. The safest type of crate for the car is a plastic or fibreglass one. What these plastic crates lack in visibility for the dog, it makes up for in safety.

There are some Jack Russell Terrier puppies that will become ill the first few times they ride in the car. I suggest that the first-time car ride should be on an empty stomach, and this should minimise any upset that may occur. Normally car sickness will diminish with frequency and age. If it does not, it is probably wise to have your puppy checked by your veterinarian. See Chapter 5 'Training the Jack Russell' for more details.

VACCINATIONS

Vaccinations are critical for your puppy's long-term health and safety. Eight-week-old puppies have usually been given two vaccinations, either by the breeder or by a veterinarian. Most puppy vaccinations are given in two to three week intervals, from the time the puppy is six weeks of age until the time he is 18 to 20 weeks of age, but you will want to discuss any vaccination schedule, and the type of vaccines to be used, with your vet. Chapter 12 'Health Care' gives more details.

Your vet will advise on a suitable vaccination programme.   *Photo courtesy: Mary Strom, Snow Wind.*

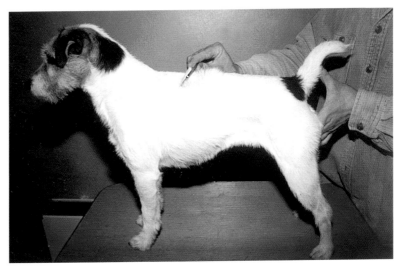

If you accustom your puppy to grooming from an early age, he will learn to stand quietly and accept the procedure.

Photo courtesy: Mary Strom, Snow Wind.

WORMING

Parasites will greatly impact your puppy's growth and maturation process, as any parasite will take away nutrition that should be going to the puppy instead. The two most common types of parasites affecting puppies are worms, such as roundworms, whipworms, hookworms, or tapeworms, and two kinds of protozoa, coccidia and giardia.

Some puppies that are heavily burdened with worms may exhibit signs such as being pot-bellied, with dull, dry coats or excessive shedding. Puppies with tapeworm may scoot their bottoms along the floor, and show a marked weight loss, or you may see rice-like segments in your puppy's stool. To treat tapeworms effectively you will also need to consider the source, which is the flea; unless the fleas are eliminated, then you will continue to have problems with tapeworm.

With coccidia or giardia, a puppy may have either constant or intermittent bouts of diarrhoea, both of which may be bloody. Both coccidia and giardia are single-celled organisms that infect the intestinal and digestive tracts of dogs. In the case of coccidia, unsanitary conditions such as overcrowding can be one cause. However, once a breeder has had a problem with coccidia it can tend to recur in subsequent litters, and most veterinarians will suggest

using a different whelping box, as well as a new run or play yard for future litters. Adult dogs often have some degree of immunity; however, your veterinarian may also prefer to treat all of the dogs, regardless of age, that live on an infected property. The Giardia organism can be found in some streams and water supplies and is much harder to detect. Giardia can be transmitted to humans.

It is very difficult to housebreak a puppy that has any type of parasite, so be sure and have your puppy checked for worms at the same time as he is vaccinated, and then regularly until he is six months of age. After the age of six months most veterinarians will recommend you worm your dog at least twice yearly, once in the spring and again in the autumn. If you live in a warmer climate you may need to consider additional worming.

Heartworm is another type of internal parasite, and is transmitted from mosquitoes to dogs, although they are not transmittable to humans. The only test for heartworm is a blood test that will need to be done by your vet. You will need to treat your dog for heartworm throughout the warm months of the year, usually from spring to late autumn. However, seek the advice of your vet, as there are some areas where heartworm is very rare because of the lack of mosquitoes. If you

In the first few weeks, your puppy will get sufficient exercise playing in the garden.

Photo courtesy: Rani Morningstar.

are going to do a lot of travelling with your dog from one area to another, it may be best to treat him for heartworm; that way he is fully protected no matter where he is.

GROOMING AND BATHING

Grooming should be considered as part of the routine in training your puppy right from the start. Young puppies usually need very little grooming, but it is at this young age that you set the habits for life. If your puppy is accustomed to being brushed, having his nails trimmed, ears and teeth cleaned, then he will be a pleasure to handle as an adult dog.

First make sure you always use a very soft-bristled brush on a young puppy. Do not let him struggle and get away; instead gently hold him until he settles. Remember that brushing should become a positive experience, so treats and praise during the brushing are an essential part of the process. Gently start at the top of his head and work back through the body, softly brushing and telling your puppy what a wonderful puppy he is. If you plan on showing your puppy, than the grooming is better off started on a grooming table; you will want to have him on the table a minimum of two to three times a week, with constant praise and rewards. Make sure any table or surface that you place your puppy on is secure and steady, as a wobbly table or slippery surface may frighten a young puppy. Many of these early experiences will stay with a puppy for his lifetime.

Cleaning or checking ears and teeth and trimming nails are important aspects of grooming your puppy. If you are intending to show your puppy, you will want to make sure he is used to having both his ears handled and his teeth examined, as these are both things a judge in a dog show will do. Young puppies'nails grow at a very rapid rate, and are quite sharp. It is important to handle your puppy's feet, perhaps just massaging them gently at first, and then working up to trimming his nails. If you are uncertain about how to trim their nails, ask your veterinarian; most are glad to show a new owner how and where to trim.

Baths, although often not enjoyed by dogs, are a necessity at one time or another. Never call your puppy to a bath, instead go and get him. Your puppy may consider being called

to a bath something unforgivable; you could unknowingly be setting up future recall problems with your puppy. The rule is never call your puppy to something he may deem bad. Start by bathing your puppy in lukewarm water, never hot. Young puppies are quite sensitive to temperature. You may also want to make sure you keep the puppy's collar on during the bath, just to give you a handhold in case he tries to leap from the tub. Very gently rub in the soap over his body, the first few times you may want to use just a soft cloth to wash around his face until he is more familiar with the process. Be sure and rinse your puppy thoroughly, as leftover soap residue can leave a puppy itchy and uncomfortable. It is a good idea to grab a towel when you are done and hold it in front of you as most dogs will shake off the excess water; and then gently towel him dry. Most Jack Russell puppies will run around the house leaping and jumping after a bath. If this will be a problem for you, you may want to consider keeping him in a smaller confined area or in his crate until he has settled.

Jack Russell Terriers usually have very hard coats, which naturally repel dirt and mud, so ideally they should not need to be bathed more than once a month. Bathing will soften their coat, and if you plan to show your puppy, you will want him to have the typical hard coat of a terrier. A good brushing several times a week will often allow your puppy to go longer between baths.

EXERCISE

Jack Russell puppies usually have boundless energy, and need plenty of exercise. Indeed, many of the common problems that owners experience with their dogs stem from lack of exercise.

Jack Russell puppies, because of their working background, need lots of exercise and an outlet to burn off their energy. Problems such as chewing, barking, or digging can be caused simply by a lack of proper exercise. Energy that is bottled up can be very stressful, and puppies that are not properly exercised can be more difficult to house-train.

However, turning your puppy out in the yard to play on his own cannot be considered true exercise. Interactive exercise is good for you and your puppy; games such as fetching

It is much more stimulating for the puppy if he interacts with the family during playtimes.
Photo: Anne Milne.

Consistency in approach is vital when rearing a youngster.   *Photo: Kim James, Badgerwood.*

tennis balls and retrieving Frisbees are all great fun for your puppy. Running with your puppy is probably not a good idea until he is into adulthood, as you would not want to put undue stress on a growing puppy, and it is something that should definitely be worked into gradually. Never exercise your puppy strenuously in the heat of the day – puppies and adult dogs can overheat quickly. Keep in mind that Jack Russell puppies rarely want to stop and rest, so you need to be the one to say enough. Pick the morning or late evening when it is relatively cool. A good swim can be a great idea for cooling off in the heat; however, young puppies should be carefully watched around water – not every puppy will like the water, or be a strong swimmer.

Overweight dogs have more health problems and die younger, so if you want a full life for yourself, as well as your puppy,

plenty of exercise is the key. A well-exercised puppy will be a happier and healthier puppy for your household, and like any aspect of training, exercise needs to be fun and consistent.

HOUSE RULES
Some of the most common complaints of puppy and dog owners are unwanted jumping, chewing, barking, refusal to come when called, and poor house-training habits. So the simple answer to these problems is not to get these bad habits started in the first place. Many of these top six complaints begin when a dog is very young. After all, it can be charming when a small puppy jumps up on your leg, or barks its very tiny bark to gain your attention. However, all of this becomes less charming as your dog becomes older, larger, and louder.

The most important aspect for a young puppy is consistency. So decide what your house rules are going to be before you even bring a puppy home from the breeder. Inconsistency will delay getting rid of unwanted behaviours, and may well produce psychological problems in your dog. This is where everyone in the family needs to be involved; for example, if you do not want your dog to jump up on you, then never praise or pet the puppy while he is jumping up, or immediately after he has done so. Instead, greet your puppy in a crouching position, and pet him while holding him in a sitting or standing position. You can follow the same pattern with guests; use a collar and leash on your puppy and then stand on the leash when the puppy tries to jump up on the guests. Have your guests praise him only when all four feet are on the floor, and if your guests are not quick to praise, then you should step in and praise as well.

If you want your dog to always come when he is called, never have him come to something that would be considered bad. That includes being called only to be put away in his crate, bathing, or scolding him after you have just chased him for a half-hour around the garden, trying to catch him. Instead, start out by having someone hold the puppy in another room while you prepare his food. When his food is ready, call him with a single word "come!"and simultaneously the person holding him should let go. 'Come' should always mean a reward, of either food or attention. Do not over-use the word; any training word that is overused tends to be ignored with time.

Never encourage your puppy to bark or speak for a reward of food. Consider that what he may learn from this is how to manipulate you and to gain attention. Most Russells are fairly mouthy in that they like to lick, nibble, or possibly chew on your hands. However, it is your job to teach the dog either not to do this at all, or to do it very gently, by letting your puppy know with a firm and loud "Ow!" if something hurts. If the chewing and biting behaviour is still a problem, there are bitter apple products on the market that can be applied to furniture, clothing and your hands if needed to discourage the behaviour.

Understanding how a dog learns is the key to establishing any of the house rules above. Always keep in mind that puppies or dogs need immediate feedback as to whether behaviour is appropriate or not. Correction for breaking a house rule should be firm, but not so firm as to cause physical harm or fear; praise and reassurance should immediately follow any discipline.

4 KEEPING YOUR JACK RUSSELL FIT

Nutrition has never been the sole domain of the medical practitioner or of the veterinary surgeon. It is relatively recently that the medical profession has developed clinical nutrition to the point that there are professors in the subject, and that vets in companion animal practice have realised that they have an expertise to offer in this area of pet health care. This is curious because even the earliest medical and veterinary texts refer to the importance of correct diet, and for many years vets working with production animals such as cattle, pigs and sheep have been deluged with information about the most appropriate nutrition for those species.

Traditionally, of course, the breeder, neighbours, friends, relatives, the pet shop owner and even the local supermarket have been a main source of advice on feeding for many pet owners. Over the past fifteen years there has been a great increase in public awareness about the relationships between diet and disease, thanks mainly to media interest in the subject (which has at times bordered on hysteria), but also to marketing tactics by major manufacturing companies. Few people will not have heard about the alleged health benefits of 'high-fibre', 'low-fat', 'low-cholesterol', 'high in polyunsaturates', 'low in saturates' and 'oat bran' diets. While there are usually some data to support the use of these types of diets in certain situations, frequently the benefits are overstated, if they exist at all.

Breeders have always actively debated the best way to feed dogs. Most Jack Russell owners are aware of the importance of good

Providing a well-balanced diet is a vital part of caring for your Jack Russell.

Photo courtesy: Mary Strom, Snow Wind.

bone development and the role of nutrition in achieving optimal skeletal characteristics. However, as a vet in practice, I was constantly amazed and bewildered at the menus given to new puppy owners by breeders. These all too frequently consisted of complex home-made recipes, usually based on large amounts of fresh meat, goat's milk, and a vast array of mineral supplements. These diets were often very imbalanced and could easily result in skeletal and other growth abnormalities.

Domestic dogs usually have little opportunity to select their own diet, so it is important to realise that they are solely dependent upon their owners to provide all the nourishment that they need. In this chapter, I aim to explain what those needs are, in the process to dispel a few myths, and to give some guidance as to how to select the most appropriate diet for your dog.

ESSENTIAL NUTRITION

Dogs have a common ancestry with, and are still often classified as, carnivores, although from a nutritional point of view they are actually omnivores. This means that dogs can obtain all the essential nutrients that they need from dietary sources consisting of either animal or plant material. As far as we know, dogs can survive on food derived solely from plants – that is, they can be fed a vegetarian diet. The same is not true for domestic cats, which are still obligate carnivores whose nutritional needs cannot be met by an exclusively vegetarian diet.

ENERGY

All living cells require energy, and the more active they are the more energy they burn up. Individual dogs have their own unique energy needs, which will vary, even between dogs of the same breed, age, sex and activity level. Breeders will recognise the scenario in which some littermates develop differently,

one tending towards obesity, another on the lean side, even when they are fed exactly the same amount of food. For adult maintenance, a Jack Russell Terrier will need an energy intake of approximately 30 kcal/lb body weight (or 65 kcal/kg body weight). If you know the energy density of the food that you are giving, you can work out how much your dog needs; but you must remember that this is only an approximation, and you will need to adjust the amount you feed to suit each individual dog. This is best achieved by regular weighing of your dog and then maintaining an optimum body weight. Learn how to body-condition-score your dogs. This is a very accurate method that will help to prevent under- and over-feeding. Many veterinary practices now offer a puppy growth-check service where both body weight and body condition score are monitored.

If you are feeding a commercially prepared food, you should be aware that the feeding guide recommended by the manufacturer is also based on average energy needs, and therefore you may need to increase or decrease the amount you give to meet your own individual dog's requirements. In some countries (such as those within the European Union) legislation may not allow the energy content to appear on the label of a prepared pet food; however, reputable manufacturing companies can and will provide this information upon request.

When considering different foods it is important to compare the metabolisable energy, which is the amount of energy in the food that is *available* to a dog. Some companies will provide you with figures for the gross energy, which is not as useful, because some of that energy (sometimes a substantial amount) will not be digested, absorbed and utilised.

There are many circumstances in which your dog's energy requirement may change

WORK	
Light	1.1 - 1.5 x MER
Heavy	2 - 4 x MER
Inactivity	0.8 x MER

PREGNANCY	
First 6 weeks	1 x MER
Last 3 weeks	1.1 - 1.3 x MER
Peak lactation	2 - 4 x MER
Growth	1.2 - 2 x MER

ENVIRONMENT	
Cold	1.25 - 1.75 x MER
Heat	Up to 2.5 x MER

from its basic adult maintenance energy requirement (MER).

Light to moderate activity (work) barely increases energy needs, and it is only when dogs are doing heavy work, such as pulling sleds, that energy requirements are significantly increased. Note that there is no increased energy requirement during pregnancy, except in the last three weeks, and the main need for high energy intake is during the lactation period. If a bitch is getting sufficient energy, she should not lose weight or condition during pregnancy and lactation. Because the energy requirement is so great during lactation (up to 4 x MER), it can sometimes be impossible to meet this need by feeding conventional adult maintenance diets, because the bitch cannot physically eat enough food. As a result she will lose weight and condition. Switching to a high-energy diet is usually necessary to avoid this.

As dogs get older their energy needs usually decrease. This is due in large part to being less active, either through getting less exercise, e.g. if their owner is elderly, or enforced by locomotor problems such as arthritis; but there are also changes in the metabolism of older animals that reduce the amount of energy that they need. The aim should be to maintain optimum body weight throughout old age, and regular exercise can play an important part in this. If there is any tendency to decrease or increase weight this should be countered by increasing or decreasing energy intake accordingly. If the body weight changes by more than ten per cent from usual, veterinary attention should be sought, in case there is a medical problem causing the weight change.

Changes in environmental conditions and all forms of stress (including showing), which

The amount you feed should be closely related to energy requirements.

Photo: Sheila Atter.

The working dog leads a demanding life, and this should be reflected in the nutrition provided.
Photo: Kim James, Badgerwood.

particularly affect dogs with a nervous temperament, can increase energy needs. Some dogs, when kennelled for long periods, lose weight due to a stress-related increase in energy requirements that cannot easily be met by a maintenance diet. A high-energy food containing at least 1900 kcal of metabolisable energy/lb dry matter (4.2 kcal/gram) may be needed in order to maintain body weight under these circumstances. Jack Russell Terriers can be very highly-strung, nervous individuals, and may also benefit from high-energy foods. These products are often sold as being for 'active and working'dogs. When choosing the right product for your dog, you should choose those that are high in fat and not

those that are higher in protein. Nervous and stressed adult dogs have no higher protein requirement than other adult dogs; they simply need more calories. This is best achieved by feeding more fat. Excessive energy intake, on the other hand, results in obesity, which can have very serious effects on health.

Orthopaedic problems, such as rupture of the cruciate ligaments, are more likely to occur in overweight dogs. This condition, which often requires surgical intervention, may present as a sudden-onset complete lameness, or gradually worsening hind leg lameness. Many Jack Russell Terriers exhibit intermittent hind limb lameness, often manifesting as total reluctance to use one hind leg. Some dogs alternate the affected limb. This intermittent lameness is sometimes due to a condition called Legg Perthe's disease, where necrosis of the femoral head occurs. Affected dogs tend to be between three and nine months of age and may need a surgical procedure to totally remove the affected hip joint. An excess intake of calcium in the diet during the period of growth has been suggested as one of the factors that may predispose puppies to the development of this painful condition.

Dogs frequently develop heart disease in old age, and obesity puts significant extra demands on the cardiovascular system, with potentially serious consequences. Obesity is also a predisposing cause of non-insulin dependent diabetes mellitus, and has many other detrimental effects on health, including reducing resistance to infection and increasing anaesthetic and surgical risks. Once obesity is present, activity tends to decrease and it becomes even more necessary to decrease energy intake; otherwise more body weight is gained and the situation is made worse.

Energy is only available from the fat, carbohydrate and protein in a dog's diet. A

gram of fat provides 2$^1/_4$ times as much energy as a gram of carbohydrate or protein and so higher energy requirements are best met by feeding a relatively high fat diet. Dogs rarely develop the cardiovascular conditions that have been associated with high fat intake in humans, such as atherosclerosis and coronary artery disease.

Owners may think that protein is the source of energy needed for exercise and performance, but this is not true. Protein is a relatively poor source of energy because a large amount of the energy theoretically available from it is lost in 'meal-induced heat'. Meal-induced heat is the metabolic heat 'wasted' in the digestion, absorption and utilisation of the protein. Fat and carbohydrates are better sources of energy for performance.

For obese or obese-prone dogs a low energy intake is indicated, and there are now specially prepared diets that have a very low energy density; those which are most effective have a high fibre content. Your vet will advise you about the most appropriate type of diet if you have such a problem dog. Incidentally, if you do have an overweight dog it is important to seek veterinary advice in case it is associated with some other medical condition.

CHOOSING A DIET

The first important consideration to make when selecting a maintenance diet is that it should meet the energy requirements of your dog. In some situations, specially formulated high-energy or low-energy diets will be needed to achieve this. Other nutrients that must be provided in the diet include essential amino acids (from dietary protein), essential fatty acids (from dietary fat), minerals and vitamins. Carbohydrates are not an essential dietary component for dogs, because they can synthesise sufficient glucose from other sources.

A puppy will achieve half its adult weight by four months of age.
Photo courtesy: Mary Strom, Snow Wind.

Do not fall into the trap of thinking that if a diet is good for a human it must be good for a dog. There are many differences between a human's nutritional needs and those of the dog. For example, humans need a supply of vitamin C in the diet, but under normal circumstances a dog can synthesise its own vitamin C, and so a dietary source is not essential. The amount of nutrients that a dog needs will vary according to its stage of life, environment and activity level.

FEEDING FOR GROWTH

Growing animals have tissues that are actively developing and growing in size, and so it is not surprising that they have a relatively higher requirement for energy, protein, vitamins and minerals than their adult counterparts (based on the daily intake of these nutrients per kg body weight). Birth weight usually doubles in seven to ten days and puppies should gain 1 to 2 grams/day/lb (2 to 4 grams/day/kg) of anticipated adult weight. An important key to the successful rearing of neonates is to reduce the puppies' energy loss by maintaining their

The development of a good skeleton depends on an interaction of genetic, environmental and nutritional influences.

Photo courtesy: Marcia Walsh.

environmental temperature, as well as by ensuring sufficient energy intake. Bitch's milk is of particular importance to the puppy during the first few hours of life, as this early milk (called colostrum) provides some passive immunity to the puppy because of the maternal antibodies it contains. These will help to protect the puppy until it can produce its own immune response to challenge from infectious agents. The ability of a puppy to absorb the maternal antibodies from the colostrum is greatest within the first few days of life. Failure to ensure adequate colostrum intake within the first two or three days of life can predispose to fading puppy syndrome and other infections.

Survival rate is greatly decreased in puppies that do not get colostrum from their mother. Orphaned puppies are best fed a proprietary milk replacer, according to the manufacturer's recommendations, unless a foster mother can be found. Your vet will be able to help if you find yourself in such a situation.

Obesity must be avoided during puppyhood, as so-called juvenile obesity will increase the number of fat cells in the body, and so predispose the animal to obesity for the rest of its life. Overeating is most likely to occur when puppies are fed free choice (ad lib) throughout the day, particularly if there is competition between littermates. A better method is to feed a puppy a daily ration

based on its body weight divided into two to four meals per day, the number of meals decreasing as it gets older. Any food remaining after twenty minutes should be removed. Limiting food intake in growing puppies has also been associated with fewer signs of hip dysplasia, although this is not a common problem in smaller breeds such as the Jack Russell.

Proper growth and development is dependent upon a sufficient intake of essential nutrients. If you consider how rapidly a puppy grows, usually achieving half its adult weight by four months of age, it is not surprising that nutritional deficiencies, excesses or imbalances can have disastrous results. Deficiency diseases are rarely seen in veterinary practice nowadays, mainly because proprietary pet foods contain more than sufficient amounts of the essential nutrients. When a deficiency disease is diagnosed it is usually associated with an unbalanced home-made diet. A classical example of this is dogs fed on an all-meat diet. Meat is very low in calcium but high in phosphorus, and demineralisation of bones occurs on this type of diet. This leads to very thin bones that fracture easily, frequently resulting in folding fractures caused simply by weight-bearing.

Development of a good skeleton results from an interaction of genetic, environmental, and nutritional influences.

The genetic component can be influenced by the breeder in a desire to improve the breed. The new puppy owner can control environmental influences, including housing and activity level, with good advice from the breeder. However, nutrition is one of the most important factors influencing correct development of the puppy's bones and muscles.

In growing puppies it is particularly important to provide minerals, but in the correct proportions. The calcium:phosphorus ratio should ideally be 1.2 - 1.4:1, and certainly within the wider range of 1 - 2:1. If there is more phosphorus than calcium in the diet (i.e. an inverse calcium:phosphorus ratio), normal bone development may be affected. Care also has to be taken to avoid feeding too much mineral. A diet for growing puppies should not contain more than two per cent calcium. Excessive calcium intake actually causes stunting of growth, and an intake of 3.3 per cent calcium has been shown to result in serious skeletal deformities, including deformities of the carpus, osteochondritis dissecans (OCD), wobbler syndrome and hip dysplasia. These are common diseases, and while other factors such as genetic inheritance may also be involved, excessive mineral intake should be considered a risk factor in all cases.

If a diet already contains sufficient calcium, it is dangerously easy to increase the calcium content to well over three per cent if you give mineral supplements as well. Some commercially available treats and snacks are very high in salt, protein and calories. They can significantly upset a carefully balanced diet, and it is advisable to ask your vet's opinion of the various treats available and to use them only very occasionally.

A growing puppy is best fed a proprietary pet food that has been specifically formulated to meet its nutritional needs. Those that are available as both canned and dry are specially suitable to rear even the youngest of puppies. Home-made diets may theoretically be adequate, but it is difficult to ensure that all the nutrients are provided in an available form. The only way to be sure about the adequacy of a diet is to have it analysed for its nutritional content *and* to put it through controlled feeding trials.

Supplements should only be used with rations that are known to be deficient, in order to provide whatever is missing from the diet. With a complete balanced diet *nothing* should be missing. If you use supplements with an already balanced diet, you could create an imbalance, and/or provide excessive amounts of nutrients, particularly minerals.

Nutritional management alone is not sufficient to prevent developmental bone disease. However, we can prevent some skeletal disease by feeding appropriate amounts of a good-quality balanced diet. Dietary deficiencies are of minimal concern with the ever-increasing range of commercial diets specifically prepared for young growing dogs. The potential for harm is in overnutrition from excess consumption and supplementation.

FEEDING FOR PREGNANCY AND LACTATION

There is no need to increase the amount of food being fed to a bitch during early and mid-pregnancy, but there will be an increased demand for energy (i.e. carbohydrates and fats collectively), protein, minerals and vitamins during the last three weeks. A bitch's nutritional requirements will be at the maximum during lactation, particularly if she has a large litter to feed. Avoid giving calcium supplementation during pregnancy, as a high intake can frustrate calcium availability during milk production, and can increase the chances of eclampsia (also called milk fever or puerperal tetany) occurring. All

small breeds, including the Jack Russell Terrier, are prone to the development of eclampsia. It is most common in the bitch following birth of a large litter when the puppies are about four to six weeks old. The clinical signs include collapse, excessive salivation, paddling of the legs and vocalising. This is a veterinary emergency and if you suspect your bitch may be suffering from eclampsia you should seek veterinary attention immediately.

During pregnancy a bitch should maintain her body weight and condition. If she loses weight her energy intake needs to be increased. A specifically formulated growth-type diet is recommended to meet her nutritional needs at this time. If a bitch is on a diet formulated for this stage of her life, and she develops eclampsia, or has had previous episodes of the disease, your veterinary surgeon may advise calcium supplementation. If given during pregnancy, this is only advisable during the very last few days of pregnancy when milk let-down is occurring, and preferably is given only during lactation (i.e. *after* whelping).

FEEDING FOR MAINTENANCE AND OLD AGE

The objective of good nutrition is to provide all the energy and essential nutrients that a dog needs in sufficient amounts to avoid deficiency, and at the same time to limit their supply so as not to cause over-nutrition or toxicity. Some nutrients are known to play a role in disease processes, and it is prudent to avoid unnecessarily high intakes of these whenever possible. The vets at Hill's Science and Technology Centre in Topeka, Kansas, are specialists in canine clinical nutrition and

Nutritional requirements will be at the maximum during lactation.

Photo: Sheila Atter.

Tina, dam of Imis Of Willowall, aged seventeen. Food intake should be adjusted in old age.

Photo courtesy: Sue Porter.

they are particularly concerned about the potential health risks associated with too high an intake of protein, sodium (salt) and phosphorus during a dog's adult life.

These nutrients are thought to have an important and serious impact once disease is present, particularly in heart and kidney diseases. Kidney failure and heart failure are very common in older dogs and it is believed to be important to avoid feeding diets high in these nutrients to such an 'at risk' group of dogs. Furthermore, these nutrients may be detrimental to dogs even before there is any evidence of disease. It is known that salt, for example, can be retained in dogs with subclinical heart disease, before there is any outward evidence of illness. Salt retention is an important contributing factor in the development of fluid retention (congestion), swelling of the limbs (oedema) and dropsy (ascites).

A leading veterinary cardiologist in the USA has claimed that 40 per cent of dogs over five years of age, and 80 per cent of dogs over ten years have some change in the heart – either endocardiosis or myocardial fibrosis (or both). Both of these lesions may reduce heart function. Phosphorus retention is an important consequence of advancing kidney disease, which encourages mineral deposition in the soft tissues of the body, including the kidneys themselves, a condition known as nephrocalcinosis. Such deposits damage the kidneys even more, and hasten the onset of kidney failure.

As a dog ages there are two major factors that determine its nutritional needs:

1. The dog's changing nutritional requirements due to the effects of age on organ function and metabolism.
2. The increased likelihood of the presence of subclinical diseases, many of which have a protracted course during which nutrient intake may influence progression of the condition.

Many Jack Russell Terrier owners are aware of a condition called gastric dilatation and torsion, commonly known as 'bloat'. This

potentially life-threatening condition was previously thought to be due to the ingestion of a high fat or carbohydrate meal. Current thinking is that bloat is due to aerophagia (the intake of large amounts of air with a meal), common in greedy individuals, and the predisposing factors may be:

Genetic make-up
Competitive feeding
Strenuous exercise around meal times
Excitement at feeding time.

The last three factors encourage rapid eating. Bloat is more common in large, deep-chested breeds, but all dog owners should be vigilant, as the condition is often fatal. Special highly digestible diets are available from the vet to feed to at-risk individuals.

Energy requirements usually decrease with increasing age, and food intake should be adjusted accordingly. Also the dietary intake of some nutrients needs to be minimised – in particular, protein, phosphorus, sodium and total energy intake. Dietary intake of other nutrients may need to be increased to meet the needs of some older dogs, notably essential fatty acids, some vitamins, some specific amino acids and zinc. Unlike humans, calcium and phosphorus do not need to be supplemented in ageing dogs – indeed, to do so may prove detrimental.

LABEL INTERPRETATION
Labelling laws differ from one country to the next. For example, pet foods sold in the USA must carry a Guaranteed Analysis, which states a maximum or a minimum amount for the various nutrients in the food. Pet foods sold in Europe must carry a Typical (as fed) Analysis, which is a declaration of the average amount of nutrients found from analysis of the product.

'COMLETE' VERSUS 'COMPLEMENTARY'
In the UK a pet food must declare whether it is 'complete'or 'complementary'. A 'complete'pet food must provide all the nutrients required to satisfy the needs of the group of pet animals for which it is recommended. At the time of writing there is no obligation for a manufacturer to submit such a diet to feeding trials to ensure that it is adequate. In the USA some manufacturers submit their pet foods to the feeding trials approved by the Association of American Feed Control Officials (AAFCO) to ensure that they meet the nutritional requirements of the National Research Council (e.g. the Hill's Pet Nutrition range of Science Plan products).

A 'complementary'pet food needs to be fed with some other foodstuff in order to meet the needs of the animal. Anyone feeding a complementary food as a substantial part of a dog's ration is obliged to find out what it should be fed with in order to balance the ration. Failure to do so could result in serious deficiency or imbalance of nutrients.

DRY MATTER
The water content of pet foods varies greatly, particularly in canned products. In the USA there is a legal maximum limit (78 per cent) which cannot be exceeded, but no such limit is in force in Europe, and some European canned pet foods contain as much as 86 per cent water. Legislation now makes it compulsory for the water content to be declared on the label and this is important, because to compare one pet food with another, one should consider the percentage of a nutrient in the dry matter of food.

For example, two pet foods may declare the protein content to be 10 per cent in the Typical Analysis printed on the label. If one product contains 75 per cent water it has 25 per cent dry matter, so the protein content is

actually 10/25 x 100 = 40 per cent. If the other product contains 85 per cent water, the protein content is 10/15 x 100 = 66.6 per cent. This type of calculation (called Dry Matter Analysis) becomes even more important when comparing canned with dry products, as the water content of dry food is usually only 7.5-12 per cent.

You can only effectively compare pet foods if you know the food's energy density and the dry matter analysis of the individual nutrients.

COST

The only valid way to compare the cost of one food against another is to compare the daily feeding costs to meet all the needs of your dog. A high-energy, nutritionally concentrated type of diet might cost more to buy per measure of food, but it could be cheaper to feed on a cost per day basis. Conversely, a poor quality, poorly digestible diet may be cheaper to buy, but actually cost more per day to feed, because you need to feed much more food to meet the dog's requirements. The only valid reason for feeding a food is that it meets the nutritional requirements of your dog. To do that, you need to read between the marketing strategies of the manufacturers and select a diet that you know provides your dog with what it needs.

HOME-MADE DIETS

What about home-made recipes? Well, theoretically it is possible to make a home-made diet that will meet all the nutritional requirements of a dog, and all foodstuffs have some nutritional value, but not all published recipes may actually achieve what they claim. The reason is that there is no strict quality control of ingredients, and the bioavailability of nutrients may vary from one ingredient source to another. If you feed a correctly balanced home-made diet, they are often time-consuming to prepare, usually need the addition of a vitamin/mineral supplement, and if prepared accurately can be expensive. Variations in raw ingredients will cause fluctuations in nutritional value.

The only way to be absolutely sure that a home-made diet has the nutritional profile that you want is to mix all the food ingredients plus supplements, treats, snacks, scraps etc. in a large pot, homogenise them and have a sample analysed chemically (this

A greater understanding of nutrition is proving of great benefit in the field of canine health.

Photo courtesy: Sue Porter.

costs well over £100 (US$160) for a partial analysis); then compare this analytical content with the published levels for nutrient requirements.

You may feel that feeding an existing home-made recipe passed on to you, or developed over a number of years, is adequate. But how do you know? What is the phosphorus level of the diet that you are feeding? An undesirably high intake level may take a long time before it results in obvious problems.

Sometimes the condition of your dog will give you an idea that all is not well with the diet you are feeding. One of the most common questions asked by breeders at dog shows is: "Can you recommend a diet that will keep weight on my dogs?" Unless there is a medical problem (and in such cases you should always seek veterinary attention first), the usual reason dogs have difficulty maintaining their weight is simply that they have an inadequate energy intake. This does not mean that they are not eating well – they may in fact have very large appetites, but if the food is of a relatively low digestibility, your dog may be unable to eat enough food to meet its energy needs. Large bulky faeces are an indicator of low digestibility. A poor, dull, dry or scurfy coat, poor skin and other external signs of unthriftiness may also be an indicator of poor nutrition. How many 'poor-doers' and dogs with recurrent infections are on a diet with a marginal nutritional level of adequacy?

SUMMARY
The importance of nutrition has been known for many years and yet, sadly, it is still surrounded by too many old wives'tales, myths and unsubstantiated claims. The emergence of clinical nutrition as a subject in its own right has set the stage for the future. Hopefully, we shall hear about the benefits and dangers of different feeding practices from scientists who can base their statements on fact, not merely opinion.

Already we know that a dog that is ill has different nutritional requirements to a healthy dog. In some cases, dietary management can even offer an alternative way to manage clinical cases. For example, we currently have the ability to dissolve struvite stones in the urinary bladder simply by manipulating dietary intake instead of having to resort to surgery.

Please note, dietary management is not 'alternative medicine'. Proper nutrition is key to everything that a living animal has to do, be it work or repairing tissues after an injury. It is not an option; it is a crucial part of looking after an animal properly. If you own a dog then you should at least ensure that the food you give supplies all his needs and avoids the excessive intake of energy or nutrients that may play a role in diseases which your pet could develop.

5 TRAINING THE JACK RUSSELL

I always advise people, before acquiring a puppy or young dog of any breed, to do their homework on raising a puppy and to research the breed, learning about its characteristics, its behaviour and what size it will eventually grow to. After all, buying a puppy is not like going to the supermarket and picking it off the shelf like a bottle of sauce! You have to bear in mind these little terriers can live until they are 15 or 16, so temperament is vital, especially if your dog is to be a family pet, or indeed whatever you intend.

It is important to remember that Jack Russells, being terriers, are not generally as eager to please their owners as are breeds from the working or gundog group. The desire to run and to hunt has been strongly bred into them for generations, which is as it should be, otherwise there would be no Jack Russells. However, with firm and consistent handling, they can become excellent pets and also succeed in other disciplines such as Obedience, Working Trials and Agility.

TRAINING OBJECTIVES

Whenever anyone asks me what the most important exercise you can teach any dog is, I always say, the instant down or drop on command, and to come when called. I would say the instant down is the most important as, in certain circumstances, it can save your dog's life. Other important objectives are to have a dog which will walk nicely beside you on a lead, one that will wait when told to whilst you go through a door, without barging through first. A dog that will not charge off to the other side of the park the minute you let it off the lead or go and fight with other people's dogs.

Jack Russells seem to have quite a strong guarding instinct, so they need to be taught from day one that the food bowl and toys are not for guarding – neither is the best armchair, nor the bed! They can also be quite vocal, and so need to be taught that ad lib barking is not on the agenda, either at home or in the car!

Whilst on the subject of cars, it is a good idea to teach your terrier to either ride in a crate in the rear of the car or to be secured in a properly designed harness on the back seat. How many times have we all seen cars travelling along with the dog either doing a 'wall of death' around the car or travelling along with its head hanging out of the window!

If your Jack Russell is to be kennelled, try to make sure he does not perceive this as a punishment; to keep a dog in a kennel on his own with no stimulation is extremely cruel. With proper training you will end up with a well-socialised, obedient family pet to be proud of!

Hoelio Just Jenny (left) and Snow Wind Bolt: With firm and consistent handling, the Jack Russell will be an adaptable and well-behaved companion.

Photo courtesy: Mary Strom.

EARLY TRAINING

Whilst any pups I have are well integrated with my other dogs, I always make sure that the pup spends a lot of time with me, when he is not sleeping. So all these exercises and early lessons take place for very short periods several times a day, which means that if you have other dogs and they all live together and are not kennelled, the pup will become orientated on you and not on the other dogs.

LEARNING HIS NAME

The most important first lesson for the puppy is to learn his name. I tend to use one-syllable names, as they sound sharper and cannot be abbreviated. Make sure the whole family sticks to the name being used, for example, if you are going to use the name 'Ben', do not let other people call the pup 'Benny'. Always use the pup's name when you want to attract his attention, particularly when you want him to come to you.

HOUSE TRAINING

Early lessons should start the minute you get the puppy home. An area should have already been designated as the place where the pup should be taken to go to the toilet. A pup should always be taken physically to his toilet area at first, then when he gets bigger and more used to you, he will probably follow you to the area when you call him. It is not good enough to just turn the pup out and leave him to his own devices and hope he will perform. I always use the command "be quick" for toilet training, and give lavish praise in a low voice (so as not to distract him whilst he is performing). See Chapter 3 'The Jack Russell Puppy' for more details.

WAIT

After the pup has arrived in his new home, been fussed over and had a chance to sleep, he will probably be keen for a feed. I believe in starting as you mean to go on, and dogs

respect consistency. Put the food on the floor in the area where the pup is to be fed, kneel down and restrain the pup gently with two hands in front of his shoulders and use the command "wait", count to five, tell him "good boy" and let him eat his meal. The time you make him wait can be increased as he gets older. This exercise stops the dog from jumping up at the bowl and diving in immediately it is put down. At a later stage he can be taught to sit and wait.

COLLAR AND LEAD TRAINING

Another first early lesson for the pup is to get used to a lightweight collar and lead. Whilst he will not be able to go out until after he has been vaccinated, getting him used to walking on his collar and lead around the garden will stand you in good stead later on. I always use lightweight webbing collars and leads for pups, no more than about a half-inch wide. Put the collar on the pup and, if he does not struggle or scratch it, praise him lavishly. *Never ever* leave a pup unattended with a collar on – it can be fatal. Start by leaving it on just for five minutes or so; if he starts to scratch at it, distract him by turning

his attention to something else, for example his meal, or by playing with him. He will soon learn to accept the collar happily.

Once he is happily wearing his collar under observation for around half-an-hour or so at a time, you can then attach a lightweight lead to it. Let the pup drag it around behind him – again, I stress *under close observation*. If he is ignoring the lead, gently pick it up and attract his attention by calling his name and praising him. Then try moving away a step or so, all the time attracting his attention, by having a tidbit in your hand and using his name. If the pup is a bit stubborn, move away a step or so and bend down, encouraging him all the time to come to you. With plenty of praise and encouragement, he will soon be following you around the garden on the lead. These lessons should be very short and should take place several times a day; pups have a very short attention span and get bored easily.

PLAYING

Another very important early lesson for pups is to teach them to play with you with toys. I never leave toys lying around for my dogs to

An important early lesson is to introduce your puppy to a light collar and lead.

Photo courtesy: Mary Strom.

play with ad lib; if you teach your pup to play *with you* with toys, rather than on his own, he will be more focused on you, and so you are in control all the while, in a subtle way.

Terriers in particular like to play tug-of-war games. This is fine, as long as you stay in control and the toy is then put away until you want to play with your pup again. However, I think it is a good idea to let the dog win occasionally, otherwise he will become bored. I usually let my dogs win one out of three, and I always win the final one, then put away the toy. Also, if there are no toys left out, it stops the tendency for the pup to guard them or, in a multi-dog household, stops any arguing between dogs.

The method I use to teach young dogs to play is to find a toy the pup is keen on – most of my dogs find a tennis ball irresistible. I put a hole in the ball and thread some twine through it, usually around ten feet or so. Find a smallish, enclosed space – at our last house we had a small, enclosed yard with a garden seat. I found it ideal to sit on the seat and toss the ball out on its twine for the pup and, hey presto, as soon as he has picked up the ball, gently reel him in. All the while, use the commands which you will be using when more formal obedience exercises are taught. Get the pup really interested in the ball and he will be keen to run out after it. As he picks it up, say excitedly, but in a low voice, "good boy! hold it!" Then, as you reel him in, give the command to come to you. I use either "come" or "here" . You may find the pup will be reluctant to give up his toy, so take it from him very gently and, as you do, give the command "leave". This is the basis for the retrieve exercise to be taught later. I cannot overemphasise the importance of not being rough with the pup, in particular when getting him to give up the toy, as a bad experience will put him off

Teaching your puppy to pay attention is a useful exercise.

Photo: John Valentine.

retrieving for a long while. Also, when he starts teething, his gums will be really sore, and I would recommend that this exercise be stopped for a few weeks. As with any training with very young dogs, the 'play-retrieve' sessions should be very brief, but can take place several times a day.

LONG DOWN

The 'long down'is another early exercise for pups which I find extremely useful, as it forms the basis of the 'long stay'exercise at a later date, and also I feel teaches the pup to be calm.

To begin with, choose a time of day when you are not likely to be interrupted. Sit down on the floor with the pup and gently put him into the down position, making sure he is lying comfortably. Tell him in a low voice "down, good boy". If he struggles, gently hold him in the down position. To begin with, a few minutes is enough, but eventually you will find the pup will probably fall asleep

and you will be able to work up to a goal of around half an hour for a long down.

I must emphasise, this exercise is not a 'down-stay', but reinforcement of subtle dominance over the pup. When you feel the pup has been in the down position long enough, or if you should be distracted, for example if the telephone rings, you must release the pup with a release command such as "OK". On no account should he be left to his own devices to get up on his own, as this completely negates the exercise.

CALLING TO ATTENTION

Teaching your pup to pay attention with a single command is a useful exercise. Always carry a few treats in your pocket. I find a small portion of dry puppy food excellent: it can be deducted from his diet so he does not put on too much weight, and it does not mess up your pocket like choc-drops do. When the pup is not in a sleepy mood, call his name and use the command "look" or "watch" and then immediately give him the tidbit. Once he is responding to the command immediately, dispense with the treat every time and only give it, say, once every three times or so. You will find he will work harder when he gets the treat spasmodically. The same theory applies to training your pup to come when he is called. At first I always give him the treat when I call his name and he responds but, later on, it is best to reward the pup only when obedience is immediate.

CAR MANNERS

It is necessary to teach pups 'car manners' at quite an early age. Take the pup on his collar and lead to the car, give him the wait command and hold the lead down close to his collar (or hold his collar), open the door or tailgate and, with a low encouraging voice, tell the pup continuously to wait. Whilst he is still in the wait position (it does

not matter whether he is standing or sitting), I then close the tailgate. If this is repeated two or three times, he will soon get the message that he is not allowed into the car before you invite him in. On about the third time of opening the car, the command can be given for him to jump in or, if he is very small, to be lifted in. On no account should small pups be allowed to jump in and out of cars until their bones have become strong enough to handle the impact.

The words I use for getting in and out of the car are just that – "in" and "out". Again, this lesson is repeated three or four times a day, and when the pup waits without attempting to jump in the car, lavish praise should be given.

The same theory applies to getting the pup out of the car. With a small pup I normally have him in a crate in the back of the car, so that when I open the tailgate he cannot jump out anyway. However, you can still teach him the command to stay in the car, and I find having the pup in a crate is the easiest way to do it. As you open the car, give the command "wait" in a firm voice (a firm voice does not mean a loud voice; a pup should not be shouted at as it will intimidate him). Keep telling him to wait in a low, firm voice, and then go to open the crate door. If the pup comes forward, close the door of the crate firmly. After two or three times, the pup will get the message that he is not to jump out of his own accord, and you can then lift him out or, if he is big enough, let him jump out with the command "out". I must add that you should have attached his collar and lead as he must not be allowed to wander about or, indeed, leap back into the car. Once he is out of the car again, give the command "wait". When you have closed the car and the pup is still waiting quietly at your side, you can release him by giving the word "OK". It is rather like a soldier on parade standing to attention and then being told "at ease". The

car training can be accomplished without having to take the car out of the driveway.

DOOR MANNERS

The same sort of method applies to teaching the pup not to barge through a door or gateway ahead of you. Again, put the pup on his lead and give him the "wait" command at the door. You will find, as you go to open the door, that the pup will want to move forward, so shut the door smartly and say "No, wait!" to the pup. After two or three times, he will get the message he is not to move forward, and you can gradually open the door to its full width without him moving. Then, with the pup on a slack lead, gradually back away from him through the door, all the while keeping him in the wait position by telling him "wait" in a low firm voice. I do not use the pup's name for this exercise because I have found that for wait or stay exercises the pup will find it too distracting. Indeed, I find that for exercises other than the sit, the down, heelwork and coming when called, using his name will distract him anyway.

Once you have managed to slowly back through the door and the pup is still waiting, do not call him to you but return to his side and praise him quietly for not moving. Then repeat the whole exercise again, two or three times. Then, on say the fourth time, call him to you through the doorway and praise him lavishly. Most pups are pretty sensible and realise, after having the door closed in front of them a few times, not to barge their way through. This is not really an obedience exercise, but just basic good sense. Once again this is an exercise which can be repeated three or four times a day so that, by the time your pup is old enough to start formal lessons, he is already well-versed in some of the more desirable social graces.

INSTANT DOWN

Another very early lesson I teach young pups is the instant 'down'on command; as I explained before, this can save your dog's life in extreme circumstances! It is a relatively easy exercise to teach. Have the pup close to you, preferably on the lead, say his name and give the command "down" in an urgent tone of voice whilst gently slipping a couple of fingers in his collar behind his neck and 'folding'him into the down position. Hold him there for at least a count of five, all the while praising him in a low, pleased tone of voice. Then give him the release command. The important thing to remember is to make sure that you give much more praise when you have got him into the down position than when you give him the release command, otherwise he will think he is being praised for being released and not for lying down. In fact I usually praise the pup for the down and give no praise at all when I release him.

This exercise can be repeated at odd moments during the day – as often as possible in fact – but only once or twice at each session, so as not to bore the pup or sicken him of it. Indeed, he must look on each training exercise as exciting and enjoyable – this is how to build a rapport between you and your pup. This is why what I call ad lib or informal training is so important, especially during the formative months. The pup does not realise he is being trained, and he does not become bored with it.

You will soon find the pup is dropping into the instant down on command, as long as you are in close proximity to him. Now the time has come to increase the distance between owner and pup and also to diversify the area in which the training takes place.

Take the pup into a new area in the garden or, if his vaccinations have been given, take him to the park in the car. Walk him around on the lead, talking to him and playing with

him. If the lead is six feet long or so, all the better. Let him have the full length of the lead, then when he is not expecting it, give him the down command. If he does not obey instantly, just quietly go to him and place him into the down. Under no circumstances keep repeating the command "down, down", in the hope that he will do it. This is just teaching him to become disobedient. On the other hand, do not scold him either – it is best to keep your voice as neutral as possible and not to provoke a confrontation, which is pointless. If he persists in not dropping into the down instantly, just go back to the beginning and have him closer to you when you give the command.

Once he is proficient in dropping down at the end of a six-foot lead, you are then ready to throw in a hand signal as well as a command. I use my arm raised, palm facing out; you can use this at the same time as the voice command. Also, whilst the pup is still performing the exercise on the lead, try every now and again to do away with the voice command and just use the hand signal, all the time remembering not to let the pup get up out of the down position until you give him the release command. Remember to keep him in the down for at least a count of five, and this can be increased later to a count of ten. After all, what is the use of teaching your dog an instant down to possibly save his life and having him then get up immediately and run straight into danger again?

The next step is to increase the distance even more. If you do not yet feel confident enough to practise this exercise with the pup off the lead, use an extending lead, and then, after a few days of practising on this, he should be proficient enough to try off the lead.

Once he is dropping into the instant down a fair distance from you, always make sure you go to him to release him. On no account call him out of the down, otherwise he will be anticipating this, and it takes very little time for a pup to pick up bad habits and almost forever to break him from them. Again, practise several times a day for three or four minutes a time. It can be done as ad lib training whilst you have him out for a walk.

SIT
The 'sit' exercise can easily be taught as an early lesson for the pup. Have a tidbit in your hand, call his name to attract his attention, show him the tidbit, hold it over his head, and hey presto! His bottom will pop down, and as it does, give him plenty of praise. You can then join this exercise to the recall exercise – when you call the pup to you, hold the tidbit over his head and get him to sit in front of you. You will now have

Socialisation is an essential element in training youngsters.

Photo: Kim James.

a firm basis on which to build a formal recall exercise later on.

SEND AWAY

An eight-week-old pup is also capable of learning a 'send away'. When the pup is used to you and is keen on his food, have someone show him his food bowl, whilst you restrain him. Get your helper to place the food bowl about eight to ten feet in front of you and the pup, and then to move away. Then release the pup with the away command – I personally just use the word "away!" This early exercise forms the basis of a formal send away later on. Of course you may not wish to teach your dog a send away. However, it can be useful and I feel that the more a dog is taught, the better animal he is for it later on.

SOCIALISATION

Socialisation of young dogs is very important. Any detrimental or frightening experience which occurs when the pup is going through his developmental stage can stay with him for life and colour his adulthood, as can positive experiences such as the early exercises I have just described.

These days there is a school of thought that says that, if one is thinking of buying a puppy, then the optimum age is seven to eight weeks and, if the pup has stayed with his breeder after twelve weeks or so, it is not such a good idea to have that puppy. Personally, I am inclined to think that if a pup has been raised in a home environment and has been introduced to various experiences, such as the washing machine and the vacuum cleaner, and if there are sensible children in the household, then it does not really matter whether he is eight weeks or eighteen weeks old. Indeed, most conscientious breeders will have made sure that the older pup has been vaccinated, car-trained, house-trained and lead-trained. Certainly, for people looking for a prospective show dog, or someone who does not want to go through the trauma of sleepless nights or the odd accident on the carpet, an older pup could be an excellent prospect. If you are looking for a show dog, if you choose an older pup you will be able to have a much better idea of what you will end up with. If it is a male you will be able to see if he is entire – which is required in a show dog. Also, in many cases you can see whether or not the mouth is going to be correct, and again, with

A dog that is exposed to a variety of experiences, will learn to take all new situations in his stride.

A true country dog, the Jack Russell is a familiar sight around riding stables.

CQH Daisy Mae Of Starlight CD is a stunning example of a well-trained and well-socialised dog.
Photo: Chris Cox.

a show dog, this aspect is very important.

However, if you do decide to opt for a younger puppy, and most people who want a pet do, once again I reiterate, go to a breeder who has bred and raised raised their puppies in a home environment. Let us assume you have brought your puppy home at eight weeks old. Between now and the time the pup is ready for more formal exercises, you can practise the early exercises for the pup which I have already described.

Between the time you get the pup home and the time he has had all his vaccinations, he can be accustomed to all the household noises, i.e. washing machines, tumble dryers, vacuum cleaners etc. Make sure these are all positive experiences for him. For instance, make sure you do not switch on the vacuum cleaner right under the pup's nose. If the pup is keen on his food, perhaps a good time to do the vacuuming may be when the pup is feeding. He can also go on short car journeys, just around the block, two or three times a day. Another good idea is to carry him in your arms and go into the town, so

he can meet different people and see and hear traffic, but all the while feeling perfectly secure. We were very fortunate to have lived where a major road was more or less at the bottom of our street, so all my pups were gradually introduced to this to get them used to the noise of traffic.

It is a good idea to ask friends and neighbours round so they can make friends with the pup – even better if they have well-behaved children who can play gently with the puppy. Any children of the household must be taught to respect the pup's privacy, especially if he is sleeping or eating, and that he is a creature with special needs and not a furry little toy!

Once the pup is fully vaccinated and the vet has said he can go out and mix with other dogs, he can then go on his collar and lead for very short walks along the road to get used to the noise and movement of the traffic. These very short walks can take place two or three times a day. By short I mean a couple of hundred yards. I know it is a great temptation when the pup can first go out to

take him around and show him off to everybody. However, *on no account* should puppies under six to eight months old be heavily exercised (even older in large breeds), otherwise you could find your pup will grow up spindly and with possible bone damage. Indeed, young pups, like all young things, need a great deal of sleep.

Your pup will also need to be introduced to adult dogs, but they need to be very reliable in temperament, and it needs to be done under close supervision. He will also need to be introduced to pups of his own age and, of course, older pups. I have found the best way to do this is to join a good dog training club. Visit several clubs; make sure they use kind, positive methods of training and that the instructors know what they are doing. Do not leave this until the last minute; most good clubs will have a long waiting list.

Quite a few dog clubs these days run puppy parties or kindgergarten puppy training sessions. These are mainly for very young puppies to get them used to socialising with each other, which will stand them in good stead later on. On the other hand, I feel that too much playing with other pups could possibly lead your pup to become too 'dog-orientated' later on. I have always preferred any pups I have had to be orientated towards me, and not on other dogs. However, this is purely personal preference!

Once again, I cannot stress enough how important this period of socialisation is for young dogs – some people call it the 'window of opportunity'. When you think about it, a dog that is going to be a pet has to learn to adapt and fit in with the kids, the neighbours, the non-competitive members of the family (if he is a competition dog), the visitors and the other animals you may keep. If the pup has been well socialised, he will pass this test brilliantly! If not, he may well end up as another rescue organisation statistic.

BASIC OBEDIENCE

For training a pet, there are really only six basic obedience exercises to teach your dog for him to be really well behaved. These are the sit, the down, walking to heel, wait or stay, recall and (optional) retrieve. If you have been teaching your pup the early exercises I have already described, you will find it easy when he is around six months old to teach basic obedience in a more formal way. It is down to personal preference when you start formally training your pup, and taking into account, of course, whether the individual dog is ready. I feel it is a good idea to let him just be a pup rather than start too much formal training too early and make him bored, or have to put pressure on him because he does not concentrate, which probably means he is not yet ready.

FORMAL SIT AND DOWN

To teach the 'sit', have the dog on his collar and lead (I prefer a collar to check-chains as they are less abusive). Have him next to you, then call his name and say "sit" in a fairly neutral voice. I do not believe in shouting at dogs or using a silly exaggerated voice to give commands. In any case, dogs have a very acute sense of hearing and the more quietly you speak to your dog, the more intently he is likely to listen to you.

Make sure he sits nice and straight at your left-hand side. If he does not sit immediately, do not give him the opportunity to disobey again, but take hold of the lead low down near the collar with your right hand, and with your left hand gently 'fold' his bottom under him. On no account press down on his back or his pelvis. This folding action is achieved by your left hand gently stroking down the dog's back, and so folding his bottom under him. Keep him in the sit position for a count of five or so before releasing him. Again, once he has sat, praise him in a low voice for sitting, and not when you release him.

TRAINING EXERCISES
Photos: Sheila Atter.

When teaching the Sit, stroke the dog down his back rather than applying pressure to the hindquarters.

A tidbit can be used to encourage your dog to go into the Down position.

Use a slack lead when teaching the Stay.

The Down-Stay: Build this exercise up in easy stages.

Most important of all, give plenty of praise throughout the training session.

Use a similar scenario to teach the formal 'down'. Have the dog sitting nice and straight on your left-hand side, call his name and give him the down command. Once again, if he does not do it the first time, gently hold his collar underneath and 'fold' him into the down, or if you prefer, hold his collar with your left hand, hold a titbit in your right hand under his nose and, with a sweeping motion, take the titbit out and down to the floor. As he follows it with his nose, he will automatically lie down. Praise him in a low voice, count to five and release him.

If you have been teaching sit and down as early exercises, all this should be relatively easy. We are merely formalising it by teaching him to sit tidily and reinforcing instant obedience, especially with the 'down'. During these months you should still carry on with the early exercises, such as the long down and 'going through the door' and so on. Dogs, especially terriers, have short memories and soon forget early lessons if they are not practised on a regular basis.

WALKING TO HEEL

Walking to heel is an important basic obedience exercise if you are going to enjoy taking your pet for a walk. What we are hoping for, at the end of the day, is a well-socialised, well-behaved pet.

Once again, have your dog on your left-hand side. (It is really just a tradition in dog training that one always works the dog on the left. However, if you wish to work him on the right, that is perfectly OK; indeed for agility training and show training he needs to be able to work from both sides.) Call your dog's name; and you can also use the command "look" or "watch" (remember the early lessons). As soon as your dog is looking up at you, give him the command "heel" or "close" and step off smartly with your left foot. The secret is to only walk a few paces, then break off and have a game with your dog or give him a titbit. Then repeat everything from the beginning.

If your dog's attention wavers and he looks away, just give him the 'look' command and carry on for a couple of paces before you break off and play with him. You will soon find you will be able to walk quite a few paces before he loses attention. However, do not keep repeating this exercise ad infinitum – terriers have a short attention span at the best of times and the worst thing you can do is to make him bored. This is an exercise to be practised for short periods several times a day. Eventually you can graduate to walking left- and right-hand circles and figures of eight; these are designed to keep the dog's attention on you. On no account try to marry up the heelwork and the sit just yet – that can happen later.

When you are ready to teach your dog the sit during heelwork, just have him walking to heel for two or three paces, give him the 'sit' command and, as you do so, slide your right hand to the bottom of the lead and fold his bottom underneath him with your left. Make sure you give most of the praise for the heelwork rather than the sit, as it is heelwork we are teaching, not the sit exercise. When you are walking along with your dog at heel, do not forget to use a slack lead and to talk to your dog – tell him in a low voice what a good chap he is and what a good job he is doing.

STAY

Another very useful exercise is the 'wait' or 'stay'. I personally use the command "wait" if I want my dog to wait when I am then going to call him back to me, and "stay" when I mean 'stay where you are and do not move until I come back to you'. To teach the wait or stay, put your dog into either the sit or the down and, in a low voice, tell him to "wait" or "stay". Incidentally this is one of the exercises where it is best not to use the dog's name to precede the command, as we do not want him to be ready for action and move from his position! After you have given him the stay command and he is remaining steadily at your side for around ten to fifteen seconds or so, very slowly take one pace away from him to the side, all the while telling him in a low voice to "stay" or "wait". When you have taken the pace away from him (on a very slack lead, I hasten to add – indeed there must be hardly any movement of the lead at all), count to ten, move back to your dog's side, count to five, then tell him in a low, very quiet voice what a clever, good dog he is. Then, take a pace backwards and release him with the "OK" command. On no account whatsoever should you give him any praise at all upon release. In fact the whole exercise should be kept extremely quiet and

low-key. The dog should also not be played with upon release.

I like to teach the 'stay' on a 10 ft training lead because it means you are in control all the time and, after all, 10 ft is quite a long way. You can leave the dog to the left or the right, to the front, and even, when he is steady, walk right round him in a circle, remembering all the while to keep the lead slack. I cannot stress enough how much patience you will need to teach the 'stay' or 'wait' exercise; every stage must be taken very slowly if you are going to end up with a steady dog. On no account should a dog ever be punished or even scolded for breaking a 'stay'. If necessary, go right back to the beginning and reinforce positively the lessons you have already taught him.

Only when he is staying steadily on his ten-foot training lead can you consider letting him off the lead to practise the exercise and, even then, thirty yards or so is plenty of distance to leave your dog. It really is not necessary to leave a pet dog in a 'stay' at a distance greater than this, any more than it is necessary to go out of sight of your dog. Of course, if you are going to do competition work, then you should join an appropriate training club and buy a book on training competition dogs.

FORMAL RECALL

By the time a dog is ready to start formal training, I would expect him to be reliably coming back when he is called. Therefore the formal recall exercise is purely that – a formality. When your dog is reliable in the 'wait' exercise you can then start to teach him the formal recall. This exercise should never be taught or practised immediately after a 'stay' exercise, just as a retrieve should never be taught after you have been doing 'stays'. It is a sure-fire way to confuse your dog and end up with a dog which breaks his stays.

To teach the formal recall, have your dog

Make sure you get the correct size of dumb-bell for your Jack Russell.   *Photo: Pat Baker.*

on his collar and ten-foot training lead. Do not use his name, but tell him in a quiet voice to "wait", pause for a moment, then step off with your right foot and leave him. After you have gone about four feet away, turn and face him, so that you are standing directly in front of him. Pause for the count of five then return and stand beside him. Tell him in a quiet voice "good boy", then immediately tell him to "wait" once more, pause, and then go to stand about four feet in front of him. Pause again, then in a quiet but happy voice and with a smile on your face, call him in to sit directly in front of you. Once again if you have been practising the

'look' or 'watch' exercise he should be looking up at you. Pause momentarily, then praise him in a quiet but pleased voice. Keep him sitting in front of you, swivel on the ball of your right foot and return to stand next to your dog with him on your left, and then give him the release command.

Another variation of this exercise is to tell your dog to wait, pause briefly, stand immediately in front of him, pause briefly again, then move backwards for three or four steps, encouraging your dog to come to you. After you have gone three or four paces backwards, tell him to sit directly in front of you, pause briefly, and praise him quietly. Still standing in front of him, repeat the whole exercise, then pivot on your foot so you are then standing next to him. Count to five, then give your dog the release command.

FORMAL RETRIEVE
It is really down to individual personal preference whether you wish to teach your dog a formal retrieve. If you have been following the early lessons for the puppy, you will find it easy to teach your dog a formal retrieve when he is a bit older. Before you start teaching him a formal retrieve, make absolutely sure that he has finished teething, otherwise his gums will be sore and you will put him off.

To start with, choose an article that you are going to use as a formal retrieve article and keep it purely for this exercise. On no account use it as a toy or let your dog play with it or 'mouth' it. I prefer to use a dumb-bell: for one thing it is easy for a dog pick up, the centre bar being raised off the ground. Make sure it fits the dog's mouth – the centre bar should not be so long that the device is unbalanced in the dog's mouth, nor should it be so short that the ends pinch his lips. The ends of the dumb-bell should be large enough so that the centre bar is an inch off the ground to facilitate ease of pick-up. A

Cassacre Berwick Of Gripton makes all training exercises look easy! Photo: Pat Baker.

lot of people get 'hung up' about the dumb-bell, but it is really only a stick with ends on!

Have your dog sitting on your left-hand side on his collar and lead. Slip two fingers of your left hand through the back of his collar, hold the dumb-bell by one of its ends in your right hand, and hold it close to your dog's mouth. Tell him to "hold it" in a neutral voice. If he is already play-retrieving, following the early puppy lessons, he should reach forward and take the dumb-bell from you. All the while he is holding it, praise him in a low voice, by saying "good boy, hold it". Let him hold the dumb-bell for five seconds or so, then tell him "leave" and gently take it

from him. I prefer to give all the praise for the 'hold' and hardly any at all for the 'leave', otherwise you will end up with a dog that spits out his dumb-bell to get the praise for the 'leave'.

Once he is holding his dumb-bell properly for around ten seconds or so, start to hold it about six inches away from him down towards the ground. On being given the 'hold' command, he should reach forward and take his dumb-bell from you. Always remember to give plenty of praise in a low voice. Eventually you will place the dumb-bell lower, until your dog is picking it up from the ground. Once he is as advanced as this, place the dumb-bell three feet or so away on the ground and give him the 'hold' command – your dog should go out and pick up his dumb-bell. He should still be on his training lead, so encourage him to sit in front of you still holding his dumb-bell; pivot on your right foot (remember the recall lessons), stand beside your dog, pause briefly, then take the dumb-bell from him.

Once he is happily retrieving his dumb-bell from about ten feet away, still on the training lead, the time has come to teach your dog to wait before going to retrieve his dumb-bell. Place (not throw) the dumb-bell out about six feet or so, hook a couple of the fingers of your left hand into the back of his collar and tell him, in a firm but not loud voice, "wait", count to five, then reach out and pick up the dumb-bell yourself! Repeat this at least three times, and you will soon find he is waiting rather than charging out after the dumb-bell. Remember to give him plenty of praise in a low voice. On the fourth attempt he can be commanded to go out and retrieve the dumb-bell. When he is reliably waiting when told and retrieving on the lead, you can attempt the exercise off the lead; leave his collar on, though, so you have a modicum of control and, if he regresses, go back to the beginning and use the training lead again.

The show dog must learn to stand for inspection. This is Belmorr Dash of Lenacourt.
Photo courtesy: Vera Harcourt-Morris.

Also once your dog is proficient at retrieving, other articles such as a ring or a ball on a rope can be substituted for the dumb-bell. One word of warning – never ever be tempted to throw sticks for your dog, and do not let anyone else do so. Your dog could be seriously injured or even die if he were to impale himself on a stick!

SHOW TRAINING

If you have bought your pup for show, it is always a good idea to enrol at your local ringcraft classes. The instructors there can tell you if you are moving your dog at the right speed, and conditions will simulate most of what goes on in the show ring. Your dog will become used to being handled by strangers, which is essential if he is to be steady as a show dog. Also he will get used to ignoring other dogs and concentrating solely upon you; again this is most important if your dog is to sparkle and show himself off to his best advantage. Also, hopefully, you will end up

making plenty of friends! Another thing you will need to do is to start buying dog magazines, as not only do these publications have interesting articles and notes on all the different breeds, they also advertise the various shows in which you might like to enter your dog.

It is wise to invest in a nice show collar and lead for your dog and keep it purely for ringcraft training and the show ring. I prefer to use a soft leather half-check collar and matching lead, about 3/8 inches (6 mm) wide and in black or dark brown, so as not to distract the judge's eye from the dog. If you have an older puppy and his show collar and lead will fit him, always use this when you have a training session with him. If he is a young puppy just use his soft puppy collar and lead.

If you have bought an older puppy, as I said earlier, most conscientious breeders will have made sure he is lead-trained. However, whatever age your pup is, once he has settled

into your home you can start training him for the show ring. Show ring training is not really that different from basic heelwork training, except you need to teach your dog to stand on command. He still needs to pay attention to you just as much as he does when he performs his obedience exercises. There is a school of thought that is of the opinion that show dogs should undergo no obedience training at all, just in case they sit in the show ring instead of standing. This, of course, is utter rubbish – any dog as intelligent as a Jack Russell is perfectly capable of understanding the difference between sit and stand.

STAND

Find yourself an old table about four feet long and two feet wide and cover it with a piece of carpet or a couple of large carpet tiles, so that it has a non-slip surface. Practise standing your puppy on this, pretending it is the judge's table in the show ring. Give him the command "stand" in a neutral voice, all the while praising him in a low voice; you can also have a tidbit in your hand to attract his attention. Practise this for brief periods several times a day. You will need plenty of patience at first, as a very young puppy will probably not be too keen on standing still. However, persevere and you will soon find the penny will drop and he will start to stand still. On no account should you ever chastise or scold your puppy whilst he is on the table. If you find yourself losing your patience, stop the training session and return to it later.

You will also need to teach him to stand still on a loose lead and to keep his attention solely on you. To achieve this tell your pup to "stand" and "wait" (if you have been teaching him to stand on the table he should by now know what "stand" means), step in front of him, not immediately in front as in the recall exercise but a pace or so back, and then tell him to "look" or "watch". You

should also have a small tidbit concealed in your hand, so the minute he looks up at you and wags his tail, show him the tidbit, then give it to him, of course all the while praising him in a low voice.

INSPECTION

When your pup is at the stage when he is standing still on the table, you can then go through the same routine a show judge would go through. As you gently lift his lips up to inspect his teeth, quietly give him the command "teeth". Run your hands over his body and also lift up each foot in turn and examine his pads, all the while quietly praising him.

It is also a good idea to make a measuring stick out of thin wood so you can practise bringing this up and over your pup's back, simulating conditions identical to those he will be meeting in the show ring. When you put the measuring stick over your pup's back, bring it slowly up over his hindquarters until it is level with his withers, praise him quietly, then remove the measure. Another good idea is to get friends to examine the puppy gently whilst you have him standing on the table. He then will not find strangers handling him quite so traumatic when you start ringcraft classes with him.

HEELWORK

For show ring training you need to teach your dog to walk smartly to heel on the right as well as on the left. Actually the principle is exactly the same as basic obedience heelwork, except when you come to work your dog on the right, if you have been using the word "heel" for heelwork on the left; use a different command such as "close" or "right" for heelwork on the right. You need to work your pup on a slack lead, as 'stringing him up' on a tight lead is unnecessary and will throw his front out.

Practise little and often and keep the

doorways; if he does, do not step over him to pass but make him get up and move elsewhere.

MOUTHING

If your pup is going through a phase where he has started to mouth or bite at your hands, especially whilst you are grooming him, then as soon as he starts, give a high-pitched yelp – "Ouch!"– like another pup would, and the minute he stops, give him a tidbit straightaway and praise him. On no account smack him on the nose, as this will make him snap at you and the behaviour will become worse.

DISOBEDIENCE

If your dog persists in not coming back when he is called, or worse still, running off the minute he sees another dog, on no account should you chastise him if he returns of his own accord. If it is purely a case of him not coming back when you call him, or if he comes back but stays out of reach, you will probably find this is just a phase he is going through. In this case I would keep him on a long line or an extending lead for a while; let him have the whole length of this and, while you are out for your walk, keep calling him back to you (without turning it into a formal recall). To begin with, give him a tidbit deducted from his food ration, or have a game with him with a toy. Then, after a while, only reward him when he returns to you immediately and doubly quick.

If, on the other hand, he sees another dog and disappears after it, he needs to be taught that this is undesirable behaviour. Call your dog immediately he sees the other dog, and if he returns praise and reward him lavishly. If, however, he ignores you and runs after the other dog, on no account keep calling him; this is merely teaching him to be disobedient. Do not lose your temper. Walk determinedly over to where your dog is; when you arrive on the scene, and it could be quite a distance (I know what it is like, it has happened to me), ignore the other dog and its owner, get hold of your own dog's collar and scold him severely. Put him on the lead and march him back to where he left you and practise some recall exercises on the lead – these should be rewarded, however.

If you have your dog on a long line and he is showing interest in chasing other dogs, he must be told "No!" most emphatically and praised when he stops showing interest. This is one of the reasons why I do not like any young dog of mine to play too much with other young dogs. I am not saying it is a bad idea to get your puppy to meet other pups of a similar age and older, because it is not – they do need to learn to be friendly with other dogs. However, I feel that too much playing with other dogs can make your pup keener on them than he is on you. It is my personal preference that my dog is keener on me than he is on other dogs.

I would like to think that, if you have followed the early lessons for the puppy and the basic obedience exercises, and your dog has been well socialised either by yourself or by his breeder, then you will not have any problems, but will have a well-behaved pet to be proud of.

6 THE VERSATILE JACK RUSSELL

The Jack Russell could certainly be described as a jack of all trades, and a master of many. These dogs have literally worked their way from the ground up: stable terrier to television and film star. At the same time, Jack Russells have been doing their fair share of meaningful work such as therapy, hunting, obedience, earth dog, tracking, and even drug-sniffing. With this breed's trainability and temperament, versatility is their middle name.

In talking about versatility you need to remember that an excellent temperament is essential for any breed to be truly versatile. A dog that is too independent does not tend to be a good training prospect, and a dog that lacks self-confidence can be just as difficult to train. Temperament is the one ingredient that every breeder needs to keep at the top of his or her list. No matter how well a dog is structured, or how beautiful it looks, if it cannot be trained and have its energy channelled in a positive way, it will make a very poor companion, and versatility will soon be lost.

Since, for a great majority of people, the opportunity to engage a Jack Russell Terrier in the discipline it was bred for is probably pretty remote, it has always been my opinion that any type of work is better than nothing at all. Even if you teach your dog very basic obedience *just* to be a well-behaved pet, it will benefit him and you in the long run, and any dog that has received even only basic training is a much better dog because of it.

In the UK, there are three major organised disciplines in which you can train your dog to compete in. These are Working Trials, Obedience and Mini Agility. All three disciplines are highly competitive and have a large following, with competitions being held most weekends.

UK WORKING TRIALS

Working Trials have been around a long time. Initially there were probably not that many held, as most dogs were either military or service dogs. The premier society in the UK was, and still is, the Associated Sheep, Police and Army Dog Society (ASPADS, which celebrated its 70th anniversary in 1994). In the 1920s very few, if any, of the dogs were worked by civilians. Now, most of the dogs are worked by civilians. At the present time, the Working Trials calendar is very crowded, especially during the spring and autumn, and on some weekends there could be two or three trials held in different parts of the UK.

When ASPADS was first formed, almost all the dogs that took part in trials were German Shepherd Dogs. Today, however, any dog that will lend itself to the training can take part, and they do not have to be pedigree dogs. The only criterion is that, because of

The intelligent Jack Russell can adapt to a wide variety of tasks.

Photo courtesy: Sue Porter.

the Agility section, dogs have to be 18 months old before they compete.

Small breeds can and frequently do take part in Working Trials but, because of their size, can only compete in the CD and UD stakes. So, these letters after a dog's name, what do they mean?

CDEX	Companion Dog excellent
UDEX	Utility Dog excellent
WDEX	Working Dog excellent
TDEX	Tracking Dog excellent
PDEX	Patrol Dog excellent

These qualifications are not come by easily. The training is long and arduous and requires a great deal of self-motivation; the dogs (and handlers) also need to be very fit. You need land available to go tracking on – and we all know how difficult it is to get permission to work dogs on farmland. You also need your own set of jumps and access to a set (or two) that the dog is not familiar with. The other things I nearly forgot to mention a great deal of patience and a sense of humour!

QUALIFICATION

In every stake except CD, you must qualify in an Open Trial with over 80 per cent of marks before you are eligible to enter a Championship trial. This, however, does not mean that CD is easy. Indeed, because of the anomalies in the way it is marked, it is often more difficult to obtain a qualification in CD than it is in UD. Also, your dog must earn over the minimum group qualifying mark in every group of exercises; to fail one means you fail the whole trial! Also, you must get 70 per cent of the total marks overall to qualify in whichever stake you are working, and to qualify 'excellent', 80 per cent must be obtained.

The great thing about Working Trials is that, although there are always the first four places up for grabs, you are actually competing against a standard, so you do not have to be among the first four to qualify. Nevertheless competition is still very fierce. On average, at a Championship Trial, there would be roughly 50 to 60 dogs entered in the CD stake and, out of this number, only half-a-dozen or so will actually qualify.

I have found Jack Russells to have an

extremely good nose for the track and search and they are easily able to cope with the Agility section. The control section for Jack Russells is a little more difficult; they need quite a lot of motivation and the stays can be quite difficult to train, as Jack Russells tend to lack the concentration of a Border Collie or a German Shepherd. However, if you are prepared to spend quite a lot of time motivating and training your terrier (I have found little-and-often is the best way), then there is no reason why a Jack Russell should not be able to reach the standard required to compete in CD and UD at working trials.

In the nose-work group, the search is for four articles in a 25-yard square, and five minutes is allowed for this. Each article, roughly similar in material and size to the CD articles, or even smaller, is worth seven marks. There are also seven marks allotted for style – as in CD. If the handler and dog work as a team and the dog responds well to the commands and quarters the square well, you can still earn the seven marks, even if the dog is unfortunate enough not to find all the articles.

The track is usually about half a mile long, and is always laid unseen by the dog and handler and known only to the track-layer and the judge. Marks are awarded for how the dog works the track, particularly on the corners. Ten marks each are awarded for the dog finding the two articles (he has to find at least one of them to qualify), and also marked is how the dog and handler work as a team. The dog is worked on a harness and long line.

The type of ground used for tracking at Working Trials varies according to the season and the location. Incidentally, weather conditions are not taken into consideration, land always being at a premium. If you are lucky and have good weather for the nose work, fantastic – but, if the weather is adverse, then you must learn to be philosophical.

US WORKING TRIALS

In the USA, similar titles are competed for under the umbrella of Obedience Trials. The American Kennel Club offers Obedience Trials to test your dog's ability to perform a prescribed set of exercises on which the dog is scored. There are three levels of competition. The first level is Novice, and has more to do with being a good

U-CDX CQH Daisy Mae Of Starlight CD: The first Jack Russell to win the AKC Companion Dog title.

Ashbey Photography. Photo courtesy: Chris Cox.

companion. The resultant title is Companion Dog and the initials CD are then placed after the dog's registered name.

The next two levels are called Companion Dog Excellent (CDX) and Utility level, with the title Utility Dog (UD), and then Utility Dog Excellent (UDX). The most difficult and prestigious title to earn is the Obedience Trial Champion (OTCH).

Chris Cox of Minnesota, with her dog CQH Daisy Mae of Starlight CD, was the first Jack Russell to earn her AKC Companion Dog title, in January of 1998. Her title was particularly meaningful as she left her litter of pups to compete in the first shows and was more than anxious to return to her maternal duties at home. Daisy also had earned her Canine Good Citizen title prior to her AKC debut. Daisy and her owner are currently working on a CDX title.

Kim James from Oregon routinely does obedience work with her dogs, most of which have earned their Novice titles. She feels that the obedience training is essential to her breeding programme. Her level of control is obvious when seeing the many fabulous photos that she has taken of her group of terriers. Kim is also active in Agility, Earth Dog, and conformation, and a few of her dogs are registered therapy dogs.

OBEDIENCE
In the UK, Obedience developed as a separate discipline from Working Trials. If you are really feeling up to a challenge, Obedience is another discipline in which you could compete with your Jack Russell. I always feel it is akin to dressage as, in fact, not only is the dog marked for extreme accuracy, but the handler is also marked for deportment and footwork.

There are several stages to work through before your dog is eligible to compete at the highest level, which is Test C Championship. To win three Challenge Certificates under three different judges in Championship C makes your dog up to an Obedience Champion. The lowest class is Beginners, then you work your way up the Obedience ladder through Novice, Test A, Test B, Test C Open and then Test C Championship. The competition, even in Beginners, is very fierce. Marks are lost for the slightest crooked sit, wide heelwork and inattention. There can also be anything from 30 to 40 dogs in a class and, once again, Border Collies dominate the sport. In tests A, B and C, there is a scent discrimination test as well as a retrieve.

Dogs are eligible to compete in Obedience tests once they are six months old, and, as for Working Trials, do not have to be a purebred dog to be eligible.

AGILITY
Agility will often attract a diverse and enthusiastic crowd. You can do Agility for fun, recreation, or for competition. For the Jack Russell, it is an excellent event for channelling excess energy and for providing the mental stimulation it requires. It is also a great way for your dog to keep in top shape! Agility is rather like show jumping. The dog is trained to run a course off the lead with its handler. The course consists of jumps, tunnels and other obstacles, and the fastest dog with the fewest faults wins. Marks are deducted for faults, these being either jumps knocked down or missed contact points on the obstacles, such as the see-saw, the 'dog walk' or the 'A' frame. Contact points are a certain distance from the ground on these obstacles and the dog's feet must touch them – he must not jump off the obstacle prior to this. If a dog and handler take a wrong turn, they are eliminated, as in show jumping.

The handler needs to be able to exert a great deal of control over the dog, and yet keep the dog motivated enough to get round as quickly as possible. Dogs find the sport of

EXCELLING AT AGILITY

Photos: Kim James, Badgerwood.

Agility very exciting and it takes a great deal of expertise on the part of the handlers to be able to control their dogs. The dog needs to be able to work on the right as well as on the traditional left-hand side, and he also needs to work ahead of the handler and be proficient in the instant down on command! Probably the most difficult part of the course for these dogs is the dreaded 'pause table'; stopping, even for five seconds, is not always something a Jack Russell wants to do especially when it is having such a fun run.

To learn Agility it is best to join a club or group that specialises in Agility training, so that your dog is taught safely and correctly. A reputable club will not allow dogs to start their training until they are 12 months old, and they cannot compete until they are 18 months old in the UK, 12 months old in the USA. Your national Kennel Club will have a list of recognised Agility clubs.

GOOD CITIZEN

Working Trials, Obedience and Agility are very social events and it benefits both dog and owner to work together with other people and other breeds of dogs. Of course, if you are not a particularly competitive person, you could still join a dog training club and enrol your dog in the Kennel Club Good Citizen scheme which, although there is a test at the end of the 10-week course, is completely non-competitive and purely a test of competence.

The Good Citizen scheme was started in the US under the auspices of the American Kennel Club, and has been slightly adapted for use in Britain. The tests are quite basic, and should prove no problem to the average, well-socialised Jack Russell.

RACING

Besides being bright and entertaining, Jack Russells are also very fast. If you have never seen a Jack Russell race, it would remind you

a bit of Greyhound racing. The dogs are generally run in heats, so perhaps four to five dogs run against each other per race, followed by the winners squaring off for the best time. There are a few people at the end of the race specifically to catch the terriers so they do not continue beyond the race set-up, as many of them surely could. The excitement of the spectators and the owners of the dogs once the start box has opened and the race begins is truly infectious. The dogs seem to pick up the enthusiasm of the cheering owners, which is why most race organisers require all dogs to be muzzled – with all the yelling and screaming it would be easy for a dog to take a nip or two at another terrier.

Flyball is another sort of racing event, which has the dogs running down a racing lane, with four jumps spaced ten feet apart, to retrieve balls from a Flyball box at the end. The dogs run in two separate racing lanes, usually with a very enthusiastic crowd of spectators waiting to hear "Get your Ball", which signals the start of the race. Jack Russells make fierce competitors in Flyball racing, because their prey-drive easily translates to ball-drive, and they have boundless energy. If you want to learn more about Flyball there is a whole book devoted to the sport, called *Flyball Racing*, written by Lonnie Olson, and published by Howell Book House. Contact your national Kennel Club for details of Flyball clubs.

FALCONRY

Falconry is a sport that, while not exactly mainstream, certainly has quite a following. The sport itself has a long history dating back to medieval times, and basically revolves around the training of hawks to hunt in co-operation with people.

There is certainly nothing unusual about a hawk hunting or catching a rabbit, as that is how they survive. However, the sport is in teaching the hawk to allow a human to

TERRIER RACING

Fast and determined, the Jack Russell is an enthusiastic participant at the races. Photo courtesy: Mary Strom, Snow Wind.

participate in the hunt. This is where the terriers are of assistance, particularly Jack Russell Terriers.

Jack Russells, because they are smart, trainable, agile and hard-working, make excellent partners in the sport of falconry. This sport basically requires the dogs to flush bunnies and small birds, such as pheasant and partridge, from dense cover. Falcons are able to cover large amounts of territory in a day, so the dog must also be willing and able to cover ground in an efficient and tireless manner. All of the above is what a Jack Russell was bred to do.

The Jack Russell is a baying terrier, and this is one of the reasons why they are an excellent dog for falconry. The dog and the hawk are worked in open areas, as wooded areas give poor visibility because of tree cover and are more difficult for the hawk to hunt in. If you have ever listened to a Jack Russell baying, it is quite distinctive. It is essential that the falconer knows the particular bay of his dog, so that the hawk is not released unless the dog has actually found quarry.

Russell pups are never used with a falcon, as the hawk could mistake the pups for quarry. Puppies are started on scent training and tracking at an early age, and must also have some simple obedience training. The pups must also be of good structure, and able to cover large amounts of ground; so for this reason, good length of leg is important to a falconry dog.

Since this sport is a complex relationship between hawk, human and dog, it is essential that the human has good control of the hawk, and constantly monitors the relationship between the dog and the hawk. Dave Gardiner lives in a small Eastern Washington town, where he has enjoyed the sport of falconry for many years, along with the companionship of his Jack Russell Terriers, which he occasionally breeds. He

states that the dog's role is usually thought of as supporting. However, watching a good terrier trail up a rabbit and push it hard enough so that the hawk has a good chance to catch it adds a whole new dimension of excitement to the hunt.

The following is the story of one of Dave Gardiner's trips out to hunt with his dog and hawk, to give you a better idea of the sport and how it is actually conducted.

"In one of the areas in which I hunt, there is a thick patch of large sage brush that grows between a creek and a cliff of columnar basalt. The cliff rises to a height of about 150 feet and a hawk perched at the top is in command of a lot of real estate.

I remember a clear, winter day when there was a thin covering of snow on the ground. The blue sky with its sun shining cold, the white snow, the black rock of the cliff and the vagueness of the sage brush all combined to give me a jolt and to remind me that I was alive.

I walked toward the thick patch of brush, while my Jack Russell Terrier, Pete, ran ahead scenting the air and snow. Jenny, my old red-tailed hawk, powered by and flared up to take her place at the top of the cliff. She watched in anticipation as Pete and I worked our way through the brush, but we came out the

FALCONRY
Dave Gardiner has proved that the versatile Jack Russell
can be used in this most impressive of sports.
Photos courtesy: Rani Morningstar.

other side without having flushed anything. I was feeling a little let down and Jenny was looking ahead to select her next perch when Pete's head came up and he headed back into the brush, tasting the cold air.

The hawk, alerted by Pete's evident interest, shifted position and her posture took on a certain intensity. Pete was holding his head so high that his front feet barely touched the ground as he disappeared into the brush. Then I heard the muffled bark that says " there is a rabbit in here". The next instant Pete was in full cry (well, full yip, anyway) and moving fast, sounding like a demented squeaky toy. Then he circled around and headed straight back toward me. With a few powerful wing beats, Jenny launched herself and went into a steep, fast, swept-wing glide toward a spot between the terrier and myself. Through the brush I could see a rabbit coming towards me at high speed with Pete about 30 feet behind him. The hawk banked and pulled in behind the rabbit; she folded her wings, crashed through a sage and slammed into the rabbit, almost at my feet.

As the hawk and rabbit tumbled to a stop, Pete had to put on the brakes and skid to keep from running into the hawk. The little dog looked over at me, then sat down, panted and grinned while he watched Jenny begin her meal.

I did not do a lot of formal training with Pete. I just took him to places where he could chase lots of rabbits. It took a little while for Pete and Jenny to figure each other out, but the mutual desire to catch game helped. Also I dulled Jenny's talons for the 'getting to know you'part of the relationship.

During a hunt, the hawk and the dog watch each other with more interest than they show for me. Each will respond quickly if the other locates game and sometimes the two of them will hunt an area together while I sit on a hill and just watch.

Sometimes the whole experience gives me a strange feeling and I wonder just who these two magical creatures are and what it would be like to look out through their eyes.**"**

EARTH DOG
In Earth Dog events, the dog is worked through a plywood liner system.

Photos courtesy: Mary Strom, Snow Wind..

EARTH DOG EVENTS

Many people that purchase Jack Russell Terriers are very interested in their working ability. However, if you live in an inner city, or well-manicured suburban neighbourhood, it can be difficult to find an acceptable place to work your dog, let alone someone to teach you how.

Earth Dog events are designed for a safe and positive experience in introducing a den terrier to quarry. It is both casual and relaxed and can be a very fun outing with your dog. There is no real competition in Earth Dog, as the dog is really competing for himself.

AKC Earth Dog is a controlled event where the dog is usually worked through a plywood liner system which forms a nine-inch by nine-inch hole, with rats caged at the end of the liners. The liners are buried underground to look as natural as possible and most clubs use dirt and brush to make it look so. In all tests there is a scent line and a release line for the dogs. In the Junior test, the release line is located only ten feet from the actual entrance to the liner. In both the

Justice Electra Blue: A winner in Obedience, Conformation, Earth Dog events and Agility.
Photo courtesy: Kim James, Badgerwood.

HERDING

This is not a task generally associated with the Jack Russell, but, in fact, the breed can be very effective in this line of work.

Photos courtesy: Mary Strom, Snow Wind.

Senior and Master tests the release line is substantially longer. The judges are located in an area at the end of the liners to observe whether the dog will actually work the cage where the rats are contained. Working can be defined as barking, baying, growling, digging and pawing at the cage. Intense staring or sniffing do not count as working. For the Junior Earth Dog Test, the dog must work the cage continuously for 60 seconds. Once the dog has passed the test, it has earned one part of its Junior Earth Dog Title. In order to earn the title the dog must pass the test twice.

There are two other levels of Earth Dog titles – Senior and Master. Both of these titles require a certain amount of obedience training. The Master Earth Dog test is designed to be as close to a natural hunting situation as possible, as it requires the dog to work in conjunction with another dog. There is a false den as well as one that has actual quarry in both the Senior and Master tests. In the Senior test, the quarry is actually removed from the liner and the dog must be called out of the liner. This can be one of the bigger challenges with a Jack Russell Terrier who is very focused on the task at hand.

If you are interested in participating in Earth Dog events, they are listed each month in the American Kennel Club Events Calendar, which can be purchased through a subscription or be located on the Internet through the AKC web site at:

http://www.akc.org. Remember, when you go to an Earth Dog event, leave your dress clothes at home – jeans and sweatshirts are the required attire!

POLICE WORK
The Jack Russell Terrier, being first and foremost a working dog, has even caught the eye of the police. They are beginning to be used as drug-sniffing dogs in at least one major airport.

Bob Eden of K9 Academy for Law Enforcement in the USA states: "The Jack Russell may make a good detection dog of any type. They are small, which makes them easy to work into tight places, and the handler can lift them up to high enclosed spaces. To train a good detection dog, we need a dog with confidence in working in various environments and a high retrieve instinct to train with."

Like many types of canine work, there is specific testing that is done to ascertain whether a dog will have potential for police work. The qualities that a dog must have are good temperament, courage, and a certain amount of hardness, along with sharpness and instinctive drive. Many dogs will have these characteristics, but they will not necessarily be able to produce the behaviour at the appropriate time.

One of the biggest and most enduring trends I have noticed through talking with owners about their Jack Russell Terriers is the

The police have started to recognise the talents of the Jack Russell as a drug-sniffer.

Photo: Kim James, Badgerwood.

need for an excellent temperament. This is where breeders need to be so very watchful, as any breed that loses its reputation for an excellent temperament will also lose its versatility and soon its popularity.

THERAPY DOGS

This breed has a reputation for being very active, and most of them are. However, because of the excellent trainability of the breed, a Jack Russell can go from running in the fields, chasing bunnies and squirrels, to quietly sitting in a sick or elderly person's lap.

Not every dog is suited for therapy work, although it seems there are quite a few Jack Russells registered. In the USA, these dogs are called Therapy Dogs and are registered with Therapy Dogs International. In the UK, dogs are registered with Pro-Dogs as Pets as Therapy Dogs (Pat-dogs). It takes a certain amount of training and dedication to train your dog for therapy work, and he must pass a temperament test before he will be

accepted, but the emotional rewards are very great indeed.

The job of a therapy dog is to visit various institutions such as hospitals, nursing, retirement and residential homes, special schools and hospices where residents, due to their circumstances, are unable to have a dog of their own. The dogs take patients' minds off of their problems, and more onto interactive time with the dog. It has long been recognised that the elderly live longer, happier lives when they have a pet or companion to care for. There have also been numerous studies that support the notion that a person's blood pressure actually lowers when they are in the act of petting a dog.

If you are interested in your dog becoming a registered therapy dog the following are a few things to keep in mind. Be sure that your dog has an excellent temperament, and is exposed to young children, elderly people, wheelchairs, crutches, electric beds, and general medical apparatus, that it would

Keswick Whip Of Starlight: Registered as a Therapy Dog in the US.
Photo courtesy: Chris Cox.

encounter on a visit to the above institutions. You might be surprised how many dogs are terrified by a wheelchair, or startled by the sound of a crutch or cane dropping to the floor.

Therapy Dogs International requires a dog to be at least one year of age and to have passed a training club graduation class or have an AKC Obedience title. They must be well groomed and up to date on all of their vaccinations and worming. Female dogs should not be in oestrus when doing therapy dog work.

It is always entertaining for a therapy dog to know a special trick or a series of tricks to entertain the patients. Your dog also needs to be able to interact well with other dogs, as there will be different dogs of various breeds at the institution at the same time as you.

FILM AND TV WORK

Of course, if you have a Jack Russell with a super outgoing temperament and who is a real show-off, you can always register him with an animal agency in the hope that he might get a part on TV or in films. Dogs that are used in film work need to have an absolutely rock-steady temperament. They also need to be able to be taught to give every task their complete concentration, as there are so many distractions in a film studio and even more outside on a location shoot. A potential film-work dog must be friendly and outgoing with everybody, as he might need to work directly with and take his commands from an actor. He must have the ability and temperament to build up a rapport with the person he is working with, and will probably even have to get used to being called by a different name! There is nothing worse than seeing a dog on TV looking for his handler and not obeying the actor he is supposed to be working with.

If you do register with an animal agency, be prepared for your dog to be worked by one of their animal handlers. If you intend to handle your dog yourself, the hours can be long and arduous and sometimes you may be required to go on location shoots for several weeks at a time at very short notice.

When training a dog with film work in mind, you must first teach him to be steady in basic obedience; that is, Stand, Sit, Down, Stay and Retrieve. He also needs to know hand signals for each command, as once a director has called "action", verbal commands to the dog can no longer be given. Once he knows all the basic commands, you can then teach him the more complex tricks that could be called for in a film-work dog. These generally are 'speaking' on command, begging, digging, chasing his tail, send away and redirection, crawling on his belly and playing dead.

FAMOUS JACK RUSSELLS

Ask almost any American child about Jack Russell Terriers, and they will immediately come up with the name of 'Wishbone'. Wishbone, whose AKC registered name is Willowall Soccer, was bred by Donna Maloney and is owned and trained by Jackie Kaptan. He is tricolour, smooth-coated, and surely one of the most famous son's of Blencathra Badger and Weardale Sherry.

Willowall Soccer had to compete against 100 other dogs to win the prized role of Wishbone, and perhaps his experience helped to land him the role. Soccer has been used in commercials for two dog food companies, as well as several print advertisements, including a photo shoot for Nike. We now see Wishbone on everything from bed linens, pillows, shirts, and of course the Wishbone Series of books. This little terrier has truly permeated our lives and become part of mainstream America.

Wishbone has captured the hearts and imagination of many children, and their parents, in his half-hour-long live action

Cassacre Berwick Of Gripton (Ace), trained by Pat Baker – every inch the film star.
Photo courtesy: Pat Baker.

Below: Ace filming the title sequence for Pet Power, a BBC TV series.

lessons fun; the last thing we want to see in the show ring is a dog that looks half-asleep and bored; besides, he will not catch the judge's eye unless he looks sparkling.

PROBLEM BEHAVIOUR

If your dog has been unfortunate enough to have developed a serious behaviour problem, my advice is not to try to solve it through the medium of this book. You should consult a veterinarian and he will check your dog over and be able to tell you if the behaviour problem is being caused by a medical condition, or if your dog has a psychological problem, in which case your veterinarian will refer you to a qualified behaviourist.

The type of minor problems you could encounter are, possibly, fear of noise, the pup guarding his toys or his food bowl, not coming back when he is called, or trying to bite or "mouth"your hands when you are grooming him.

NOISE SENSITIVITY

If your pup is noise-sensitive you need to desensitise him very carefully, otherwise you will inadvertently teach him to be even more frightened. If he is accidentally exposed to a loud noise and shows a fear reaction, on no account pet him and say "it's all right". This will only reinforce the behaviour. It is best to ignore the reaction and then you can start a desensitising programme. For example, if the pup is frightened of the vacuum cleaner, have someone switch it on in the next room and either feed your pup or have a boisterous game with him. Make each experience where noise is involved a positive one, and you will find, given time, that he will overcome his fear.

GUARDING

It is not uncommon for a puppy or adult dog to guard his toys if they are left lying around. If he has got into this bad habit, remove all the toys and put them away in a box, out of the pup's reach. Only allow him access to the toys when you want to play with him, and when the game is over put the toys away. Control the game and you control the dog! Terriers enjoy tug of war games; if you find your dog is reluctant to part with the toy at the end of the game, on no account continue to tug the toy to get it away from him, as you will not win. The best method is to swap the toy for a tidbit, and then do not play tug of war quite so often. This does not mean you are losing face and giving in; it is merely a case of not provoking a confrontation which, in all probability, you would not win anyway!

A similar method applies if the pup has started to guard his food bowl. Do not leave food down for the dog to eat ad lib. Have set meal times (my adults are fed twice a day), put the food down with half his ration in it and make him wait until you tell him to eat – do not let him 'dive' into the food bowl. Give him ten minutes; if he has left any, or if the bowl is empty and he is guarding it, put a few bits of food on the floor away from the bowl and encourage him to eat this while you remove the bowl. Do not leave empty bowls lying around. If your dog persists in growling when you go near his food bowl, when you feed him only put a few pieces of his ration in the bowl. When he has finished, add the rest of the ration piece by piece, so eventually, when you have repeated this for several mealtimes, he will no longer perceive you as a threat when you go near his food bowl.

Never allow your puppy to lie on the furniture or the bed; ideally he should not even be allowed access to your own sleeping quarters. Read the early lessons for the puppy and practise the 'long down' with your pup every day; this can also be done with an adult dog that has developed dominant behaviour. Also, try not to allow your dog to lie in

WISHBONE: WINNER OF FOUR EMMY AWARDS

Above: Wishbone as Aeneas in the 'Roamin' Nose'.

Right: Wishbone as Faust in 'Flea-bitten Bargain'.

The Jack Russell Brewing Co.

Vogue Italia Front Cover.

Photo: Steve Meizel.

Hoelio Just Jenny showing star quality in an advertising photo session.

Photo: Bruce Andre.

television show. The basic idea behind the show is to introduce children to the classics of literature, such as *Romeo and Juliet*, *Faust*, and the *Aeneid*. Each episode is a mix of fantasy and reality as the classic story being told parallels the events in Oakdale, USA, the home of Wishbone's television family. The attention to detail and the dog's obvious willingness to wear such complex costumes adds to the show's overall appeal. There is nothing much more amusing or appealing than a handsome Jack Russell dressed in costume! It is no wonder that the *Wishbone* series has won so many awards, including a total of four Emmy Awards.

A Jack Russell Terrier named Moose and known as 'Eddie' on the NBC television comedy *Frasier* is another of the more famous dogs to come to the attention of the American public. Like Willowall Soccer, Moose has appeared in television commercials and on the covers of such prestigious magazines as *Life*, *TV Guide*, *Entertainment Weekly*, and he even has his own calendar. Moose is soon to make the leap from primetime television to the big screen with his first starring role in a movie, to be titled *Moose on the Loose*.

The charm of the Jack Russell Terrier has certainly not been lost on the media. The fact that they are very photogenic, with a great deal of expression, makes them ideal candidates for the job. However, both Wishbone and Eddie are older, more settled Jack Russell Terriers with a great deal of obedience training behind them, so that while they are amusing to watch, their model behaviour is not necessarily typical of the breed.

ADVERTISING
The Jack Russell now appears on everything from cards to calendars.

Justice Hill Electra Blue is gracing the cover of the Jack Russell Calendar for 1999. She is owned, loved and trained by Nell Rux of Maine. Electra is an American Rare Breed Champion, and does Obedience, Earth Dog, and Agility – an excellent example of the breed.

Jack Russells have been sighted in some of the top magazines in the United States and have even made the front cover of Italy's *Vogue* Magazine. The photo, with several Jack Russell puppies and their happy human companions is very eye-catching. Sue Porter of Honey Hill Jack Russell Terriers bred all of the puppies, except the one with the black ribbon.

The list of companies that use these dogs to sell products and or attract attention is a very long one, so suffice it to say we will most likely continue to see the Jack Russell in television, print, and commercial advertising for many years to come.

7 *THE WORKING JACK RUSSELL*

Fox hunting is as much a part of the traditional English scene as is Big Ben or red London buses. People who live in towns and who have never seen a fox in their life send Christmas cards depicting horses and riders gathered in an attractive country setting, snow on the ground and hounds ready to be off. Often, there will be a terrier or two in evidence.

Idealised as these images may be, it is entirely right and fitting that the terriers should be pictured along with hounds, for this is where the Jack Russell was first created and refined into the working terrier of today. In the early 19th century, any terrier that worked with a pack of foxhounds was known as a Fox Terrier – whatever its colour or shape. Then began the heyday of hunting. Vast fields of riders, most usually accompanied by a groom riding a spare horse, would meet in the expectation of a good day's sport, consisting of some hard riding in pursuit of the fox. It follows, logically, that no foxes meant no hunting. A gentle hack from covert to covert was not what they had in mind! However, no self-respecting fox would put his nose above ground when hounds were about, and if he did find himself in view, he would dive into the nearest hole and stay their until the hunt got tired of waiting and looked elsewhere.

Enter the terrier! By harnessing the terrier's natural instincts to dig and to bay at his quarry, the fox was encouraged to leave his sanctuary and to try elsewhere. With the huntsman holding hounds off some little distance from the earth, the fox was allowed to make his escape safely, and the hounds put on the line when he had gone a little way, thus ensuring a good hunt across country and satisfying the riders. The huntsman who regularly showed little sport did not stay in his position long.

Not only was this the high point of hunting, it was also the golden era of Foxhound breeding. Packs had kept careful records for many generations (predating the Kennel Club records of purebred dogs by nearly a century), and great store was set on breeding a uniform pack of hounds. The spectacle of hunting is part of the overall picture. A ragtag pack of hounds, of different shapes and sizes, accompanied by a couple of riders in jeans and sweatshirts mounted on ungroomed horses might be just as efficient at hunting foxes, but would not fill the eye in the same way as does a pack of disciplined, well-matched hounds accompanied by riders in hunt livery on horses that are turned out to perfection. At a time when hounds were being selected so rigorously for their looks as well as their hunting ability, it was natural that attention should be turned also to the terriers. Their contribution to the certainty of

At the Meet: The Jack Russell is built on athletic lines, so he is capable of keeping pace with the horses.

Photo: Sheila Atter.

a good day's hunting cannot be over-emphasised. In the golden years of hunting, terriers often lived with hounds in the kennel, and the most traditional packs took much care in ensuring that the overall picture was not let down by the appearance of these terriers. Indeed, it was in the fashionable hunt kennels, most particularly the Belvoir and the Grove, that the art of breeding Fox Terriers reached perfection. Names such as Belvoir Joe and Grove Nettle were behind many of the best smooth-coated terriers found in the ring as the newly invented sport of dog showing became more widespread.

Despite the fact that many Hunt Terriers forsook their original home and opted for the more glamorous life of the show dog (and inevitably changed their make and shape into the elegant Fox Terriers of today) terrier work was still vital, and terriers remained in the kennels. These rather more workmanlike specimens were still bred with great care, but with different priorities in mind than mere good looks.

Intelligence, instinct and correct

conformation combine to make the working terrier an efficient fox-seeker. It cannot be emphasised too often that the purpose of the Hunt Terrier (and the rough-coated Fox Terrier of the type bred by Parson Russell is the Hunt Terrier par excellence) is never to kill a fox. Riders out hunting want to enjoy a day's riding across country. They gain no pleasure from waiting around on a cold winter's day for hours whilst a terrier is firmly ensconced down a nice warm hole with a very dead fox! The terrier's job is always to bolt the fox so that hunting can continue.

Jack Russell, although now remembered mainly for his terriers, was a man to whom hunting was a passionate interest. He loved the thrill of the chase and his followers, knowing the character of the man, expected (and almost invariably enjoyed) a very hard ride across the bleak Exmoor countryside. It was only to be expected that he would realise the value of a good terrier very early on in his hunting career, as indeed we know that he did, buying his first terrier, Trump, whilst still

Instinct, intelligence and the correct conformation are the key ingredients in a working terrier.

Photo: John Valentine.

a young man at university. He gave so much thought to the breeding of his terriers, and was so successful in this task, that it is hardly surprising that the name of Jack Russell was very quickly synonymous with the white-bodied Hunt Terrier.

WORKING TERRIERS TODAY

The role of the terrierman and his terriers is as important today as it ever was. Nowadays, most working terriers do not live with hounds, but are kept by the terrierman and brought along on hunting mornings to do their work for the pack. The terrierman is often expected to combine his position with other tasks – stopping earths in the area the night before the meet, so that the fox cannot go to ground too easily, and mending any fences that are damaged during hunting. All good terriermen are incredibly knowledgeable about the countryside and the animals that live there.

Fox hunting, then, is the true vocation of the Jack Russell, but the number of terriers that can truly work in the manner for which the breed was created is obviously limited by the number of Foxhound packs in existence, and some of those, because of the nature of the country that they hunt, have little opportunity to use terriers in this way. Jack Russells (and their owners), being practical

and resourceful creatures, have found other outlets to channel their energies in a constructive manner.

Fox hunting is a winter sport. Traditionally, some terriers would find occupation in the summer along the riverbanks, hunting otter. These have been replaced by Minkhound packs, and terriers are still used, and work in much the same way – bolting mink, so that the hounds can hunt them.

Apart from the spectacle that it provides, hunting is a practical means of controlling the fox population at an optimum level, rather than exterminating the fox altogether. Since, in the UK, the fox has no natural predators (other than man), without some sort of control the number of foxes would increase to an unacceptable level (as has been seen in our cities, where the urban fox is now a common sight in some areas). In parts of the country where hunting with hounds is not carried out to any great extent, or when foxes are causing specific damage, it sometimes becomes necessary to actively pursue and kill foxes. By far the most efficient and humane way to do this is with terriers. The terrier is put into the earth and bolts the fox. Again, just as when working with the pack, he should not attempt to kill the fox (Jack Russell himself said that his terriers 'never tasted blood'). His task is to

The terrierman: There is still a place for the working terrier in rural life today.

Photo: Sheila Atter.

bark and to threaten, and generally to make life underground so unpleasant that the fox decides to take his chance elsewhere. When the fox bolts, he is quickly and humanely dispatched with a gun. This is a far more reliable and less cruel method than other forms of culling, such as gassing or the use of traps.

The owner of a Jack Russell should never ever just take himself and his terrier off into the countryside in the hopes of encouraging the dog to work. In the UK, every piece of land, however small and however remote, actually belongs to someone, and permission must always be sought before entering the terrier. At the present time, it is still legal to work terriers to fox (but never to badger), but legislation changes. The Countryside Alliance fought a strong campaign in 1997/8 against Michael Foster's proposed Hunting with Dogs Act which would, amongst other things, have made a criminal of the owner whose terrier merely chased a rabbit whilst out for a walk across a field. Terriers do have a very strong working instinct, and it is up to the owner to take responsibility for his animals and to ensure that they only work when and where such activity is permitted.

Anyone who is interested in terrier work and who takes their terriers, even occasionally, into an area where they might, even inadvertently, find themselves in a position where the terrier goes to ground, should make the effort to discover as much as possible about terrier work. This is something that cannot be learned from books. The would-be terrierman should take every opportunity to go out with the experts. Those who do work their terriers will usually give every encouragement to the novice who genuinely wants to find out more, but they are naturally wary of anyone who might bring about others' disapproval of their work and of the terriers that they love. Once his confidence has been gained, a good terrierman will pass on so much knowledge about the Jack Russell, the way he works, and indeed about the countryside and the animals that live therein. But this confidence and trust must be earned, for it will not be given lightly.

Before taking terriers out with the intention of working them, owners should ensure that they are members of both the National Working Terrier Federation (NWTF) and the Fell and Moorland Working Terrier Club. Many breed Clubs (including both the Jack Russell Terrier Club of Great Britain and the Parson Jack Russell Terrier

THE JACK RUSSELL AT WORK
Photos: Sheila Atter.

*Strong and determined, with a nose as keen as his nature, the
Jack Russell has a tremendously strong instinct to work.*

Club) are members of the NWTF, but individuals can also join. It was founded in 1984 ' to promote the efficient and humane use of working terriers for pest control purposes'. The NWTF has produced a Code of Conduct for Terrier Work, which is accepted as a measure of good practice. It is a condition of membership of the organisation that this Code is adhered to at all times. The Federation has also introduced a National Identification Card available to terriermen of good standing.

The Fell and Moorland Working Terrier Club acts both as an umbrella organisation for its members and, most importantly, provides a network of terriermen who are prepared to drop everything when a call is received giving notice of a terrier trapped underground. Club funds are used to hire digging equipment where necessary, and every effort is made to ensure that no terrier dies underground.

THE WORKING INSTINCT

Throughout history, man has found it necessary to control certain animals which, because they conflict with farming interests, are regarded as pests. The terrier, small-bodied but strong, intelligent and with a nose as keen as its nature, was selectively bred over many generations for just this work. This natural instinct is so strong that it is difficult to deny it, and is reflected in the increasing numbers of pet terriers rescued by the working terrier clubs. These can be terriers which, despite being from 'non-working'stock, have gone off hunting of their own volition and become trapped in underground earths. Jack Russells are no longer seen mainly as the typical countryman's dog – it is probable that more live in urban surroundings than in the countryside. Along with a change in the type of owner has come a change in attitudes to the countryside and to terrier work. Many of

those who own Jack Russells today would probably declare themselves to be anti-Field sports. To take such a position is a contradiction. The terrier's working instinct is so deeply ingrained that a few generations of urban living will not breed out the desire to go to ground at the first opportunity. The wise owner will take the trouble to find out as much as possible about the breed's heritage, even if they have no intention of encouraging their own Jack Russell to work. It is, after all, a breed's character that attracts people in the first place, and the Jack Russell's character – the intelligence and gutsy determination – has been forged by the terrier's role as a hunter.

USA

Originally, Jack Russell Terriers, like most working terrier breeds, were simply working dogs, and were rarely they kept as pets. Today, the opposite is more the norm, especially for American terriers. Most are kept primarily as family pets and rarely see work. In the United States, the Jack Russell has tended to follow the equine hobbyist and is known as 'the stable terrier'. The breed has enjoyed enormous popularity due to its intelligence and temperament. This versatile, talented little fellow is a very entertaining and beloved companion dog – also a formidable varmint dog, ridding barns of mice and rats. It is easy to understand how these little terriers have worked their way into the American landscape and lifestyle, as Americans have long admired and adopted British traditions and craved British goods and services. Relatively inexpensive travel fares between the two countries, coupled with ease of importation, made the Jack Russell readily available to the Anglophile interests of Americans. The Jack Russell, master of manipulation, has had no difficulty securing his special place in the American heart.

Photos: Pam Simmons.

Despite differences in terrain and quarry, the Jack Russell has proved a valuable worker in the USA.

Game though he is, the American Jack Russell Terrier, percentage-wise, has enjoyed more pet service than hunt service. Of late there has been a tremendous resurgence of interest in working terriers in America, as well as in the many other countries where Jack Russells are found. The entire future of the working Jack Russell lies squarely on the shoulders of the men and women dedicated to preserving the traditional working terrier.

There are many factors that contribute to the small percentage of working Jack Russells in America. First, the historic English country life, which for hundreds of years has been steeped in the rich tradition of horse, hound and hunt, has never truly existed in American society. As a result, there are obvious differences between hunts in the UK and American Hunt Clubs, where so much of the tradition has been lost, having no relevance or practical application in America.

Secondly, the hunt clubs in America, abundant in years past, are now beginning to decline in number. The financial burden of maintaining a pack of hounds, horses, and staff continues to escalate, while interest in fox hunting and membership declines. Even if Hunt Terriers had ever enjoyed the same rich heritage in America as they do in England, maintenance of a terrierman and his dogs would soon prove too costly for most clubs. The British Red Fox has no natural enemies, and so the fox population has truly exploded in the British countryside, and the local farmer considers the fox 'vermin'. If the hunt does not 'account for' or kill their quarry, the farmer will not endure them galloping across his fields.

In Britain the hunt has abundant quarry in one small area, and hunt staff frequently go out the night before a hunt to stop up the entrances to all the earths or the dens in the area to be hunted the next day. In America, however, the sheer vastness of the landmass and distances that can be travelled has tended to spread the fox population. Thus, the British practice of stopping up holes the night before a hunt is impractical in North America. In addition, the American Red Fox is not as quick to take to ground as his British cousin and as a result, the use of Hunt Terriers has never been necessary to insure a good day's hunt in America.

Unfortunately, the urban and suburban sprawl of American cities is rapidly eroding available hunting country. Hunt clubs must venture ever further afield to secure quantities of usable land and, because of this, the very nature of the hunt is changing. In addition to this, the 'bigger, better, faster' attitude for which Americans are so famous is evident in the game of choice now favoured to hunt. Today, the popular choice for pursuit is the American Coyote, a bigger, faster animal than the American Red Fox. The Coyote, a supreme opportunist, is present throughout North America, and has even established itself in urban areas. The Coyote not only competes successfully for the same food as the fox, it preys upon him. Nowadays, if the terrierman were to be functional with the American hunts, he certainly would not choose to put his Russell up against the much larger Coyote. Jack Russells would be considered a nice-sized meal for the Coyote, and needless to say, most do not survive the encounters.

American breed and working clubs have heavily promoted the working aspect of the Jack Russell and have garnered serious interest in terrier earthwork. Still, serious earthworkers comprise a very small percentage of total Jack Russell enthusiasts; rather, pet and show homes make up the majority in America. The rich tradition of mentoring, alive and well in the United Kingdom, is seriously limited by the absence of the knowledgeable professional terrierman in America. Thanks primarily to the efforts of organisations such as the American Working

Terrier Association, and many working terrier enthusiasts, the future of many working terrier breeds is indeed bright.

Mentors are crucial to the survival of the working Jack Russell, as there are virtually no written 'how to' publications for individuals to study. Serious earthworking men and women give countless hours of their time and skill to the endless task of teaching novices to hunt the terrier, truly a labour of love. Despite the fact that many American people are very serious earthworkers, not even a dedicated group such as this can stem the tide of anti-hunting sentiments so prevalent in America, nor can they overcome the societal trends eliminating employment for the terrier. On the bright side, however, the preservation of the working Jack Russell may be assured through the diligent efforts of serious earthworking individuals, breeders and breed clubs all coming together in a concerned push to initiate, educate, and train newcomers in this rich tradition.

The essence of terrier earthwork is a verbal legacy passed down by word of mouth from person to person. If at all possible, enthusiasts should take advantage of the deep tradition still available in Britain, the breed's country of origin. Nothing can be more instructive, and inspiring, than a walk through the British countryside with a terrierman, shovel in hand and terrier at his side. Those interested who make the trip to Britain to view terrier work first-hand come home with a new perspective, and further insight about the Jack Russell and what he was bred to be – a working dog, form following function.

EARTHWORKING TOOLS
The methodology of terrier work in America remains much the same as it is in the UK, and has changed little over the years. One important exception in both countries is the use of locating collars and boxes, a very recent innovation. The use of collars has helped to ensure safer hunting for all concerned, especially the dogs. With a locating collar, the dog can more easily be found and extricated from the earth, thus saving countless hours of trenching and digging to locate a terrier in trouble or entombed in the earth.

Tools employed in earthwork have changed very little over the years; the standard shovel and bar are universal. Specific tools may vary from individual to individual and the local terrain may require modifications or additions to the old standbys. In America the use of the post-hole digger has been adopted, much to the amazement and amusement of the British terrierman. The British are not aware of the American landowner's aversion to having huge holes dug in the earth for his livestock to wander into. Posthole diggers allow a much smaller hole to be dug.

QUARRY
By and large, earthworking itself has remained unchanged. North American quarry, however, differs radically from the traditional British fox and badger. Due to the vastness of North America, and its geographic diversity, several different varieties of fox exist. Most Jack Russell hunting enthusiasts seek out the red and gray varieties.

RED FOX: The Red Fox, much smaller than its British cousin, flourishes throughout Canada and most of the United States. During the 1800s, the European Red Fox was imported to the Northeast by fox hunters, accounting for the heavy concentration of fox in that area. Red Fox are omnivorous, which simply means they will consume and thrive on almost anything. They are intelligent, very shy, and can adapt to any habitat. Rarely does the American Red Fox use a den; even in winter they prefer to curl up under brushy cover. Mating occurs from January to March; during this time pairs take over old marmot and groundhog holes or

badger setts, abandoning them in August when the young disperse to begin life on their own. Red Fox dens are easily identified by the characteristically large earth 'drags' or 'kick-backs' surrounding the holes, as well as cache piles of stored food, accompanied by copious amounts of litter strewn about. Red Fox prefer to locate on a slight rise with a clear view, and will bolt away at the slightest sign of danger. In more arid regions, due to sparse food sources, the fox utilises a much larger hunting area and as a result, is more nomadic than his European cousin. Serious earthworkers wishing to put their Jack Russells to the traditional quarry may be required to travel across the continent to areas of heavy fox concentration. In addition, fox hunting is strictly governed by law and is only allowed in certain seasons, as fox is considered a fur-bearing animal and as such is protected by statute.

GRAY FOX: The Gray Fox is much smaller than the Red Fox and is much more elusive. Very few hunters will encounter the Gray Fox on a day's excursion, and your chances of coming across him are slim, unless of course you know just where he may be found. Gray Fox inhabit all of the eastern United States, much of the south-west, into and along the California coastline. They are also found in the Dakotas and Nebraska. Grays prefer thick woodlands and rocky areas, and are often seen climbing trees. Winter finds the Gray Fox in his den, unlike the Red Fox. Due to the rough and rocky terrain – the preferred habitat of the Gray Fox – most earthwork of this variety of fox is left to a very few hardy experts, who by necessity, must be half mountain goat and half mountain man.

AMERICAN BADGER: The American Badger is an even more elusive target for anyone wishing to work with his or her terrier. Its range covers most of the western

United States from the Texas border into the southernmost parts of western Canada. The Mississippi River limits its eastern range for the most part; however, badger populations are found in the upper Midwest states through to the Great Lake states, where the species is considered endangered and is rigidly protected by law. The badger is nomadic and elusive, ranging many miles foraging for food and burrowing at will. The presence of rattlesnake, a favoured food of the badger, makes terrier work quite hazardous in these areas, and few Jack Russell earthworkers seek to put the terrier to badger. The badger's disposition is ferocious when encountered, although it prefers to dig away when threatened. Its digging capabilities are more than a match for a person with a shovel and a dog; its burrowing prowess having been described as 'swimming' through the ground. Most often, the badger will disappear before any real encounter occurs.

GROUNDHOG: North America does provide several other species of wildlife that give sport to earthworkers and employment for the Jack Russell. These include the groundhog or marmot, raccoon and opossum. The most commonly found is the marmot (in the west) or groundhog (in the east). Western marmots, the Yellow-bellied and the Hoary, prefer rocky mountainous areas for habitation. They can be found from as far north as the provinces of British Columbia and Alberta, and their range extends southward into California and as far east as Colorado. Mountainous habitat makes digging for marmot an arduous task.

The eastern variety is referred to as the woodchuck or groundhog; it is also named the 'whistle pig', due to its melodious whistle when threatened. Groundhog populations abound in the plentiful grassland areas of the east, providing much in the way of sport for

illustrated in the twelve plates, one of which features five different terriers.

The rougher-coated dog, predominantly white but with patches of colour on its head and at the root of its tail, is similar to the Bewick terrier in type, and is shown wearing a baiting collar with padlock, the style of which was popular for some two centuries. This dog was obviously intended for use against badgers. The sleeping terrier on the left of the plate, with colour just on its head and with cropped ears, more closely resembles what became the Fox Terrier of the late 19th century, and the type preferred by the Reverend John Russell.

PHILIP REINAGLE

Philip Reinagle RA (1749-1833) was one of a family of twelve artists whose father had arrived in Scotland in 1745 as a supporter of the young pretender. Philip Reinagle became one of the best known of the sporting artists of his era and his dog portraits are some of the most important. It is generally considered that his work is a reasonably accurate representation, rather than just being portraits painted just how a patron would

wish them to be. His pictures also have a fluidity to them, often lacking in earlier works. It was Colonel Thornton who really established Reinagle as a great sporting artist, and his painting of Major, the Colonel's famous Greyhound, was exhibited at the Royal Academy in 1805.

In the dog world, Reinagle is best remembered for a series of paintings which were engraved by John Scott and which appeared in William Taplin's *The Sportsman's Cabinet,* published 1803/4 – the third dog book in the English language. The plate of the three terriers shows a central dog that is very similar in conformation to the legendary Trump, the Reverend Russell's first terrier, and with the same characteristic head and tail markings and coat which identified him. Trump's picture was acquired by the Prince of Wales (later King Edward VII) and hung in the harness room at Sandringham. Reinagle could well have based his terrier on those he would have seen at Colonel Thornton's home, and Russell most certainly would have wanted to emulate such a great sportsman as Thornton.

Philip Reinagle RA (1749-1833). Reinagle's terriers engraved by John Scott for 'The Sportsman's Cabinet'. Col. Thornton was Reinagle's chief patron and the centre dog shows similarities to Thornton's Pitch, and also to Russell's first terrier, Trump.

Richard Andsell (1815-1886). Men rabbiting at Starr Hills on the Ribble estuary.

SIR EDWIN LANDSEER

The predominantly white dog with a strong, weather-resistant coat and head patches and, often, tail patches, came to epitomise the Fox Terrier of the 19th century, and, in particular, those associated with the Reverend Russell. One sees such dogs featured over and over again in paintings throughout the years. Perhaps a sign that such dogs had 'arrived' was the portrayal of one by Sir Edwin Landseer RA (1802-1873). Landseer will forever be associated with Queen Victoria, and lifted the dog in art to a position previous artists had failed to do. His pictures were frequently anecdotal and his dogs were often given human characteristics.

In 1828, Owen Williams, landowner and Member of Parliament, of Temple House, Buckinghamshire, commissioned Landseer to paint his terrier, Jacko. The dog, with his cropped ears and black head-markings, was shown wearing a typical steel terrier collar of the period and was teasing a hedgehog. The dog is shown against a typical dramatic Landseer landscape, with perhaps Loch Laggan in the background. Prints after the picture were engraved by T. L. Atkinson and published in 1889. The original now hangs in Milwaukee Art Museum.

THE TURN OF THE CENTURY

George Armfield (1810-1893), Edward Armfield (operating c.1864-1875) – no relation to George – and Paul Jones (op. 1855-1888) were all prolific artists working in the second and third quarters of the last century who specialised in dogs, and in particular, working terriers and working spaniels. Although all three artists painted with a certain skill, their work is very stylised and their output was prodigious, and many of their paintings repeat a standard pictorial formula. Their works, in my opinion, are all too easily discounted by dog historians for not being accurate portraits of individual breeds, which, of course, to some extent is true. Nevertheless, their output does record the working terriers and spaniels that were evolving at that time, clearly showing the different types evolving into breeds standardised by the clever Victorian breeders of livestock.

Edward Armfield (op. c. 1864-1875). Terriers in an Interior.
This shows terriers as they were evolving during the middle years of the 19th century. The white dog is of a type that has changed little over 200 years, and would be instantly recognisable to Col. Thornton, Rev. Russell, and Parson Jack Russell owners today.
Coutesy: Christies, South Kensington.

S.E. Shirley founded the Kennel Club in 1873 and was a contemporary of the Rev. Russell. On the left is Shirley's terrier Bristles, similar in type to the dogs kept by Russell.

If we take, for example, the terriers, we see dogs whose descendants we know today as the Fox Terrier, Parson Jack Russell Terrier, Welsh Terrier, Irish Terrier and others. It is interesting to note that the Armfields and Paul Jones also painted terriers with both docked and undocked tails. All this, perhaps, indicates that it was the formation of the

Bronze after Pierre-Jules Mene (1810-1871) showing two smooth-haired and a wire-haired terrier rabbiting.

Kennel Club in April 1873 and the formulating of Standards for the individual breeds that created the fashion for docking.

Whilst the 18th century and the first half of the 19th century were noted for the number of fine sporting artists working in the British Isles, the latter years of the 19th century brought with them a proliferation of artists who would specialise in dog portraiture, as well as other sporting subjects. The men who had formed the Kennel Club in 1873 and the dog breeders of the last quarter of the 19th century were all men of considerable wealth. They bred dogs without the restraints of modern-day legislation and sentimentality, and kept large numbers of dogs and very many staff. They experimented in a way today's breeders could not or would not, and they wished to record the results of their efforts.

Interestingly, the Parson was a founder member of the Kennel Club, and although forever associated with working Fox Terriers, he did exhibit some of his dogs at the early dog shows and was himself a judge of the breed. S. E. Shirley, who founded the Kennel

Club, kept a large number of breeds (being perhaps best known for his Flat-Coated Retriever), but he also owned Fox Terriers and, from the painting, his dog Bristles was a similar type to the dogs Russell kept. The Reverend John Russell was himself an artist and, as there never seems to be any mention as to who painted the picture of his first dog, Trump, it is just possible that Russell himself did.

TYDDESLEY DAVIS
Tyddesley Davis (op. 1831-1857) painted a number of hunting pictures, one of which was of Samuel Beale, Huntsman to the Carew family, mounted on a grey hunter, surrounded by hounds in a landscape. In the foreground of the picture is what is claimed to be the first terrier bred by Russell and used with a hunt. Just how true this is we will probably never know. The Carew family was a great West Country sporting family and we do know that Russell knew them well, so even if this dog is not the first of his terriers used with a hunt, it could well have been bred by Russell.

John Emms (1843-1912). Emms was particularly fond of hunting and all dogs associated with it.
Courtesy: Sara Davenport Fine Paintings.

JOHN EMMS

Artists like John Emms, Maud Earl and Arthur Wardle owe their very reputations to the monied and influential dog breeders. Of the three, John Emms (1843-1912) is considered primarily as a sporting artist. He was the son of an artist and studied under the neo-classical painter, Frederick Leighton. Emms at one time lived a Bohemian life in London, frequently seen wearing a long black cloak and a wide-brimmed black hat. He was passionately fond of hunting, and through it he found many clients for his work. Although he painted many breeds, his output is perhaps most closely associated with hounds of the chase. In studying for such pictures, he would have seen many working Fox Terriers of the period.

Emms's work is recognised by strong brushwork and generous applications of paint, a technique which very much complimented the Fox Terriers he painted.

The dogs are always shown with short, thick, harsh coats, which would have appealed to the Reverend Russell.

ARTHUR WARDLE

Perhaps the artist most associated with the Fox Terriers that were only just a few generations on from the dogs the Reverend Russell was breeding, and which no doubt shared common ancestry with the Parson's dogs, was Arthur Wardle (1864-1949). Wardle was born in London and started painting at a very early age. He became known to millions of people through the work he did for tobacco companies, which were reproduced on the cards issued in packets of cigarettes. He is perhaps the best known of all the dog artists working in the

Arthur Wardle (1864-1949). Wardle's portraits were not always confined to showing the whole dog. Here are two alert head studies.

Arthur Wardle (1864-1949). Wardle sometimes deserted the warrens and burrows to show us terriers with their arch enemy – the cat.

Courtesy: Christie's South Kensington.

Arthur Wardle (1864-1949). A classic dog portrait showing highly-prized dogs set against an appropriate background. Wardle's work is much admired by collectors of Parson Jack Russell art. Courtesy: Christie's, South Kensington.

Adrienne Lester (early 20th century). Patiently waiting for the right moment.

20th century. He painted virtually every breed of dog, but, artistically, his large cats undoubtedly account for his better work; they were far more imaginative, rather than simply being naturalistic.

In the dog world, his work will forever be synonymous with Fox Terriers at earths and burrows. His output was considerable, and the dogs are, in many cases, portraits, the backgrounds being used to set off what were, in many cases, highly prized dogs.

Wardle's painting of Francis Redmond's Fox Terriers, of which two copies exist, both painted in 1897, is classic dog portraiture. Known as *The Totteridge XI*, each dog is individually placed to emphasise its balance and type. Such paintings are, in fact, representational rather than totally accurate studies. Redmond is known to have supervised throughout the painting of this picture, making suggestions as to how he thought each dog should be portrayed, rather than allowing Wardle to paint them as they actually were. The same can be said for Wardle's *Land Spaniels*, in which some of the dogs in the painting bear little resemblance to

their photographs entitled *Realisation*.

Arthur Wardle's painting is of a basically white terrier, with head markings and a coat far less developed than today's Fox Terriers. Undoubtedly, the Parson would have approved, and the painting typified what was considered the ideal Parson Jack Russell Terrier in the show ring at Crufts in 1997, where the breed first had Challenge Certificates in the United Kingdom. The painting shows a dog standing over a dead rabbit, and has far more realism than many of Wardle's similar subjects. It was at one time owned by the Lakeshore Kennel Club in America, and now forms part of the collection of the American Kennel Club Museum of the Dog. Arthur Wardle's paintings epitomise the Fox Terrier of the turn of the century and show just how close in type the Parson Jack Russell Terrier of today is to these earlier dogs.

The relationship between dogs and cats has always been uneasy, and never more so than when terriers have been involved. Arthur Wardle occasionally deserted the burrows and earths to show us that there was no love lost

between the two species. The terriers usually hold the trump card and the cats were disadvantaged, being trapped up trees, on chairs, or other high objects, their faces always displaying hate and contempt for the terriers. Occasionally an artist would bring humour into such conflicts, such as Adrienne Lester (early 20th century), with a cat in a wicker basket intently watching a somewhat passive terrier and obviously waiting its moment to escape.

MAUD EARL

Maud Earl (1864-1943) is today the most respected of all the late 19th century and 20th century dog artists. She was taught by her father and quickly developed her own distinctive styles. She numbered most of the leading dog breeders in the United Kingdom as her patrons. Because of her dislike of war, she moved to America in 1916, where she remained until her death in 1943. Her oeuvre may be loosely divided into four styles. Up until 1900, her paintings were richly painted in a naturalistic style. Typical of this period was a painting she completed for the Duchess of Newcastle. The dogs portrayed were Ch. Cackler of Notts and Christopher of Notts, shown gazing intently over a fallen tree. Cackler was the first of the Wire Fox Terrier

champions owned by the Duchess, and is considered the ancestor of every show Wire Fox Terrier. From Maud Earl's painting, he exemplifies what today would be considered ideal type in the Parson Jack Russell Terrier ring. As with Wardle's *Realisation*, this painting is also in the American Kennel Club Museum of the Dog.

Maud Earl's second period up to 1915 is characterised by a looser, more sketchy style. Her painting *Old Sport* is a typical example. It shows the head and forechest of a Foxhound and a Fox Terrier and indicates that the Fox Terrier was, at that time, still highly regarded as a working terrier, even though, by then, it was a very successful breed on the show bench.

King Edward VII's dog, Caesar, along with the French Bulldog, Peter, was a favourite of the King. Caesar was of the working type, with the thick weather-resistant coat so prized by the late Parson Russell, and would not look out of place in the Parson Jack Russell show ring today. Caesar was immortalised by such artists as Maud Earl and Herbert Dicksee (1862-1942).

GEORGE EARL

Maud Earl's father, George Earl (op. 1856-1883), was an active sportsman and as an

George Earl (op. 1856-1883). Ch. Oakleigh Topper portrayed as the archetypal ratter of the 19th century.

artist he excelled in the depiction of dogs. His series of oil paintings entitled *Champion Dogs of England* were among the first to portray celebrated show dogs. He exhibited at the Royal Academy and his works have been reproduced in a number of important books, including *Dogs by Well Known Authorities*, edited by Harding Cox and published (although never completed) 1906/8. In this work, Earl shows us Ch. Oakleigh Topper, a dog born in 1880 that had been owned by Harding Cox. The dog is portrayed as a typical working terrier, being shown in an old outbuilding standing over a dead rat and with a rat cage behind him. Although the Fox Terrier was the terrier of the hunt, many artists liked to portray it as

the ultimate ratter. George Earl was by no means alone. The dog has a short, wire, weather-resistant coat, and is all white except for black on his ears and around his eyes. Topper is of a similar type to Vixen and others from the early 19th century, and also similar to the Parson Jack Russell of today.

CHOCOLATE-BOX ART

It is only by being able to study such pictures that one can appreciate the existence of a uniform type of terrier that spans nearly twenty years. Surely, no other terrier breed could make such a claim. With the formation of the Kennel Club and the proliferation of wealthy breeders of purebred dogs, a great many people became aware of the diversity of

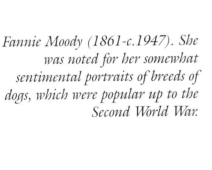

Fannie Moody (1861-c.1947). She was noted for her somewhat sentimental portraits of breeds of dogs, which were popular up to the Second World War.

Edgar Hunt (1876-1953). Inquisitive terriers in farmyards were popular subjects for Hunt.

William Stephen Coleman (1829-1904). Mischievous terriers have long served as companions for children.

breeds of dog. Added to this awareness was the popularity of works by Sir Edwin Landseer and Queen Victoria's devotion to "all dumb creatures", and all these things contributed to the popularity of the dog in both literature and art. Pictures that featured dogs were amongst the most popular and this resulted in a great wealth of artists eager to take advantage of this popularity. The era saw the birth of 'chocolate box' art, where dogs were portrayed with endless tolerance, sympathy and courage, and were frequently given human characteristics. Large dogs were companions to small children and the most unlikely of canine bedfellows all lived happily side by side. Terriers were frequently portrayed as mischievous, inquisitive little characters, and both smooth and wire working terriers became favourites.

EDGAR HUNT

Edgar Hunt (1876-1953) preferred painting farmyard subjects which he painted in meticulous detail; so when it came to him painting dogs, terriers in old buildings, or in straw-filled barrels converted into kennels became obvious choices. His painting of four terrier puppies, one of which is predominantly white, watching intently a pigeon as it moves carefully to investigate their biscuit, is typical of a number of paintings which Hunt painted.

As an example of just how popular Hunt's paintings of terriers are, an oil showing three puppies playing outside an old kennel while their mother watches from her straw bed within the kennel, was the most expensive picture sold by Bonhams in their 'Dogs in Art' sale in 1995.

WILLIAM STEPHEN COLEMAN

Terriers and children have long been favourites with artists. *The Ferry*, painted by William Stephen Coleman (1829-1904), which shows two small children being led by an older one through a flower-filled garden to an old wooden ferry, is the type of Victorian picture which has always been popular. It shows member of the lower classes without even hinting at hardship or squalor. In the background is an idyllic cottage with smoke rising from the chimney and, as a focal point to the picture, a Fox Terrier-type of dog gallops on ahead of the children.

WILLIAM HENRY HAMILTON TROOD

William Henry Hamilton Trood (1860-1899) was the master when it came to portraying a great variety of breeds all amicably agreeing,

William Henry Hamilton Trood (1860-1899).
The Rhubarb Patch.
A Victorian sentimental rendition with a mother offering affection to her child.
Courtesy: Christie's, South Kensington.

135

or of one dog showing sympathy and understanding towards another. As one critic said of his work, "Usually accompanied by a large dollop of Victorian sentimentality."

His painting, *A Domestic Scene*, is one of the best known of all Victorian pictures. The group of dogs all amicably agreeing, includes a litter of five terrier puppies, all predominantly white with a few head markings. Three of the terriers are playing with a whip, a fourth sleeps at the paw of a Mastiff, whilst the fifth looks on over the Mastiff's back. The other players in the idyllic Victorian scene include a Bloodhound, a Dachshund (interestingly a dapple one), a Poodle and a Newfoundland. As with so many other important dog pictures, this too is in the American Kennel Club Museum of the Dog.

Staying with Trood, but on a less grand scale (although lacking nothing in sentimentality) is his study of a bitch comforting her puppy under the large leaves of a rhubarb plant. Philip Eustace Stretton (1884-1915) and Valentine Thomas Garland (op. 1868-d.1914) are two other artists whose work, like that of Trood's, was both sentimental and anecdotal, and both painted terriers which are today collected by lovers of the Jack Russell Terrier.

JOHN ALFRED WHEELER
Apart from the sporting artists already mentioned, many others painted Fox Terriers/working terriers. John Alfred Wheeler (1821-1903) specialised in portrait studies of Foxhounds and terrier heads, and his paintings are some of the most popular in this genre. Rarely shown singly, his dogs are grouped together in twos, threes and sometimes more, and when it came to painting terriers, he usually liked to feature more than one breed. They are always the keen working ratters of the last half of the 19th century – Manchester, the now extinct

John Alfred Wheeler (1821-1903). Wheeler's studies of terriers are always popular with the collectors of Jack Russell art.
Courtesy: Sara Davenport Fine Paintings.

White English Terrier (a victim of the ban on cropping) and Fox Terriers, both wire and smooth – never the show dogs of the period. Auction houses frequently catalogue such pictures as 'Jack Russell Terriers', for in all honesty, they more closely resemble what people think of as the 'Jack Russell'and without fail, they always readily find buyers.

So popular were Wheeler's paintings when they were painted that many artists copied his theme. Wheeler lived for much of his life at Bath in the West Country, so could well have been conversant with the Parson's terriers. Included amongst his well-known sporting patrons was the Duke of Beaufort, so Wheeler would at least have come into contact with some genuine working terriers.

THE PARSON IN ART
The Parson himself featured in a number of paintings and in E.W.L. Davies'book *Memoir of the Reverend John Russell and his Out-of-*

Door-Life, the 1902 edition is illustrated by Nathaniel Hugh John Baird (1865-1936) and coloured by hand. Baird was a portrait and landscape painter who was born in Roxburghshire, Scotland, and it was he who drew the frontispiece, of Russell with three terriers, from a photograph. The photograph was of Russell alone, and Baird added the terriers, which, unfortunately, do not resemble greatly the terriers Russell would have kept. The first edition of this book was published in 1878, when Russell was still alive and was illustrated by H. B. Young (op. 1870s), sportsman, draughtsman and etcher.

TWENTIETH CENTURY

As the 20th century progressed, the Fox Terrier with strong working instincts, which had been established on working terriers which were dear to Russell and other sportsmen, gave way to a show terrier. Pockets of Fox Terriers, which the Parson would have approved of, did remain, and were perpetuated by sportsmen. These

Nathaniel Hugh John Baird (1865-1936). The frontispiece to E.W.L. Davies' 'Memoir of the Rev. John Russell and his Out-of-Door Life', 1902 edition – and the edition which is of most interest to Jack Russell collectors.

Vic Granger (b. 1931). The Ratpack. *Courtesy: Vic Granger.*

Vic Granger (b. 1931). Jack Russell Terriers. *Courtesy: Vic Granger.*

terriers formed the stock on which the Parson Jack Russell Terrier we see in the show ring today is based. 20th century sportsmen developed a short-legged terrier, both smooth and wire, affectionately known as the 'Jack Russell Terrier' and, with their coat and colouring, they very possibly share common ancestry with the Fox Terrier. An old short-legged terrier 'breed' was the Cowley Terrier, kept by the Cowleys of Buckinghamshire. They appear from the painting by Arthur Wardle to have been basically white, wire-coated dogs, with markings similar to those of the Reverend Russell's dogs, and were said to have been exceedingly game. The so called short-legged 'Jack Russell' could also descend

from these dogs – all in turn, no doubt, descending from the working terriers we first saw being depicted in art over 200 years ago.

Parson Jack Russell Terriers, Jack Russells and the short-legged dogs, often known as Hunt Terriers, are today favourite subjects with contemporary sporting artists. Mike Cawston, who won The Fine Arts Trade Guild Published Artist of the Year Award in 1998, Michelle Pearson Cooper, who has done commission work for Prince Sadruddin Aga Khan, Sir Tom Stoppard, Countess Bismarck and others, and Vic Granger, the Norfolk-based sporting artist, are just three who find these working terriers irresistible subjects.

Michelle Pearson Cooper (b. 1957).
A favourite Jack Russell.

Courtesy: Michelle Pearson Cooper.

9 THE BREED STANDARDS

Perhaps it is useful to start with a quote from *A Memoir of the Reverend John Russell and his Out-of-Door Life* by the Reverend E.W.L. Davies, published in England in 1878. Describing an oil painting of Parson Russell's Trump, he writes:

In the first place, the colour is white with just a patch of dark tan over each eye and ear, while a similar dot, not larger than a penny-piece, marks the root of the tail. The coat, which is thick, close, and a trifle wiry, is well calculated to protect the body from wet and cold, but has no affinity with the long, rough jacket of the Scotch Terrier. The legs are straight as arrows, the feet perfect; the loins and conformation of the whole frame indicative of hardihood and endurance; while the size and height of the animal may be compared to that of a full-grown vixen fox.

"I seldom or ever see a real fox-terrier nowadays," said Russell recently to a friend who was inspecting a dog show containing a hundred and fifty entries under that denomination; *"they have so intermingled strange blood with the real article that, if he were not informed, it would puzzle Professor Bell himself to discover what race the so-called fox-terrier belongs to."*

"And pray, how is it managed?" inquired the friend, eager to profit by Russell's long experience in such matters. *" I can well remember Rubie's and Tom French's Dartmoor terriers, and have owned some of the sort worth their weight in gold. True terriers they were, but certainly differing as much from the present show dogs, as the wild eglantine differs from the garden rose."*

"The process," replied Russell, *"is simply as follows: they begin with a smooth bitch terrier; then, to obtain a finer skin, an Italian greyhound is selected for her mate. But as the ears of the produce are an eyesore to the connoisseur, a beagle is resorted to, and then little is seen of that unsightly defect in the next generation. Lastly, to complete the mixture, the bulldog is now called on to give the necessary courage; and the composite animals, thus elaborated, become, after due selection, the sires and dams of the modern fox-terriers. This version of their origin,"* continued he, *"I received from a man well qualified to speak on the subject."*

The bulldog blood thus infused imparts courage, it is true, to the so-called terrier; he is matchless at killing any number of rats in a given time; will fight any dog of his weight in a Westminster pit; draw a badger heavier than himself out of his long box, and turn up a tom-cat possessed even of ten lives, before poor pussy can utter a wail. But the ferocity of that blood is in reality ill-suited – nay, is fatal to fox hunting purposes; for a terrier that goes to ground and fastens on his fox, as one so bred will do, is far more likely to spoil sport than promote it; he goes in to kill, not to bolt, the object of his attack.

Besides, such animals, if more than one slip into a fox-earth, are too apt to forget the game,

and fight each other, the death of one being occasionally the result of such encounters. Hence, well may Russell have been proud of the pure pedigree he has so long possessed and so carefully watched over. Tartars they are and ever have been, beyond all doubt: going up to their fox in any earth, facing him alternately with hard words and harder nips, until at length he is forced to quit his stronghold, and trust to the open for better security.

A fox thus bolted is rarely a pin the worse for the skirmish; he has had fair play given him, and instead of being half strangled, is fit to flee for his life. The hounds, too, have their chance, and the field are not baulked of their expected run.

This excursion into history is very informative, in that it describes the Parson's terriers, gives his opinion on crossbreeding, and also gives a detailed picture of how the terrier was and is supposed to work.

The Parson Jack Russell Terrier is the original working Fox Terrier, and, as such, is a very old breed, or strain. People in the breed call it the 'unimproved Fox Terrier',

and anyone who has seen old prints or paintings of the Fox Terriers of the last century will be struck by the similarity with present-day Jack Russells.

THE FIRST STANDARD

The use for which a dog was bred is almost always the basis for its Standard. Aside from the previous quote from Davies's memoirs, the first known Standard for the breed was a similar description written by the Parson himself in 1871.

A small energetic terrier of from 14 - 16 lb in weight, standing about 14 inches at the withers, legs straight as arrows; a thick skin, a good rough weather-resisting coat, thick, close; and a trifle wiry, well calculated to protect the body from cold and wet, but with no affinity to the wiry jacket of the Scotch Terrier. It is certain that a good horse or dog cannot be a bad colour, but I prefer a white dog. The bitch 'Trump' was white with just a patch of dark over each eye and ear, with a similar dot not larger than a penny-piece at the root of the tail. Feet should be perfect, the loins

The Jack Russell Terrier: "Every inch a sportsman."

Photo: Sheila Atter.

141

and conformation of the whole frame indicative of hardihood and endurance. The size and height of the animal may be compared to a fully grown vixen. Every inch a sportsman, the dog must not be quarrelsome. As regards height, some people prefer them to be rather more on the leg if they are to run with the hounds all day.

THE SECOND STANDARD

The second Standard that has relevance to present versions is Arthur Heinemann's 1904 Standard. This apparently was used as a model for the Parson Jack Russell Standard submitted to the Kennel Club.

HEAD: The skull should be flat, moderately broad, gradually decreasing to the eyes. Little stop should be apparent. The cheeks must not be full. Ears V-shaped and small, of moderate thickness and dropping forward close to the cheek, not by the side. Upper and lower jaws strong and muscular and of fair punishing strength. Not much falling away below the eyes. The nose should be black. The eyes dark, small, and deep set, full of fire, life and intelligence, and circular in shape. Teeth level, i.e. upper on the outside of the lower.

NECK: Clean and muscular of fair length gradually widening to shoulders.

SHOULDERS: Long and sloping, well laid-back, fine at points, clearly cut at withers.

CHEST: Deep but not broad.

BACK: Straight and strong with no appearance of slackness.

LOINS: Powerful, very slightly arched, fore ribs moderately arched, back ribs deep. The terrier should be well ribbed up.

HINDQUARTERS: Strong and muscular, free from droop, thighs long and powerful, hocks near the ground, dog standing well up on them. Not straight in the stifle.

STERN: Set on high, carried gaily but never over the back or curled. Of good strength and length. A 'pipe cleaning' tail, or too short, is most objectionable.

LEGS: Perfectly straight, showing no ankle in front. Strong in bone throughout, short and straight to the pastern. Fore and back legs carried straight forward when travelling, stifles not turned outward. Elbows should hang perpendicular to the body, working free to the side.

FEET: Round, compact, not large, soles hard and tough, toes moderately arched, turned neither in nor out.

COAT: Dense, a trifle wiry, abundant. Belly and undersides not bare.

COLOUR: White, with acceptable tan, grey or black at head and root of tail. Brindle or liver markings are objectionable.

SYMMETRY, SIZE AND CHARACTER: Terrier must present a gay, lively and active appearance. Bone and strength in a small compass are essentials, but not cloggy or coarse. Speed and endurance must be apparent. Not too short or too long in leg. Fourteen inches at the withers ideal for a dog, thirteen for a bitch. Weight when in working condition about fourteen pounds, but a pound more or less entirely acceptable. Conformation that of an adult vixen.

*Junior World Ch. Heythrop Trailblazer Of Snow Wind: Workmanlike
and agile, the Jack Russell is built for speed and endurance.
Photo: T.M. Strom.*

DISQUALIFYING POINTS: Too short, too leggy, legs not straight. Nose white, cherry, or spotted considerably with these colours. Ears prick or rose. Mouth under or over shot. Excessively nervous or savage.

RECOGNITION

The Parson Jack Russell Terrier Club was founded in 1983 in order to preserve and promote the old type of West Country terrier that had been bred and worked during and since the Parson's lifetime. It was this organisation which took the initiative and applied for Kennel Club recognition and, after several refusals, its efforts were crowned with success. The Kennel Club (KC) of Great Britain recognised the Parson Jack Russell Terrier on the 22 January 1990. The Fédération Cynologique Internationale (FCI) published a provisional Breed Standard on the 2 July of the same year. While the Kennel Club accepted the Parson Jack Russell Terrier as a variant of the Fox Terrier, rather than the other way around (which might have been more historically correct), the FCI, which is obliged to adopt the Standard of the breed's country of origin, added a clause accepting a dog of not less than 10 inches (26 cms) "for a period of time not yet determined". This was an acknowledgement of the fact that there were thousands of short-legged Jack Russells on the provisional registers of many of the FCI member countries. American Kennel Club (AKC) recognition came on January 1 1998, with The Jack Russell Terrier Association of America (JRTAA), becoming the parent breed club.

COMPARISON OF BREED STANDARDS

Comparing the KC, FCI and AKC Standards, one immediately notices the extreme detail of the AKC Standard. The revised FCI Standard No. 339, dated 1 December 1997, apart from a historical introduction, follows the KC Standard very closely, and in fact is merely a rearrangement of the points. The AKC Standard has a different format, and has only twelve headings as compared to the Kennel Club format, which has eighteen.

GENERAL APPEARANCE
KC and FCI: Workmanlike, active and agile, built for speed and endurance.

This terminology stems largely from the Heinemann Standard, and, to my mind, exactly defines the type of dog a Parson Jack Russell should be. A heavy, short-legged, wide-chested dog can never be so described.

AKC: The Jack Russell Terrier was developed in the South of England in the 1800s as a white terrier to work European red fox both above and below ground. The terrier was named for the Reverend John Russell, whose terriers trailed hounds and bolted foxes from dens so the hunt could ride on.

To function as a working terrier, he must possess certain characteristics: a ready attitude, alert and confident; balance in height and length; medium in size and bone, suggesting strength and endurance. Important to breed type is a natural appearance: harsh, weatherproof coat with a compact construction and clean silhouette. The coat is broken or smooth. He has a small, flexible chest to enable him to pursue his quarry underground and sufficient length of leg to follow the hounds. Old scars and injuries, the result of honorable work or accident, should not be allowed to prejudice a terrier's chance in the show ring, unless they interfere with movement or utility for work or breeding.

The statement that it was a white terrier bred to work red fox seems to me a mistake,

as nowhere is it recorded that the terrier had to be entirely white. It also seems to me that the words 'compact construction' do not appear in either the KC or the FCI Standards, and could easily lead to misunderstanding, possibly describing a cobby, heavier or short-coupled dog. The sentence on old scars and injuries, which is not featured in either of the other Standards, is nevertheless covered by the words 'essentially a working terrier' (see below). It is understood that a working terrier may have a blemish or two, be they honourable or otherwise.

CHARACTERISTICS

KC and FCI: Essentially a working terrier with the ability and conformation to go to ground and run with hounds.

This second heading in the KC Standard further describes type, and clearly stipulates that this is, and always has been, a working terrier. The same words are used by the FCI under its third heading, 'Behaviour and Temperament'.

SIZE, SUBSTANCE, PROPORTION

SIZE

KC: Height minimum 33 cms (13ins), ideally 35 cms. (14ins) at withers for dogs, and minimum 30 cms (12ins), ideally 33 cms (13ins) at withers for bitches.

FCI: For dogs, ideal size at withers 35 cm. For bitches, ideal size at withers 33 cm.
NB For a period of time not yet determined, the size of males and bitches should not be less than 26 cm. Dogs which have not the ideal height at withers should not be penalised for this reason and are accepted for breeding purposes without any restriction.

AKC: Both sexes are properly balanced between 12" and 14" at the withers. The ideal height of a mature dog is 14" at the withers, and bitches 13". Terriers whose heights measure either slightly larger or smaller than the ideal are not to be

Ridley Pilot: The first FCI Champion.

penalized in the show ring provided other points of their conformation, especially balance and chest span, are consistent with the breed standard. The weight of a terrier in hard working condition is usually between 13-17 lb.

The discrepancies that exist between the KC Standard on the one hand and the AKC and FCI Standards on the other, in my opinion make a farce of many of the other points in these two Standards. The FCI Standard lists the dog in Group III, Terriers, under 'Section 1 – Large and medium sized Terriers.' A 26 cm (10 in) animal is not medium-sized, and certainly not large. Even though this is stated as 'for a period of time not yet determined', there seem to be no plans to delete this passage, even though the breed will be listed on the permanent register for the foreseeable futre. The AKC Standard is almost equally illogical on this point, stating that both sexes are properly balanced between 12 and 14 ins, and then goes on to say that terriers whose heights measure 'either slightly larger or smaller than the ideal' are acceptable. This in fact allows a dog to be two inches under but only one inch over the ideal height. Bitches, it follows, are only allowed to be one inch under the ideal height, but are allowed to be two inches over the ideal height.

The AKC Standard further stipulates that the weight be between 13 and 17 lbs, something which is not mentioned in the other two Standards. Weight, however, is mentioned by both the Parson (14 to 16 lbs) and the Heinemann (around 14 lbs) Standards. Perhaps this is not a bad idea, in order to be more precise in the description of the dog. The British point of view is that there is no maximum height and no mention of weight, as a dog that is too large and too heavy is not spannable. There is a lot to be said for this point of view, but nonetheless, I find that some of the dogs at British shows

are getting a bit big. A maximum height in the KC Standard might not be a bad idea.

PROPORTION
AKC: Balance is the keystone of the terrier's anatomy. The chief points of consideration are the relative proportions of skull and foreface, head and frame, height at withers and length of body. The height at withers is slightly greater than the distance from the withers to tail, i.e. by possibly 1 to 1.5 inches on a 14 inch dog. The measurement will vary according to height, the ratio of height to back being approximately 6:5.

This is in complete contradiction to the KC Standard, which demands that the length of back from withers to root of tail is equal to height from withers to ground. The FCI considers this measurement so important that it is incorporated in its second heading, 'Important Proportions' (see below). It is difficult to understand how the AKC Standard could have gone so terribly wrong on this point, as this measurement not only changes the whole look of the dog, calling for a short-backed animal, but is also completely detrimental to the working ability of the dog, in that a short-coupled animal is not nearly as flexible as one with a longer back. The short-coupled terrier will not be able to turn itself around in a foxhole, and will be inhibited from easily leaving an earth.

IMPORTANT PROPORTIONS
FCI: Well balanced. Length of back from withers to root of tail equal to height from withers to ground (longer than high). Length from nose to stop slightly shorter than from stop to occiput.

In the KC Standard, these points are covered under the headings 'Head and Skull' and 'Body', which seems more logical,

A correctly proportioned head, with typical expression.

Photo: Sheila Atter.

as a judge, when examining a dog, normally starts at the head and then goes over the rest of the body. However, this is largely a rearrangement of the KC Standard, as the wording is exactly the same.

HEAD

KC and FCI: Head and Skull: Flat, moderately broad, gradually narrowing to the eyes. Shallow stop. Length from nose to stop slightly shorter than from stop to occiput. Nose black. Eyes: Almond shaped, fairly deep-set, dark, keen expression.

AKC: Head: Strong and in good proportion to the rest of the body, so the appearance of balance is maintained. Expression: Keen, direct, full of life and intelligence. Eyes: Almond shaped, dark in color, moderate in size, not protruding. Dark rims are desirable.

Here again, the AKC Standard varies from both the FCI and the KC Standard on two important aspects. Whereas the KC calls for eyes which are almond-shaped, fairly deep set, dark, and with keen expression, and the FCI Standard is identical, the AKC Standard is more precise and stipulates that the eyes also be moderate in size and not protruding. Nowhere is it mentioned that the eyes should be fairly deep-set, even though this is essential in a terrier who works underground. Perhaps 'not protruding' covers this necessity. The AKC Standard further says that dark rims are desirable, which is a purely cosmetic quality and is not mentioned in either of the other Standards. Dark-rimmed eyes may be more attractive, but rarely exist in white dogs or dogs with asymmetrical head markings. What is a judge to do – penalise an otherwise well constructed dog, only because its left eye might not be pigmented?

EARS

KC and FCI: Small, V-shaped, dropping forward, carried close to head, fold not to appear above top of skull.

AKC: Button ear. Small 'V'-shaped drop ears of moderate thickness carried forward

close to the head with the tip so as to cover the orifice and pointing toward the eye. Fold is level with the top of the skull or slightly above. When alert, ear tips do not extend below the corner of the eye.

Here the AKC Standard again varies from the KC and the FCI Standards, and is much more descriptive. Nonetheless, the original KC Standard particularly states that the fold of the ear is not to appear above the skull. By tolerating ear folds slightly above the skull and demanding that the ear tip points toward the eye, the AKC Standard seems to call for an ear which is similar to that of the Fox Terrier or Lakeland Terrier, and that look is foreign to the breed.

SKULL
KC and FCI: Head and Skull: Flat, moderately broad, gradually narrowing to the eyes. Shallow stop. Length from nose to stop slightly shorter than from stop to occiput.

AKC: Flat and fairly broad between the ears, narrowing slightly to the eyes. The stop is well defined but not prominent.

Here, again, it seems to me that the terminology of the AKC Standard is open to misinterpretation. 'Narrowing slightly to the eyes'does not mean the same as 'gradually narrowing to the eyes'. The AKC Standard can be interpreted to allow a much boxier, less wedge-shaped head than the Parson Jack Russell should have. This again would let the head appear more like that of the modern Fox Terrier, and the breed would lose its strong head and powerful jaws, and above all, it would lose distinctive type.

MUZZLE
KC AND FCI: Length from nose to stop slightly shorter than from stop to occiput.

AKC: Length from nose to stop is slightly shorter than the distance from stop to occiput.

MOUTH
KC and FCI: Jaws strong, muscular. Teeth with a perfect, regular and complete scissor bite, i.e. upper teeth closely overlapping the lower teeth and set square to the jaws.

AKC: Jaws: Upper and lower are of fair and punishing strength. Bite: Teeth are large with complete dentition in a perfect scissors bite, i.e. upper teeth closely overlapping the lower teeth and teeth set square to the jaws.

Teeth should meet in a complete scissor bite. Photo: Sheila Atter.

Correct placement of incisors. Photo: Sheila Atter.

NOSE
KC and FCI: Nose black.

AKC: Must be black and fully pigmented.

The AKC, Kennel Club and FCI Standards all call for more or less the same things (though in the FCI Standard this phrase is found under the heading 'Important Proportions'). The muzzle to skull proportion should be roughly two-fifths to three-fifths. A muzzle that is too short is reminiscent of a Border Terrier; if too long, it resembles a Fox Terrier's. One exception again is to be found in the AKC Standard, which calls for large teeth with complete dentition, states that missing teeth are a fault, yet permits three missing teeth (four missing teeth constitutes disqualification). The KC and FCI Standards call for a complete scissor bite, and leave the question of missing teeth to the discretion of the judges. It is important here to note that in Europe, most judges are emphatic about dogs having every one of their 42 teeth and, in some countries such as Germany, dogs are banned from breeding if they do not have a complete set of teeth.

NECK AND TOPLINE
KC and FCI: Neck: Clean, muscular, of good length, gradually widening to shoulders.

AKC: Neck: Clean and muscular, moderately arched, of fair length, gradually widening so as to blend well into the shoulders. Topline: Strong, straight, and level in motion, the loin slightly arched.

Again, although the wording is slightly different, all three Standards call for the same construction.

When the three Standards call for a slightly arched loin (AKC as above; KC and FCI

under 'Body', below), they mean that the topline cannot be completely straight, as is that of a Fox Terrier. This slight arch is produced by the set of the pelvic bone. If the pelvis is too horizontal, the terrier might look smart, but it will have lost some angulation of the stifle, thereby sacrificing a lot of the extension, which produces the necessary drive for an effortless ground-covering stride.

BODY
KC and FCI: Chest of moderate depth, capable of being spanned behind the shoulders by average size hands. Back strong and straight. Loin slightly arched. Well balanced, length of back from withers to root of tail equal to height from withers to ground.

AKC: Body: In overall length to height proportion, the dog appears approximately square and balanced. The back is neither short nor long. The back gives no appearance of slackness but is laterally flexible, so that he may turn around in an earth. Tuck-up is moderate. Chest: Narrow and of moderate depth, giving an athletic rather than heavily-chested appearance; must be flexible and compressible. The ribs are fairly well sprung, oval rather than round, not extending past the level of the elbow.

The KC Standard calls for a well balanced body, length of back from withers to root of tail equal in height from withers to ground, whereas the FCI Standard adds succinctly 'dog 3D longer than high' under its 'Important Proportions' heading. The AKC Standard, in calling for a square dog, again opens the door for interpretations.

The KC and FCI Standards here do not go into such detail about the chest, and merely call for a 'chest of moderate depth', leaving that measurement to be controlled by

The Jack Russell should appear square and balanced, with a moderate depth of chest.

Photo: Sheila Atter.

spanning, a heading which comes at the end of the AKC Standard. Slightly confusing is the wording in the AKC Standard, which calls for ribs 'not extending past the level of the elbow'. This should read 'not extending below the level of the elbow'.

TAIL
KC and FCI: Strong, straight set on high.

Customarily docked with length complementing the body while providing a good handhold.

AKC: Set high, strong, carried gaily but not over the back or curled. Docked so that the tip is approximately level to the skull, providing a good handhold.

The tail is customarily docked, with the length complementing the body. Photo: John Valentine.

In a number of FCI countries, docking is now banned. Photo: Sheila Atter.

Here again the AKC Standard is much more explicit than either of the others. Docking is also cosmetic, and is now forbidden in many FCI countries, and no dog should be penalised for a tail which is either too short or too long. Nowhere in any other Standard is a tail called for which is level with the skull.

FOREQUARTERS
KC and FCI: Shoulders long and sloping, well laid back, cleanly cut at withers. Legs strong, must be straight with joints turning neither in nor out. Elbows close to body, working free of sides.

AKC: Shoulders: Long and sloping, well laid back, cleanly cut at the withers. Point of shoulder sits in a plane behind the point of the prosternum. The shoulder blade and upper arm are of approximately the same length; forelimbs are placed well under the dog. Elbows hang perpendicular to the body, working free of the sides. Legs are strong and straight with good bone. Joints turn neither in nor out. Pasterns firm and nearly straight.

Once again the FCI and KC Standards are identical. Since dogs do not have collarbones, their front assemblies are attached to the ribcage only by muscles. And since the forequarters of a dog support about 60 per cent of its weight, therefore absorbing the push and drive which stem from the hindquarters, it is eminently important that the proportions and angulation be correct in order to ensure smooth, effortless movement. The shoulder blade (scapula) should be the same length, or slightly longer than, the upper arm (humerus). The angle of the scapula, measured up the scapula ridge, should be about 30 degrees off the vertical. This angulation allows the dog to extend its forelegs adequately, while a steeper shoulder

Correct angulation will ensure smooth, effortless movement. Photo: Sheila Atter.

(i.e. a shorter humerus) does not. This leads to a stilted gait or pounding. When an upright shoulder in an unbalanced dog goes with angulated hindquarters, the rear stride will be longer than the front, resulting in hackney action, as the dog has to get its forelegs out of the way. These faults in construction inhibit the dog from moving effortlessly, and a dog which tires easily will not be a good worker. The qualities called for under the heading 'General Appearance': 'Workmanlike, active, agile, built for speed and endurance'will have been lost through incorrect front structure.

FEET
KC and FCI: Compact with firm pads, turning neither in nor out.

AKC: Round, cat-like, very compact, the pads thick and tough, the toes moderately

arched pointing forward, turned neither in nor out.

As usual, the AKC Standard is more explicit, stating that toes should turn neither in nor out. Personally, I have never seen a dog with cat-like feet. Nonetheless, the dog walks and runs on its feet, and pads should certainly be tough and resilient, and it stands to reason that a dog with correct front assembly will have feet that point straight forward.

HINDQUARTERS
KC: Strong, muscular, with good bend of stifle. Hocks short and parallel, giving plenty of drive.

FCI: Strong, muscular with good angulation and bend of stifle. Hocks short and parallel giving plenty of drive.

AKC: Strong and muscular, smoothly molded, with good angulation and bend of stifle. Hocks near the ground, parallel and driving in action. Feet as in front.

The construction and angulation of the hindquarters should be a mirror image of the front, giving an impression of perfect harmony and balance. Since it is the hindquarters which give drive to movement, the angulation of the stifle, the strength of muscle and the shape of hocks are all most important. Cow hocks and spreading or barrel hocks both inhibit straight movement and also put a strain on muscles and ligaments and tire the dog, and should be penalised. All three Standards could be a bit more explicit under this heading.

COAT
KC: Naturally harsh, close and dense, whether rough or smooth. Belly and undersides coated. Skin must be thick and loose.

The coat should be harsh, close and dense, regardless of whether it is rough or smooth.

152

FCI: Skin: Must be thick and loose. Hair: Naturally harsh, close and dense, whether rough or smooth. Belly and undersides coated.

AKC: Smooth: Double-coated. Coarse and weatherproof. Flat but hard, dense and abundant, belly and undersides of thighs are not bare. Broken: Double-coated. Coarse and weatherproof. Short, dense undercoat covered with a harsh, straight, tight jacket which lies flat and close to the body and legs. There is a clear outline with only a hint of eyebrows and beard. Belly and undersides of thighs are not bare. Coat does not show a strong tendency to curl or wave. No sculptured furnishings. The terrier is shown in his natural appearance not excessively groomed. Sculpturing is to be severely penalised. Faults: Soft, silky, woolly or curly topcoat. Lacking undercoat.

The FCI Standard puts 'Skin' under a separate heading, thus emphasising an important point. A terrier that is meant to go to ground to face a fox must have skin which is thick enough and loose enough to take the brunt of any injuries, thus protecting the organs underneath. While the mention of wavy or curly coats is certainly useful, as this sort of coat is evidence of foreign blood, the wording again implies that a slight tendency to curl or wave is permissible. Since Americans seem to be much more prone to over-groom, colour, trim, and sculpture their show dogs, penalising these actions is probably a good thing. I personally would like to have dogs shown in a much more natural state. Even over-stripping makes it difficult for a judge to assess what kind of a coat a dog has.

COLOUR
KC: Entirely white, or predominantly white with markings which are tan, lemon or black, or any combination of these colours, preferably confined to the head or root of tail.

FCI: Entirely white or with tan, lemon or black markings, preferably confined to the head or root of the tail.

Ideal markings including a tail spot.   *Photo: Sheila Atter.*

AKC: White, white with black or tan markings, or a combination of these, tri-color. Colors are clear. Markings are preferably confined to the head and root of tail. Heavy body markings are not desirable. Grizzle is acceptable and should not be confused with brindle.

The AKC Standard calls for clear colours, but then goes on to accept grizzle, which, to me, is a contradiction. Lemon does not seem to exist.

GAIT/MOVEMENT
KC and FCI: Free, lively, well co-ordinated, straight action front and behind.

AKC: Movement or action is the crucial test of conformation. The terrier's movement is free, lively, well coordinated, with straight action front and behind. There should be ample reach and drive with good length of stride.

Here, the AKC Standard is superior. The mention of reach, drive and length of stride should certainly be incorporated in to the other two Standards.

TEMPERAMENT
KC and FCI: Bold and friendly.

AKC: Bold and friendly. Athletic and clever. At work he is a game hunter, tenacious and courageous. At home he is playful, exuberant, and overwhelmingly affectionate. He is an independent and energetic terrier and requires his due portion of attention. He should not be quarrelsome. Shyness should not be confused with submissiveness. Submissiveness is not a fault. Sparring is not acceptable. Fault: Shyness.

Disqualification: Overt aggression towards another dog or human.

It is difficult for a judge in the show ring to assess the working qualities of a dog, or whether he is playful at home. It is difficult enough to judge temperament, but certainly the words 'bold and friendly' mean that the dog should not be shy or overly aggressive. I personally think that submissiveness is not a characteristic found in the Parson Jack Russell, and I also think that shyness should be judged as harshly as aggression. Both traits make the dog unfit for the work he was bred to do. All three Standards call for a bold and friendly dog. A shy dog is not bold, and an aggressive dog is not friendly. The Parson would not have given houseroom to either.

SPANNING
AKC: To measure a terrier's chest, span from behind, raising only the front feet from the ground, and compress gently. Directly behind the elbows is the smaller, firm part of the chest. The central part is usually larger but should feel rather elastic. Span with hands tightly behind the elbows on the forward portion of the chest. The chest must be easily spanned by average size hands. Thumbs should meet at the spine, and fingers should meet under the chest. This is a significant factor and a critical part of the judging process. The dog can not be correctly judged without this procedure.

The Kennel Club Standard merely states, under its heading 'Body', that the chest must be of moderate depth, capable of being spanned by average-size hands. The FCI Standard is exactly the same. The effect of these three directives is similar.

DISQUALIFICATIONS
AKC: Height under 12 inches or over 15 inches. Prick ears, liver nose. Four or more missing teeth. Overshot, undershot or wry mouth. Brindle markings. Overt aggression towards other dogs or humans.

I have already commented on most of the points listed above. The Kennel Club and the FCI do not list any disqualifications, but state 'Any departure from the foregoing points should be considered a fault and the seriousness with which the fault should be regarded should be in exact proportion to its degree.' This means that a judge is able to assess a dog more subjectively, perhaps putting type over other considerations. The above sentence is the same for all KC Breed Standards. The KC and FCI Standards end with a note: 'Male animals should have two apparently normal testicles fully descended into the scrotum.' The AKC Standard covers this issue as a blanket requirement for all breeds on a par with being able to see and hear. It is not, however, included in each Breed Standard.

All in all, it seems to me that, although the AKC Standard is more precise and descriptive in many points, it describes a different type from the British dog. Both judges and breeders should familiarise themselves with the Parson's and Heinemann's Standards and study as many old books, prints, and paintings as possible in order to recognise the correct type.

10 COAT CARE

For the vast majority of purebred dogs, colour and coat type are essential to breed type, and the Jack Russell Terrier is no exception. For many breeds of dog, coat density, texture and length are also essential points to consider when assessing the suitability of the individual dog for the purpose originally intended. Again, the Jack Russell Terrier is no exception.

TEXTURE AND LENGTH

For the Jack Russell Terrier, there are three accepted coat variations. All are equally correct, providing the depth and texture are of good quality. The Jack Russell Terrier can be either smooth, broken, or rough coated. The only important consideration should be that the coat is weatherproof and protective. The three coat types are essentially the same, and consist of a dense undercoat and a weatherproof topcoat. It is only the length of the topcoat or guard hairs that vary, giving three distinctly different-looking terriers that are still obviously the same breed. Coat type has little bearing on the terrier's ability to work, as long as the texture and thickness of the coat are correct. As a functional breed of terrier, the Jack Russell's coat should protect it from the cold and wet, and against some degree of superficial injury. Texture and thickness, being of vital importance in helping to protect the working terrier, are obviously more important than superficial appearance.

A good protective pelt consists of a dense, soft, insulating undercoat, interspersed with a hard (but not harsh), straight, oily, and thus waterproof, top coat. The topcoat will vary in length, from approximately, 2 to 6 cm (0.5 to 2.5 inches), especially around the neck and across the shoulders. Profuse feathering or an open and thin coat are more likely to contribute to ill health as a result of exposure to the elements. The Jack Russell Terrier's coat must be virtually water resistant to help to prevent the terrier from weather-related ailments, such as painful and stiff joints, especially in old age. He is also more likely to suffer from superficial injuries to the body if the coat fails to provide adequate protection.

Although the length of the topcoat, even in the smooth-coated Russell, is variable, the undercoat is always the same and acts like a layer of insulating and protective foam. The topcoat even in the smooth-coated russell, should be longer and appear more concentrated around the neck and over the shoulders. This will help to give the terrier protection against its foe underground, and is a common feature of many unexaggerated breeds. The coat should be perfectly straight and lie flat to the body, effecting the best protection possible to the terrier, regardless of coat type.

COAT TYPES
Photos: Sheila Atter.

Broken-coated: The outline is clean, with a slightly more ragged appearance around the neck and shoulders.

Smooth: This coat is still weather-resistant with its dense undercoat.

Rough-coated: The topcoat is longer, but it should still lie flat to the body.

While the vast majority of Jack Russell Terriers today spend a great deal more time than their ancestors relaxing in the warmth of their owner's home, the important aspects of a breed's heritage should never be forgotten. As a working terrier first and foremost, or rather, a breed that should still be capable of performing the same day's work as its ancestors, the key characteristics of the breed should always take priority in any breeding programme.

The outline of the Jack Russell should be clean and easy to identify, regardless of whether the coat is smooth, broken or rough. This is an important aspect of the Jack Russell, for it is believed that the Reverend John Russell preferred all his terriers to look smooth from shooting distance, regardless of coat type. This reference would have been to the Jack Russell Terrier in its natural state, without any trimming or stripping. Of course, the broken and the rough coated Jack Russell will have a more ragged outline around the neck and shoulders, but these should be the only areas where the outline is less defined. Legs should be clean and smooth, covered by thick, short and protective hair. The belly and undersides should be well covered, with little or no hair or skin visible.

COLOUR

The Standard for the Parson Jack Russell Terrier defines the only acceptable colour as white, either entirely or with patches. Any colour other than white should, ideally, be confined to the head and the root of the tail. Colour should be a secondary consideration, but it is an essential aspect of correct breed type. Acceptable colours for markings are lemon, tan, or black, or a combination of black and tan or lemon, i.e. tricolour – that is, a terrier with patches of black and tan or black and lemon on a white background. Colour mutations such as blue (where any

black colouring on the terrier occurs as anything from grey to steel blue, (including the nose) or chocolate (where any black colouring appears as chocolate brown, including the nose) do occur from time to time, and are caused by a defective gene for the colour black. No black colouring will be apparent on the terrier anywhere, and this includes the nose. Eyes on such terriers tend to be grey or greenish as opposed to dark hazel or black, and the nose is always grey or brown respectively. Recessive genes normally gives rise to such characteristics and, consequently, both parents should be suspected of carrying the characteristic. Blue or chocolate-coloured patches and/or noses are considered highly undesirable features in the Jack Russell Terrier and, ideally, neither parent should be bred from again. In the case of a white and tan or white and lemon marked Jack Russell Terrier, the nose and eye rims will be the only areas where the presence of a genetic colour mutation will be apparent. A terrier with dark brown patches but a black nose is not the same and, although uncommon, does appear from time to time.

The white and lemon coloured terrier, although essentially a lighter variation of the white and tan terrier, tends to be born white and the coloured areas develop over a couple of weeks. The tan colour will vary, and in some Russells may be even sable, or, sometimes, grizzle, but will always appear basically the same when viewed from a distance.

White and tan puppies are born with tan patches which seldom change colour, while sable or grizzle coloured patches usually appear black at birth and develop over a week or two. Rich red colouring is considered undesirable, as is brindle, which should never be confused with grizzle. Tricoloured Russells have markings from one of three patterns, each referred to as tricolour, but each quite different in terms of both genetics and

A tricolour bitch.

A tan and white male.

These markings are also referred to as tricolour.

appearance. Almost all tricoloured puppies, when born, are (or appear to be) black and white with a hint of tan around the eyes and cheeks. As the puppies develop, the amount of tan in the coat markings will increase to varying degrees, depending on the breeding. In some tricoloured Russells with just head markings, the mature terrier will appear white and tan as opposed to tricolour, but this is only due to the absence of body colour, in which case more black would be evident on patches along the back. White Russells with black markings are relatively uncommon, but Russells with black markings and tan spots on the cheeks, above the eyes, inside the ears and under the tail are a little more common. These terriers are also classified as tricolour, although, again, such Russells are quite different, both genetically and in appearance, to the more common 'hound'-marked tricolour.

Eye rims and lips should ideally be of dark-pigmented skin, and as a result many white and tan or white and lemon Jack Russell Terriers are born with a black mask. This will fade as the puppy develops, and the black may all but disappear except at the corner of the mouth and around the eyes. However, these terriers are classified as white and tan or white and lemon and not tricolour, as the mask is only an indication of good eye and lip pigmentation.

In fact, the colour of any patches on your Jack Russell Terrier will give some insight into any other breeds which may have been influential in that particular dog's background. Smooth Fox Terriers, Border Terriers and Beagles are all breeds that can enhance, or at least contribute, characteristics desirable in a Jack Russell. Indeed, as puppies, some Smooth Fox Terriers and Parson Jack Russell Terriers are quite indistinguishable to the inexperienced eye until the heads begin to develop. All have coats of similar texture and depth but they differ in colour and markings. Wire Fox Terriers, Lakeland Terriers and Sealyham Terriers are also breeds that may appear to have influenced certain lines from time to time. These breeds tend to contribute more in the way of undesirable characteristics that have a direct affect on the terrier's ability to fulfil the purpose for which it was intended. The Lakeland Terrier, Sealyham Terrier and Wire Fox Terrier all have profuse and, in the case of the Wire Fox and Lakeland, wavy or curly coats. The Sealyham Terrier is also shorter in the leg than the ideal Jack Russell, and the Lakeland has very different temperament. All of these characteristics are considered highly undesirable in the ideal Jack Russell Terrier and give rise to a very different sort of terrier.

GROOMING
Grooming should form a fundamental part of

Grooming equipment.

any dog's health care programme. It is an activity that provides an ideal opportunity to spend time with your dog and check for parasites such as fleas and ticks, lesions, lumps, bumps, etc. Regular grooming also helps to establish your relationship with your dog, tone up its muscle condition and keep the coat clean. The Jack Russell Terrier, as a breed, needs relatively little grooming to keep its coat in good condition. As a result, the grooming equipment needed is minimal, and reasonably inexpensive.

Obviously, the exact amount of grooming your Jack Russell Terrier requires will depend on the type of coat he has. All dogs benefit from regular brushing, so this is a routine that should be established from day one. Regular grooming helps to remove loose hair and dead skin, subsequently promoting new coat growth, while also keeping the skin healthy. For the smooth-coated Jack Russell Terrier, regular grooming will be sufficient. The broken-coated and rough-coated varieties will also benefit from 'hand-stripping' or 'plucking' in the spring of each year. This is a process where the loose topcoat is removed by pulling, using only finger and thumb. The procedure greatly reduces the amount of hair shed around the animals' living quarters and encourages healthy, even new coat growth.

EQUIPMENT
You will need the following grooming supplies: grooming table, slicker brush, horsehair glove or hound glove, metal comb, flea comb, scissors, stripping knives, stripping stone, nail clippers or nail grinders, shampoo, mouthwash and a mirror.

GROOMING TABLE: There are many different brands of grooming table on the market, and the type that you purchase is rather dependent on whether it will stay in one place, such as your home or kennel, or whether you will be taking it with you to dog shows. If you are going to be taking it with you and setting it up often, then perhaps a lighter-weight table is better, or one that has wheels and is meant for travel. Many people invest in two – one for travel and one for home use.

A grooming arm with a noose to slip around the dog's neck as an added accessory can be invaluable in helping to control a busy terrier – almost like having a third hand. However, you should never leave any dog, adult or puppy, in a noose on a grooming table. There is a quick-release safety clip, sold through several of the canine catalogues, that you can purchase which can be attached between the arm and the noose to keep a dog from accidentally choking if he jumps from the table. It will release the noose if enough weight is put on it, and it is adjustable. There have been several cases of dogs dying as a result of slipping off the table and strangling in the noose – do not let yours be one of them.

If you plan on showing your puppy, the grooming table should become part of his routine on a weekly basis. Early experience and training on the grooming table should be limited to treats and praise, with soft brushing. Building a positive experience is the most important aspect of working with your puppy on the table.

This breed, when shown in conformation, is required to be examined on the table so the judge can properly evaluate the dog. The more comfortable your dog is with being on the table, the easier it will be in the show ring, and at the vet's too.

SLICKER BRUSH: This is a very fine wire-bristle brush on a flat back with a handle. Slicker brushes come in several varieties, usually from softer to harsher. The softer versions should be used on young dogs, with the medium version used for adult dogs. Take care never to be too heavy-handed with a

slicker brush as it is easy to scrape the skin and make it a most unpleasant experience for the dog.

HORSEHAIR GLOVE OR HOUND GLOVE: Your hand will fit right inside the glove, with the brush part lying in the palm of your hand. Go over the body in the same direction as the hair growth of the dog, never against, just as if you were wiping down your Jack Russell. This glove keeps the coat neat and polished. It also gives the skin a massage.

METAL COMB: The most useful comb is a seven-inch comb with one-inch teeth, coarse (wider spaced) at one end, and fine (closer spaced) at the other end.

FLEA COMB: This comb can be useful for keeping a short coat flat, and for picking up signs of flea infestation.

SCISSORS: Use small blunt-nose curved scissors for trimming the pads of the feet, and thinning scissors to tidy up any areas necessary when defining a profile. Thinning shears when grooming a broken or rough-coated dog are extremely useful. The most efficient type of thinning shears has one solid blade and one with teeth. Never buy a pair of shears or scissors without first trying them in your hand, as every person has a slightly different hand, and what is comfortable for one may not be for another. You will also tend to use a pair of scissors more if they feel comfortable and are easy for you to use.

STRIPPING KNIVES: There is a wide variety to choose from, and they come in several different blade sizes – coarse, medium and fine. Make sure that you test the feel when you hold it, as stripping knives are the same as scissors, in that you want to make sure they are comfortable in your hand. A medium-fine blade is a good one to have on

hand; if not for stripping it can be used for raking through the coat. However, the best stripping is done with your fingers.

STRIPPING STONE: These are black in colour and are actually called lava stone. They are quite inexpensive and are an excellent tool for removing dead or loose hair.

NAIL CLIPPERS OR GRINDERS: Nail clippers or grinders are a must for grooming a dog, whether it is for show or a pet. Only use nail clippers that are specifically made for canines. If you are somewhat nervous about clipping your dog's nails, perhaps a nail grinder may be helpful, as it only shaves off a small amount, depending on how much pressure you use. Because of the speed of a nail grinder it will actually tend to cauterise the nail if you reach the quick. However, the grinders do make more noise, and many dogs can be uncomfortable with this. Using nail grinders is best started when your dog is a puppy. Always have a blood stop powder on hand in case you do take a nail down too far.

SHAMPOO: A basic flea shampoo and a terrier coat shampoo are good to have for your complete baths. Waterless shampoo can be used in between baths in areas that need attention, such as the genital area or the face.

MOUTHWASH: A listerine mouthwash, in a mixture of one third mouthwash to two thirds water, can be used to clean and freshen up the coat without taking away from its natural texture. A squirt or spray bottle is handy for this, or a small bucket and sponge, depending on how much needs to be done.

MIRROR: Placing your grooming table in front of a mirror will be an added asset. As you go over your puppy, you can then see the judge's side as well as your own. A mirror will also help you to see how your puppy

looks best when he is stacked, and you can experiment with different ways of stacking him to his best advantage. Most American judges will like to see your dog stacked and positioned with his front toes just touching the front edge of the table.

ROUTINE CARE

A Jack Russell is considered a low-maintenance dog, and if you are spending a great deal of time grooming yours, then perhaps you are over-grooming. Grooming sessions should be short, particularly if you are starting with a young dog.

When you start a young puppy, make each session fun and upbeat. Pick a time when you are rested and can relax, as your puppy will feel your tension and begin to dread both the table and grooming.

When the puppy is comfortable on the table you will want to carefully go over him. First check his teeth, then move on to the pads of his feet, the nails, which may need to be trimmed, and the ears, which need to be cleaned or the excess hair trimmed under the ear flap. Run your hands over the coat with a flea comb to check for parasites.

If you are training for show, run your hands over your puppy in the same manner as the judge will, praising him often. It is also good to have a family friend or someone your dog does not know go over him too. The more different people that go over him, the more relaxed he will be on the table in the show ring. If you have a male dog, make sure he is accustomed to having his testicles checked as this will be something the judge will do each time he is on the table.

EYES AND EARS

The nature of a Jack Russell is to be very inquisitive and curious, digging in dirt and rooting through brush, so special attention should be given to keeping the eyes clean and free from debris. Wipe them with a damp cotton pad or ball, cleaning up the inside corners and any matter that may build up. If the eye has an excessive amount of tearing or weeping, it may be a good idea to have your veterinarian check your dog's eyes for allergies or irritation.

The ears should be cleaned with an ear-cleaning solution made especially for dogs. Be careful not to probe deeply into the ear so as to avoid damaging the ear canal or eardrum. If you notice any abnormal smell, discharge or build-up, you may want to consult your veterinarian. Jack Russells that do a lot of working may get either cheat grass or foxtails in their ears. If you notice your dog scratching or shaking its ears, it is a good idea to have your veterinarian examine them. Both cheat grass and foxtails can burrow into the ear, causing a great deal of discomfort, and they may actually pierce the eardrum itself if left untreated.

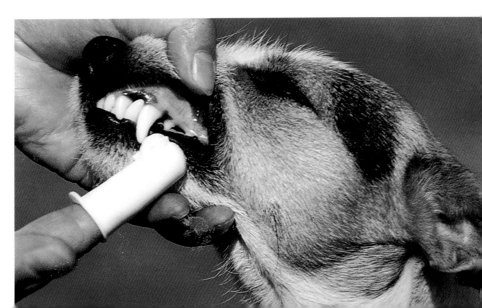

Teeth will need to be cleaned if tartar accumulates.

Photo: John Valentine.

Nails will need to be trimmed on a regular basis.
Photo: Sheila Atter.

TEETH

The teeth and gums on your terrier should be checked every week, particularly when your puppy is teething. The gums should be pink or dark, depending on the amount of pigmentation your dog has. Check the teeth for tartar build-up, as this can lead to future dental problems. Dog show judges normally dislike seeing dirty or yellow teeth on a show dog.

Like humans, some dogs will have more tartar build-up than others. There are a variety of ways to keep the gums healthy and the teeth clean. Raw bones are excellent, as the dog, by chewing, will remove a great deal of tartar. There are also chew toys with bristles that work to keep the teeth clean. Then there is simply using a toothbrush designed for canines to clean the teeth once a week, which can also be used in conjunction with toys and bones.

Although it is an added expense, having your dog's teeth professionally scaled and cleaned by your veterinarian once a year is a very good idea. As your veterinarian cleans, he will also check for loose or badly worn teeth, which can lead to future health problems.

NAILS AND FEET

The nails on your dog should be kept short. Cut the nail on an angle perpendicular to the long axis of the nail and about one-quarter inch (three quarters of a centimetre) away from the pink mark indicating the quick or blood supply. If your dog's nails are black in colour, cut small amounts off at first on a weekly basis, as that will encourage the quick or blood supply to recede, so you can gradually shorten them. If you should cut into the quick, use your blood stop powder, dabbing it at the end to stop the bleeding. Alternatively, use a bar of softened soap and run it along the edge of the cut to stop the bleeding.

If you are using a grinder, grind off the nail leaving one-eighth of an inch (half a centimetre) between where you stop and the pink indicating the blood supply. With a nail grinder, you can also lightly grind the bottom or underneath part of the nail to encourage the quick to recede in order to be able to keep the nails a bit shorter, particularly for the show ring.

Trimming toenails can be a chore if your puppy or dog is not accustomed to it; it may be the better part of valour to enlist help from a professional groomer or your veterinarian. If your dog has had a bad experience with nail trimming, try using treats and perhaps do one paw at a time with some play-time in between.

Check the skin around the nails and the pads of the feet for debris, infections, splits or stickers. Dogs can easily work brush or debris, particularly grass seeds, between their toes and be unable to get them out.

Trim the hair around the feet and in between the pads of the feet. If there is substantial hair growth on the feet of a terrier it can make their feet appear sloppy or not as neat as they should be. The Jack Russell should have feet that are cat-like, so their feet should be tight and compact, rather than splayed with open space between the toes. Feet can often be improved if the dog is run on pea gravel, which will actually improve the strength and overall condition of the feet.

STRIPPING

The broken and rough-coated Jack Russell Terrier will need to be 'stripped out' at least once a year, usually in the spring. Stripping is the removal of the loose topcoat, by hand, and is common practice for most terrier breeds. Hand stripping or 'plucking'is a relatively straightforward and painless procedure, providing it is done positively and while the dog is shedding. The process not only reduces the amount of hair shed around the animal's living quarters, but also results in neat, even regrowth, and in the short term gives the terrier a slick new appearance. Grooming with the slicker brush will remove the loose undercoat, and it is only the topcoat that subsequently needs further attention. A pet terrier only requires an annual stripping, or, at the most, two strippings per annum. The show dog, however, requires a little more regular trimming, and a little more attention to detail in order to keep the outline clean and defined.

Most breeds of dog shed their winter coat in the spring of each year, and this is when the coat will need the most attention. Some terriers seem to become quite irritated by the loose winter coat, and will seem almost relieved when it has been stripped out. The coat will fall out anyway, to make way for the new growth, although it may take a few weeks, during which time your Jack Russell Terrier may look positively bedraggled.

Prior to stripping your Jack Russell Terrier, the coat should be brushed and combed using the slicker brush and comb to remove loose hair and dirt. It should not be necessary to bathe your Jack Russell Terrier prior to stripping, but it can be beneficial to bathe the terrier in a mild antiseptic and anti-bacterial shampoo after the coat has been completely stripped. This will help to remove dirt, bacteria and excess oils from the skin and coat, especially in a particularly grubby, oily-coated or thin-coated Russell and should, consequently, avoid any discomfort and irritation that the terrier may be likely to suffer from a subsequent skin infection. For quite a number of dogs, shedding appears to cause some degree of irritation, and the most likely cause of this irritation is bacterial. The dog will, most probably, return to normal as soon as the new coat comes through.

In short, a good Russell coat will be easy to strip, and will not cause any distress to the dog. Stripping should leave a naturally clean and protective undercoat and make way for the new coat.

STRIPPING STEP BY STEP

To be suitable for hand stripping, your terrier's coat should easily come away when pulled, and, ideally, the dog will have begun to shed hair itself already. If the hair is difficult to pull, it may not be ready to come out yet, and is best left another couple of weeks. However, it may be that stripping is not the most feasible option to control the growth, especially if your Jack Russell has an abundance of hair; in which case it would be best to seek the advice of a good professional dog groomer. As an alternative, electric clipping may be the most appropriate form of trimming for a pet. Stripping knives are also useful to give purchase when taking out the loose coat.

If the coat is of the correct texture and thickness, then hand stripping is the best way to control the coat. Clipping a good coat only serves to shorten hair that is to be shed, and, in most cases, gives the subsequently shed hair a sharp point. However, rarely do all examples of a breed represent the ideal, and, from time to time, the general rules for trimming that particular breed will not apply to the individual dog. If the coat is not of good texture or particularly profuse and it does not seem feasible to strip out the dog by hand, then it may be better to first try

STEP BY STEP GUIDE TO TRIMMING
Photos: Sheila Atter.

1. The untrimmed dog.

2. Start by thoroughly brushing through the coat.

4. Groom against the lie of the coat.

3. Use the large slicker brush for the next stage.

5. The comb is used in the same way.

6. Comb the coat through thoroughly.

9. Grasp the hair with finger and thumb.

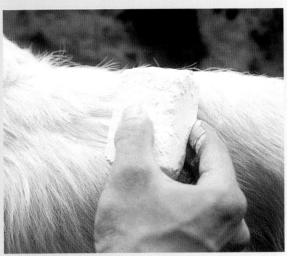

7. Chalk is applied to the coat.

10. Pull with the lie of the coat.

8. Comb the hair up before stripping.

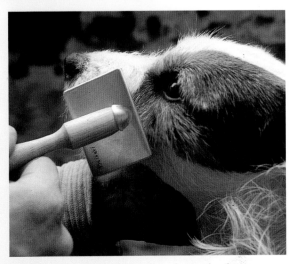

11. Use the small slicker brush on the face.

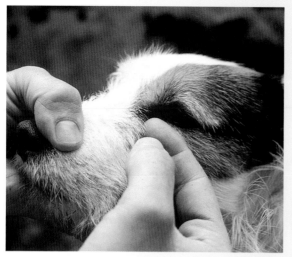

12. Pluck the hair from under the eyes.

15. The small slicker brush is used on the knees.

13. The hair from under
the eyes has been removed.

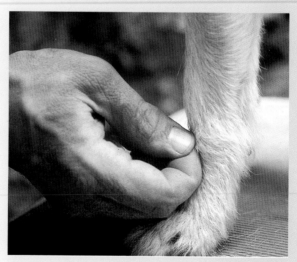

16. Excess hair is stripped from the knees.

14. Move on to the straggly hair around the neck.

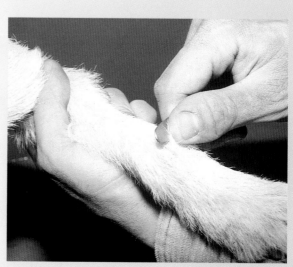

17. It may be easier to use the stripping knife.

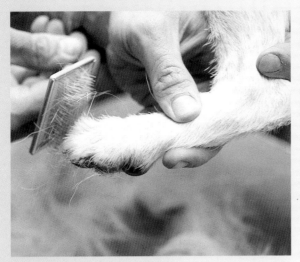

18. The feet need to be tidied with the small slicker brush.

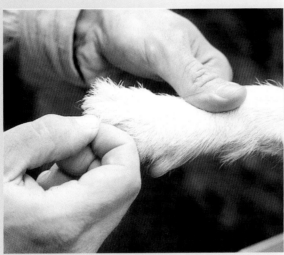

19. The feet are neatened with finger and thumb.

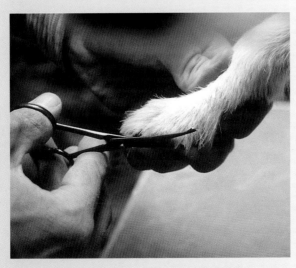

20. Scissors are used to trim round the feet.

21. Halfway there!

22. Tidy up around the elbows.

23. Now move to the underside.

24. *The aim is to achieve a smooth line.*

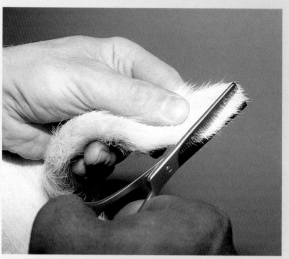

27. *Thinning scissors can be used to neaten the tip of the tail on an undocked animal.*

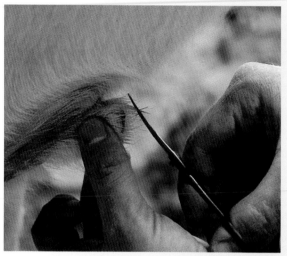

25. *Trim carefully around the penis.*

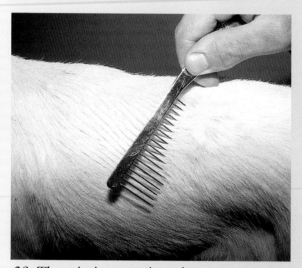

28. *The stripping stone is used.*

26. *The tail must be neatened. This dog has been docked.*

29. *The wide-toothed comb is used to groom through the body coat.*

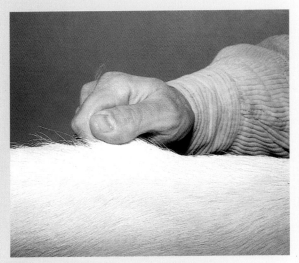

30. *The new coat growth can be seen.*

32. *A firm grip will be needed for this.*

31. *Before a show, remove the longer hairs.*

33. *Ready for the show!*

splitting the stripping into several sessions, until all the excess coat has been removed. Hand-stripping does serve to improve a poor coat over time, and should always be considered as the only form of coat control for the Jack Russell Terrier, providing, of course, that the animal does not become unduly distressed. An experienced and capable groomer should be able to complete a full annual strip on a good Jack Russell Terrier coat within a maximum of three hours. Hand

stripping should be thought of as a procedure that, essentially, only speeds along a natural process, effecting a neater finish in the short term. It should never be an ordeal for either dog or owner.

Assuming the hair is falling out, then the coat needs to be prepared thoroughly by brushing, both against and following the direction of growth, using the slicker brush and then the comb. This will remove the loose undercoat and the worst of the topcoat.

This procedure should certainly not cause your dog any concern, providing the animal has been accustomed to grooming from day one.

Having thoroughly groomed the terrier from top to toe, the remaining dead hair should be removed using finger and thumb to pull out the long hairs (the topcoat) only. Beginning at the neck, brush the coat up against the direction of growth and begin to remove the rough stuff by gripping the longer hairs just above the undercoat (i.e. about 1 to 1.5 ins/2.5 to 4 cms from the skin) firmly, with clean hands. Pull positively away from the dog in the direction that the coat is growing (i.e. away from the head, towards the tail). Dusting a little hard chalk over the coat can give a better grip to the hair and make pulling it out easier for both dog and groomer.

Continue pulling out the long hairs down the neck, across the shoulders and along the back, always pulling in the direction that the hair is growing. If the coat is a good thick double coat, this should leave a short covering of hair (the undercoat), and the terrier should begin to resemble a short-coated Russell.

To continue the stripping, use the comb to rake the hair against the direction of growth, (i.e. combing from the tail towards the head), and, still using only finger and thumb, pull out all the long hairs that do not automatically spring back and lie close to the body. The undercoat and the topcoat should be easy to identify in the broken or rough-coated Jack Russell Terrier, making it easy to see the hairs that need to be pulled out. The growth on the sides of the dog will be less profuse than on the topline and shoulders, and should not take long to completely strip out. The thighs and front legs should be covered in short hair and will not need much attention, except perhaps to remove the odd long hair, unless your Jack Russell is being

prepared the show ring, in which case it will need to be a little neater. For best results, the longest hairs around the feet should first be plucked out, and then, if necessary, trimmed with scissors. Toe trimming scissors for dogs are fairly widely available, and it really is wise to purchase a pair, ideally with rounded tips. These will need specialised sharpening from time to time. Using blunt scissors to trim feet, apart from giving an unsatisfactory finish, is also more likely to contribute to errors. Great care should always be taken when using scissors on any dog, for a nick will not be forgotten easily. The result is a more apprehensive 'patient', which, as a result of its more nervous behaviour, will be more likely to end up being cut again.

To trim the feet, first pluck out all the long hairs around the toes, and then, if necessary, trim the outside edges of the toes by snipping off any remaining hairs that grow below the line of the pad. To achieve the best results around the feet, the hair should first be brushed up away from the toes with gentle use of the slicker brush. This makes it easier to identify the hair that needs removing.

The hair from under the tail and along the tummy may take a little longer to strip out in the rough-coated Jack Russell Terrier than in the broken coated version, where there may be little or no extra growth in these areas. By holding the terrier's front end up and standing him on his hind legs, it will be easier to trim the tummy and inside the thighs. It is important to always try to pull the hair in the direction that it appears to be growing. This ensures that the hair comes away quickly and painlessly.

Having plucked all the long hairs from the tummy and inside the thighs as much as possible, it is now best to use scissors to finish off. Gently and very carefully trim off any long hairs from around the genitalia using the toe trimming scissors. The use of

scissors on the Jack Russell Terrier should always be kept to a minimum, in keeping with the breed's natural appearance. Toes and genitalia are the only areas where scissors are required.

After about eight to nine weeks, the new coat will begin to grow through. As it does, your dog will usually shed a little more hair. This is generally undercoat, and is making way for the new coat. The coat should be brushed and combed as normal, but afterwards it will help to rub the coat with dampened hands, first against, and then with the direction of growth. This will help to loosen the hair that is to be shed. The terrier should be then be brushed again from top to toe. This procedure will need to be carried out every day for a few days while the animal is losing coat. Three to four weeks after this, your Jack Russell will be showing a healthy, neat new coat, thick and clean.

GROOMING FOR THE SHOW RING

In order to achieve success in the show ring with any exhibit, it must appear at its best, both physically and superficially Attention needs to be drawn away from those features which may not be the exhibit's best, while enhancing and defining those features where the exhibit does excel. Knowledge and understanding of conformation will help you to assess the good and bad points of the potential exhibit, ensuring that the terrier is presented to the judge looking at its best. In no way should the Jack Russell Terrier ever appear exaggerated or over-trimmed; he should look neat and tidy, with still enough coat to distinguish between the three coat variations. As a breed, balance, suitability for work and (as a result) temperament are of prime consideration when assessing the credentials of any Jack Russell Terrier in the show ring. Trimming of the coat for the show ring, ideally, should not be necessary. It is purely cosmetic, and should only be

practised with a view to enhance and clarify the exhibit's outline. The Jack Russell Terrier is a breed of moderation and should never appear sculpted or sharp in outline. As coat density, distribution and texture all have a direct bearing the individual's ability to perform well as a foxing terrier, they will be of prime consideration for any judge at any level of show competition. Excess and profuse feathering is uncharacteristic in the Jack Russell Terrier and will directly affect the terrier's ability to hunt day after day without ill effect. Some Jack Russell Terriers, which may otherwise be fine examples of the breed, do have rather profuse coats. Stripping and exhibiting such a terrier may be rewarding, but the coat is of vital importance to the Jack Russell Terrier and breeding from such dogs needs careful consideration. Profuse coats are highly undesirable. The characteristic 'moustache 'and 'eyebrow' in the broken and the rough-coated Jack Russell are completely natural features of the breed and not the result of skilful trimming. The only hair that may need removing from the head in preparing the Jack Russell for exhibition will be that growing up at the inner corner of each eye, and perhaps a little from the area around the occiput where some terriers will grow a little tuft or two.

If your potential exhibit has not been stripped for some time, or has begun to shed coat, it is best to strip the terrier out completely and wait for the new coat to come through before beginning to show the dog. Until the new coat has at least become evident, it is impossible for any judge to make an accurate and fair assessment of your terrier's coat. Consequently, should you show the terrier before the topcoat has begun to regrow, your exhibit is likely to be penalised unduly. It takes around eight to twelve weeks for the topcoat to grow back sufficiently after stripping. Obviously it is best to plan ahead if your potential exhibit has not had much work

done on his coat for some time.

Once the new coat has come through, it is a good idea to adopt a routine of regular grooming to keep your exhibit in top form. While skilful routine trimming should not be necessary for the Jack Russell Terrier, allowing the coat to grow through to the point where it needs to be completely stripped out again would be unwise, and is likely to inhibit your exhibit's chances in the show ring. As the terrier begins to look the part and the coat type has once again become evident, it is a good idea to routinely remove any stray long hairs, especially from around the neck, toes, tummy and, if necessary, from just between the ears. Particular attention needs to be paid to the terrier's outline, and it does not do any harm to go back to these areas until you have removed almost all the long hairs. The area around the shoulders also needs to be kept neat for the show ring, as excess growth around here can give a false impression as to angulation and balance.

If the potential exhibit is a puppy, then trimming can be left until nearer the date of the show. Any long hairs sticking out from the neck should be plucked out using finger and thumb, as should any unsightly long hairs around the shoulders, tail and tummy line. It is important to remember not to make the only time your puppy spends on the table the time that he is being groomed. While stripping your puppy is a relatively pain-free procedure, most youngsters quickly become bored and will not relish the thought of standing still on a table, especially if it involves a procedure that is not much fun. However, at the show it is likely that your exhibit will be assessed for the main part on a table, where he should look relaxed and interested. It is a good idea to feed the puppy on the table, for example, so that he does not constantly associate being put on a table with boredom.

Of course, it is important to begin grooming sessions from day one to accustom your puppy to the procedure, but this does not mean that the puppy will exactly enjoy it. Grooming should not be an ordeal for any animal, but some dogs quite simply do not like being worked on. Grooming sessions on puppies should always be kept short, but should be frequent.

The Jack Russell puppy should not need a great amount of work done on his coat until he has reached at least one year old, as the correct coat will take around a year to develop. Assuming that your puppy has a good double coat, it should be tidied at least two to three weeks before the show, depending on the amount of coat there is, and then just neatened the night before. In contrast to many of today's terrier breeds, the Jack Russell's coat can theoretically be prepared on the day of a show without any prior work being needed. However, do not leave the grooming until the last minute or your puppy will lose its sparkle on the judge's table in anticipation of another trimming session.

Start at the neck by plucking out the long hair that grows in a line from the ear to the shoulder, perpendicular to the body. Remove this from each side of the neck by pulling the hair away from the dog two or three at a time, leaving the shorter hair untouched. Continue down the front of the shoulders by combing the hair forward and plucking out the longest ones. Continue along the sides of the dog in the same manner, only plucking out the longest hairs where necessary. Remember that the intention is only to clarify the puppy's outline and to neaten him up, not to completely remove the coat. It is important to begin plucking out coat from around the outline of your terrier before touching the body, because, more often than not, this will be all that is necessary. To storm in and start taking coat out on the main body of the animal only serves to ensure that your

puppy will be a good couple of months late in beginning a show career. It is always good practice to concentrate first on the outline of the dog before taking any coat out from the back, whatever age the dog is.

To keep the coat neat between shows and to prevent it from becoming too heavy, your dog will benefit from short but regular grooming sessions. 'Rolling' the coat is a good way of keeping the terrier looking at his best for as long as possible. This is an easy process, but may take a couple of attempts to master. Lift the skin at the base of the neck by pinching with finger and thumb on either side of the shoulder blades. As the skin is lifted, the hair will stand on end and any really long hairs can be plucked out. Massaging the skin through your fingers towards the tail, plucking out any long hairs all the way down the back, should serve to leave a neat and tidy terrier, still with enough coat to establish whether the exhibit is broken or rough coated.

SPECIAL SHOW RING DETAIL
When preparing your Jack Russell for the show ring, it is an excellent idea to have the Standard firmly in mind or refer to it as you groom. The judges will be looking for a dog that best fits their perception of the breed Standard.

Picture in your mind the defined outline of the profile the Standard describes as the ideal dog. The Jack Russell should appear "workmanlike and moderate, totally without exaggeration, with a sturdy, slightly racey appearance."

If you have been following your weekly grooming routine, then you are over halfway to your finished product. Basically, you will only be tidying up your terrier for the show ring.

HEAD
The head and skull should be "flat and moderately broad, gradually narrowing to the eyes". So, in order to follow the breed Standard you need to strip away any excess hairs on the top of the head to emphasise the flat part of the skull, which may be best done with a fine stripping knife. You may also need to tighten up the look of the hair on the sides of the skull towards the eyes, to show the gradual narrowing. Stripping and pulling the hairs between the eyes around the stop will help to define that area more clearly.

With broken coated dogs, the colour and or the furnishings can deceive the eye as to how strong or weak the head actually is. If your dog has a very dark face you may want to leave a little more hair and whiskers to give a stronger appearance, as the darker the head, the smaller it will appear.

"Ear tips should extend to just below the outer corner of the eye." If the ear on your dog is a bit longer and the hair or outline falls below the eye, trim the hairs on the outer edge following the natural outline of the ear. If the ears have a tendency to lift, sometimes trimming the hair underneath the ear fold can help them to drop better.

Because not all dogs in this breed have full eye pigmentation, the area around the eye where they lack colour will often appear to weep and to show tear stains. This area should be thoroughly cleaned before show time. There are a variety of products used and sold through grooming catalogues to disguise and hide tear stains, as many breeds have this same problem.

NECK AND CHEST
"Clean and muscular, of good length, gradually widening to the shoulders." On some Jack Russells, the hair around the neck and shoulders grows quite thick and is abundant. To help to create the correct look, you will need to take your stripping knife as a rake or a comb and tighten up the hair on the neck, removing any extraneous hairs, and

then gradually blending the neck into the shoulders to present a smooth and flowing line. The stripping stone can also be used to help blend and tighten this area.

Work down the fore-chest and do the same, taking off any stray hairs that stick outward, and form a smooth line down the neck and through the front legs into the chest.

"The chest should not extend below the elbow." To present a clean profile, use your thinning shears to clean up the underline at a gentle angle from the loin to the elbow. From the front view, the long hairs hanging down below the elbows under the chest can be pulled out, or trimmed carefully with your thinning shears.

FEET

Check to make sure that the feet are clean and trimmed. When you are showing on a concrete or tile surface where your dog's traction may be an issue, there are products made to help the dog to grip the floor when the product is applied directly to the pads of the feet. These products can be found through a grooming supply catalogue, or vendor.

TAIL

"The tail length should complement the body." Extra hair can be left on the end or it can be trimmed shorter, whichever is needed to balance the look of your terrier. Trim the hair around the anal area and any stray hairs going up the back of the tail.

BATHING

Five days before the show, bath your dog in a textured or terrier coat shampoo. Rinse thoroughly, as any soap residue may cause skin irritation for your dog. Bathing your dog just a day or so before a show will often leave your dog with a coat that will be very soft in texture and appearance, so it is always good to plan ahead.

Two days before the show, check over all the fine points covered above and in the routine care section. Now look at the profile of your Jack Russell, and make sure the outline looks clean. Go over your dog again and pull any wild hairs from the throat and chest area and from the back of the tail to the bottom of the hocks. Walk around your dog from all angles and pull any long hairs that distract you from their outline.

Remember: your Jack Russell should look natural and clean with a neat, tidy and workmanlike appearance. Be careful not to over-groom or sculpt your dog, as they are not Wire Haired Fox Terriers and should not look as if they are.

11 BREEDING JACK RUSSELLS

Breeding in general should be thought of as an act of borrowing, and as my grandmother always told me: "When you borrow something be sure and return it clean, and in the same condition or better than when you borrowed it."

When you decide to breed your first litter, you will inevitably be borrowing from all of the individual breeders named on your dog's pedigree. The resultant litter will be a combination of the strengths and faults that they bred for or started with. For this reason, it is essential that you be a bit of a historian, and ascertain as much about the grandparents and great-grandparents of your dog as possible – the past will always come to the fore.

In order to have the most consistent quality in a litter, there needs to be consistently high quality dogs as ancestors of the dogs being mated. Rarely, if ever, do two pet-quality dogs produce an exceptional show-quality puppy – Although when an exceptional dog is produced from two pet-quality dogs, that is what most breeders would refer to as a 'one off'. That individual dog will not reproduce itself, or have any consistency in the traits that it passes on.

Keep in mind there can be a great deal of difference between a show dog and a good breeding dog. A show dog is not always a good breeding dog, and a good breeding dog is not always a good show dog. A show dog wins despite its faults. Attitude, excellent

Representatives of three generations: The aim of a breeding programme is to produce quality dogs of a similar type.

Photo courtesy: Jo Ballard.

grooming and training will often disguise faults that one would not want in a good breeding programme. A good breeding dog or bitch passes on consistent qualities, and complements and improves the animals they are mated with.

There are many factors that enter into breeding a litter, and financial gain should never be one of them. For the most part, Jack Russell Terriers are easy to breed, and relatively few have whelping problems. However, when there is a whelping problem, it can be quite costly, and you may well risk losing an entire litter of puppies, and possibly the bitch as well. You cannot possibly breed a proper litter – with excellent nutrition, genetic testing, vaccinations, worming, the time and effort put into socialisation, finding proper homes for your puppies – and expect to turn much of a profit. Raising a litter should truly be a labour of love, not financial gain.

INHERITED CONDITIONS

When breeding the Jack Russell Terrier you not only must be a historian, you also need to be a bit of a detective. Because this is a breed that is relatively new to Kennel Club recognition, records that many other breeds have kept for years are just now being established with the Jack Russell Terrier. As was mentioned before, it is our job as breeders to leave the breed as free from genetic defects as possible. In order to do this, genetic and health testing must be carried out wherever possible. Remember: when you breed two dogs with the same fault, you only increase your chances of that fault appearing in the resultant puppies. See Chapter 14 'Breed Associated Diseases' for details.

Genetic defects that can be tested for and identified simply do not go away; many are recessive in nature and even with consistent testing they may still occur from time to

time. Genetic testing, health and structural screening are some of the most important tools a breeder has to ensure the integrity of a breeding programme and the general overall health of the breed.

BREEDING FOR TYPE AND STRUCTURE

Most breeders, after having been in the breed for a number of years, home in on a look or type that they prefer. Each dog they breed will carry this special look, and will often be quite recognisable because of its unique type. A good example of this would be the Ridley lines of Sheila Atter. Her dogs, although different in such things as coat type, height and markings, were unmistakable because of their head shape, expression and overall appearance, or 'breed type'.

While type is very important and should never be overlooked, it is also important to start with relatively sound and well-structured dogs. All dogs have faults, and there is no perfect dog. However, a realistic evaluation of your dog's faults is critical to a good breeding programme. If a dog has lovely type, but is unable to move smoothly and correctly, then your chances of success in the show ring will be quite limited. It is not uncommon for a breeder to have a difficult time finding fault with his or her own dogs. The best approach is to find an experienced person to evaluate your dogs and to begin to see the dogs through a fresh pair of eyes, rather than your own.

GENETICS

Knowing when, where and how those traits surface in a breeding programme is just as important. Traits are usually referred to as being either 'recessive' or 'dominant'. Figure 1 gives trait comparisons for the Parson Jack Russell Terrier. This list of traits will give you an idea of what points in this breed are dominant and what points are recessive.

DOMINANT	RECESSIVE
Long head	Short head
Long ears	Small/short ears
Low-set ears	High-set ears
Wide ear leather	Narrow ear leather
Coarse skull	Fine skull
Short foreface	Long foreface
Erect ears	Drop/tipped ears
Dark eyes	Light eye
Normal eye	Large bulging eyes
Brown eyes	Blue eyes
Wire coat	Smooth coat
Short coat	Long coat
Curly	Straight coat
Poor shoulder layback	Good shoulder layback
Poorly angulated stifle	Well angulated stifle
High tail-set	Low tail-set
Heavy bone	Light bone
Deep chest	Shallow chest
Straight topline	Swat back
Good spring of rib	Poor spring of ribs
Short stifle	Long stifle
Light pigment	Dark pigment (on skin of white dogs)
Normal hearing	Deafness
Good eyesight	Night blindness
Good eye pigment	Wall eyes
Self-colour-colour	Parti-colour
Black nose	Dudley nose
Good mouth	Overshot/undershot
Normal palate	Cleft palate
Normal lip	Hare lip
Straight tail	Kinked/bent tail

Figure 1: Trait copmarisons.

Recessive traits that a dog carries are basically hidden traits, ones that are not dominant or visible on the dog standing in front of you. The only way to know whether a dog carries a hidden or recessive trait is by breeding that individual. Brown noses are a perfect example of a recessive trait, as most breeders would not knowingly breed a dog that had a brown nose. However there are dogs that will repeatedly produce brown noses because they carry the recessive gene for it, although both parents would have to carry the recessive or hidden trait in order for it to become dominant or visible in a puppy. Recessive traits such as an overshot or undershot mouth, deafness, cleft palate, etc., are all serious faults in any dog, and they are difficult to get rid of in a breeding programme, because they will continue to come forward generation after generation.

As you can see from Figure 1, not all of the recessive traits listed would be considered

Never under estimate the importance of temperament when selecting breeding stock. Photo courtesy: Marcia Walsh.

faults; good shoulder layback, dark pigment and smooth coats are all examples of recessives that would be desirable in a breeding programme. This, again, is why it is necessary to have as much information as possible on the parents and grandparents. Something as simple as listing the coat types and colour in a pedigree of a Jack Russell Terrier can be very helpful for future breeding decisions. For example, a curly coat is a dominant trait, and a straight coat is a recessive trait. If your bitch hads a poor-quality coat, being either too heavy or curly, you would then want to breed her to a smooth-coated dog, or a broken-coated dog that carries the recessive gene for smooth coats. You could then experience substantial improvement with coat quality in the litter of pups from your bitch. However, you have gained nothing if you do not then take the best structured, correctly coated pup from the litter and then breed on from that. Coat quality is one of the easiest things to improve in a breeding programme. Poor dentition, on the other hand, because it is a recessive or hidden trait, is more difficult to overcome in any given breeding programme.

It is also crucial to start with sound temperament in a dog, because no matter how well structured a dog is, its primary role is that of a friend and companion, particularly when the show and breeding career are over. However, you will have to make your own assessment about whether temperament is genetically based or caused by poor socialisation. Genetically based shyness or aggressiveness is very difficult to breed away from.

Breeding a litter is a blend of complex genetic combinations between the stud dog and the bitch. There are 78 chromosomes, or 39 pairs in each dog. So when those pairs are combined from two different dogs, there are several million combinations possible. It is not a wonder, then, why repeat matings of excellent dogs often do not work. It is simply very hard, given the mathematics, to make a carbon copy of any individual dog.

PHENOTYPE AND GENOTYPE
Two other terms that any breeder should be familiar with are phenotype and genotype. The physical characteristics that a dog possesses, such as expression, height, coat type, and colour make up his phenotype, or those dominant traits that have expressed themselves in the dog that stands before you. What you cannot see is that totally transmittable potential that a dog carries, and will pass on to his offspring, called his genotype. For this reason, what you see in a dog may not always be what you will get. Looking at their offspring will give you a much better idea of what traits specific animals will pass on. Many times the dog

that is the top show winner may not be the one to breed to, or from, as perhaps their sire/dam may be better, particularly if the sire/dam has other quality sons and daughters.

The phenotype and genotype can certainly explain why full litter brothers or sisters may not produce equal quality, although they have identical pedigrees and look quite similar. When you really begin to research the offspring of two littermates you may find, depending on the bitches or dogs that they were bred to, that one simply passes on more consistent qualities to his/her offspring than the other.

EVALUATING A BREEDING PROGRAMME

When you are looking for a breeder or breeding programme that is producing the type of dog that you prefer and want to go forward with, you must again become a bit of a detective. Most breeders are happy to share past history regarding their dogs with you, but you must first ask specific questions. If you are purchasing a puppy, have the breeder go over the parents of the puppy with you, showing and explaining their strengths and faults. Ask the breeder to evaluate your dog as a puppy, and then again as he has matured into an adult. Serious breeders will want to help you to be successful in your own breeding programme, as it will be a reflection of their own.

Be wary of a breeder who constantly outcrosses to other lines, because every time you outcross, you reduce the prepotency of your own family lines. In defining outcrossing, it is generally considered to be two dogs mated which have no common ancestry in the first five generations of the pedigree. When you outcross you take on a new set of virtues and faults into your breeding programme. For instance, you may be looking to bring down size in your breeding programme. However, if you outcross and breed to an individual from smaller lines, you may reduce size, but you may give up your nice heads or straight fronts to do so. In dog breeding there are really no short cuts, and you must be dedicated and willing to be critical in the selection process of what puppies you keep and then go forward with.

Pedigrees are certainly part of the equation for finding a quality dog, but it is not the

A good stud dog stamps his type on his progeny.

Photo: Sheila Atter.

total picture. Because of the fairly recent recognition of the Jack Russell, there are relatively few dogs that have earned their Championships at the time of writing. Purchasing a dog on the basis primarily of the virtues of its pedigree can be a terrible mistake in any breed. A poor-quality dog is still a poor-quality dog, even though he may come from a long line of Champions. Certainly, in this breed there are dogs of very high quality that come from a pedigree with a number of excellent quality dogs that may simply have never been shown or earned any titles, because there were virtually none to be earned, other than at a possible Rare Breed show. It can certainly be more of a challenge to breed high-quality dogs from a less established breed.

CHOOSING A STUD DOG

There are probably far too many dogs that are left intact as stud dogs; a stud dog, because he can have so much of an impact on the breed, needs to be of a very high quality, and you should not settle for less. An average stud dog will sire several litters per year; the average bitch should only have one litter per year. So it becomes very clear that a stud dog will make the larger impact on the breed just on numbers alone.

A stud dog can only really be expected to improve one to two faults in a given mating. If you are looking for a stud dog to improve more than a couple of faults in one mating, you may need to rethink the breeding, as perhaps your level of expectation is too high. After all, in the world of dog breeding it is perhaps a greater honour to have bred the sire of a top winning show dog than the dog himself.

Never choose a stud dog just because he is close by; you may sacrifice quality if you only confine yourself to using local dogs. You will also want to choose a stud dog that complements your bitch. Moderation is the key here, as breeding extremes, although it may work in the first generation, will only cause more disparities to deal with in the successive generations.

A good-quality stud dog should always present a picture of overall balance. Keep in mind such things as length of leg vs. height, as they are not the same. A stud dog can be 15 inches (38 cms) in height, and have very poor length of leg, having most of his height in the body and depth of chest. A 13-inch (33 cm) dog can have very nice length of leg, with the height carried in the leg rather than the body. I have even had a 10-inch (25 cms) bitch, and although her height did not conform to the breed Standard, she had such lovely length of leg and proportion that when photographed you would think she measured 12 to 13 inches (30 to 33 cms). Her secret was excellent proportions, despite her lack of overall correct height. This is one of the reasons not to choose any dog simply on the basis of photos.

Defects produced in a given litter should be carefully examined from both sides of the pedigree. A reputable stud dog owner will allow you to use his stud dog only if he believes the breeding will bring improvement. Over time, it has always seemed that the stud dog gets a fair amount of the blame any time a litter with faults is produced. No stud dog is a miracle worker; he is of course only half of the genetic composition of the litter. It is important to learn from mistakes or faults in a litter. Certainly you will not want to repeat a mating that produced a litter where most of the puppies had poor conformation or temperament.

PLANNING THE MATING

When you are looking for a stud dog, you need to consider the reputation and integrity of the owner as well as the dog. After all, your bitch will most likely spend at least a

week at the stud dog owner's home or kennel. It is good to determine where and how your bitch will be kept, if there will be a charge for her board, and what type of exercise and care she will receive. Work out all of the financial dealings with a stud dog owner ahead of time. Some will want the breeding fee up front, others will want half at the time of breeding, and the other half after the bitch has whelped. Other owners will want to see the litter before deciding on whether to charge a stud fee or to take a 'pick puppy' from the litter as payment for the breeding. If a pick puppy is the option chosen by the stud dog owner, make sure you have clearly arranged when the puppy will be taken home and who will pay the transportation costs, if any.

Not every bitch will conceive on a mating, so it is probably better to determine in advance whether the stud dog owner has any guarantees. In the case of a missed breeding it is common for breeders to offer a return service at no charge. Some will even offer one return service if there is only one to two pups in a litter. It should be the goal of any stud dog owner to have quality puppies that represent their stud dog, so it is in their interests to be somewhat flexible with guarantees and returns.

Most breeders will require any bitch to have been tested and to have a negative result for brucellosis before being mated to their stud dog. This is done by means of a simple blood test, and the results are usually sent back to your vet within 48 hours. Brucellosis is an infectious disease that affects dogs as well as other animals, including humans, and causes abortion, resorption, stillbirths, and sometime sterility. At the same time vaccinations should be checked to make sure they are up to date and current, as it is not wise to vaccinate after your bitch has been bred.

YOUR BITCH

When you decide to breed your bitch you will first want to take her age into consideration. It is never a good idea to breed a bitch under the age of one year. Many of the inherited defects in this breed are not seen until a dog is 16 to 24 months of age. So breeding a Jack Russell bitch before that age could be a terrible mistake if she were to have an eye defect such as lens luxation. It is quite common in the United States for serious breeders to have health contracts on dogs they sell that expressly prohibit using them for breeding until all the health clearances have been completed, or until they have reached a certain age, usually around 18 months to two years.

Raising a litter takes a great deal of a bitch's resources, and it is not a good idea to breed her season after season. Most bitches can benefit greatly from a year's rest between litters, and bitches that are bred on successive seasons will generally have smaller litters. For the same reason most bitches are not bred after the age of eight years, depending on their individual health. Breeding after the age of eight can certainly increase the bitch's chances of developing uterine infections, experiencing difficult births and other health problems. A particular concern in older bitches is pyometra, a uterine infection, which becomes more likely each time she cycles. This condition, if left untreated, can cause death, and at the very least the bitch will usually need to be spayed. For this reason, it is advisable to spay any bitch whose breeding career is over, as spaying a bitch that has developed pyometra is dangerous.

Breeding should only be undertaken to improve a breed. With that in mind, I truly believe that repeating the same mating over and over does the breed a great injustice – particularly with a breed that is not well established, as you will want to have as many breeding options available for future

Somervale Jessie: An important brood bitch whose name can be found on many pedigrees.
Photo courtesy: Mr & Mrs E. Rich, Somerwest.

generations. It is also my belief that when you have bred a litter, and you have been fortunate enough to breed a puppy that is an improvement on the bitch, you should then go forward with breeding the better quality dog. When you breed the same bitch over and over, and do not go forward with one of the resultant pups, you begin to stagnate yourself as a breeder. If your bitch is not improving herself on successive litters, then perhaps you need to give careful thought to the merits of continuing to breed that particular bitch.

THE SEASON

Jack Russell Terrier bitches generally have very regular seasons, which means they are in season approximately every six to eight months. Females are usually in season for 21 days or three weeks at a time. There is the occasional bitch that will stand for a few days after the normal 21; however, they are generally not breedable after day 21. There is also the occasional bitch that will have what is referred to as a 'split season'. The bitch will

appear to be coming into a normal oestrus and then suddenly drop out of season after five to seven days for no apparent reason – although stress can certainly be a causal factor. The bitch may then come into season again, any time from several weeks to a month later, and will then be breedable on this second season. Any bitch with a prolonged season (one that lasts well over 21 days) should be checked by your veterinarian.

When a bitch comes in season there is the normal vaginal swelling and discharge, usually a darker red at first, gradually changing to a lighter pink colour when she is in standing heat. However, because most Jack Russell bitches are very clean about themselves, it is very easy to miss the first few days they are in season. Bitches that are heavily coated, or that have a history of very little swelling and discharge, need to be watched a bit more carefully. One of the best ways is simply to keep a box of tissues by her crate, and when she emerges from it, simply swipe her bottom with a tissue; even using white bedding can be helpful.

It is important to note the first day your bitch is in season.

Photo courtesy: Mary Strom, Snow Wind.

Bitches are certainly individual in the way that they move through their cycle; some are in standing heat at day five, others not until day 11 or 12. I have had a bitch in standing heat at day nine, and she did not ovulate until day 19. If we had bred her on the normal assumption that ovulation occurs somewhere between days 10 and 14, then we would most likely have missed her altogether. If the breeding is important to you, it is best to do either repeated vaginal smears or a progesterone test, particularly with maiden bitches.

False pregnancies can happen regardless of whether a bitch has been mated or not. The bitch may well show all the signs of a typical pregnancy right up to preparing a nest, delivery, and producing milk, yet there are no puppies. Giving your bitch a toy to mother and towels to nest in will certainly help her to cope. Alternating hot and cold packs on swollen mammary glands will aid in making her more comfortable. If the behaviour is extreme or prolonged, a vet should see her. Normally bitches that have a false pregnancy can be bred on successive seasons and whelp a healthy litter of pups.

There is also the occasional bitch that will have what is called a 'silent season', meaning simply that the bitch will show no outward signs of being in season, such as the swelling and bleeding that accompany a normal season. These seasons can certainly be fertile, and sometimes the only one that will know for sure is the stud dog. Silent seasons can also be a sign of hypothyroidism.

THE IN-WHELP BITCH

Once you have bred your bitch you will want to make sure she is not exposed to another intact male. Bitches have been known to mate with a second male, resulting in a litter of pups sired by two different fathers. The only way then to sort out parentage is by DNA testing, which can be costly for an entire litter of pups.

Each bitch can be quite different in her pregnancy; some lose their girlish figures early, others quite late. Some will eat continuously through their pregnancy, and others will have a touch of morning sickness and go off of their food for a few days when they are around three or four weeks in whelp. If you really want to know sooner rather than

later whether your bitch is in whelp, ultrasounds are probably the best. An ultrasound, because it is a non-invasive procedure, is quite safe, and can be done as early as 18 days, although it would be more accurate at 25 to 30 days in whelp. The ultrasound may give you an approximate idea of the numbers of puppies as well, but they are not as accurate as x-rays. X-rays should not be taken until the bitch is over 45 days in whelp, and to be safe we have always waited until 55 days. This way you are sure that you are over the 45-day mark, since it would be difficult to know the exact day your bitch became pregnant. The reasoning behind this is foetal development. When the pups are over 45 days their bones have begun to calcify, and there should be no radiation damage to the developing foetuses.

DIET AND EXERCISE

If your bitch is one of those that does experience some nausea or a small amount of vomiting, you might try offering her a bland diet for a few days, consisting of cooked chicken and rice. If for any reason her nausea continues for more than a week, or she is vomiting profusely, then your veterinarian should see her. When she is feeling a bit better, you can add back in her regular kibble.

A pregnant bitch will need to eat a high-quality premium dog food. Some breeders will often add or gradually change to a puppy-type of food to provide extra calories and a higher fat content. With all of the premium foods on the market this is probably not necessary, as you can certainly supplement her diet yourself with hard-boiled eggs, raw liver, cottage cheese or yoghurt.

High-quality food and moderate exercise are the key factors for a healthy pregnancy.

Photo: Kim James, Badgerwood.

When giving supplements to a dog be sure to keep size in mind – a large teaspoon of any of the above should be adequate for a Jack Russell bitch. Water-soluble vitamins such as Vitamin C or B complex are probably fine; however, be careful with feeding calcium, as too much can lead to eclampsia after whelping. Some breeders have found that raspberry leaf powder assists in easing labour, if given in very small quantities daily for three weeks prior to the due date.

While a bitch's food should be increased by about 20 per cent in the last weeks of pregnancy, be careful that she does not become too fat. It is the tendancy of many bitches to want to eat far more than they should, and obesity can make pregnancy and delivery very difficult. As she becomes heavier in whelp she will have less room for food so you may want to divide her food into two or three meals per day rather than one.

A healthy pregnancy has many of the same requirements as a healthy life – high-quality food and moderate exercise. However, after your bitch is three or four weeks in whelp, the type and amount of exercise should be watched – if she likes to hunt and work in the field, that should probably be curtailed at this stage. Most Jack Russells become so excited over the hunt that all reason can be lost. Leaping off high places and trying to fit through very small holes are characteristics of the breed, and it is no different when they are in whelp. There is nothing more tragic than losing a litter to a bitch taking a hard tumble at the wrong time in her pregnancy.

WHERE TO WHELP
Several weeks prior to your bitch's due date, you will want to think about where she will whelp and raise her puppies. Some breeders let their bitches whelp in their crates, as they are familiar with them and already call them home. Other people prefer to have an actual whelping box.

A whelping box need not be too large, and should only be slightly larger than her crate. For the Jack Russell Terrier, a 36 x 36-inch (96 x 96 cm) box is more than adequate. The box should be raised a few inches off the floor, if possible, to prevent chills from dampness or drafts. The most important aspect of puppy survival is warmth, as they are unable to regulate their own body heat for the first few weeks.

Most Jack Russell bitches are fairly careful about their babies so it may not be absolutely necessary to put up rails in the interior of the whelping box. However, there is the occasional mother who is just not as careful as she should be, and accidents can and will happen, especially with first-time mothers. The ideal rails, sometimes called pig rails, are approximately three inches (eight centimetres) above the bottom of the box, though you may need to allow for thick bedding. The rails should go all the way around the box and should extend out from the box by approximately two-and-a-half inches (six centimetres) from the sides. If a whelping box is designed and made from wood, it should be sealed and/or painted with non-toxic paint to prevent liquid from being absorbed into the wood.

If you are going to have an open whelping box, then you have the option of using a heat lamp as well. If you are using a closed crate then there are heated pads made especially for puppies, with an even temperature distribution throughout, and the cords are usually protected from chewing. Never use a heat pad made for humans as they are not meant for spills and wetness, nor are they protected from chewing. Heat should be moderated too. If it is too hot, the bitch may become dehydrated and not want to stay with her pups. A good benchmark is 80 degrees – higher than that will be too warm for most new mothers, and probably for you too. Common sense and observation of the

THE NEWBORN LITTER
Photos courtesy: Mary Strom, Snow Wind.

The new mother soon learns to cope with her puppies.   *This is Barsetta Polmanta with her day-old litter.*

pups will tell you a lot about how comfortable they are. If the pups are all lying far apart, panting or crying, they are probably too hot.

FIRST STAGE SIGNS

Due dates are often hard to figure, even with the progesterone testing available, estimates can still be a day or two off. Jack Russell bitches on the whole rarely seem to go the full 63 days. The average has seemed to be about 59 to 60 days. However, with any average there are always those that will be earlier or later, so the best course is to be observant, and keep good records.

Within a week of whelping it is good idea to take your bitch's temperature approximately three times a day, but at least twice. You will begin to see her normal temperature pattern. When you see a sharp decrease of a couple of degrees, so that her temperature is 98 degrees or below, you will know that she is within 24 hours of whelping. Once her temperature has dropped it is wise not to leave her alone, particularly if this is her first litter.

There are usually are a few other indications to whelping time, such as refusing to eat. If your bitch's eating habits are very poor for several days before her due date it is probably best to try some favourite foods, just to make sure she keeps up her strength for what lies ahead. A clear vaginal discharge, usually stringy in texture, is another sign. However, if your bitch has a greenish or yellowish discharge, your veterinarian should see her.

WHELPING

It is such an asset to be able to have an experienced breeder with you upon the delivery of your first litter. There is no substitute for experience and knowing what is normal behaviour. Each breed is different in the way (and, sometimes, the speed) they whelp, so if at all possible find someone familiar with the breed. If you cannot have someone with you, remember your bitch will need you to be calm, as it is easy for her to sense your nervousness and then begin to believe that there is really something to be worried about. Bitches that are nervous can actually delay labour for up to 24 hours if they feel that conditions are not right.

When your bitch begins actual labour, she may be restless, circling and nesting in her box. She will pant, sometimes tearing at towels or bedding before delivery of the first pup. For a maiden, the first pup is often the most difficult, and it is wise to pre-plan and have all the necessary whelping tools at hand. Latex gloves and a water-based lubricant are some of the most essential things to have. You can often smooth some of the lubricant along the edge of and just inside the vaginal opening to help an emerging pup through a tight area. If your bitch is having a tough time pushing and the pup is partially emerged you can gently pull, but only in time with a contraction and in a gentle downward arc. Never pull straight out, as this is against the natural direction of an emerging pup. If a pup should start to be presented face-up, this is against the natural direction, and the pup should be rotated so that the head is facing downward. The bitch will often retract the pup back up into the birth canal and may be able to turn it herself. Many pups will be born 'breech', with the feet coming first; however, the pup's legs should be facing downward rather than up. If a bitch has been seriously pushing and trying to deliver a pup for over an hour and has had no luck, then it is best to seek the help of a veterinarian or pet emergency clinic in your area. Having the forethought to have the phone numbers and location of the nearest pet emergency clinic in your area at hand can save precious time when you need it most. It is always better to err on the side of concern.

Other supplies, such as a baby nasal aspirator, small syringe, or even a small eye-dropper, can be very helpful to rid the newborn pup of any excess fluid it may have breathed in or aspirated in the birth canal.

If your bitch is having a difficult labour and doing a lot of thrashing about, it may be wise to have a small box inside with a heat lamp or pad to move the new pups to while she is having another, so as to prevent any accidental injuries. The actual time between puppies can vary greatly; some bitches will have their pups in assembly line fashion, resting just a very short time between pups, while others will take up to an hour between pups. Neither is more normal than the other. However, if your bitch should go several hours between pups, there is cause for some concern.

In a normal delivery the bitch will promptly tear the sac away and lick the pup to stimulate it, drying it as she does so, and will then consume the placenta. Do not try to take the placentas away. Russell bitches are quick and can be somewhat argumentative over eating them. It is their natural instinct, and it gives the bitch nourishment, extra energy, and oxytocin, which stimulates further contractions. Another great extra source of energy for a bitch to have between pups is a rich vanilla ice cream – perhaps some for her, some for you.

If your bitch for some reason does not tear the sac right away, you must do it for her. Then encourage her to lick and take care of the pup herself. She should also tear or shred the umbilical cord, but if she does not, you can use a piece of dental floss to tie it off, leaving at least an inch of cord attached to the pup. Try to gently shred the cord with your fingers, because when you cut it with sharp scissors there may be more bleeding. Iodine can be used on the end of the cord for disinfecting.

If the bitch will not do her job of licking and drying, then you can use some small towels to vigorously rub the puppy dry, hopefully stimulating the pup to cry and move some air through the lungs. If at all possible keep the pup directly in front of her where she can see it at all times, and give it back to her as soon as the pup is looking in the pink. She should continue to lick the pups and clean their bottoms, and soon they will be using that wonderful sense of smell to find the milk and be nursing with enthusiasm.

If you have a puppy that is born purple and having a difficult time breathing, knowing how to 'swing it' may be very helpful. While I can describe the method here, it is really best to have someone like an experienced breeder or your vet to show you how. Swinging a puppy will often dislodge mucus blocking the nasal passages or throat that sometimes a nasal aspirator will not. To swing the puppy, use a towel and cradle the puppy in both hands carefully with a firm enough grip to hold but not to harm. The puppy's head should be upwards, tummy facing towards you, as you raise the puppy above your head-level, and then swing the puppy downwards in an arc type motion. Gravity tends to dislodge fluids and mucus, and you can then alternate the swinging with the use of a nasal aspirator.

AFTER WHELPING
After all the pups are born, licked clean and nursing, it is very likely that your bitch will want to take a long nap. It is best at this point to make sure her bedding is clean and dry and then leave her to her nap. Do not stress your bitch by inviting anyone over to see the pups, as you will be stressing her at her weakest moment. It is not a good idea for her or the pups to have visitors until the pups are at least three or four weeks of age.

Make sure that any bedding you put in with newborn puppies is free from ravelling

Make sure the mother and her puppies are left relatively undisturbed for the first few days.

Photo courtesy: Mary Strom, Snow Wind.

threads, holes, stuffing that can be torn out, etc. You would be amazed at what a two-day old puppy can crawl into. There has been a pup or two that managed to get a very small thread wrapped around its neck, so tight that it had to be cut off. Simulated sheepskin or some of the poly fleece-type bedding is wonderfully warm and safe for newborn puppies.

IF THE WORST HAPPENS
Although Caesarean sections are generally rare, it can happen on a bitch's first litter or after she has had several trouble-free litters. Jack Russell bitches normally recover very quickly from a C-section and the pups will do very well. However, there is unfortunately always the possibility of losing a bitch, and having orphan pups to rear, so you should be prepared, as this is part of the commitment of breeding a litter.

Should you lose your bitch, if you can possibly find another bitch that has just a few pups, and could nanny yours, that would be the best of all possible worlds. It does not necessarily need to be a Jack Russell bitch either. Another terrier or even a larger breed can be an equally good mother to orphan pups.

One of the largest obstacles for a bitch taking another bitch's pups is the scent of the pups themselves, as they will not smell like her own. A simple way of making the transition is to spread peanut butter on the pups. It sounds silly, but most bitches like the flavour of peanut butter and it is very strong in aroma – strong enough to cover up the scent of another bitch. Most bitches will begin licking the peanut butter off the pup, thereby covering the pup with their own scent. You will still have to watch carefully for any signs of rejection on the part of the new mother.

I would encourage anyone who loses a litter to ascertain why. If your bitch actually gives birth to stillborn pups or simply pups that are too immature to survive, it is really necessary to know why, so the same mistakes are not made again. Most veterinarians can do simple post mortems, and if need be, send pups to the nearest university for evaluation. Some of the reasons for abortion can be injury, infection, malnutrition, hormone imbalance, or even poor immunity to what we normally vaccinate for. Any of the above may cause a breeder to give thought to changing the way in which they manage their dogs. Likewise, failure to conceive can result from a hormone imbalance, and any bitch that is bred and found not to be pregnant between 28 and 35 days should have her progesterone level tested.

CARE OF THE NEW MOTHER

Most of the mothers will want to stay with their puppies continuously for the first few days; some will even need to be carried outside for a quick potty break. Be cautious of other dogs in the house, as new mothers are very protective, and may bite and snap at other animals coming too close to their new puppies. This protectiveness and unwillingness to leave the pups will gradually subside as the pups age, and by the time the pups are three or four weeks of age it is likely she will only be with them when it is feeding time or bedtime.

For the first few days after a bitch has whelped it is a good idea to check her temperature at least twice daily. Mastitis can come up quite quickly, although it is usually preceded by a fever. If you suspect that your bitch has retained several placentas, it may be wise to have your vet give her what is sometimes referred to as a 'clean-out' shot. The clean-out shot of oxytocin is given routinely by some breeders after their bitches have finished whelping, usually within the first 24 hours. The oxytocin encourages the uterus to contract and expel any retained placentas, and it will also stimulate your bitch's milk production.

Jack Russell Terrier bitches on the whole are very good mothers; however, any litter is a tremendous drain on a bitch's resources. It is after the pups are born that your bitch will really need the extra food and calories. An average-sized litter is around four or five puppies; however, there are bitches that have eight or nine pups as well as those with two or three. With the larger litters you may find it necessary to supplement the pups early on. The puppies' behaviour will be your best indicator of that: if they are doing a lot of crying or fussing, it is one sign they may not be getting enough milk.

It is advisable to monitor the weight of the puppies to ensure they are getting sufficient nourishment.
Photo courtesy: Mary Strom, Snow Wind.

CARE OF THE NEWBORN

Normal newborn puppies will sleep approximately 90 per cent of the time. Healthy, happy puppies' muscles will twitch, and they may look as if they are chasing bunnies in their sleep. Puppies should spend the rest of their time nursing enthusiastically. Pups that are squirming around the whelping box away from mother and the littermates should be examined, as they may be ill. Sick puppies will also cry excessively, and or may appear weak and listless. Body temperature is the first thing to check, as warmth is critical for the newborn pup. If the puppy is chilled, weak, or both, warm it and give a drop or two of glucose or corn syrup which may help to give it the energy needed to nurse. With a large litter, you can always help a bit by starting the smaller pups on the rear teats where there is normally a greater volume of milk.

I always weigh my pups when they are first born, and then daily for the first week after, to make sure the weight gain is steady and consistent. Some bitches may come into their milk at a slower rate for a variety of reasons. Extra food, with supplements such as raw liver, raw beef, cottage cheese or yoghurt, can certainly be helpful to aid milk production. Weighing the pups twice daily will give you a good idea how they are doing. By the time the pups are three days old they should look filled out, with rounded little bellies. If they do not, you may need to give them a supplement.

There are several ways in which to give supplements to very young puppies. One would be to try the small puppy nurser bottles; however, I have not always had good luck using them. Many times if a pup is weak, it will be unable to suckle and it is sometimes more helpful to try an eye-dropper or small syringe to slowly drop the mixture into its mouth, letting it swallow each drop before another is given. Keep in mind that for the first 24 hours, what a puppy needs most is warmth and energy. Energy can be gained by feeding a solution consisting of one teaspoon of light corn syrup to four tablespoons of warm water, mixed thoroughly, with a few grains of salt added. Tube feeding is also an alternative, but it is not always easy to learn and can be fatal to the pup if it is done incorrectly. It is best to have your vet go over the procedure with you and help you to do the actual feeding the first time around, until you are comfortable with it.

If a pup is not nursing on its dam after 24 hours of using the glucose then it may need further supplementation. A commercial milk-replacer could be used until the pup is stronger and can be put back with its dam. If the puppy does not begin to gain weight it is always best to consult with your veterinarian.

REARING THE LITTER

DOCKING AND DEWCLAWS

Once you are sure your pups are on a steady course, gaining weight, and growing stronger, it will be time to think about docking tails and removing dewclaws. Usually this procedure is done between three and five days of age; after five days it becomes very difficult in terms of the amount of bleeding and discomfort for the pups. Jack Russell Terriers will often have rear dewclaws, so it is always best to check.

Study your puppies carefully and you will find that the tail lengths in a litter of pups will vary greatly – some longer, some shorter. This is why it is impossible to cut the same amount off each pup's tail. When you dock a tail it is better to err on the side of generosity leaving a tail a bit too long rather than too short. Your vet will usually want you to mark the spot to cut. There are many ways to ascertain the proper length of tail for a Jack Russell Terrier; some people use particular coins, others count the number of vertebrae in the tail. The best method is to look at the pup itself, cradling them into a standing position and holding the tail up. Draw an imaginary line from the top flat of their head straight across to their tail, as the cut should be even with the top flat of the head to give a balanced picture. With female pups you can also pull the tail between the legs and mark the spot on the tail where the tail just covers the tip of their vulva. You can use the same method with the boys; it would just have to be an imaginary vulva.

Trimming the pups' razor-sharp nails will be greatly appreciated by your bitch and is a part of early puppy training. Puppies that have their nails trimmed early and regularly will be very easy to trim as adults.

WORMING AND VACCINATION
At three weeks of age your puppies will

usually be up on their feet, and the first worming should be done, for both the puppies and the bitch. Depending on your vet's advice, you will want to have your pups'first vaccinations done at around five or six weeks of age, with a second vaccination at eight weeks, just before they are ready to go to their new homes. Worming should also be done again at five to six weeks, as well as at eight weeks. At this point it may be wise to take a faecal sample from one of your puppies to your vet to be analysed. The veterinarian can screen for Coccidia, as you would then have plenty of time for proper treatment before the pups go to their new homes. Usually, if one puppy has it, the rest will too. (For more detail see Chapter 3 'The Jack Russell Puppy'.)

Weaning should be under way at three weeks, but the puppies will continue to feed from their mother for as long as she will tolerate them.
Photo: Sheila Atter.

DIET

At three weeks it may also be time to start the litter on puppy gruel, usually goat's milk with some baby rice cereal. Never use cow's milk, as it is usually harder for a puppy to digest. You can then gradually introduce a softened puppy kibble that has been soaked in water and then made into a mush. If they do not take to the puppy gruel right away, try adding a teaspoon of light corn syrup, as it can sometimes do the trick.

When you first start feeding solid food it is best to offer it several times a day, possibly up to four times a day just to get them started. If they are beginning to eat well you can probably cut it down to three times a day, moving it down to twice a day by the time the pups are eight weeks of age and ready to go to their new homes. Few families will be able to realistically handle feeding more than twice daily.

Be observant of your puppies. They can tell you a lot about themselves if you simply watch them. When a puppy is poorly nourished you begin to see it very quickly. At the same time when their food quality is

Little and often is the rule with weaning, and the newly-weaned puppies should have at least four meals a day.

Photo: Sheila Atter.

improved, the change for the better is just as rapid. Many commercial foods are loaded with inexpensive grains – with dog food it is often a case of 'you get what you pay for'. Some other supplements we add to our puppy food are flax oil for a good coat, and vitamin C for the immune system, and yoghurt is great for the digestive tract.

There are many pros and cons about using raw meats; however, a small amount used in conjunction with a high-quality kibble will give the pups a good start. It also has the extra advantage of making puppy stools very firm and easy to clean up. We have always used small bits of cut-up steak, as I like the higher quality meat for young dogs, where the ground meats are fine when they are older. It is quite common in Europe to use tripe, either raw or canned, as a supplement to the biscuit.

TOYS

We do not suggest rawhide and some types of rope toys for your puppies. Both of these have the potential to cause intestinal blockages if eaten in large pieces. We had an older Russell bitch go to her new home, and the owners called to check in and mentioned that she was coughing a lot. I asked them what they had given her to chew on and they mentioned rawhide strips. As it turned out, there was an immediate trip to the vet's, as the rawhide strip had become caught on one of her back molars and was dangling down her throat – hence the coughing trying to bring it back up. The same thing could happen to a puppy. My vet used to recommend rope toys until recently, when he had to surgically remove pieces of one from a dog. We have also had a dog that was having cramping and diarrhoea; on an X-ray, we could see the large chunk of rawhide. Medication was given to break down the

At four weeks of age, the puppies will be inquisitive and will start to explore their environment.

Photo: Sheila Atter.

rawhide, but it is just better to be safe than risk a trip to the vet's. Dogs can and will eat the strangest things.

EARLY LESSONS

Touch is very important to any animal, and although your pups in the first few weeks can neither hear nor see you it is important to handle and stroke them. Cradling them in your hands and gently rocking, turning them over on their backs and gently rubbing their tummies are all part of getting them accustomed to human touch.

Mental and physical stimulation are very important for a healthy, happy puppy, although most homes can be a veritable obstacle course for a puppy. Toys, tunnels and small puppy-sized obstacle courses are great too. Keep things simple at first so there is a high rate of success for the puppies. Things need to be challenging, but not so much so that there is a high rate of failure. Small six- to eight-inch-round plumbing pipe is wonderful for young puppies to crawl over and through. Small step stools are great for puppies to learn to climb, and if you have no stairs in your house you can set up a few from lower to higher to mimic stair-climbing. Some of the best shopping for puppies is through garage sales and, second-hand toy and clothing stores.

ASSESSING PUPPIES
Photos: Sheila Atter.

At the four-week stage, puppies can be assessed for conformation.

Sight and sounds for young puppies are wonderful for patterning and conditioning. Small baby mirrors can go in with the pups at around three weeks of age, once they are able to focus. Make sure the mirror has no sharp edges and is securely mounted. When the puppies are between three and five weeks the television and radio are good for sound stimulation. Sounds of all different varieties – loud bangs and vacuum cleaners – should be introduced at approximately five weeks of age, though you should never make a loud banging or clapping noise as a puppy is approaching you. Continue to add new and varied sounds, such as recordings of heavy traffic, cows mooing, trains, babies crying, etc.

By the time the pups are six weeks, their mother willl probably not want much to do with them. After all, their teeth are very sharp by now, and bitches will often growl and snap at the pups when they try to nurse. It is still vital that she is with them, not for food so much as for discipline and to set parameters. Pups that are taken away from their mothers too soon do not get this very important influence, and the lack of it may follow them throughout their lifetime. In the pack young pups are often flipped onto their back and pinned by their mothers. The pups soon learn that the adult dogs must be treated with respect. They will then approach the adult dogs in the proper posture of submission, slightly crouching, head low, ears back, tail down but wagging. They will usually keep their head low, licking at the bottom and sides of the adult's muzzle. These are all signs of respect, not fear, and it shows the puppies'subordination to the adult.

Introduce your puppies to a variety of floor surfaces, as many young puppies that have been raised on carpet or rugs will be wary of concrete or tile. Different textures outside are also good: grass is nice; however,

Above: Play is a means of developing the senses, and soon individual personalities will begin to emerge.

Photo: Kim James, Badgerwood.

a puppy pen with pea gravel is excellent for easy clean-up, solid footing, and easy digging too. Pea gravel is a good surface for adult dogs too; it can actually tighten and improve the overall condition of their feet.

This is a good time to start puppy collars as well. Chapter 5 describes collar and lead training in detail, but if you find the pups are chewing on each other's collars, you can take the collars and soak them in bitter apple spray and this should take care of the chewing problem. However, you may need to re-apply the spray after a few days. It is so nice for a new owner to have a pup that is accustomed to a collar, and has some familiarity with a lead as well.

CHOOSING THE RIGHT HOMES
Over the years it has been the tried and true saying that not everyone needs a Jack Russell puppy. However, if you give some thought to this it is a rather empty statement, as there are many breeds where that would be the case. It is up to the breeder to choose the new owners and place their puppies carefully. A good breeder will always tell a new owner that a puppy is welcome to come back if for any reason the situation does not work out. However, careful matching of puppy to owner is essential to the puppy being successful in its new home.

Puppies come in a variety of temperaments, structural soundness and abilities, and it is up to the breeder to know their puppies well enough to know what will be best for that particular puppy. For instance, a shy puppy is probably not going to be good for a family that will baby him and play into an already existing shyness. A shy puppy needs confident owners that will be willing to build confidence without picking him up and saying "poor little puppy" every time he falls or fails to succeed. A puppy that is very independent will not be successful in a home where he does not have adequate structure and training – these are the puppies that have the potential to end up in rescue associations or

shelters by the time they are adults.

Structural faults also need to be taken into consideration. A puppy with a ewe-neck will not be a good bet for someone wanting to show in obedience, for no matter how willing the puppy is to please, because of its neck construction it will not be comfortable in a collar and leash. With a ewe-neck, the arch or shape of the neck is actually reversed so each time a collar and leash pulls against the neck it is pulling the neck into an uncomfortable position, and the puppy will most likely struggle against it. Likewise, a puppy with slipped hocks or hocks that collapse forward is not a good agility prospect, as its ability to jump will always be compromised.

TEMPERAMENT TESTING

So, if you are a new breeder, how do you tell which puppy should go where? This is where a good mentor can be very helpful.

Temperament testing of some type is essential to determine if a pup will be shy, bold, fearful or friendly and willing to please. Someone very experienced should do the temperament testing, and you may be able to locate someone through a local dog club.

There are some very simple tests you can do at home. Start by picking up your puppy and securely cradling him on his back, which

is referred to as a puppy inversion test. To be most successful, someone who is a stranger to the puppy should do the puppy inversion test. When you gently cradle the puppy on its back, look it in the eye, speak to it in a soft and kind voice, then watch its reaction. If the puppy is fussing and will not look you in the eye, struggling to right himself and to be free from you, it may be quite independent and will need a home that will give the necessary structure and obedience training that is required. If the puppy holds your gaze, and is content to be on its back, body relaxed, and looking at you adoringly, then this puppy is likely to be quite confident and will be willing to please and easy to train. When a pup will look at you but has that unmistakable look of fear in its eyes, and clutches on to your hand, this is a puppy that may well be fearful and insecure as an adult. This puppy will then need someone that is willing to build confidence, in a firm and gentle way, and will be a clear leader for the puppy.

Just like people, there are all types of personalities in puppies. The best for showing will be the pup that is confident, head held high, and who thinks quite a lot of himself. A dog can be extremely well structured, but if he does not have the attitude to be the extrovert and the showman

The breeder must attempt to match potential owners with puppies which are most likely to suit their lifestyle.

Photo courtesy: Mary Strom, Snow Wind.

PUPPY WATCHING

The more time you spend watching puppies, the more you will understand about temperament, conformation and movement.

Photos: Mary Strom, Snow Wind.

then it is difficult to gain this later. Remember, a dog wins in the show ring in spite of his faults. A pup's attitude, how he carries himself and uses his body is very important to the total picture.

Never underestimate the power of puppy watching. Having puppies is one of the biggest time-consuming events I can think of. However, careful watching of puppies – how they behave, the way they approach new situations and how they use their bodies – is one of the greatest ways to learn about your puppies and your breed.

GOING HOME
When you have sorted out the which-puppy-goes-where decisions, it is good to have put some thought into giving the new owner some type of puppy booklet or other printed information to take home. Jack Russell Terrier puppies are usually very good at making the transition to their new homes, and they will be running them in no time. It is important for the new owner to have information on what the pups are eating, where to purchase the food, and how much to feed. If the food you feed is hard to find and the new owners will need to change the puppy's food, send a small bag home with them so that there is as little digestive upset as possible. Making a list of suggested toys is also helpful.

A copy of the pedigree and the registration papers will need to be gone over with the new owners. In the United States there is a choice between full or limited registration. Pet puppies should be sold with limited registration. If the puppy turns out to be better in quality than anticipated, then the breeder can always write a letter stating that and asking for registration to be changed to full privileges. Limited registration still gives the pet owner the ability to show in performance events such as Earth Dog, Obedience, and Agility, and to earn titles in

those events. However, any offspring from a dog with AKC limited registration will not be able to be registered with the AKC.

It is also very nice for new puppy owners to have photos of the sire and dam of their puppy, and perhaps a little history of your breeding programme or the breed in general, plus any information on how to get connected to such things as suitable obedience trainers, Earth Dog events, fun days or trials, and an all-breed dog club, or breed club.

Vaccination and worming records should be given for each individual puppy, along with a discussion about when and what additional vaccinations should be given. If you have a health contract, it is best to go over this with the prospective owner in advance to make sure there are no misunderstandings.

After a puppy has gone home, it is a good idea to give the new owners a call after they have had the puppy for 24 hours to see if they have any questions or concerns. Often new owners are embarrassed to call, and many potential puppy problems can be prevented with good communication.

Puppies are a lifetime responsibility. No matter how careful a breeder is about placing their pups in the proper homes, life for any family is in a constant state of flux. Divorces, deaths, and moving are all part of life, and so, as a breeder, you must be willing to take the responsibility for the puppies you breed for their lifetimes.

IDENTIFICATION
Permanent identification is one means of ensuring that you are able to get the dogs you have bred back. No matter what types of guarantees and contracts a person has signed, promising they would never dream of dropping their dog off at a shelter or rescue association, it will happen. For that reason, it is essential that puppies be permanently

identified with either a tattoo or a microchip, so that you have an opportunity to re-home the puppies you have bred. It is now required that any puppy or dog being imported into the United States and registered with the American Kennel Club must be identified with either a tattoo or a microchip.

There are several different brands of microchips, and most shelters and rescue associations now own scanners that will scan for a variety of different brands. The microchip has the advantage over the tattoo, as tattoos can fade over time or be unreadable, whereas the microchips, unless there has been substantial movement, can always be read by the appropriate scanner.

SHIPPING A PUPPY

If you are shipping a puppy by plane, then you will first need to make sure the puppy is very familiar with his crate. Also, give thought to the owner on the receiving end – instead of shipping a puppy in towels that will most likely be soiled when the pup arrives on the other end, ship him in at least one large roll of wadded-up paper towels. Paper towels are very absorbent and if the puppy has a bowel movement, it is likely to be enveloped by the paper towels. It is so disappointing for the new owner on the other end to receive a dirty puppy, and meanwhile the puppy will not understand why no one really wants to give him lots of hugs and kisses.

Make sure puppy has a light meal on the evening prior to his departure, and only water for the morning that he travels. Over the years we have given every puppy that travels by plane some drops of a natural flower essence called Dr Bach's Rescue Remedy. There are several homeopathic remedies to calm and reassure a puppy or dog under stress. Some are made specifically for dogs; others can be used by both humans and animals. Be sure and tape a bag of your puppy's regular food to the top of his travel crate. That way, if the puppy is delayed, he will be able to have his regular food, and not be further stressed by a change in diet. I also attach a slip of paper to the top of the crate with the puppy's name – you would be surprised how many of the airline people will use his name if it is provided. This can be such a comfort to a young puppy flying for the first time.

Many airlines will permit a small dog or a young puppy to be transported inside the passenger cabin; however, most will only allow one per travel class, so reservations need to be made well in advance. The best type of carrier to use if your puppy is to accompany you inside the plane is a soft-sided one with adequate ventilation that is specifically designed for dogs. Most of these carriers have a solid flat bottom, so the wadded-up paper towels will still work very well for absorbency. Make sure to take extra towels and a plastic bag along, just in case your puppy should become airsick. If you are worried about water on the flight, ice cubes are great to entertain the puppy as well as hydrate him. Smoked pig ears are also a great chew toy for a travelling puppy; they last a very long time.

A RESPONSIBLE BREEDER

Each time you breed a litter of puppies, you widen your circle of contacts and friends, and with this comes a bigger responsibility to keep track of those contacts, friends, and puppies you have bred. One of the best ways to keep in communication is to keep track of your puppies' birth dates, and then send out birthday cards to the pups at a year of age, and on through if possible. It is something every pet owner will appreciate, and many times they will respond in kind with pictures and news of their friend and companion. By keeping in good contact with your puppy owners, you are more likely to avoid and be

As a responsible breeder, you must regard yourself as a guardian of the breed and your duty is to safeguard it for the future.   *Photo courtesy: Kim James, Badgerwood.*

able to solve any difficult situations that may arise with a puppy you have bred and sold.

Being a thoughtful and responsible breeder is one of the hardest jobs I know. There are unbelievable commitments of time, energy and finances. There will always be new things to learn, especially from your mistakes, so being open-minded and willing to learn is a must. It is never an easy job and if you are looking for a fast and easy success, dog breeding is not it! There are always highs and lows with breeding dogs. However, the calls that give me the most satisfaction are the puppy owners who call just to share with me how wonderful their dogs are – healthy, happy, and their best friends in the world.

12 *HEALTH CARE*

Much of health care is aimed at preventing disease rather than going to the expense of treating well-established or chronic conditions. Visits early on in life to the veterinary surgeon are aimed at preventing animals becoming ill in the first place. In Jack Russell Terriers brought in as puppies, preventive care involves a vaccination programme, administering appropriate worm doses and checking on the feed given to help growth. Measures such as hygiene in the home and providing a rewarding environment for the puppy to grow up in can be considered positive health care measures. Visits to the vet when there are no painful procedures and when rewards can be offered by the veterinary staff for good behaviour will make any future visits all the easier. Simple tasks such as weighing the puppy in the surgery or handling him to trim his nails during first visits will make the dog more trusting and easier to handle in the surgery when adult.

Between visits, you should inspect your terrier for any changes in coat condition, breath odour or for any unusual lumps or swellings. Daily brushing and grooming helps you to get to know the dog and pick up any early signs of disease. Improved diet and preventive vaccinations are contributing to a much longer life for all domestic animals. The dog's weight should be observed, and weighing at three-monthly intervals, if suitable scales can be found, helps to detect any gradual change in condition.

SELECTING A VETERINARY SURGEON

The choice of a veterinary surgeon may be based on accessibility, especially if you like to walk your dog to the surgery. Dogs excited by car travel may be frustrated if, after a journey, they are deposited in a waiting room full of other dogs' odours, and no opportunities to work off pent-up energy. If there is no immediately close practice that the dog can be walked to, some people will make enquiries of other Jack Russell owners they meet before deciding which veterinary practice will have the greatest sympathy for their dog and their requirements for veterinary care.

Treatment prices will vary, and it is fairly easy to phone around and enquire about the cost of a booster vaccine or the cost of neutering to judge the level of charges, especially if you are new to an area. Facilities in practices are not all the same. A practice or veterinary hospital with 24-hour nursing staff residing on the premises and equipment for emergency surgery will have to charge more than the smaller surgery, which adequately provides for vaccination and other simple injections, but requires you to go elsewhere for more complicated procedures. Remember,

Photo: John Valentine.

one day you may need a vet in a hurry if your dog has been involved in a road accident or has a very acute illness, so try to find out how good the 'out of hours' call-out is in the veterinary practice before you choose.

INSURANCE

Pet insurance has proved a great incentive to vets to provide additional equipment and veterinary experts with specialist knowledge of your breed. Once it is known there is insurance cover, the veterinary surgeon is confident that payment will be made for all treatments given to the dog, and is less likely to be cautious about embarking on expensive treatment. With large breeds, treatment costs are often higher because of the larger doses of drugs, which are based on body weight (unlike humans, who have a standard dose regardless of their weight). Just as the vet should be chosen to provide the type of health attention needed, each insurance company's provisions should be compared to find the one with an annual premium that will deliver the most help in times of difficulty. The excess you have to pay on each claim is not as important for a small dog, but

there are additional premiums requested by some companies for ensuring the giant breeds. Caution in asking for treatment for some disorders is necessary, as inherited disorders are not covered by insurance in the UK, nor are booster vaccines, routine neutering and some chronic or continuing disease states. Many companies do not pay for veterinary visits to a dog in your home, nor do they pay in full for prescription diets that could be part of your dog's treatment.

GENERAL GROOMING AND HYGIENE

Jack Russells have relatively easy coats to maintain but they do require daily grooming, especially when they are moulting. This is the ideal time to inspect the body closely, to look for any abnormalities and at the general condition. The sooner a health problem is noticed, the quicker the veterinary adviser can be asked for an opinion, and the better the chance of a full recovery in the case of a progressive disease or a tumour.

The puppy should be brushed and groomed from the earliest age so that he will associate such handling with a pleasurable experience. Procedures will be easier to carry out if this is started early in life. If a dog is

used to being handled in this way, it will be far easier for a veterinary surgeon to make an examination, and a visit to the surgery becomes less stressful for the owner as well as the dog.

Before you start to groom the dog, carry out a physical examination to check for any abnormalities. Always start at the head end, as the hands are cleaner looking at the orifices on the head before handling the dog's feet and the anal region.

EYES: Inspect the eyes first for matter or discharges in the corner. There should be no excessive watering, and the white of the eye should be briefly checked to see that it is not red or discoloured. The surface of the eye should be clear and bright, and the expression one of alertness. There are specific diseases that affect the eyes, so any abnormal signs should be noted and reported to the veterinary surgeon.

EARS: A painful ear can be a very irritating complaint for your dog, so preventing ear problems is important. If there is a noticeable build-up of wax in the ear canal, this can be easily removed by first softening the wax with an ear cleaning fluid and then wiping gently with cotton wool (cotton). The use of cotton buds in the ear is discouraged, and all cleaning should be the most gentle possible. There is a range of ear cleaners suitable for the terrier, and your veterinary surgeon will advise on the one most appropriate for routine use.

If there is an excessive amount of wax in the canal or if the ear is hot, reddened or swollen, this is an indication of infection or inflammation, and veterinary attention should be sought quickly. Should an infection be left untreated, the dog will scratch the affected ear repeatedly, often introducing other infections carried on soiled hind toenails. Oozing and the multiplication of harmful bacteria in the moist discharges will make the ear much worse, and treatment becomes more difficult.

MOUTH: Check your dog's gums each day for redness or inflammation. Gum diseases can develop as the tartar builds up on the teeth and food particles get caught at the gum margin. The decaying food will produce breath odour if not removed, and mouth bacteria can produce even worse halitosis. The teeth and gum margins have pain receptors, so any tartar build-up can lead to disease, which puts the dog off its food and even causes bad temper.

Canine toothpastes are now available, which can be used to help prevent a build-up of tartar. If the dog's teeth are cleaned regularly, you will avoid a state of dental neglect so advanced that your old terrier needs a general anaesthetic to have his teeth scaled and polished at the veterinary practice. Start brushing a dog's teeth at about four months of age, but avoid the areas where the permanent teeth are about to erupt. At first the puppy will want to play, but little by little will become used to having all his teeth cleaned. Better to start while your puppy is young and small, rather than waiting until you have a fully-grown dog that objects to the procedure.

Puppies lose their milk teeth at between four and six months, and sore gums should be noted at that age. Persistent milk teeth or temporary canines are quite common, and extraction by eight months of age is advised if they have not come out by themselves. Massaging the skin just below the eye will help when the molar teeth are about to erupt. While grooming the older dog, look for signs of abnormality such as mouth warts, excess saliva or white froth at the back of the mouth.

NOSE: Again, remove any discharges and

look for cracking or fissuring. There is little point in worrying about the traditional 'cold wet nose' as a health indicator.

SKIN AND COAT: Examine the whole of your dog's body when grooming. Tell-tale black dirt or white scurf may indicate a parasite infection. Patches of hair loss, redness of skin and abnormal lumps may first be found during grooming. Your terrier's coat will normally have a slight shine, and oil from the sebaceous glands will provide the waterproofing grease that gives a smooth feel as you run your hand over the hair.

NAILS AND FEET: Nails should be kept short, as over-long nails may splinter painfully, especially in cold weather when the nail is brittle. The dewclaw may be a particular problem in the Jack Russell, but regular inspection should stop the point of the nail growing so long that it penetrates the flesh and causes a painful abscess. If the dog is regularly walked on hard surfaces such as concrete, paving stones or rocks, the nails of the feet will wear down naturally. Tarmac and grass do little to wear nails down at exercise times. If the nails are left to become too long, they are then difficult for the dog to wear down, whatever the surface. As a result, the heel takes more of the weight of the leg and the nails may split, with painful consequences.

Clipping nails is a delicate task. If you cut too short, into the quick, blood will flow and the dog will find it painful. He may then become very wary of anyone who tries to get near his feet with nail clippers. Exercising on concrete may be safer for the beginner than attempting to cut across the nail with new sharp clippers.

Make a habit of feeling the area between the toes, where tufts of hair attract sticky substances, clay soils can form little hard balls, and tar or chewing gum can be picked up on a walk with equally damaging effect.

You will notice any cuts and pad injuries when handling feet for grooming.

PERINEUM AND GENITAL AREA: Check for swollen anal sacs or unexpected discharges. Segments of tapeworms might be seen near the rectum. A bitch's vulva should not discharge, except when signs of heat are present. The prepuce of the male dog should have no discharge and the penis should not protrude except if the dog is inadvertently excited during grooming or handling.

PREVENTIVE CARE

VACCINATIONS
The use of vaccines to prevent disease is well established for human as well as animal health. The longer life of the animal, and the comparative rarity of puppy disease and early death, are things that have become taken for granted in the last 40 years. Yet many older dog breeders remember puppies dying of distemper fits, or left twitching with chorea for the rest of their lives. The appearance of canine parvovirus in 1979 was an unpleasant shock to those who thought that veterinary treatment could deal with all puppy diarrhoeas. There were many deaths in puppies under 12 months old – some affected pups died of sudden heart failure caused by the parvovirus damaging the heart muscle – until they developed immunity either through their mother's milk or when the puppies' own defences became mature enough to respond to an injected vaccine.

Your veterinarian is the best person to advise on the type of vaccine to use and at what age to give them, since he or she will have a unique knowledge of the type of infection prevalent in a locality and when infection is likely to strike.

An example of this is in the Guide Dogs for the Blind Association's breeding programme where, for over 25 years, an early

vaccination was given to the six-week-old puppy. No isolation after this early vaccination was needed. This was contrary to general advice given in the 60s and 70s when figures for puppy disease were acceptably low. Later, when the parvovirus infection was widespread in the early 80s, the mortality rate of GDBA puppies was much lower than amongst breeders who kept their puppies in kennels until they were eight to 12 weeks of age before selling them. The puppies already sent out to homes were much less likely to go down with disease than those puppies held back by breeders in their kennels.

Additionally, the temperament of some breeds was suspect, because a longer enforced isolation after vaccination meant that proper socialisation did not take place. New owners of such puppies were advised not to take them out until they were four months of age, when a final booster had to be given. This meant that there were no opportunities to mix with people and other dogs until an age when the older puppy had already developed a fear of being handled by strangers or was suspicious of other dogs met outside the home.

DISTEMPER: This is the classic virus disease, which has become very rare where vaccine is used on a regular basis. From time to time, it is seen in larger cities where there is a stray or roaming dog population. This may subsequently lead to infection of show or other kennel dogs that do not have a high level of immunity.

The virus may spread though saliva, nose and eye discharges, diarrhoea faeces or urine. It has an incubation period of seven to 21 days, and infection is followed by a rise in temperature, loss of appetite, a cough and, often, diarrhoea. The virus causes immunosuppression, so that the dog becomes more susceptible to the bacteria that cause diarrhoea and pneumonia. Discharges from the eyes and nose may be watery at first, but often become thick mucoid, with a green or creamy colour due to secondary infections. The teeth are affected when a puppy of under six months of age is infected by the virus: enamel defects show as brown marks – they last for life and are known as 'distemper teeth'.

The 'hard pad' strain seen in the 60s is now considered to be nothing more than the hyperkeratosis of the nose and footpads that occurs after all distemper infections, although the name is still in use when dog illness is written or talked about. In over half of all dogs affected with distemper, damage to the nervous system will manifest itself as fits, chorea (twitching of muscles) or posterior paralysis. Dogs in old or middle age may develop encephalitis (ODE) due to latent distemper virus in the nervous tissue.

The vaccines in use today are all modified live vaccines, and highly effective in preventing disease. The age for a first injection will partly depend on the manufacturer's instructions and partly on knowledge of the amount of protection passed by the mother to the young puppies. Maternally derived immunity (MDI) might block the vaccine in the young puppy, but blood sampling of bitches during pregnancy is now used as a method of estimating how soon the puppy will respond to vaccine. The use of a first vaccine at six weeks is becoming more widespread, and this allows for the all-important early socialisation period of the puppy's development.

PARVOVIRUS: This is probably the second most important virus disease in Europe and, like distemper, is largely preventable by the correct use of vaccination. The speed at which an infection could spread from kennel to kennel surprised many, but the disease is caused by a very tough virus that can be carried on footwear that has walked through

virus-infected faeces. It may then survive for up to a year, untouched by many commonly used kennel disinfectants. The sudden death of puppies, caused by damage to the heart muscle, is no longer seen, but the gastro-enteritis form of parvovirus still occurs from time to time.

This sudden illness takes the form of repeated vomiting in the first 24 hours, followed by profuse watery diarrhoea, often with a characteristic sour smell and a red-brown colour. The cause of death was often from the severe dehydration that accompanied this loss of fluid, but once it was understood that puppies should be treated with intravenous fluids similar to the treatment of human cholera victims, the death rate fell. Fluids by mouth are sufficient in less severe cases, provided they contain the electrolytes that need to be replaced. The traditional mixture of a level teaspoonful of salt and a dessertspoonful of glucose in two pints of water has saved many dogs'lives.

Vaccination of the young puppy is recommended, though the MDI may partially block the effectiveness of the vaccine, as seen with distemper. A live vaccine at six weeks, followed by a further dose at 12 weeks, will protect most puppies. The four-month booster is no longer in common use, but it is most usual to see parvovirus in the recently weaned puppy or the five-month-old puppy, where immunity no longer protects that individual against infection.

HEPATITIS: The disease produced by an *adenovirus* is now quite rare, but one form (CAV-2) is often associated with kennel cough infection in dogs. After infection, the virus multiplies in the lymphatic system and then sets out to damage the lining of the blood vessels. It was for this reason that the cause of death was liver failure. The name hepatitis was given because, on post mortem, the liver was seen to be very swollen and

engorged with blood. Other organs are also damaged, and about 70 per cent of recovered dogs are found to have kidney damage. The eye damage, known as 'blue eye', seen on recovery is not recognised in the Jack Russell, but was quite common in certain other breeds. Vaccination at six and 12 weeks using a reliable vaccine that contains the CAV-2 virus is very effective as a preventive measure against this disease.

LEPTOSPIROSIS: This is caused by bacteria, and as such it differs from the previous group of viral infections. Protection has to be provided by at least two doses of a killed vaccine, and a 12-monthly repeat dose is essential if the protection is to be maintained. It is for this disease that the annual 'booster'vaccine is most essential. The type of leptospirosis spread by rats is the most devastating to the dog and frequently results in jaundice, then death from kidney and liver failure unless early treatment with antibiotics is available. The other serotype of leptospira that damages the dog's kidneys is less often seen since vaccination and annual boosters have been regularly used. Gundogs and all dogs that work in the country where rats may have contaminated water courses are especially at risk, as are terriers working in buildings populated by rats. Terriers kept outdoors in kennels with yards have been known to die of jaundice, as rats cross the exercise yards and leave infected urine traces in pools for the dog to sniff at or lick up.

KENNEL COUGH: Now very common, especially in the summer months, this is a troublesome infection that causes harsh coughing originating from the trachea and bronchial tubes. Kennel cough is one of the best known diseases to Jack Russell owners. Traditionally, dogs became infected in boarding kennels, but any dog coming within droplet infection distance of another dog's

Photo: John Valentine.

coughing at a show or in public exercise areas may catch the illness. There are five known viral and bacterial agents that may all (or perhaps two of them at a time) cause the disease known as kennel cough. Vaccination by nose drops of a *Bordetella* vaccine can be offered to give protection, and is often given just a week before a dog goes into kennels. The normal booster injection given contains protection against three of the other known causes.

The disease develops within four to seven days of infection, so it may not be evident until after a dog has left the kennels. The deep harsh cough is often described as "as if a bone or something was stuck in the throat". The dog coughs repeatedly. Even with treatment, coughs last for 14 days, but in some dogs the cough lasts for as long as six weeks. Infection may then persist in the trachea, and if the dog is a 'carrier', he may get subsequent coughing attacks when stressed. This explains why some non-coughing dogs put into board may cause an outbreak of kennel cough. Once a summertime disease, kennel cough outbreaks now occur at any time of the year, often after a holiday period when more dogs than usual are boarded.

RABIES: This virus disease is almost unknown to most UK veterinarians due to a successful quarantine policy that has kept the island free of rabies in dogs and in wildlife such as foxes. This mandatory quarantine policy cannot be maintained, as the six-month period of isolation does not have a strong scientific basis. The Swedish Government's switch to a compulsory vaccination and identification policy for all has provided a basis for modification of the UK laws on importing dogs.

In countries such as the Philippines, where very recently rabies was widespread and causing human deaths, it was found that at least 75 per cent of a dog population had to be compulsorily vaccinated (including rounding up all strays) to delay the spread of this disease. It must always be rigorously controlled in animals because of the devastating effect of one human becoming infected with rabies. Rabies control also involves vaccinating foxes, and this will be provided for once the disease enters the UK.

Inactivated rabies vaccine is available in the UK and has been used for many years for dogs intended for export. Elsewhere in the world, both live attenuated vaccines and inactivated vaccines are used on an annual basis.

BOOSTERS

Thanks to the development of effective canine vaccines by the pharmaceutical industry, most of the diseases described above are now uncommon in Europe and North America. The need for an annual booster is essential to keep up a high level of immunity where killed vaccines are used, and with live virus vaccines it probably does no harm to inject repeat doses every year. There has been a suggestion that thrombocytopenia occurs after repeated vaccine administration, but this does not seem a major problem and should not be used as an excuse for not making the once-a-year visit to the vet's. It is easy to become complacent about the absence of infectious disease in Jack Russells and it is false economy to overlook the need for re-vaccination.

INTERNAL PARASITES

ROUNDWORMS: the most common worms in puppies and dogs up to a year of age are *Toxocara* and *Toxascaris*. Puppies with roundworms start to pass worm eggs as early as three weeks, and most are passed when puppies are about seven weeks of age. This is the most dangerous time for the environment to be contaminated with eggs, especially for young children, who play with the puppies so that the slightly sticky worm eggs get on their hands, then lick their fingers and catch *zoonotic Toxocariasis*.

Adult dogs also pass roundworms, which have been seen emerging from the rectum of a nursing bitch that develops diarrhoea. Worms may also appear in the vomit if the worm moves forward from the intestine into the stomach by accident.

Control of worms depends on frequent dosing of young puppies from as early as two weeks of age, repeated every two to three weeks until three months old. To prevent puppies from carrying worms, the pregnant bitch can be wormed from the 42nd day of pregnancy with a safe, licensed wormer, such as fenbendazole. The worming treatment can be given daily to the bitch until the second day after all the puppies are born. Routine worming of adults twice a year with a combined tablet for roundworms and tapeworms is a good preventive measure. With young children in a household, even more frequent worm dosing may be advisable to reduce the risk of migrating roundworm larvae in the child, and possible eye damage.

TAPEWORMS: These are not known to kill dogs, but the appearance of a wriggling segment coming through the rectum, or moving on the tail hair, is enough to deter all but the most non-squeamish dog lover. Regular worming is needed to avoid the harm that dog worms can do to other creatures. The biggest threat is from the *Echinococcus* worm that a dog obtains if feeding from raw sheep offal. The worm is only six millimetres ($1/4$ in) long, but several thousand could live in one dog. If a human should swallow a segment of this worm it may move to the liver or lungs, in the same way as it would in the sheep. A major illness of the person would be the unpleasant result – another example of a zoonotic infection.

The most frequently found tapeworm is *Dipylidium caninum*. It is not a long tapeworm compared with the old-fashioned *Taenia* worms, but when segments break off they may be recognised, as they resemble grains of rice attached to the hairs of the dog's tail. The tapeworm has become more common in dogs and cats since the number

of fleas has increased, as the intermediate host of this worm is the flea or the louse. When dogs groom themselves, they attempt to swallow any crawling insect on the skin surface and in this way may become infested with tapeworms even though worming is carried out twice a year. Flea control is just as important as worming in preventing tapeworm infection. Three-monthly dosing with tablets is a good idea, less frequently if the dog is known to be away from sources of re-infection.

The other tapeworms of the *Taenia* species come from dogs eating raw rabbits (*T. serialis* or *pisiformis*) or from sheep, cattle or pig offal (*T. ovis*, *hydatigena* or *multiceps*).

HOOKWORM: Hookworms are less frequently a cause of trouble in the UK. They damage the intestine by using their teeth on the lining. *Uncinaria* may be the cause of poor condition and thinness. The other hookworm, *Ancylostoma*, may be found to be the reason for anaemia and weakness. Exercising dogs over grass used by wild foxes for excretion and scent marking allows the dog to re-infect itself with hookworm eggs.

GIARDIA: *Giardia* is a parasite that occurs in dogs in kennels. It should be investigated in dogs with diarrhoea that have come through quarantine. It is a protozoal organism that likes to live in stagnant surface water, and is of special interest because a similar strain is a cause of dysentery in humans, especially where water-borne infection is blamed for the illness. It may be necessary to routinely treat all dogs in a kennel with a drug such as fenbendazole to prevent a continuing problem.

OTHERS: Whipworms, found in the large intestine, may be identified when faeces samples are examined after mucoid dysentery affects a dog. Treatment is effective using a reliable anthelminthic. Heartworms are almost unknown in most of the UK, but are a great problem in other countries. Bladder worms are only detected when urine samples are examined. They are similar to whipworms and, fortunately, are rare. Any obscure illness in a dog should require the examination of fresh faeces samples.

EXTERNAL PARASITES

Ectoparasites may cause intense irritation and skin diseases from scratching and rubbing. In recent years, the cat flea has become by far the most common ectoparasite of the Jack Russell, but more traditional sarcoptic mange, demodectic mange, lice and ringworm skin infections do appear from time to time. Demodectic mange may have a hereditary basis associated with low immunity, as it is seen more frequently in certain strains and litters.

FLEAS: the flea's hop may never be seen in longer-haired dogs, but its presence may be detected by flea dirt or excreta containing dried blood. Grooming your dog over white paper or a light table-top may reveal black bits that have dark red blood stains if moistened. Once the flea dirt is found, a closer inspection of the dog may show fleas running though the coat at skin level. At one time, they preferred to live in the hair down the spine towards the tail head, but now they are found in the shorter hairs of the abdomen or the neck. This may be due to the fact that cat fleas are the most commonly found variety in UK dogs. Such fleas prefer a softer hair structure for their 'living space'. All fleas are temporary visitors who like to feed from the dog by biting to suck blood, but in their development and egg-laying stages they may live freely off the dog, thereby escaping some of the anti-parasitic dressing put on their host's coat. Re-infestation then becomes possible and many flea treatments appear to

Photo: Kim James, Badgerwood.

be ineffective unless the flea in the environment is eliminated at the same time as the flea on the animal.

There is a wide range of anti-parasitic sprays, washes and baths available and the Jack Russell owner may well be confused as to how and when to apply these. There is the further problem that some dogs seem able to carry a few fleas on them with very little discomfort, whilst other show intense irritation and bite pieces out of themselves in an attempt to catch the single flea. A cat in the household or one crossing the garden may drop flea eggs, and in a warm place these eggs can hatch out and develop into more fleas waiting to jump onto the dog. The new injection for cats that stops flea eggs hatching out due to chitin interference seems to constitute a major advance in flea control for the dog household with a cat in it.

Flea eggs and immature larvae may lie dormant for months, waiting to complete their development and become ready to bite. Adult fleas too can wait for months off an animal, until they are able to find a host to feed from, so treating the dog is only tackling part of the problem – the kennels or the house must be treated as well. Vacuum cleaning and easy-to-clean dog sleeping quarters help enormously in dealing with a flea infestation, once an environmental spray has been applied. The choice of aerosol spray, medicated bath, tablet by mouth or agent that stops larval development is a wide one, and experience will show which method is most suitable for each dog affected.

LICE: These may be found in the dog's coat occasionally, especially in a dog leading more of an outdoor life than the average pet dog. Lice spend their whole life on the dog, and fairly close contact between dogs is necessary to spread the parasites. Large numbers of lice cause intense irritation with hair loss. Biting

lice can produce anaemia when they are present in large enough numbers to remove blood continuously, at a rate similar to a bleeding ulcer. Liquid treatments applied as a total bath soak are best. Lice eggs can be transmitted from dog to dog on grooming brushes. The lice and their eggs are visible to the naked eye, and should be spotted during the normal grooming routine.

MANGE MITES: These mites cannot be seen during grooming. If they are suspected, scrapings from the skin surface are sent for examination under the microscope. The two forms of mange, *Sarcoptes* and *Demodex,* can be distinguished in this way, but bare skin patches of low-grade mange infection may at first seem similar when a dog is examined. A new blood test for *Sarcoptes* recently became available, and this helps to pinpoint why a dog may scratch a lot but not appear to have mange. There are a number of differences in the two forms of mange that need not be detailed here, but there is one simple distinction. Sarcoptic mange is very itchy and spreads from dog to dog, whilst demodectic mange in the older dog usually remains as a scaly hairless patch, and although an obvious blemish, does not cause a lot of itching. Anti-parasitic baths with pyrethroids or amitraz and topical applications of organo-phosphorous washes will have to be repeated, but are usually effective. The antibiotic Ivomectin in the food has also been used to treat sarcoptic mange, but great care is needed as fatalities have been recorded when this product is used in some dogs.

TICKS: Ticks are large enough not to be missed, and can be expected in those dogs working where sheep, wildlife etc. leave tick eggs about. Applications of pyrethroid or other 'spot' liquids on the neck and rump will keep ticks off a dog for a month. Baths are also effective. Ticks may be removed by first soaking them in vegetable oil, and then gently coaxing and lifting the tick's head away from the dog's skin.

CHEYLETIELLA: These cause surface irritation to dogs and intense itching to humans who happen to get bitten. The so-called 'moving dandruff' show up as white flecks on a black dog's skin, but may be more difficult to see on a light-coloured dog. Anti-parasitic shampoos will kill the surface feeder, but carrier dogs in kennels may show very few symptoms at all.

MALASEZZIA: This is a yeast-like surface organism that appears in dogs with low resistance to infection. A patchy coat and dull hair appearance should make the Jack Russell owner suspect the presence of this organism in unusually large numbers. Malasezzia occurs in moist skin areas in greatest numbers – places such as between the toes and under the tail are used for sample taking. Once identified, baths and general hygiene, with improved nutrition, help the dog to overcome the problem. The yeast will also be found in the ear canal and can multiply to cause a type of discharging otitis. Malasezzia may be shown to be present under the microscope on a stained smear, often in large numbers. Baths with a preparation of Miconazole are effective and should be repeated as often as the veterinary surgeon directs.

RINGWORM: Ringworm is found in dogs as a fungal infection of the hair. The signs of a 'ring' are not always present, and some dogs show quite a violent itchy skin response once infected. Cattle ringworm can be transmitted to country dogs. Ringworm spores can remain in the environment and old woodwork for a long time. Diagnosis by skin test is slow but reliable, as the 'Woods'lamp, which uses ultra-violet light,

does not identify all types of ringworm. Treatment with anti-fungal washes, or the antibiotic griseofulvin, may be used to eliminate the mycotic infection.

ACCIDENTS AND FIRST AID

I do not suggest that there are no other things that can be done as 'first aid' apart from the few simple procedures described here, but in most cases the sooner the patient gets to the veterinary surgery, the better the chance of a full recovery may be. For this reason, splinting broken bones is now out of favour, and more pain may be caused than if the dog is quickly transported to a place where any shock and pain can be treated professionally. X-rays will better show the nature of a fracture and the best method for treatment.

TRAFFIC ACCIDENTS: Jack Russells, being solidly compact dogs, may go underneath vehicles, and so tend to get severe leg and chest injuries if hit in front, or pelvic limb injuries if struck on the side. Fractures of the long bones of the leg are common

results of injuries with a fast-moving car. Any dog hit by a car will be distressed, and because of fright and pain will tend to bite, even when its familiar owners attempt to help. After an accident, first assess the injuries by noting any gaping holes and where blood is being lost. Do this before touching the dog's head. Some frightened dogs may try to run away at that point, so a lead or scarf round the neck will help to steady the dog, and a tape muzzle may have to be used before a dog is lifted into a vehicle for transport to the surgery.

A pressure bandage applied to a bleeding area is the best way of staunching blood flow, but improvisation with whatever cloth is to hand is acceptable in a life-saving situation. The dog may be breathing rapidly or gasping with 'air hunger' signs. In this case, the mouth and nostrils should be wiped free of dried blood or saliva to help the airway. If you suspect a spinal injury, slide a board under the dog before picking him up. Otherwise, a blanket is the best way of allowing two or more persons to pick up an injured dog without aggravating the injuries.

CHOKING AND VOMITING: Try to find out the cause of any sudden attack. Grass awns may enter the throat and airways in the summer months, and at any time of year, a dog that has been playing ball or stick retrieval games may get an obstruction at the back of the throat. Even a fine bamboo cane may become wedged across the upper molar teeth. Lamb bones are the most common foreign body found in the mouth. Poisonous substances may cause retching and vomiting, and thirsty dogs have been known to drink from toilet bowls, and so unsuspectingly to drink bleach and other cleaning substances.

Having initially looked for a foreign body, your first-aid measures should be to provide as good an air supply as possible. If there is any blistering or soreness of the lips or tongue, use honey or salad oil to coat the inflamed surfaces. A vomiting dog should be prevented from drinking water and regurgitating it as fast as it is swallowed. Ice cubes in a dish left to melt may be a way of helping the dog, as it will drink the iced water more slowly.

COLLAPSE AND UNCONSCIOUSNESS: As for a road accident, assess the dog before touching to determine the cause of the incident, so that appropriate first aid can be given. A dog running in a field on a warm day may have had a circulatory collapse; another dog convulsing may be throwing an epileptic fit; an elderly dog found semi-conscious in the morning after voiding urine and faeces may have had a stroke or vestibular disease. Acute enteritis, as with a virus or *Clostridia* infections, will also cause dogs to appear collapsed. Each condition in turn will need different treatment, but as a general rule, pull the tongue forward to ensure there is an airway to the lungs, keep the animal cool and avoid unnecessary noise and commotion. Look for any drugs or poisons that the dog may have swallowed;

gently feel the left side for gas distending the abdomen – does it feel gas-filled? Look at the pupils of the eyes and their response to a bright light. The veterinary surgeon will be better able to deal with the situation if a timetable of events and any contributing factors can be given in a concise manner.

WASP STINGS: Stings occur more often in the late summer. Usually the foot swells rapidly, or if the dog has caught a wasp in his mouth, the side of the face swells up and the eye may become partly shut. Vinegar is a traditional remedy to apply to the stung area. If an antihistamine tablet is available, this can be given to the dog immediately to stop further swelling.

Other biting flies cause swellings on the body and may be the cause of the 'hot spots'or acute moist eczemas that Jack Russells can suffer from. Calamine lotions cool the skin, but the dog should be discouraged from attacking his own skin. If licked, the calamine causes vomiting.

SHOCK: This occurs to a greater or lesser extent with nearly all accidents. Keep the patient warm, wrapping a blanket, coat or wool garment around his body. Unless you have reasons to think an anaesthetic will be given, or other contraindications exist, such as throat damage, offer fluids by mouth in small quantities. Oral rehydration solutions can be obtained from your veterinary surgeon, and a packet should be kept in every emergency first-aid kit. As an alternative, a solution of half a teaspoon of salt and half a teaspoon of bicarbonate of soda dissolved in a litre of water may be given a few dessertspoonfuls at a time. There are certain conditions, such as acute pancreatitis collapse, where nothing must be given by mouth.

SKIN DISEASES

PARASITIC SKIN DISEASES: Fleas are probably still the most common problem, but there are many other causes of skin disorders. Flea bites may not be obvious, especially in a dense-coated breed. Once a dog becomes sensitised to the proteins injected by the flea when it first bites, any subsequent contact with flea saliva may bring on an itchy rash, even though no live fleas are found on the dog. The other causes of parasitic skin disease have already been outlined in the section on external parasites.

OTHER PRURITIC SKIN CONDITIONS: Anal sac irritation will cause a dog to nibble at the hair around the tail base, or to lick and nibble anywhere around the hindquarters. The glands may be so impacted that they cannot be emptied out during the dog's normal straining to pass faeces. An infected lining of one or both sacs may be the cause of irritation, and this can often be detected by a fruity odour to the sac's contents, or, at its worst, a smell like rotten meat.

Bacterial dermatoses result from multiplication of skin bacteria such as *Staph. intermedius*. Red blotches and ring-like marks around a central pustule are most clearly seen when the hairless areas of the abdomen are inspected. Skin swabs may be used to identify the bacteria present, and this information can then be used to choose the most appropriate antibiotic for the infection causing the irritation.

HAIR LOSS AND ALOPECIA: A Jack Russell's coat is normally shed twice a year, but sometimes the growth of new hair is delayed and the coat appears thin and lifeless, and if it is groomed excessively, bare patches develop. Investigations into the possibility of thyroid disease may be needed when there is

Photo courtesy: Mary Strom.

a failure of hair to grow. Cushing's disease is another possible cause, especially in the older terrier with an increased thirst and a rounded abdomen. Other hormonal skin diseases may cause symmetrical hair loss in the flanks of a bitch, or bare tail-head areas (stud tail) in some dogs. Feminisation in the older male dog will have hair loss as one of the signs of a Sertoli cell tumour. Veterinary advice should be sought.

DIGESTIVE SYSTEM DISORDERS

SICKNESS AND DIARRHOEA: Occasional sickness is not a cause for concern in the younger dog. The dog is adapted to feeding from a wide range of different foods, and part of his protection against food poisoning is the ability to reject unsuitable foods by returning them from the stomach by reflex vomiting. If there is a yellow colouration to the vomit, it means that the bile from the liver that normally passes into the small intestine after leaving the bile duct,

has for some reason been passed forward to enter the stomach. The bitter bile acids will cause reflex vomiting as soon as they reach the stomach wall and will be vomited up together with any food left in the stomach.

Bacterial infections such as those of *Salmonella and Campylobacter* can only be detected by the culture of faeces. *Helicobacter* are known stomach bacteria that have become of recent comparative interest, but Helicobacteriosis is not known as a cause of disease in dogs. *Clostridia,* which are spore-forming resistant bacteria, have been known to cause fatal toxic enteritis. The importance of strains of *E. coli* as a cause of dog diarrhoea is an interesting development. Renewed interest in this organism, that was at one time thought to be harmless, is accompanied by a number of human deaths from the 0157 strain in cooked and raw meat. Certain viruses are also known to cause gastro-enteritis.

Repeated sickness, starting off with recognisable food followed by slime, or food followed by mucus alone, is a more serious sign. It may be associated with obstructions due to a foreign body or to infection such as pyometra or hepatitis. Some outbreaks of diarrhoea will start with food being vomited, as it will stimulate the intestine. As soon as food enters the small intestine, the stomach empties itself by reflex vomiting any food remaining within the stomach. Sometimes a reversal of normal flow of food will cause the appearance of a faecal vomit.

Diarrhoea is the passage of frequent loose or unformed faeces. Diarrhoea is associated with infections and irritation of the intestine. The rapid transit of food taken in by mouth means that water cannot be absorbed by the large intestine, and a soft or runny product results from the incomplete digestion and water re-absorption. When blood is present, it may appear as streaks from the large intestine. If blackish and foul smelling, it

means that the blood has come from the small intestine and has been subjected to some of the digestive fluids. The condition is then known as dysentery.

Chronic diarrhoea is a problem where the looseness of faeces lasts more than 48 hours. It may be associated with malabsorption, where the lining of the intestine is incapable of absorbing digested food. There are other diseases such as food intolerances, bacterial overgrowth, lymphoid and other tumours that may cause maldigestion, where there is some failure of the digestive juices to break down the food. Other causes are Exocrine Pancreatic Insufficiency (EPI), inflammatory bowel diseases or any disturbance in gastric or liver function. Investigations by the veterinary surgeon will include blood tests and faecal laboratory examinations. These may be followed by X-rays or endoscope examinations.

The treatment of sickness and diarrhoea involves, firstly, withholding solid food for 24 hours, giving small quantities of replacement fluids as soon as the dog stops vomiting – proprietary electrolyte fluids are probably best. Then, introduce a highly digestible food in dogs – low-fat is best – in small quantities, about one third of the normal amount fed on the second day of the illness. The amount should be increased slowly until, by the fourth day, a full ration of food is given again. In the recovery period, fats should be avoided, as well as milk and dairy products, because of the dog's inability to digest lactose.

GASTRIC DILATION: This disease is better known as 'bloat', and can be a problem in any breed, but it is fortunately rare in terriers. Greedy feeders that swallow air as they gulp down their food are considered at greatest risk, but it does seem more associated with dogs that have large deep chests and thus loosely suspended stomachs.

Photo courtesy: Mary Strom.

The bloated stomach may rotate as a torsion or volvulus, and become a Gastric Dilation and Volvulus (GDV) condition, which means an acute emergency. The dog needs to be rushed to the veterinary surgery for treatment for shock and for the deflation of the stomach. Affected dogs look uncomfortable, become depressed and look at their flanks with expressions of disbelief. At first, the left side just behind the ribs is the only side to bulge; percussion with the fingertips will produce a drum-like resonance over the left rib-cage edge and over the distended abdomen behind. Within a few hours, both sides of the abdomen appear distended behind the rib-cage, the dog becomes more uncomfortable and lies down a lot as the pain increases. The gas-filled stomach presses on the diaphragm, restricting the breathing; the colour of the tongue becomes more purplish, and breaths are more frequent and quite shallow. Sometime at this stage, the weight of the enlarging spleen attached to the greater curvature of the gas-filled stomach makes the stomach twist in a clockwise direction. The signs of discomfort become more noticeable as the stomach's exit to the oesophagus is pinched off by a 180-degree rotation. If a stomach tube is passed through the mouth down the oesophagus at this stage, the tube can be pressed down no further than just beyond the entrance level of the oesophagus into the abdomen. No gas will pass back up the tube, even though the stomach is still tight-filled with gas.

Emergency treatment at the veterinary surgery will usually mean setting up an intravenous drip to deal with the shock. Frequently, a laparotomy will be necessary to empty the stomach or to provide a means of fixing the stomach to the abdominal wall, so that an adhesion will make it less likely that the gas distension will appear again. A number of operation techniques are used; some involve suturing the stomach wall to a rib, whilst others rely on a tube to vent gas from the stomach. The aim is to have a permanent adhesion to prevent rotation of the stomach at a later date. Some veterinary surgeons believe that feeding a complete canned food diet to the dog is the best preventive available.

Photo: Kim James, Badgerwood.

CONSTIPATION: This disorder usually occurs either through the dog eating too many bones, when a chalky residue clogs up the rectum, or, in older male dogs, it may be associated with enlargement of the prostate gland. Occasionally, a tumour inside the rectum will cause straining and apparent constipation. Treatment with oily lubricants and enemas should be followed by high-fibre diets. Soluble fibre, as found in oatmeal, is thought to add to the moist faecal bulk and thus to retain water from the large intestine lumen so that the faeces are not bone-hard and painful to pass. Allow exercise, or place the dog in the garden 30 minutes after feeding, as this will stimulate the reflexes for normal defecation.

BREEDING AND REPRODUCTION

There are no specific problems in the terrier breeds, and both mating and whelping should proceed with the minimum of trouble. False pregnancy seven to 10 weeks after the end of the heat seems to be an increasingly frequent problem in terriers, and behaviour and temperament problems may be encountered at this time. There are several effective treatments (see Chapter 11 'Breeding Jack Russells').

THE OLDER DOG

GERIATRIC CARE: The Jack Russell breed has a long life-span, commonly living to 12 years and often going on to 18 years or more, provided they avoid arthritis and injuries. Some of the oldest dogs are the leanest dogs, so dietary control helps if you wish your dog to live longer. After about seven years of age, it may be of advantage to divide the daily ration into two small feeds to help absorption and digestion, and any tendency to overweight must be checked – regular weighing helps to control the dietary intake. The older dog will use up less energy in exercise, and if housed for most of the day, fewer calories will be burned up to keep the dog warm. Some reduction in calorie intake is desirable, and there are special diets prepared for the older dog that are higher in fibre and lower in energy than the diet for the younger dog,

219

Keep a careful watch on the condition of the mouth, as breath odour is one of the first signs of dental disease or decay of food trapped between the gums and 'ledges' of tartar that may have built up on the teeth. Terriers may have cracked teeth from chewing bones or iron bars earlier in their life, and only in old age does the tooth root become infected, followed by the development of an abscess. The back upper molar teeth are often affected, and an abscess will show as a swelling immediately below the eye if the carnassial tooth has infected roots. Chewing as a form of jaw exercise is one method of keeping the teeth healthy, but when there is a build-up of plaque on the tooth surface, cleaning the teeth using an ultrasonic scaler, followed by a machine polisher, is the better way of keeping a healthy mouth.

Monitor the length of your dog's nails, since less exercise and possible arthritis sometimes lead the older dog to put less weight on the affected leg, and nail overgrowth occurs. Be careful not to cut into the quick or live part of the nail.

URINARY INCONTINENCE: This is one of the problems found in many older dogs. Leakage from the bladder, resulting in damp patches in the bedding overnight, may be remedied by taking up the water bowl after 7pm to prevent evening drinking. Also effective is the use of one of the sympathomimetic group of drugs to promote bladder storage. A urine sample should be examined: sometimes mild cystitis bacteria will be found, and treatment with an appropriate antibiotic will reduce bladder sensitivity and storage will be better. If large quantities of urine are being voided day and night, then investigation of urine concentrations and blood biochemistry tests are necessary to look for major disease. Diabetes Insipidus or Mellitus, Cushing's disease, liver disease and nephrosis may all be first indicated by the dog being 'incontinent' when left shut indoors for more than a few hours. Blood tests are necessary to distinguish many of these conditions in the older Jack Russell.

13 BREED ASSOCIATED DISEASES

As the Jack Russell Terrier breed originated from a working strain of hunting dogs, a sound dog with stamina and a strong constitution was essential to fulfil its duties. Fitness involved good eyesight, rapid movement and a large lung and heart capacity for active work. Only the best performers were used for breeding, so many disorders were avoided. The smaller terrier breeds were all ultimately related, and by introducing blood from Smooth Fox Terriers, Wire-Haired Fox Terriers and Sealyham Terriers, inherited eye disorders may have been introduced inadvertently. Mixing several genetic groups should allow for improved health, but a recessive mode of inheritance may allow an old problem to reappear in certain litters from time to time.

INHERITED EYE CONDITIONS

CATARACT
Cataract is defined as any opaqueness in the lens or the capsule surrounding the lens. The young terrier is rarely affected by cataract, unless there has been some injury to the eye that causes the lens to become opaque. Any penetrating injury of the cornea, such as a blackthorn spike, may cause a cataract to form. A blunt injury sustained in a fight may produce uveitis of the iris, and this too leads to cataract.

The most commonly found eye disorder in the old Jack Russell is a cataract. Metabolic diseases such as diabetes may result in cataracts; toxins and some drugs can also produce cataract, as can inappropriate diets, and there is always the natural ageing process in the delicate parts of the eye. Accurate diagnosis and a discussion on the advisability of removing a lens with cataract should be considered for even the elderly dog.

PRIMARY LENS LUXATION
Subluxation and luxation of the lens are conditions where the ligament or zonule that holds the lens at the centre of the eye weakens, the lens lacks support and a partial displacement may occur. Both eyes may be affected, but usually one eye shows disease in advance of the other. The displaced lens may eventually become a cataract, and the eye opaque. Frequently, the loosened lens falls forward to touch the inner side of the cornea, with oedema seen as a white patch that suddenly develops on the cornea, at the front of the eye. There is potentially a risk of fluid building up within the eye (glaucoma) after the lens luxates. Once again, accurate diagnosis of the condition may save the sight of the eye – even when one eye is opaque, having the lens removed before irreversible changes take place can save the second eye. Modern techniques give good results, and

although the procedure is relatively expensive, a number of veterinary centres perform this service. A second opinion is always advised if there is any doubt about a sudden blindness.

EYE CONDITIONS WITH A HEREDITARY BASIS

EYELID DISORDERS
The eyelids normally protect the sensitive surface of the eye. Any deviation of eyelid structure can lead to a red eye, excessive watering and, through rubbing, blindness after corneal ulceration.

Distichiasis is an eyelash condition where the eyelashes have an extra row encroaching upon the cornea. Inward turning of the upper or lower lids, known as entropion, may be an inherited defect of the eyelid structure, but it is injury to the eye that may most often cause the problem in this breed: seen as a continuously watering eye, the eyelids may be found to be inward-turning at the site of an old scar. If diagnosed, the severe cases will need surgery to evert the eyelid edge.

Ectropion (the opposite condition to entropion) is a looseness of the eyelids with undue exposure of the pink lining of the lid, and it too, may develop after a facial injury. Ectropion can be a hereditary disease in some breeds with loose skin on the head, but in the terrier breeds, it is usually the result of injury. The lower lid edge can be torn, and if not repaired by stitching, will lead to a loose fit and the ectropion problem as described.

RETINAL ATROPHY
Retinal atrophy is now well known as a cause of poor vision and blindness in working gun dogs and collies. It is not normally found in the young or middle-aged Jack Russell. Retinal atrophy is normally only seen in the Jack Russell over ten years of age, and degenerative changes in the retina may lead to eventual total blindness. Regular inspections of the older dog's eyes and attention to diet may help to delay the onset of such a condition.

RETINAL DYSPLASIA
A severe eye disease, at one time common in Sealyham Terriers, causes haemorrhage and loss of sight in quite young puppies. It is not known to be a problem in Jack Russells, but the possibility of this gene having been introduced should always be remembered. Puppies may be found to be blind from birth, as was seen in the Sealyham Terrier and, to a lesser extent, in the Bedlington Terrier. Milder forms are seen with the ophthalmoscope as folds of the retina, and in some breeds 'rosettes' are characteristically found in the multi-focal form, but these are less likely in terrier-sized animals.

BONE AND JOINT DISEASES WITH HEREDITARY INFLUENCES

CRUCIATE LIGAMENT RUPTURE
The stifle, or knee joint, is not robustly constructed, but as long as terriers are kept well muscled and not roughly exercised, there is not a great risk of this injury. Once a dog becomes overweight, the stifle, which depends on a number of ligaments and cartilages to hold it together and give free movement, may become at risk. The stifle is used in jumping and for forward propulsion, so overweight dogs that are suddenly asked to perform tasks, even those as simple as jumping out of four-wheel drive vehicle or hatchback rear door, may land heavily and damage the ligaments. Similarly, when the older dog chases around in a field with a faster animal, sudden turning may lead to separation of the ligament and a sudden lameness.

The cruciate ligaments are those crossing

the centre of the stifle joint, and there are two other collateral ligaments that support the sides of the joint. The kneecap, or patella, also has ligaments that run at the front of the joint, and these too can fail to support the stifle joint, throwing a greater strain on the two ligaments at the centre. It is usually the front ligament in the centre of the stifle joint – the anterior cruciate ligament – that takes the greatest strain when the dog jumps or turns awkwardly and this may tear or, at the worst, completely break in half. The tearing of the ligament happens because a weakness has been developing in the fibres, so after partial tearing and stretching, the ligament ruptures. The result is a very lame dog. Often the stifle joint is so unstable that the two bone ends that form the joint can be slid over each other. This instability is used in the 'draw forward' test. Some ligaments will heal themselves in dogs weighing less than 10 kg (1.5 stones), with rest. But many dogs will require a surgical operation to repair the torn ligament. There are a number of techniques employed, but most require a ligament implant inserted through or around the joint. Provided the operation is done before arthritic changes develop in the joint surface, the results are very good, since the joint is stabilised again.

PATELLAR LUXATION

Otherwise known as slipped kneecap, this is a congenital abnormality especially found in terriers with bowed legs. In the Jack Russell, the displacement is always medial; the patella, in slipping to the inside of the knee, 'locks up' the joint and the dog has to hold the leg up high. Often, as the muscle spasm weakens or the affected leg is gently manipulated, the patella falls back into the central groove and the dog can again run. The patella normally runs in a groove, called the trochlea, at the end of the femur, and attaches to the tibial crest. The tibial crest may also be abnormally

situated, pulling the patella out of the straight line. Affected dogs may be intermittently or persistently lame.

Surgical correction is usually essential. The operation to deepen the groove is known as sulcoplasty, and the attaching ligaments may also have to be released on the inside and tightened up on the outer side of the joint. Another procedure is to transplant the tibial crest.

HIP DISEASES

PERTHE'S COXA PLANA OR CALVE-LEGGE PERTHE'S DISEASE: A not uncommon condition in short-legged terrier breeds, this is the cause of many such dogs running on three legs but walking on four legs when the pace is slower. The normal round-shaped head of the femur that sits neatly in the hip socket as a 'ball and socket' joint has a defect. Often, before birth (as it may be a congenital defect) the blood vessel supplying the growing head of the bone fails to provide sufficient nourishment. The head of the femur has a flattened surface and cannot run smoothly in the hip joint socket. Some dogs can manage without corrective surgery, but with others an operation becomes essential. Early use of the limb after the operation is advised as too much scar tissue may cause lameness due to reduced range of movement in the hip or pressure on the sciatic nerve.

HIP DYSPLASIA: This is not generally considered a problem in Jack Russell Terriers, and the breed does not appear in the official score list maintained by the Kennel Club. The problem of Hip Dysplasia was a major consideration in the breeding of many larger breeds, and is still widespread, despite years of selective breeding. Hip Dysplasia is not entirely hereditary. Environmental factors such as feeding, exercise and even the

223

position the young dog is made to sit in may all may be responsible for up to 60 per cent of the occurrence of the hip dysplasia changes as seen on X-ray, as the disease has only a moderate heritability of 30 to 45 per cent.

OTHER JOINT DISEASES

OSTEOARTHRITIS

Not necessarily a hereditary disease, osteoarthritis is more common in active dogs that have received small joint injuries in their earlier life. Usually seen in the older dog, this condition, which limits joint movement, starts as an erosive joint disease due to a loss of the cartilage on the joint surface. As the disease progresses, additional bone may be laid down round the edge of the joint, possibly as a result of inflammation and in an attempt to support the joint. The disease develops slowly, leading to lameness, pain, the grating feeling known as crepitus, and then to joint instability. The joint feels thickened from the outside, and there is limited movement when the joint is bent to stretch it or flex it. If a joint is not moving, then the muscles around it weaken or atrophy so that the leg becomes wasted.

X-rays should be taken to assess the degree of new bone building up around the joint. A management plan for the dog can be drawn up; pain control is the first priority in treatment. Osteoarthritis is thought to be aggravated by the dog being overweight, and dietary control is an important way of helping a dog with joint pain or swelling.

OSTEOCHONDROSIS

A disease with a hereditary basis, this is seen in many large and giant breeds of dogs. The Jack Russell is unlikely to suffer from elbow osteochondrosis, which may be detected in breeds such as the German Shepherd. Rapid bone growth is considered a factor in delaying the mineralisation of the cartilage at the growing joint ends of the long bones. Restricting exercise and not feeding a puppy to full appetite demand may help to reduce the incidence of osteochondrosis. Supplements should not be given, as most dog foods are balanced and contain sufficient Vitamin D. Calcium supplements are now very much frowned upon as they upset the calcium-phosphorus ratio of the diet so bone formation cannot proceed normally.

SKIN DISORDER WITH A POSSIBLE INHERITED BASIS

ATOPIC DERMATITIS

The terrier breeds are fairly resistant to skin disease, and most skin problems in the breed are probably the result of skin parasite infections. There is no known hereditary basis for such infections. The nature of the short coat and bare abdomen skin may lead to contact allergy through exposure to plant and other allergens. There is also a dietary type of skin allergy often associated with wheat gluten. Atopy is the name of an inherited type of skin allergy where dogs develop rashes and itchiness. The allergy can be dealt with, but bacteria such as *Staphylococcus intermedius* may cause redness, and this encourages the growth of Malasezzia, especially in the moister skin folds of the body. Jack Russell Terriers with white coats seem more prone to skin disease than those with predominantly dark coats.

14 *SHOW KENNELS*

Until comparatively recently, there was little interchange of stud dogs between breeders of Jack Russell Terriers in the UK. A strain would be established in one part of the country which could loosely be called line-bred, in that the terriers would all come from the same foundation stock, with breeding being carried out by a group of enthusiasts in the same area interchanging stud dogs and puppies. Only rarely did that group go out of its own circle, and then usually always to the same alternative strain. Thus in several different areas of the country very homozygous lines were established.

The terriers of the South West, the South, the Midlands and the North East all had their own distinctive look, just as, on a smaller scale, the strains of different breeders can be recognised by the educated eye. Probably the most far-reaching effect of Kennel Club recognition of the Parson Jack Russell Terrier is that, as people have travelled throughout the country to attend shows on a regular basis, so they have widened their horizons with regard to buying puppies and using stud dogs. In the long term, this should be for the good of the breed. In the short term, however, this random breeding leads to all sorts of problems – problems which, it must be stressed, were always there, but were hidden deep within each strain. Outcrossing

to other lines that carry the same fault has brought out these unwanted faults. This is no bad thing, in that it is then possible, with openness and sensible breeding, to eliminate them from the breed, but this only occurs when breeders are open and honest, and admit their problems.

The Parson Jack Russell has seen an explosion in ownership in recent years. Most of these new owners will, at some period, wish to breed. It is imperative that before taking this step they should consider not just their own bitch and her faults and virtues, but also research her pedigree in depth. All experienced breeders know that some lines, however excellent individually, just do not 'nick' together. Modern Parson Jack Russells come from such diverse origins that it is not surprising that different strains do not necessarily combine together satisfactorily. Random use of a dog, just because he is successful in the show ring, does not bring about long-term improvement within a breed. On the contrary, it merely increases the variety of type within that breed. The mark of a good stud dog is that he can 'stamp his type' on a selection of bitches, so that his progeny are recognisable.

INFLUENTIAL STUD DOGS
In considering the Parson Jack Russell, as recognised by the UK Kennel Club, one dog

Ridley Robber Of Belmorr: Top Stud Dog 1991-1996.

Photo: Sheila Atter.

stands out under this criterion as the most influential stud dog. Under the points system used by the weekly British newspaper *Dog World*, Isobel Morrison's Robbie (more formally, Ridley Robber of Belmorr) is head and shoulders above the rest, winning the title Top Stud in the years 1991-6 consecutively. He is the sire of many winners, and perhaps more importantly his own sons have gone on to sire top winners. The first Champion in the breed, Mark and Tina Allen's Winnie the Witch of Hardytown is his grand-daughter (and her sire, Clive Harrison's Ardencote Top Notch, looks like taking over his father's mantle); the first Champion male, Cass Samways' Cassacre Boatswain is a son of Isobel Morrison's Robbie son, Glenholm Erik of Belmorr, whilst the third Champion, first Championship Show Group Winner (and top winning dog for three years before CC status was awarded to the breed), Gladys and Douglas Philps' Mindlen Hoolet of Muhlross, is a Robbie son.

Robbie has produced many other winning progeny at Championship show level. The first bitch to win BoS at Crufts Dog Show was his daughter, Ridley Replica; the first

Junior Warrant winner in the breed was his son, Mindlen Hairy Minnow. More important, for the long-term strength of the breed, is that all of these winners are from totally different bitch lines.

However, just as Robbie has proved himself to be not merely the sire of winners, but also the sire of successful stud dogs, his own sire and grandsire should not be ignored, since they too have had a very important part to play in the development of the breed. Ridley Red Alert (Hursley Pilot ex Ridley Redwing) won the title of Top Stud Dog in 1990 (the year the breed was first recognised by the KC). His daughter, Ridley Rebecca of Cassacre, won the overall Top Dog title that same year, and she went on to produce the first Champion male, Cassacre Boatswain (sired by a Robbie son). A repeat mating produced his son, Susan Haigh's Ridley Renegade of Westbeck, who, although little shown, was to prove a very influential sire, particularly for George Simpson's Howlbeck kennel. Bred three times to Ground Hill Midge, he produced a series of winners, including Howlbeck Marine Diver, Muddy Rastus, and the lovely bitch, Howlbeck Mighty Mandy. Many of the most

Clystlands Legend: A representative of the well-known Clystlands kennel which was founded on West Country lines.

successful terriers bred from Howlbeck bitches go back either to this mating or to crosses to the two Robbie sons, Mindlen Hairy Minnow and Ardencote Top Notch. Ch. Winnie the Witch of Hardytown and the CC-winning Fellshied Top Talent are both by Top Notch out of Howlbeck-bred litter sisters, whilst Howlbeck Izzi-Rite for Jagen, also a CC winner, is by the very successful Howlbeck Piper out of Howlbeck Just Rosie, a grand-daughter of Renegade. Similarly, Howlbeck Matuka Mindlen (BoB, Crufts 1995) is by Hairy Minnow out of Howlbeck Pebbles, litter sister to Piper.

Red Alert's litter sister, Ridley Red Flight, was the foundation bitch of the Foxhazel (originally Redwood) kennel of Jann Ibbett. Garon's Oakley Sailor mated to Red Flight

Quarrymist Mr Fudge for Pacolito, bred by Geoff and Andrea Roden.

Photo: A. C. Roden.

Ardencote Tittletattle.

Photo: Sheila Atter.

produced Redwood Pilot, a dog who has influenced the breed both in the UK, and, perhaps more significantly, in Europe, especially through his son, Finnish & Estonian Ch. Redwood Tackles Ridley.

In the ten years since the breed was recognised, the type of dog shown has altered quite markedly. Very few of the terriers to be seen in the ring today can really be called the 'old-fashioned' sort. Almost all of the successful show winners are a combination of different lines: the smaller, showier Howlbeck breeding combined with the more traditional Ridley or Clystlands lines seems to be the favoured combination, which gives a smart eye-catching Jack Russell. Amongst others bred this way are Quarrymist Mr Fudge for Pacolito (1 CC), by Clystlands Reveller out of Howlbeck Principle Dance of Quarrymist, litter sister to Matuka. The Clystlands/Ridley combination which produced Ridley Rebecca and Renegade has given, in Mr Fudge, a fairly 'typey' terrier who has nonetheless inherited from his Howlbeck dam a positive attitude to the show-ring.

Clystlands Reveller is another terrier who, whilst not being a very enthusiastic show

dog, has more than started to prove his worth as a stud dog. Apart from Mr Fudge, he has sired two very successful youngsters in the litter sisters Alne Pirton Gorse and Alne Withycombe at Hindlewalt, out of Clystlands Wayfarer. Ruth Hussey-Wilford's very long-established Clystlands kennel is founded on old West Country lines, mainly through the breeding of Sid Churchill and Bernard Tuck. In recent years she has gone out to other kennels, perhaps most successfully in the litter out of her Crufts BoB winner Clystlands Crackerjack to Ripling Revel. Clystlands Reveller and his litter sister, Frolic, have both been good producers.

From Jan Wood's Ardencote kennel has come a steady stream of 'typey' dogs that have combined several lines. Like his sire, Ridley Robber of Belmorr, Ardencote Top Notch (out of the top-winning bitch Ardencote Tanager) seems to be able to add a dash of quality to a variety of soundly constructed but quite ordinary bitches. In addition to his Champion and CC-winning daughters, he is the grandsire of the dual CC-winning bitch Ardencote Tittletatle, who has a very interesting pedigree. Her dam,

Ch. Clystlands Belinda Ridley: Top Brood Bitch 1990/91.
Photo: Sheila Atter.

Ardencote Trisco, is out of Ridley Renaissance (a Robbie grand-daughter) by Top Notch, whilst her sire, Ardencote Twiss, has a high proportion of West Country breeding through the Clystlands, Somerwest

and Galebern lines. In addition, both Twiss and Trisco go back to Ardencote Tanager. The Ardencote kennel is now producing quite a distinctive type, with Twiss, Trooper, Tristar and Tarboosh all out of the same mould.

INFLUENTIAL BROOD BITCHES

Whilst a successful stud dog is the half of the partnership that is remembered, a good brood bitch is worth her weight in gold. Often it seems that the really successful bitches from a show point of view do not go on to produce puppies that equal or surpass their own achievements. Rather, it is usually the less flamboyant bitch, soundly constructed and sensibly bred, who will herself go on to breed the future stars. However, the successful showgirls should not be completely disregarded – often their qualities will surface again in their grandchildren or even great-grandchildren.

Bitches that can be found back in the pedigrees of many of today's Parson Jack Russell Terriers include Ardencote Tinker, Clystlands Belinda Ridley, Cobstone Lucy of Clystlands, Exmoor True, Galebern Twinkle, Ground Hill Midge, Heliwar Skat of

Fin. Ch. Barsetta Smitten.

Glenholm Erik Of Belmorr.

Photo: John Valentine.

Glenholm, Howlbeck Pebbles, Raeburn Suzie and Somervale Jessie. None of these were high-flyers in the show ring, yet between them they have bred Top Dogs (*Dog World* Competition) Ardencote Tanager, Ridley Rebecca of Cassacre, Mindlen Mizpah, Crufts BoBs Clystlands Cracker Jack, Ch. Mindlen Hoolet of Muhlross and Howlbeck Matuka Mindlen. They are behind all the Champions to date and all of the CC winners.

BREEDING TODAY

Obviously, individual breeders have different approaches to breeding programmes. Some have a long-term plan, others flit about from top-winning dog to top-winning dog, but may be lucky enough to produce a high-flyer. Breeders are producing individual dogs of quality, but very few have, as yet, a recognisable kennel type. Whilst this is leading to instant success, such breeders will

Hoelio Calum Of Glenholm.

Photo courtesy: Anne Milne.

Glenholm Crazlie For Bridgegard.
Photo courtesy: Anne Milne.

almost certainly find it very difficult to stay at the top in the long term, because these randomly bred winners are unlikely to produce terriers as good as themselves. Breeders will need to produce several more generations, line-breeding to their best stock, in order to produce a consistent type.

Breeders who have, in the main, stuck to very close line-breeding and have consequently established a very recognisable kennel type, are Ray and Mary Cutler of the Trumpmoor affix. They have based their breeding programme on West Country stock, and their terriers all work with the Exmoor Hunt (the old 'Stars of the West' – one of the packs the Parson himself supported). The CC-winning Trumpmoor Exmoor Truelass is by their consistent winner Able out of the lovely bitch Tamar, and is Exmoor-bred for several generations.

Where breeders can work together, exchanging stud dogs and running on puppies, it is possible to recreate the opportunities open to a larger kennel, whilst each individual only keeps a small number of terriers. Such is the case with the Glenholm, Belmorr and Cassacre kennels of Anne Milne, Isobel Morrison and Cass Samways respectively. Based almost entirely on Ridley and Heliwar breeding and with very occasional outcrosses, to Blencathra, Somerwest and Bridevale studs, they have produced consistent stock – most successfully in Ch. Cassacre Boatswain, by Glenholm Erik of Belmorr out of Ridley Rebecca of Cassacre.

Two kennels that are beginning to produce recognisable types (although very different from each other) are the Fellshied kennels of Norman Handy and Barbara Richards's Barsettas. The latter, living right down in the south-west of Cornwall, finds it difficult to attend UK shows with any regularity, but has exported terriers very successfully to Europe, Australia and to the USA. Having brought in foundation stock of Kenterfox, Somerwest, Tutmur, Foxwarren, Hoelio and, more latterly, Trumpmoor breeding, Barbara has blended these very different lines into a very recognisable Barsetta type – perhaps a little smaller than those usually found in the UK show ring, but ideally suited to Hunt Shows, and to the USA and Australian exhibitors, who prefer a slightly neater terrier.

Norman Handy is a successful exhibitor, who again has taken stock from different breeders and is turning out a succession of show winners. His two foundation bitches, Howlbeck Tina Turner and Ardencote Treat, came from very different lines, but by judicious use of good stud dogs (Ch. Cassacre Boatswain, Ardencote Top Notch, Clystlands Aston Rebel and Quarrymist Mr Fudge for Pacolito) he has produced three CC-winning bitches in Fellshied Telltale Top Talent, and Tiara, and a youngster who has already taken Best Puppy awards, and will surely go on to greater things, in Listen To Us.

Ten years is a very short time in considering the overall picture of the breed, yet it has been said that, on average, show exhibitors only sustain an interest in their hobby for around five years. Some of course are involved for decades, others lose heart after a year or two. Every single litter that is bred can make a contribution to the overall picture of the breed. It is impossible to mention all successful breeders, and any sort of list is quickly out of date as some give up and others come to the fore. Those who have

yet to purchase their first puppy may, in the fullness of time, prove to be the breeders of the most significant dog in the history of the Parson Jack Russell Terrier! Thorough and thoughtful research into the history of the breed and the qualities introduced into the various lines by the stud dogs and brood bitches used by others, can only make their own decisions easier. It will also lead to a more consistent overall standard of the breed than is seen at present.

USA

In the United States, Kennel Club recognition for the Jack Russell Terrier came on January 1 1998. 2,019 dogs went from the American Kennel Club's Foundation Stock Service into the American Kennel Club main registry, so there was no lack of terriers registered. Registrations continue to grow, mainly from litter registrations, and a few from dogs that had American Kennel Club-registered parents but, for whatever reason,

were not originally registered.

The one thing that that American breed clubs had in common was the pursuit of a high-quality, well-structured terrier, regardless of whether the pedigree was from Kennel Club-registered stock or registered with the other Jack Russell breed clubs. Because of the immense popularity of the dog and the desire for quality, breeders from both Jack Russell breed clubs imported a great many of their foundation dogs from the UK.

The UK Kennel Club recognised the breed in 1990, eight years before American Kennel Club recognition. For this reason, us breeders continued to import both dogs bred from Kennel Club-registered dogs and those bred from non-registered dogs. Those dogs now make up the foundation for the breed in the United States, and, genetically speaking, the longer recognition time has probably helped to serve the breed in allowing a wider base from which to breed.

Ailsa Crawford, owner and founder of the American Jack Russell Terrier Club of America, used this picture, showing Jack Russells and Hunt Terriers to advertise her Hamilton kennel in the 1970s.

Photo courtesy: Mary Strom.

Paul Ross judging one of the early Jack Russell Terrier Club of America shows.

INFLUENTIAL LINES

Some of the imported lines that have had the most influence in the American breeding programmes are those of: Eddie Chapman (Foxwarren); Derek Hume (Shotley); David Jones; Bridget Sayner; Roma Garon; Barry Jones (Heliwar); Martyn Hulme (Rushill); Wief Hulme (Russue); Ann Brewer (Tarsia); Greg Mousely (Meynell); Alf and Marilyn Edmunds (Maven); Ernie and Betty Rich (Somervale); Sheila Atter (Ridley); and Roger and Linda Bigland (Heythrop). It is a long and varied list, as certainly not all of these breeders bred for the same type of dog. The combining of some of these lines has led to a very attractive terrier of correct size and type for the American Breed Standard.

Because of the immense popularity of the dog, it would simply be impossible to mention all the breeders in the United States. For that reason, I will try to highlight the accomplishments and bloodlines of breeders from different sections of the country, as well

as giving an idea of the foundation lines that have been used in their individual breeding programmes. Since the United States is so large, you will find that certain bloodlines are more common in different areas of the country. However, with the advent of semen transport, this may lessen in years to come.

In researching this chapter and studying the pedigrees from different breeders that have provided information, it has been interesting to note the amount of blending of different lines within a pedigree. When you have such varied bloodlines, while a dog or bitch may be a very nice individual, it is doubtful that they can then reproduce themselves.

Because of the recent popularity of the Jack Russell Terrier, there has been an incredible increase in the people wishing to breed their dogs. I do not necessarily consider this good for the breed unless breeders are willing to truly study the pedigrees of their dogs, consider the faults and strengths of their

Eddie Chapman with his Foxwarren Jack Russells. Many American kennels based their breeding programme on these bloodlines.

dogs, and be responsible for the puppies that they raise and place in new homes. Additionally, with all of the mixing and blending, different and varied genetic faults will come forward, and any breeder must be willing to test for these faults, and spay and neuter those that have a genetic fault in order to help eliminate those faults from the breed.

Simply said, not every bloodline crosses well with another, and it wise to study the pedigrees of successful breeding beforehand to know what worked and what did not. Dogs that are produced by breeders with a strong sense of type and those that are line-bred will be better bets for breeding than those dogs that come from a pedigree with little common ancestry. For that same reason, breeding to the latest and greatest show winner may not move your breeding programme ahead if he is a total outcross to the lines you already have.

Many of the long-time breeders are located on the East Coast of the United States, primarily in the New England States, although recently there have been several regional Jack Russell Terrier Association of America (JRTAA) affiliated clubs started in the Midwest, South and Western parts of the country. If you are looking for a specific breed line, or for information on membership of a regional club, contact the JRTAA, either through their web page at http://www.jrtaa.org or through the club secretary.

INFLUENTIAL DOGS

BLENCATHRA BADGER

Certainly one of the better-known Jack Russells, whose progeny still has a continuing influence in the American show ring, is Blencathra Badger, bred by Paul Ross. Badger, a tan and white, broken-coated dog, was whelped in 1984. He won at working terrier shows and trials as well as at the prestigious Crufts Centenary Show. In the United States, Badger won the Jack Russell Terrier Association Trial in 1985 in Virginia. The trial was judged by Derek Hume, and was certainly not lacking in competition, with over 400 entries. Badger won his class, and then went on to win the Grand Champion award as well.

In 1986, it was Blencathra Nettle's time to shine by winning the North East Regionals. Her son Blencathra Nipper, sired by Blencathra Trimmer, won the Jack Russell Breeders Association National Trial, also in 1986. In 1987 Badger continued his winning ways and won the Jack Russell Breeders Association Grand Champion award. Blencathra Nettle, sired by Foxwarren Tigger and out of Blencathra Dorset, certainly gave Badger a bit of competition.

Paul Ross lived in the United States for many years, but he chose to return to England in the late 1980s, along with Blencathra Badger and Blencathra Nettle. After going through a six-month quarantine,

Blencarthra Badger: This dog had a profound influence on the breed in the USA.

Photo courtesy: Paul Ross.

Badger and Nettle were ready to continue their show careers in the UK.

Although Paul Ross is no longer breeding Jack Russells, the legacy his dogs have left is quite unmistakable. Keenlyside Tangle, bred by Kaja Donovan, who won the Jack Russell Terrier Association of America 1997 National Trial, is a great-granddaughter of Blencathra Badger. Willowall Angus, who is the sire of Keenlyside Tangle and the grandson of Blencathra Badger, has continued the tradition of excellence in his progeny, with his daughter JRTAA Champion Honey Hill Tamsyn, owned by Sue Porter of Honey Hill Farm.

TINA AND GRAVEL

Imis of Willowall, bred by Donna Maloney and currently owned by Pat Wilcox of Blackbriar Terriers, is another stud dog with a long record of excellence. Imis of Willowall was sired by Gravel, who was bred by Derek Hume (Shotley), and out of a bitch named Tina bred by George Simpson (Howlbeck). This combination of the older English working lines was very successful and has continued to produce outstanding progeny. Many of the breeders in the Eastern United States have both Tina and Gravel in their pedigrees either through Imis of Willowall, Willowall Angus, Shotley Pentaginous, or Shotley Thorn. Keenlyside Tangle, who won the JRTAA Nationals, is both a daughter of

Willowall Angus, and a granddaughter of Shotley Pentaginous, which again leads back to both Tina and Gravel.

KLAUS JONES

Sage of Wyndcroft (bred by David Jones, and owned by Bob and Linda Miller of Pennsylvania) is another name that will appear in many pedigrees in the United States. Sage is a son of Klaus Jones out of a bitch named Spinney Jones. Klaus Jones has had quite a lasting effect, both in the United States and elsewhere. He appears as a background dog in many pedigrees from breeders such as Bridget Sayner (UK), Roger Bigland (UK) and Nancy Dougherty (USA). Klaus Jones was the Great Yorkshire Supreme Champion and has many winning children and great-grandchildren, including Heythrop Trailblazer of Snow Wind, who was the Junior World Winner in Puerto Rico for 1997.

Klaus Jones appears as a background dog in many pedigrees.

PATHFINDER SATAN

Pathfinder Satan was the father of Scrap, who sired David Jones's Klaus, Jasper and Pieman. Satan is a foundation dog that can certainly be found in a variety of pedigrees across the country. This line then comes back to Dodger, who Nancy Dougherty says is one of her "all-time favourite terriers". Mrs Dougherty states that "Mrs N. Irwin of England bred Dodger, under the recommendation of Eddie Chapman." Pathfinder Satan was lovingly cared for by Mrs Dougherty until his death. "He was a tricolour, rough-coated terrier, approximately 13.5 inches tall and very flexible. He had to be the best working terrier I will ever own" were Nancy's comments on Satan. Mrs Dougherty now stands two other stud dogs, Pengelli Bullet, bred by Bob Clough of Wales, who goes back to the lines of David Jones through his sire Jasper, and Chalky, also bred by David Jones.

Sage of Wyndcroft: A son of Klaus Jones.

ARBA Ch. Blackbriar Executive Decision, sired by Imis Of Willowall.

Photo courtesy: Pat Wilcox.

INFLUENTIAL BREEDERS

CYNTHIA BLIVEN

Cynthia Bliven, a past president of the Jack Russell Terrier Breeders Association, has based her breeding programme on combining the lines of Imis of Willowall and Chalky, owned by Nancy Dougherty. Cynthia lives in Connecticut and has a small but very high-quality breeding programme where she truly considers her dogs as part of her family. Cynthia bred Woodland Harley, who is a JRTAA Champion, and is also the sire of JRTAA Champion Stone Island Brick, and past JRTAA Grand Champion in 1996. Her foundation bitch, Willowall Rebecca, goes back to Blencathra Dorset, who is a half-sister to Blencathra Badger.

PATRICIA WILCOX

Mrs Patricia Wilcox, who also lives in Connecticut, has based her breeding programme on combining recently imported English bloodlines with that of Imis of Willowall. She states:

❛ When I was first introduced to Jack Russell Terriers about ten years ago, I was impressed initially with the intelligence, the amenable temperament, and the soundness of the breed. When I decided to get involved with the breed, I was determined not to lose these marvellous attributes. Through luck, and admittedly some trial and error, I settled on a line that I felt gave me the balanced motion with the correct reach and drive that I was looking for, along with a temperament that was easy to live with. In my opinion, if you don't have good temperament, it does not matter what you have. An aggressive, confrontational dog does not make a good working dog, a good show dog or a pet. I believe that a Jack Russell must have the ability to get where it needs to go with ease, and to focus on the job once he gets where he must go, and must also have the temperament that allows anyone to handle him in a working situation. A dog that lacks these qualities has no place in my breeding programme, no matter how pretty the face. I like a pretty dog, with a 'typey' head, but I am not willing to sacrifice what I feel is more important to achieve it. No dog works,

ARBA & JRTCA Ch. Blackbriar Nevada. Photo: Bruce and Jeane Harkins. Courtesy: Pat Wilcox.

thinks, or loves with prettiness.

The line that is my foundation comes from Derek Hume's old Gravel and Tina cross, mainly Imis of Willowall. Crossing that with Steve Parkin's Foxgrove working line from England has given me the working instinct coupled with a marvellous temperament to go with the consistent good motion. The Imis and Foxgrove descendants are also producing lovely, typey heads, a definite

added plus. I also believe that the new tests for genetic problems are a boon to all ethical breeders. We can keep problems from running rampant in our breed through their use. **'**

HONEY HILL

Susan Porter of Honey Hill Farm based her breeding programme on Blackbriar through Blackbriar Attila, who is the dam of JRTAA Champion Honey Hill Tamsyn, who was sired by Willowall Angus. Blackbriar Attila is a very athletic bitch, having never been beaten in the racing events at JRTAA Nationals. Susan also used Sage of Wyncroft, and Treehouse Daisy bred by Katarina Hartig, and has recently crossed out to Crabtree's Petey Q owned by Sally Yancey and Carolyn McGaughey. Sue says, about her introduction into the breed:

' I did not intend to become a breeder of dogs, it happened because of a small white Jack Russell Terrier named Oliver who was given to me by a long-time friend. Oliver was the dog my daughter had been asking for. At the time, I thought you could only have two dogs; that would soon change. Oliver was the third. I loved Oliver's spirit, but he was not a healthy dog – he suffered from a form of hydrocephalus. His life was filled with seizures, pills and vet visits. What our family went through with Oliver was devastating and the end came when he was about 14 months old. He left his mark on all our lives and we missed him so much that I began my search for another Jack Russell Terrier.

Dogs have a short enough life span as it is, so my first priority was health, and I chose a bitch rather than a dog this time. I was given the name of a breeder in Maryland – Katarina Hartig. As luck would have it she had a litter of puppies with three bitches. I asked Katarina to pick out the best bitch puppy of the litter, and sent her a deposit. That puppy

Hoelio Truim: Imported from the UK.

Loblolly Tanglewood (Treacle Jones – Crosswinds Allison). *Photo courtesy: Myrna Potter.*

MYRNA POTTER

Myrna Potter of Indiana has been involved with Jack Russells since 1992 and has a small breeding programme. She has started her lines from Nancy Dougherty through Windy Hill Willow, whom she then bred to Rex of Windy Hill, and then subsequently to Camelot Derby, who was twice JRTCA National Trial Champion. Myrna has recently purchased Loblolly Tanglewood (a tan and white dog sired by a David Jones dog out of Crosswinds Allison) and Pine Acres Woodruff (by Parson's Dragon Fly out of Pine Acres Jessica, who goes back to Foxgrove Bentley). In addition to Windy Hill Willow, and her daughter Spring Rain Sequoia, she also has two full sisters, Windy Hill Magick and Windy Hill Batik, both sired by Pengelli Bullet.

PAM SIMMONS

Pam Simmons, breeder and owner of Corn

Row Tyler, who won the 1997 JRTCA Nationals and 1998 JRTAA Nationals, gives her thoughts on breeding:

❜ I have a great reverence for the breed Standard and feel every effort should be made to adhere to its precepts. It is the breeders' 'Bible' and must be thoroughly studied and understood in order for it to be effectively utilised. My direction when breeding and when evaluating the terrier is very simply 'structure first'. Proper structure allows for correct movement, overall structural balance and soundness, resulting in good breed type. Always in my mind is the phrase 'Form follows Function'. No less important in my priorities for my Jack Russells are gameness and tractability. These three things are, in my opinion, critical to breeding the proper Jack Russell Terrier. If he is close to the Standard in terms of conformation, then he is suited perfectly for

his work. If he is tractable he has the intelligence and temperament to perform his task. If he is game he will surely perform when presented with the opportunity.

As a breeder, I consider breed type as the combination of specific characteristics which makes that breed different and the individual dog uniquely recognisable as a representative of that breed. Breed type for me is critically important, for with out it you do not have a breed. However, to me structure and breed type go hand in hand. Structure, however seems harder to manage. If you have correct structure it is difficult to keep; if you lack it, it is very difficult to add. It is my feeling that when you breed for a pretty silhouette, without regard to soundness, you do detriment to the future of the breed. What good is a pretty stylish terrier if he cannot function as a working dog?

When breeding I never breed fault to fault; I weigh the strengths and weaknesses of both individuals involved in a mating, then couple that information with research on the lines that I am dealing with. When it is all said and done, it is still a matter of luck, but hopefully the odds of success are in my favour. I have chosen breeding lines exhibiting strengths in areas where I feel my dogs have weaknesses and/or which complement the existing strengths present in my breeding stock. Several of my dogs go back to Riverview Flare and Tek of Windermere. Others go directly to Blencathra Nettle, Beacon Sam, and Scrap. The blend of these lines gives me most of what I aim for but the work is never done. **,**

EARL AND NELSINE ELLSWORTH
In Southern California, Earl and Nelsine Ellsworth have based their programme on the British lines of Heliwar and Ridley, and have recently outcrossed to Heythrop Trailblazer. The Ellsworth's foundation bitch, Somerset's Rockbend Abagail, is an American

Corn Row Tyler: Winner of the 1997 JRTCA Nationals.   Photo courtesy: Pam Simmons.

Corn Row Ravage.
Photo courtesy: Pam Simmons.

Rockbends Cosmo (right) and Rockbends Pepper.

Rare Breed Champion, who was sired by Somerset Finnegan (a son of Ridley Poacher) and out of Heliwar Tip. Several West Coast breeders have used the Heliwar/Ridley crosses with great success to produce a very 'typey' dog with an excellent temperament.

The Ellsworths then bred American Rare Breed Association (ARBA) Champion Somerset's Rockbend Abagail to Hoelio Washington of Snow Wind (a Ridley Robber grandson) to produce ARBA Champion Rockbend's Cosmo and Rockbend's Pepper, who was recently bred to Heythrop Trailblazer.

KIM JAMES
Kim James of Molalla, Oregon breeds under the name of Badgerwood, and has based her programme on some of the Horsemasters dogs, particularly Sayners Wager and Horsemasters Kitty, who was sired by Foxwarren Scamp and out of Foxwarren Vixen. Horsemasters Sweep, whom she has shown in conformation, is sired by Pilot Jones and out of Horsemasters Dazzle.

RANI MORNINGSTAR
Although Rani Morningstar of Northern Idaho has acquired most of her foundation stock within the United States, it descends from British-bred lines, predominantly Hoelio (Heliwar), Heythrop, Ridley, and Barsetta. Beacon and Meynell have also influenced some of her brood stock. She states:

❛ I have recently imported a male from the Barsetta Kennels in England, and am well

245

pleased with the puppies that Barsetta Ultra (Knickers) has produced so far. Barbara Richards has made a terrific contribution to the breed with her line-bred programme to produce a terrier that carries the Barsetta stamp. Either line-bred through Hoelio or out-crossed to other lines, Knickers is proving a strong, positive addition to the outcome. His puppies carry a definite mark of his kind disposition and strong hunting instincts. He recently attained his AKC Junior Earthdog title, and a Best of Breed, and Terrier Group One at the Seattle American Rare Breed show.

Snow Winds Cosy Morningstar is a wonderful addition to my breeding programme, and brings many of the attributes that I desire. Sired by multi-champion Heythrop Trailblazer and out of Belmorr Carina, Cosy possesses an elegance and soundness that should cross well with my existing lines. Mary Strom of Snow Wind Farm has given the United States a wonderful gift in her importation of some of England's finest bloodlines. From those terriers, her breeding programme has produced a lovely, winning type and style equated only with Snow Wind Farm.

Several things come to mind when thinking of my breeding programme: Temperament, soundness/movement, hunting instinct, versatility and type. Temperament is paramount at Morningstar, and has been for more than three decades. The dogs are part of the household – harmony is essential, not only with the human members, but with the animal population as well. It is a joy to watch a pack of terriers running together with a compatible and respectful attitude toward one another. I also consider gait, movement and structure at the top of the list. A dog that moves well is not only a delight to

Horsemasters Sweep (Pilot Jones – Horsemasters Dazzle), bred by Kim James.
Photo: Kim James, Badgerwood.

Snow Wind Cosy Morning Star and Barsetta Ultra.

Photo courtesy: Rani Morningstar.

observe, but also shows balance through the correct physical combination of well laid-back shoulders, topline, and good rear angulation with well-placed hocks.

On the West Coast we have become quite creative in hunting our terriers, as we do not have access to the same type of terrain and quarry that the East Coast enjoys. As my friend Elsa Jensen at Barksalot Kennel in Central Washington says, "if skunks and coyotes count as quarry, then we have an abundance!" In Northern Idaho the most typical topographies are valleys surrounded by mountains. In the valleys we can walk the fields with our dogs, but in the mountains the safest way to travel is by horseback, due to the steep terrain and profusion of trees and brush, not to mention the predators – cougar and bear. It takes a steady, well-trained dog to hunt in the mountains, willing to recall and take direction. ❯

Rani further states that her lines must not only possess versatility in hunting, but as the family pet.

❮ My friends Doug and June, who have a 150-acre farm in our valley, acquired a Ridley Rifleman daughter from me a few years back. I think that their only expectation was to have a family pet, never realising that she would become such a viable part of their farm life. Morningstar's Cindy Roundtop has a seat on every motorcycle, snowmobile and tractor, and Doug is more than willing to come to a halt if Cindy spies a gopher trespassing in his field. Off she runs to dispatch the gopher, and then returns to assume her vigilance. Cindy keeps the fields and irrigation ponds clear of varmints and the granary free of mice. When the grandchildren come to visit, June frequently hears the question: "When is grandpa coming home, so we can take Cindy hunting?" Cindy enjoys house time with the family, and at bedtime, a welcome place at the foot of the bed.

Although breeding to the Standard, personal type certainly enters into my programme. We all have our personal favourite traits that separate us from the other breeders; however, it is that pizzazz, or keenness, or "Hey, look me over" attitude that always earns my second look. ❯

Ridley Rifleman Of Snow Wind: Bred by Sheila Atter in the UK.

Photo courtesy: Mary Strom, Snow Wind.

SNOW WIND FARM *Mary Strom*

❛ For my own breeding programme at Snow Wind I have concentrated heavily on importing the best dogs I could find from England, researching and studying carefully what crosses had worked in the past. The bloodlines that we finally settled on were those of Ridley, Heliwar (Hoelio), Glenholm, Belmorr, Somerwest, Clystlands, Barsetta, and Heythrop. For me these lines have crossed well, and combine to have excellent structure, wonderful temperaments, and trainability, which are important aspects to consider in starting any breeding programme.

ARBA Champion Ridley Rifleman was one of our earliest show winners, having won his American Rare Breed Championship and several Terrier Group placements. Rifleman, or 'Perkins' as we call him has produced some lovely sons and daughters with his same

excellent temperament and loving personality. His sire Galtress Baliff Ridley, is an Australian Champion; his dam Ridley Replica, was the first Parson Jack Russell Terrier bitch to win a Championship Show in England. His youngest daughter Snow Winds Rosey recently won Winners Bitch at the age of six months at the Seattle American Rare Breed Show. Perkins' daughters have, and will be bred to Heythrop Trailblazer, one of our recent English imports.

Heythrop Trailblazer, bred by Roger and Linda Bigland, was our first Junior World Champion – 1997 – and he has recently continued his winning ways, with three Junior Championship titles, a well as placing Group One in the American Rare Breed Shows. 'Blazer' was High Point Parson Jack Russell Terrier for the ARBA Point System in 1997, and has won several JRTAA Regional

*ARBA Ch. Hoelio Just Jenny Of Snow Wind.
Photo courtesy: Mary Strom, Snow Wind.*

Specialties. His most recent win was a Best in Show at the ARBA Micro Classic 1998, held in Seattle, Washington.

Trailblazer's sons and daughters are beginning their careers in the show ring. One of his eldest daughters Snow Winds Cosy Morningstar (out of Belmorr Carina), owned by Rani Morningstar, has earned her Junior American Rare Breed Championship at the Cherry Blossom Classic in Washington DC, Spring 1998. Cosy also won Best of Breed at the ARBA Show in Seattle. Her mother, Belmorr Carina, has a pedigree that is crossed back four times to Ridley Robber, and one can easily see the resemblance between Ridley Robber's son Glenholm Erik Of

Belmorr, and his granddaughter Snow Winds Cosy Morningstar.

Another import is Barsetta Polmanta from Barbara Richards. Polmanta, or 'Halsey' as we call her, brings in another line from Heliwar as she is sired by Hoelio Prince and out of Barsetta Make Mine Mink who goes back to some of the older Foxwarren lines.

A very successful cross that many breeders have tried is that of Ridley and Heliwar. Hoelio Just Jenny is an excellent example of that cross, she is both an American Rare Breed Champion, many times placing first in Terrier Group. Jenny is the daughter of Heliwar Pip, and sired by Glenholm Percy Of Foxwater, who is a brother to Glenholm Erik, and a son of Ridley Robber. Jenny is not only a wonderful show dog, she is also a keen worker, with a very trainable mind.

We have in the last few years imported Galebern Twinkle, bred by Bernard Tuck. Twinkle herself is line bred and crossed very well with a grandson of Ridley Poacher to produce Snow Winds Little Star. Twinkle crossed equally well with Snow Winds Redwood, a Ridley Rifleman son, to produce Snow Winds Zodiak, and Snow Winds Wishful Star.

The Clystlands lines of Mrs Ruth Wilford-Hussey have also blended well with those of Heliwar and Ridley, mostly through a daughter and son of Clystlands Legend. Hoelio Wanda (Clystlands Legend – Hoelio Kirsty) was mated back into Heliwar lines to Heliwar Ben. That cross produced Snow Winds Emma. Heliwar Ben's daughters and granddaughters have all produced lovely litters in type, temperament and excellent structure.

Many of the English breeders such as Sheila Atter, Roger and Linda Bigland, Barry Jones, Anne Milne, Isobel Morrison, and Ruth Wilford-Hussey have been very kind over the years to take the time and effort to help me research the lines that I now have,

Hoelio Washington Of Snow Wind.

Photo courtesy: Mary Strom, Snow Wind.

and I certainly owe them a gratitude of thanks.

I truly encourage anyone wishing to start a breeding programme to thoroughly research the breed lines they plan to use. Each breed line has its faults and attributes, but knowing what those faults are, ahead of time, can save you a great deal of future disappointment. I firmly believe in line breeding as that is the way you solidify the type of dog you desire. People often confuse line breeding with in-breeding, but it is simply not the same, as in-breeding should only be undertaken by the very experienced breeder who is knowledgeable of their lines.

Constant out-crossing and using a wide variety of bloodlines will rarely produce a dog capable of reproducing himself. The stronger breeding dogs are those that come from a specific breeding programme that has used line breeding as a way of producing quality in both structure and temperament. When you do need to out-cross, it is wise to breed your bitch with a dog that is similar in type to the type you already have, as it is hard to have a consistent breeding programme with too many divergent types.

Speaking from experience, Jack Russells are a very collectible breed, and there are many very attractive types, each one just a little different than the next. However, consistency in any breeding programme will require a breeder to focus on a specific type of dog that they prefer. For me, structure and temperament have to come before type, as, without these, it is hard to breed a dog that will be a quality companion, show dog, or a working dog for anyone.

Genetic testing is a costly matter for any breeder, but without it you risk sacrificing the excellent health of the dogs you produce. It is true that even with the very best of breeding programmes and genetic testing, you can produce a dog with serious heritable faults. However, if you never test, you will never know, and the responsible breeder should be aware of all faults within a breed line. ❜

THE FUTURE

Because of the recent AKC recognition and the fact that the breed is currently not eligible to be shown to AKC conformation championships, there are at present few people interested in showing in the USA. This will most likely change when the breed is moved into a specific AKC Group and awarded the chance to earn Championship titles and Group Placements. It is simply too early to say which breeders will have the most influential kennels, or which type will

win in the show ring. However, the most important aspect of breeding is surely the overall well-being of the breed, the temperament that becomes most prevalent, and the form that allows this breed to function appropriately in a pet, show, or working situation.

AUSTRALIA

In Australia, as in other countries, we are caught up in controversy over the naming of the Jack Russell Terrier and the Parson Jack Russell Terrier. It is similar, in a way, to the problems which faced the King Charles Spaniel and the Cavalier King Charles. In both cases, the breeds go back to common ancestors and the disparities are less discernible, in some lines, than the similarities.

However, there is another problem with reference to naming in Australia, and that is, should the Jack Russells bred in Australia and registered with the Australian National Kennel Control be called Australian Jack Russells? This is based on the premise that Australia claims it is the country of development, and JRTs in the show ring are judged to the Australian Standard. Or should the breed be called some other name which would still reflect its history and reason for being? This would possibly help to prevent confusion with the Parson Jack Russell Terrier which is recognised by the Kennel Club and many other national Kennel Clubs throughout the world

At the present time, Australia and New Zealand, South Africa and Japan are the only countries which separate them into two different breeds. No inter-breeding is allowed, and they are judged in the ring by two different Standards. The JRT uses the Australian Standard and the PJRT is judged by the English Standard which has been adopted by the ANKC.

Three generations of Parson Jack Russell Terriers, Owned by Jo Ballard in Australia.   Photo: Robert Lane.

The most obvious difference between the two breeds is in the height. The JR's ideal is 10-12 ins (25-30.5 cms), while the PJRT's Standard has a height minimum of 13 ins (33 cms), ideally 14 ins (35 cms), for dogs, and 12 ins (30 cms), ideally 13 ins (33 cms), for bitches. There are, of course, a number of other differences, including a difference in outline.

Australia has several associations and/or clubs for the two breeds, each of which plays a part in the JR and PJRT world, and they perform separate but overlapping functions. The two main bodies are the ANKC and the original club, the Jack Russell Terrier Club of Australia Inc. Another club which has just formed is the JRT Breeders and Workers Association of Australia Inc. These three have their own registers, but only the ANKC separates the two breeds in the strictest sense.

PARSON JACK RUSSELLS

Although the Jack Russell Terrier has been in Australia for many years the Parson Jack Russell Terrier, as classified by the ANKC, is very much a newcomer. Over the years, a number of taller Jack Russells have been imported, but they were all registered as Jack Russell Terriers with the JRT Club of Australia Inc. When England recognised the Parson Jack Russell Terrier in 1991, Australia followed suit adopting the English Standard.

However, the ANKC would only recognise a PJRT if it was on the English PJRT Club's foundation register. Whelps born to parents which fitted these criteria and which were already in Australia could also be registered. No existing Jack Russells in Australia could be registered as Parsons. All the other JRTs in Australia, if they were registered with the JRT Club of Australia Inc. And if their owners so wished, were registered with the ANKC as JRTs.

KAPALDO

Alan Lewis and his wife were the first owners to have registered PJRTs as they brought a number with them from England in 1986 amongst which were several on the foundation register in England.

MISSIGAI

Di and Mike Cross acquired their first PJRT from Alan Lewis, who lived in Queensland, in 1988. Trixie, as she was known, was registered as a JRT but as she fitted the criteria laid down by the ANKC she was subsequently re-registered as a Parson with the RNSWCC. In 1988 they acquired Kapaldo Ragamuffin (Trixie's dam) and Kapaldo Bandit from Alan, both registered as PJRTs in England. Ragamuffin subsequently had two litters and the puppies were the basis of their stock. Bandit only sired two litters in NSW before he died.

Since then Missigai kennels have bred intermittently over the years. The highlight to date, was winning Best of Breed at the British Terrier Club Show under the British PJRT specialist Mrs Jan Wood (Ardencote). Runner-up was another bitch whose sire and dam were bred by the Missigai kennels. The winning bitch, Aust. Ch. Missigai Belvoir was sired by Aust. Ch. Galtres Bailiff Ridley (Imp. UK) out of Kapaldo Ragamuffin (Imp. UK).

SWYMBRIDGE

In 1992 Carol and Robin Makeef imported Kenterfox Jean which was in whelp to Barsetta Bruce, from Barbara Richards in the UK. Kenterfox Jean whelped five puppies in quarantine and it was not long before she gained her Australian title. In 1997 Mrs Richards sent out Barsetta Jerome; he too soon gained his title. These two terriers make up two of the four bloodlines on which they are building their kennels.

Another import, again with English

bloodlines, is planned and will be selected to complement their existing lines. As Robin writes, recognition and success in the show ring against other well-known and established breeds has been achieved by a great deal of hard work and persistence. Continuing success in recent times has been a great encouragement.

YARANUIP

In 1993 Jo Ballard imported Galtres Bailiff Ridley from England. Sadly he arrived too late to be mated to Shasta, the kennel's foundation bitch. He has not been used very much at stud but the Yaranuip kennels now have his daughter and his grand-daughter. The youngest, Wasp (Aust. Ch. Yaranuip Thistle), is now persevering with Obedience but much prefers the winter months when she and her dam Twig and Bay go hunting.

There are a small number of other owners beginning to breed their PJRT's in Australia: in WA Rob Taylor and his wife (Sunset); in Victoria Mrs Wagstaff (Pureoz), whose homebred dog Ch. Pureoz Aden won Best of Breed at Melbourne Royal 1997; in NSW John Mills and his wife (Parsonage), who have based their kennel on Missigai bloodlines, and Dennis Harvey who has both Parsonage and Swymbrige lines; in the ACT Andrew Hutton and Tracy (Culloden) have started a breeding programme.

JACK RUSSELLS

KARRELL
Jann Trout writes:

❛ It is our intention at Karrell to blend the combination of recently acquired English bloodlines with our tried and tested Australian lines to produce sound quality stock, which fits nicely into the Australian Standard. Our first generation of mixing

Aust. Ch. Karrell Gallant Sophie. Owned and bred by Jann and Ron Trout.

Aust. Grand Ch. Myrmidon Jack Lairdsley. Owned by Jann and Ron Trout.

253

Aust. Ch. Carisbrooke Casablanca: A prolific winner in the show ring.

these lines has produced some very pleasing puppies. Ch. Karrell Gallant Sophie was awarded Puppy of the Year for 1997 by the Jack Russell Terrier Club of New South Wales, and commenced 1998 by being awarded Best Bitch and Runner-up Best in Show at the Jack Russell Terrier Club of Queensland's Open show in March. **'**

CARISBROOKE
Rita Frances-Little says:

' My first ANKC Australian Champion, Carisbrooke Dior, was whelped in 1989 but had to wait for recognition as a pure breed before attaining her title. In January 1988, I bought a male from Malung Kennels in Victoria as an outcross. His name was Ch. Malung Orinoco. He proved to be a most

exceptional producer of bitches. For six consecutive years, his daughters have either won on been awarded Runner Up to Best of Breed at the Brisbane Royal and The Sporting Terrier of Queensland Shows.

Orinoco won six Best of Breeds at the East Coast's biggest Royals: Sydney, Melbourne and Brisbane (average dog entries 5,500). In 1993, he became the only Jack Russell to be Runner Up Group 2 (Terriers) at Sydney Royal. Another son also won Group 2 at Darwin Royal in the Northern Territory. **'**

MYRMIDON
Jocelyn Cansdell says:

' In the last fifteen years I have bred over 60 Australian Champions over those years and am the breeder of the only two Australian

Pictured (left to right): Aust. Ch. Myrmidon Jack Danni, Myrmidon Jack Niz, Aust. Grand Ch. Jack Cam, Aust. Ch. Myrmidon Jack Quint and Aust. Ch. Myrmidon Jack Tasse, with owner/breeder Jocelyn Cansdell.

Grand Champions in the world – the famous Australian Grand Champion Myrmidon Jack Cam, a broken coat of outstanding soundness and nature, and the smooth coat Myrmidon Jack Lairdsley.

I breed to our official Standard, and use only dogs that are within this Standard, and I am becoming more and more happy with my breeding results. To me, one of the most worrying aspects is the loss of 'spannability' in the breed and the ensuing 'cloddiness'. If we do not adhere to the lithe and flexible image, we are taking the breed away from its physical ability to perform its original functions. 9

BAYLOCK
Curly Sullivan writes:

6 My wife and I had been given a Jack Russell as a present; that dog was Malung Jim Bean. 'Jim' became the foundation of the Baylock strain of Jack Russells.

At the Melbourne Royal show in 1991, Jim Bean was Best of Breed and Chum Creek Sweet Sherry, his daughter, was Runner Up Best of Breed.

One of our greatest thrills was at the Adelaide Royal show in 1993, when a grandson of Jim's took Runner Up Puppy in Show under highly respected terrier judge Harry Jorden from the UK.

Since then, Baylock Jacks have gone from strength to strength, winning under international judges from all over the world. We have bred dogs that are Champions in Japan and New Zealand and in every state in Australia. In 1997 Baylock owned, bred or sired Best of Breed or Runner Up Best of Breed at every Royal Show in Australia. We have a young team and we are looking forward to achieving the same success in the future as we have had in past years. 9

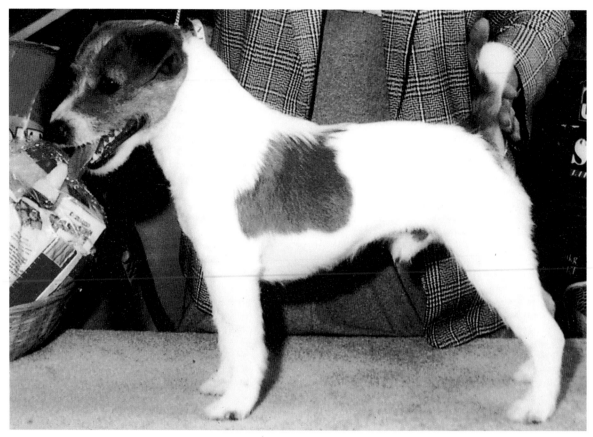

Aust. Ch. Pineview Poacher, sired by Aust. Ch. Tarsia Monocle Of Bohunt (imp. UK).

PINEVIEW

Maryke Franceschi writes:

❛ I was most fortunate to acquire a wonderful tan and white smooth-coated dog, Australian Champion Wypanda Jacko. This little dog, bred by my very good friend Ian Grigg of Ballarat, Victoria, was the base sire of all the Pineview dogs. He was hunted on fox, and also most successful in the show ring. He won Best in Show in three Australian States, as well as producing many quality winning puppies, stamping them with lovely heads, good bone and movement.

As time went on, it was quite apparent to me that the gene pool for the Jack Russell in Australia was fairly limited. I also felt that the dogs were becoming too 'cloddy' in type and losing the athletic requirement of a working Jack Russell. A trip to the UK in July 1994 saw the successful tan and white broken coat hunt champion Tarsia Monocle Of Bohunt brought into Australia. Since his arrival, he has gained his Australian Champion title. He has produced some lovely puppies with excellent fronts, easily spanned. Forward, outgoing temperaments have also been acquired. These puppies, I feel, are more to the type Parson Russell would have had in his kennels and which, as committed breeders, we should be trying to preserve. ❜

CELEBRATE RICHMOND

Compiled and Edited by

Elisabeth Dementi & Wayne Dementi

with Narratives by

Corrine Hudgins

Second Printing, 2000

Copyright® 1999
ISBN: 0-87517-109-5
Library of Congress Catalog Card Number: 99-074790

The Dietz Press
Richmond, Virginia

IN DEDICATION

*C*elebrate Richmond is dedicated to the early photographers of the Dementi family who have passed from this life, having left a treasure of images of Richmond and Richmonders. First, Anthony L. "Tony" Dementi, who had the vision to start this business in 1924, and the artistic talent to ensure its success over the ensuing 50 years. Second, his brother, Frank A. Dementi, who added to this photographic treasure with the opening of Frank Dementi's Colonial Studio in 1942. Frank ran Colonial Studio until 1984, leaving a collection of over 300,000 negatives with the Valentine Museum. Finally, this dedication goes to Robert A. "Bob" Dementi, who served as President of Dementi Studio until his passing in 1986. It was in 1972 that Bob purchased Foster Studio, thus expanding the photograph collection with images dating back to 1881. A special thank you is also extended to the Virginia Historical Society which maintains a considerable portion of this collection in its archives.

INTRODUCTION

Remember the ice cream sundaes at the Clover Room? How about the food baskets at Chicken-in-the-Rough? Who recalls swimming in Shields Lake in Byrd Park? What about the holiday excursions to Miller & Rhoads to view their Christmas windows? Eddie Weaver on the organ at the Byrd Theater? Bowling at Tiny Town? The Tobacco Festival Parades and football games at City Stadium? That special moment when the Richmond Virginians beat the New York Yankees in an exhibition game at Parker Field? Go V's!

I always thought that being a photographer's son was special in that my Dad was always being invited to photograph special occasions of all types. After all, everyone knows that when a photographer is invited, something special is going on! I frequently was able to tag along. Tagging along was something that came with being my Dad's son. So, it is perhaps easily understood that my childhood years were formative of my belief that Richmond was a special place!

I left Richmond in the mid-sixties, destined to return in the mid-nineties. I was worried that Richmond would be far different than I remembered...larger and colder, I presumed. Delightedly, my fears were unfounded. Richmond's growth had been phenomenal. When I left Richmond there was no Powhite Expressway, no Interstate 295, no Willey bridge...and, Short Pump was halfway to Charlottesville! So much had changed, but I was happily discovering that it was nearly all for the better. My old alma mater, the University of Richmond was now universally recognized as one of the finest schools in the country. Virginia Commonwealth University had assumed "major player" status for both education and metro area business and economic development. The Shockoe Bottom and Cary Street neighborhoods had become "happening places". Richmond's Riverfront development initiative was well underway, holding the promise of revitalizing downtown once and for all. The James Center and Riverfront Plaza had redefined the downtown business district in a very upscale way. The museums were collectively engaged in improvements to make Richmond a major attraction for visitors who wish to experience one of America's most historic cities.

On a personal level, I was experiencing friendly and inclusive Richmonders. A wonderful array of restaurants had emerged. And, I was enjoying the explosion of cultural and recreational activities which the Richmond of the nineties was offering.

As we were considering the idea of publishing an end-of-century book, I found the exercise of sorting through the Dementi negative archives to be particularly joyful, giving rise to a sense of celebration. The spirit of this book was right before me...my memories and our photo archives recall Richmond being a great city, then; and I was experiencing Richmond to be an even a greater city, now! So, we are hopeful that we might incite within you that same feeling that we are having — a joyful spirit which justifiably announces that the time has come to Celebrate Richmond!

F. Wayne Dementi
President, Dementi Studio

FOREWORD

CELEBRATE RICHMOND

I was born in 1930 at the old Johnston-Willis Hospital on Kensington Avenue and grew up on Gloucester Road in Sherwood Park, a brand new subdivision of Ginter Park, during the bottom-most days of the Great Depression and the queasy lull between the first two worldwide wars in human history. Being a mere speck in the cosmos, I was aware of none of these developments. Every couple of weeks or so one hobo or another—there were no "homeless" during the Great Depression, only "hobos" and "tramps"—one hobo or another would roll out of a freight car in the Acca railroad yards and come trekking about a mile to the east and knock on our kitchen door and ask for food. My mother would fix him a sandwich and wish him well and send him on his way. These encounters were always peaceful. I drew no conclusions other than that there were some people in this world who were poor, raggedy, unwashed, and hungry, and needed better shoes if they planned to do all that walking.

As for me, I felt sublimely—no, *divinely*—fortunate. Every night I got down on my knees beside my bed and closed my eyes and thanked God for placing me where He had. We had a Rand McNally globe in the house, and I thought of all the thousands, maybe millions, of places where He might have had me be born. In an igloo up inside the Arctic

Circle, for example; or in a thatched hut on one of those little islands about a thousand miles from New Zealand, judging by the globe, where they probably didn't have funny papers or Philco radios, those being my two greatest pleasures at that time. No, God had placed me in not only the greatest nation on earth, the United States of America, but also in the greatest state in the greatest nation, namely, Virginia—after all, what other state could boast of eight Presidents, starting with the father of our country?—and in the greatest city in the greatest state, Richmond, which after all, was Virginia's capital, and in the greatest neighborhood in the greatest city in the greatest state in the greatest nation. And why did I think Sherwood Park was the greatest neighborhood on earth? Because from my bedroom window I could watch the fireworks displays every night during the State Fair, which was held in September on that enormous triangle of land between Hermitage Road and the Boulevard known as The Fairgrounds, the site today of The Diamond. I was one of the handful of children in the entire world who could watch those fireworks from his own bedroom.

The State Fair! What an exciting time! And what innocent days those were... At Ginter Park Elementary School, the principal, Mr. Toms—a heroic figure to all of us because he was also a tree surgeon, and after school we would see him way up in a maple or an elm in somebody's yard standing on a branch, saw in hand, with his sleeves rolled up, revealing his forearms, which were the size of Popeye's or Superman's—Mr. Toms always gave us one day off to go to the Fair. Here we were, nine or ten years old, in the fifth or sixth grade, and my

GINTER PARK ELEMENTARY SCHOOL

mother would give me twelve nickels, and Mike Moncure's or Jerry Gumenick's mother would give him twelve nickels, and the two of us would head off by ourselves at 7 a.m. for a day at the Fair. To reach the Fairgrounds we had to walk across Brookland Parkway and through some woods that stretched on for three quarters of a mile. Mere babes we were, heading off through the woods for the greatest annual concentration of strangers in the entire Commonwealth of Virginia, the State Fair, and no one worried for a moment about our safety. Nor did we ever have to endure an anxious moment. Well...that's not completely true. One morning we were deep into the woods when we came upon a large black touring car that had somehow snaked its way between the trees to the spot where it now rested—silent and with its shades down. In those days a proper sedan had shades you could pull down. We stopped and stared—and somehow, without a word, we realized that whatever was going on inside that car, we shouldn't be the ones who found out. We walked on at a faster clip. Today an elevated segment of Highway I-95 now runs right through the land where all those trees and that mysterious black touring sedan once were.

At the Fair we didn't devote so much as a flick of the eyes to the livestock and produce exhibitions that were the Fair's original *raison d'être*. Instead, we headed straight for the carnival midway. With twelve nickels you could enter the Fairgrounds (5¢), get two snowballs (scoops of crushed ice with fruit flavors poured over them), and ride every one of the carnival rides. One time we got to the Fair so early, there was not a single other soul waiting to ride the Ferris wheel. So we got on, just the two of us, and instead of the usual five times around, the roustabout running the Ferris wheel—we could tell he was a roustabout by the immense cluster of keys that hung from one of his belt loops—everybody knew about such things—the roustabout let us have *sixty* of those stomach-thrumming circuits. What bliss! Every time we came down the far side we would be staring at a lurid mural painted across the entire side of one of the midway tents. "SECRETS OF THE THIRD SEX RE-VEALED!" it said. Sixty times we came down the far side and sixty times we stared at the legend, "SECRETS OF THE THIRD SEX RE-VEALED!" We hadn't a clue what *the third sex* might possibly be, and you had to be sixteen to enter the tent. Years later, being sixteen and men of the world, we found out it referred to a creature called the Hermaphrodite, a colleague of those other two staple monsters of the carnival midways of the 1930s, the Hydrocephalic Baby and the Geek. The Geek ate live chickens, starting with the feet, the feathers, the beak and the head.

No, the deadliest danger to the children in those days was bacteria. Prior to antibiotics, germs ruled. At the age of two I had come close to dying from a strep infection that had started in my throat and ears. Forever afterwards my mother put me to bed and kept me out of school if I had the slightest sore throat, earache, or for that matter, stuffy nose. As a result I got to listen to a lot of daytime radio. By noon all the soap operas were over, and I would turn the dial to WRNL, where you could hear Douglas Southall Freeman, the editor of the *Richmond News Leader*, deliver the news of the day and a few comments. Don't get me wrong. I was a normal child. I didn't have the faintest interest in any news from beyond the block where I lived, the school where I went, or the baseball diamond—the diamond survives today beneath the belly of the elevated I-95—where every Saturday us boys from Sherwood Park and Brook Road and Seminary Avenue played the boys from over toward Laburnum. (Who needed Little Leagues?) No, it was not the news, it was Douglas Southall Freeman's voice that got me. It was mesmerizing. It was the most totally *Southern* voice I have ever heard. It was such a soft, thick, slow, ponderous voice, I imagined this august solon with his three names to be a man with a beard, eighty years old if he was a day, the patriarch of a religion known as The Old South. If he said it, it was gospel. Every day, rain or shine, he started off his broadcast the same way: "Good afternoon, ladies and gentlemen, it's a beautiful day here on the Riviera of the South." I was eighteen years old before I realized that the Riviera was not a capital city with seven hills, one of which was crowned with a Greek Temple-like capitol and an equestrian statue of a famous general, and a bunch of pungent tobacco warehouses down by a wide, muddy river that was terribly flood-prone.

I was also eighteen before I realized that Douglas Southall Freeman had written one of the great works of Southern history, *Lee's Lieutenants*, although, needless to say, that didn't surprise me. About that same time, I was told that every morning at dawn, Freeman drove down to the *News Leader* via Monument Avenue, stopped along the circle at Monument and Allen Avenues, got out, saluted the magnificent four-story-high statue by Jean-Antonin Mercié of General Lee on his horse, Traveller, then continued on to the newspaper, invigorated anew for his mission as pastor of the religion of The Old South. In all those years I never laid eyes on the man. I never even saw a picture of him. So imagine how startled I was this spring when Wayne Dementi sent me this picture of Douglas Southall Freeman. How unremarkable he actually looked! How clean-shaven! How bald was my patriarch! Thank God for one thing. That deep, rich, gumbo voice is literally unforgettable. I can hear it even now as I write, sixty years later.

DOUGLAS SOUTHALL FREEMAN

Looking back, I realize that it would have been a gaffe for Freeman to have decked himself out like some sulfurous bewhiskered eminence from another time and place. He was instead the perfect Richmond gentleman, and a Richmond gentleman neither dressed nor cultivated the tonsorial arts in order to call attention to himself. The Richmond gentleman wanted to fulfill the code of gentility precisely, no more and no less. The code dictated that no gentleman appear on the streets of Richmond without a jacket, a necktie, and a hat, no matter what. O Summer Days Downtown! O Heat, which wrapped itself around you like an octopus! The asphalt paving turned to fudge. The brass doorknobs became tacky to the touch. Air conditioning? Didn't exist. Every respectable man wore a starched collar. Any unstarched collar housing a necktie pulled up smartly to the Adam's apple would have wilted as the sweat poured down the gentleman's face from beneath the leather band of his straw boater or cream-colored Panama. Seersucker was the fabric of choice for a Richmond gentleman's summer suit. One of my earliest memories of downtown Richmond, where my father worked, is of men walking along Broad or Main or up Ninth, the street that led up past Rueger's Hotel and Capitol Square on the steep climb from Main to Broad. The sweat gleamed on their faces. They mopped their brows beneath their boaters. By 10 a.m. dark half-moons had soaked through the seersucker beneath each armpit. I was so young, I thought seersucker suits came that way, with the half-moons. I assumed that if you went to the men's department at Miller & Rhoads or Thalhimers or Berry-Burk you would see them hanging in rows on the rack, seersucker suits in every imaginable size, all with dark half-moons woven in under the armpits.

My father favored the less common but by no means rare white linen suit for summer. His were fabulous, at least the way I saw them. A tailor on Main Street, Sam Savage, made them for him Norfolk-style, i.e., with a mock belt in the back and bellows pleats on each side from the shoulder blades to the waist. His white suits were so fabulous, in fact, I assumed that men all over the world must be lined up at the tailors' to get white suits made. I was mistaken; in due course it fell to the lot of the next generation, me, to undertake a crusade to make it so.

Not even Richmond, the last redoubt of Southern gentility, has been able to maintain the standards that once made it the gentleman's fashionplate of the western world. If you care to shed a tear over a Lost Cause, turn immediately to page 111, where you will see the men of Richmond massed on Fourth Street between Grace and Franklin at 2:45 one October afternoon in 1926 to hear a radio broadcast of a World Series game between Babe Ruth's and Lou Gehrig's New York Yankees and the St. Louis Cardinals. Commercial radio broadcasting in Richmond was barely a year old at the time, a point not nearly as interesting as the fact that virtually every one of the thousands of men jammed into that one block of downtown Richmond wore a jacket and a tie and a felt hat with a six-inch-high crown, a $2\,^3/_4$- to 3-inch brim, and a $1\,^1/_2$- to 2-inch hatband or else—and these were merely a fraction of the total display of headgear—a cap, but a real gentleman's cap, not a baseball cap (*O fin de siècle!*) but a proper Windsor cap cocked with the then fashionable Beatty Tilt. Just take a look at that picture! *Ecce gloria Richmondae!* Behold Richmond in all her glory!

Speaking only for myself, I insist on hats like that to this day, and I hereby tip the most broad-brimmed, high-crowned one I own to Dementi Studio in awe of the irresistible tide of nostalgia you have created in the pages that follow...for our ineffably glorious Riviera of the South.

Tom Wolfe
New York City

CHAPTER 1

SAME SCENE
Then and Now

The close of a century serves naturally as a moment to pause and reflect upon the life and times of the past decades. When looking back one cannot help but draw parallels between today and yesterday. Simply comparing yesterday's modes of travel, fashion designs, or even grocery prices to those of today, for example, illustrates just how everyday life has changed over the course of this century.

Similarly, in the life of a city, the scenes are ever changing. In the streetscapes, trees are planted, grown, or removed, and buildings are constructed, enlarged, restored, or demolished. Around each corner the physical comparisons of the present to the past are limitless.

The following pages feature images of Richmond buildings and scenes as they once appeared, accompanied by photographs of their current appearance. The present-day views were taken from as near as possible to the original vantage points, so true comparisons can be made. In some instances, additional images have been included, to give the viewer a more complete picture of the site as viewed then and as seen now.

EAST MAIN STREET, *View west from 11th Street, 1912.*

A dozen years into the new century, William Howard Taft was in the White House, soon to be succeeded by Virginia-born Woodrow Wilson. Richmond's Main Street witnessed a flurry of activity—chugging motorcars, rumbling streetcars, clattering horse-drawn wagons—and the capital city's financial heart boasted a building boom. On the south side of the street were the Virginia Fire and Marine Insurance Company building at 1015 East Main; Henry S. Hutzler and Co. Bankers at 1013; the E.B. Taylor Company, specializing in china and glassware, at 1011; Southern Dental Rooms at 1009; and Owens and Minor Drug Co. at 1007. The American National Bank Building stood at the corner at 10th Street. Further west, the Mutual Building occupied the corner of 9th and Main, and the First National Bank Building, at 823, was still under construction. High-rise commercial building had arrived in Richmond. The American National Bank and the Mutual Building had just expanded to ten and twelve stories, respectively, and were being surpassed in

EAST MAIN STREET, *View west from 11th Street, 1999.*

height by the eighteen-story First National Bank. The north side of the 1000 block included the Richmond Bank and Trust Company at 1016 and the U.S. Customs House and Post Office, which had just completed an expansion of its own.

Eighty-seven years later, the Ironfronts on the south side remain, along with the Mutual and First National Bank buildings. The streetcar rails are gone. The American National Bank Building, most recently known as the Heritage Building, has been remodeled but still stands on the corner opposite the old U. S. Customs House, now the Federal Courthouse. Looking west up Main Street, aside from the addition of street landscaping, most noticeable is the height of the present construction as compared to that of the earlier scene, especially the Crestar Bank at the southwest corner of 10th and Main and the more recent high-rises further up Main. The character of Main Street in 1999 is a result of the successful blending of the varied architectural styles of both yesterday and today.

GRACE AND 6TH STREETS, *Northeast corner, ca. 1926.*

LOEW'S THEATRE, *Grace and 6th Streets, 1937.*

CARPENTER CENTER FOR THE PERFORMING ARTS, *Grace and 6th Streets, 1999.*

The mid-1920s scene illustrates a typical downtown corner in the days of flappers and Prohibition. Grace Street leads to the right, and 6th Street disappears to the left towards Broad Street. Among the businesses on the east side of 6th Street are the Boys Shop and the Odeon Theatre, with the arched entrance midway between Grace and Broad. To the right is the old YMCA building at the corner of 7th and Grace, and the "Thalhimer Brothers" rooftop water tower is just visible over the corner house. Thalhimers department store at this time occupied the opposite side of the block. The YMCA moved to its present location at Foushee and East Franklin Streets around 1940.

By 1928 Loew's Theatre and its adjoining shops stood on this site and along 6th and Grace Streets. Designed as a movie palace by architect John Eberson, the theatre was noted for its ceiling featuring a re-creation of the sky, complete with moving stars and clouds—a perfect ambiance for the fantasy of the motion picture. The Loew's Theatre showed major films for decades. In the 1980s, the movie house was remodeled for live stage performances and concerts and reopened as the Virginia Center for the Performing Arts, then renamed the Carpenter Center for the Performing Arts for its benefactors, E. Rhodes and Leona B. Carpenter. A major focal point of the Sixth Street Marketplace, the theatre now serves as a venue for performances by the Richmond Symphony, the Virginia Opera, and the Richmond Ballet as well as traveling theatre companies, bands, choirs, orchestras, and recording artists, such as the May 27, 1999, Bruce Hornsby concert advertised on the marquee in this recent photograph.

BROAD STREET STATION, *West Broad Street at Davis Avenue, ca. 1945.*

Designed and built from 1917 to 1919 by John Russell Pope, noted architect of the Jefferson Memorial and the National Gallery in Washington, Union Station, commonly known as Broad Street Station, continuously provided the capital city with passenger rail service for fifty-six years. The commanding edifice was constructed for the Richmond, Fredericksburg, and Potomac Railroad on the site of the original Hermitage Golf Club. Prior to the golf club, the property was the site of the Virginia State Fair.

In the early 1970s the administration of passenger service was transferred to Amtrak, and by the middle of the decade, the station closed. In 1976 Amtrak moved to a more modest station north of the city on Staples Mill Road in neighboring Henrico County. The same year the Commonwealth of Virginia purchased the old station, and preparations began for its adaptation as a museum. The next year the Science Museum of Virginia opened its doors. Since that time the Museum has

SCIENCE MUSEUM OF VIRGINIA, *2500 West Broad Street, 1999.*

gradually worked in phases to renovate and restore the old structure, including the train sheds, which had fallen into disrepair. Today, this institution furthers science education through its exhibitions and varied programs.

The present view of the facility looks very much the same as it did fifty-odd years ago. The white dome on the west side of the building houses the Museum's noteworthy Ethyl Corporation IMAX® DOME and Planetarium, featuring planetary shows and nature and science-related wide-angle 70mm films presented via the OMNIMAX™ projection system. Directly across Broad Street from the station is the William Byrd Hotel, which opened in 1925. When built, it stood alone as a high-rise hotel on the western fringe of the downtown area. After several years of multi-purpose use, the building was recently renovated and converted to apartments for senior citizens.

TREDEGAR IRON WORKS, *Near riverfront from the west, mid-1920s.*

TREDEGAR IRON WORKS, *From the east, 1865.*

The Tredegar Iron Works were established in the 1830s. After a few lean production years, Joseph Reid Anderson took over the foundry in 1841. Within a decade Richmond led the South in iron production, largely due to Tredegar's successful operations. Among other uses, the works manufactured iron for military, railroad, and architectural purposes. During the Civil War, Tredegar was the iron works of the Confederacy, and production concentrated on Confederate military supplies, including ordnance and the plates for the CSS *Virginia*, the famed Confederate ironclad converted from the USS *Merrimack*. The foundry functioned throughout the war, closed briefly at the end of the conflict, and resumed shortly thereafter with the assistance of Northern investors.

Northern photographer Alexander Gardner, former employee of Mathew Brady, is credited with the widely published April 1865 view of Tredegar Iron Works. Gardner was one of several photographers who rushed to Richmond at the end of

FORMER HERITAGE BUILDING, *10th and Main Streets, 1999.*

Company was located just down 10th Street at the corner of Cary.

The institution became known as the American Bank and Trust Company around 1929 but closed during the Depression. Thereafter the commercial high-rise was called the American Building. In the 1960s and 1970s the exterior was extensively remodeled, creating a dramatic transformation from the old to the new appearance, and the interior was renovated. The name changed to the Heritage Building during this time. Still standing tall on one of Main Street's more prominent corners, the structure continues to house offices and small retail shops at street level.

HOTEL RUEGER,
9th and Bank Streets, 1951.

HOTEL RUEGER, *9th and Bank Streets, 1920s.*

COMMONWEALTH PARK SUITES HOTEL, *901 Bank Street, 1999.*

Built in 1912 on the site of Louis Rueger's Lafayette Saloon, the Hotel Rueger was known for its highly touted restaurant with its expansive, richly carved mahogany bar. In 1952 the establishment became the Raleigh Hotel. The 1950s view includes the State-Planters Bank and Trust building, later the United Virginia Bank building, now used for state offices, and the Mutual Building to the right, down 9th Street.

Renovated in the early 1980s, the hostelry reopened as the Commonwealth Park Suites, a luxury hotel which, as its predecessors, continues to serve the Capitol area and financial district.

17

CITY HALL, *10th and Capitol Streets, 1920s.*

In the wake of the 1870 Capitol Disaster, when the collapse of a crowded gallery and floor killed and injured scores, the early-19th-century Robert Mills City Hall on this site was taken down for fear of the occurrence of a similar calamity. In 1887 the massive, granite "new" city hall was begun. It took nearly seven years to complete the design of Detroit architect Elijah Myers. This new building was the seat of city government until the opening of the white-marble-clad new City Hall at 900 East Broad in 1971. Myers's masterpiece, known for some time as the Courts Building, is presently used as commercial office space.

OLD CITY HALL, *10th Street and Capitol Square, 1999.*

In the 1920s photograph the building is flanked on the west by the spire-less Broad Street Methodist Church and on the east by First Baptist Church. In the foreground is Capitol Square and the statue of William "Extra Billy" Smith, one of Virginia's governors during the Civil War.

Trees now mask the site of Broad Street Methodist Church, demolished in 1968, and the vista to Old First Baptist. The latter still stands at 12th and Broad Streets, but its bell tower has since been dismantled, and the building is now owned and used by the Medical College of Virginia.

DOOLEY MEMORIAL LIBRARY, *1st and Franklin Streets, 1930s.*

After the Civil War, Confederate veteran James H. Dooley returned to his native Richmond and became one of the city's most prominent businessmen and industrialists. Before the turn of the century, just west of town he built his Victorian estate, Maymont, named for his wife, Sallie May. In the first quarter of the century, there had been interest in establishing a free city library, where dues were not required. The Lewis Ginter House at Shafer and Franklin housed Richmond's first public library in 1924 but soon was deemed inadequate for the task. Major Dooley's death in 1922 was followed within a few short years by that of Mrs. Dooley,

RICHMOND PUBLIC LIBRARY, *100 block East Franklin Street, 1999.*

who bequeathed a sizeable sum for the construction of a new public library in memory of her husband. The architectural firm of Baskervill and Son designed an appropriate Art Deco memorial, and the Richmond Public Library, or Dooley Memorial Library, opened in 1930 at the southeast corner of 1st and Franklin Streets.

In 1972 a new library was erected, extending east to 2nd Street and enveloping the original library building, whose interior is still intact in the James H. Dooley Wing, at the western end of the building. The present view, from the northeast corner of 2nd and Franklin Streets, shows the extent of the expansion.

THOMAS JEFFERSON HIGH SCHOOL, *4100 West Grace Street, 1930s.*

The city's West End developed rapidly in the early 1920s. The need for a new high school was met with the construction in 1930 of Thomas Jefferson High School, the stately Art Deco structure designed by Richmond architect Charles M. Robinson. With this new arrival, soon to be known as Tee-Jay, Richmond was being served by three high schools—Thomas Jefferson, John Marshall, and Jackson Ward's Armstrong High School, with an all-African-American enrollment.

This 1930s photograph captures the Tee-Jay student body going home after a typical school day. At the time the West End was still quite countrified, as the scene illustrates. The intersection in the immediate foreground is that of Monument and Malvern Avenues.

From the start Tee-Jay's administration and faculty strove to develop a high standard of academics, and the tone was set by Ernest Shawen, the school's first principal, who would serve for a dozen years, retiring in 1942, the same year the institution's Cadet Corps was founded. Coalter C. Hancock was principal for the

THOMAS JEFFERSON HIGH SCHOOL AND THE GOVERNOR'S SCHOOL, *4100 West Grace Street, 1999.*

next sixteen years, followed by William Brock in 1958, who by the time of his retirement in 1976 had guided the institution through the desegregation and court-ordered busing of the 1960s and 1970s. Brock was succeeded by Morgan Edwards III, the school's first African-American administrator, who saw Tee-Jay through the 1980s and the end of busing. In 1991 the Governor's School for Government and International Studies was established at Thomas Jefferson. The program for highly motivated students from Richmond and its outlying counties permits in-depth independent study in addition to satisfying the basic requirements for graduation.

Today, in a marked comparison, residential development has surrounded the school on three sides, with commercial expansion running along both sides of Broad Street. The school block has pushed northward and now features a baseball field and tennis courts. Thomas Jefferson High School and the Governor's School presently continue to share the educational facility, soon to enter its seventieth year of serving the needs of area students.

DOWNTOWN BUSINESS DISTRICT, *ca. 1940.*

This late 1930s aerial view of Richmond captures the capital city when its skyline was dominated by the Central National Bank Building, to the left, near 3rd and Broad, and the wide-corniced First National Bank Building, to the right of center, at the southwest corner of 9th and Main. Railroads, vital to Richmond's industries, had filled in and built over the canal's Great Turning Basin, and warehouses and industrial buildings extended south from the financial district to the James River. In the center foreground stands Byrd Street Station, at 7th and Canal Streets, built in 1887 and closed at the opening of Broad Street Station in 1919.

The early 1970s added their share of skyscrapers to the city skyline, with new City Hall at 9th and Broad and the Fidelity Building at 9th and Main in 1971 and

DOWNTOWN BUSINESS DISTRICT, *1999.*

the F&M Center—now Nationsbank—at 11th and Main two years later. With the 1975 opening of Interstate 195, the Downtown Expressway connected Richmond's near west end with the city's central business district. The highway's construction cut through downtown between Byrd and Canal Streets. Soon after more high-rise offices were built—a Skidmore, Owings, and Merrill building at 8th and Main and the new Federal Reserve and VEPCO (now Virginia Power) buildings. The State's Monroe Building, the Crestar headquarters, the Bell Atlantic building, and the James Center were added in the 1980s, with Riverfront Plaza in the 1990s, all contrasting markedly with the view of sixty years ago and giving Richmond the profile of a city preparing to welcome a new century.

STRAND AND LITTLE THEATRES, *116-118 West Broad Street, ca. 1929.*

BOOKER-T THEATRE, *118 West Broad Street, 1934.*

THEATRE IV, *116-118 West Broad Street, 1999.*

From the days of vaudeville to the golden days of motion pictures, Broad Street was lined with theatres sporting names like Bijou, Bluebird, Lubin, National, Colonial, and Lyric. The Empire Theatre was built in 1911 for legitimate theatrical productions and vaudeville, and among the performers to grace its stage were distinguished stage actor Otis Skinner and the unforgettable early film actress Mary Pickford. The following year the adjacent Little Theatre, later known as the Regency, was constructed expressly as a movie theatre, and it is believed to have been the first such theatre in Richmond.

In 1915 the Empire changed hands and became the Strand, which offered both movies and live stage productions. The Little Theatre failed the next year, largely due to competition with larger cinemas. Over the next decade, the Strand also fell upon hard times and closed its doors in 1927. The Strand and Little theatres are depicted here in the late 1920s, at a time when both were vacant.

Seven years after closing, the Strand returned to operation, under new ownership, as the Booker-T, exclusively a movie theatre. The building was accordingly remodeled. Eddie Cantor's "Kid Millions" and "Romance in Manhattan" with Ginger Rogers are on the bill at the Booker-T for the week of March 10th in this 1934 photograph. The brackets for the letters of the word "Strand" can still be seen over the pediment, and the former Little Theatre, just visible to the right, is a used furniture and appliance shop. After two decades of multiple uses and occasional periods of vacancy, the refurbished Little became the Maggie Walker Theatre in 1936, the second cinema on the block—along with the Booker-T—to serve the African-American community. The Maggie Walker Theatre featured movies until ceasing operations in the late 1960s, and the Booker-T soon followed, closing in 1974.

Both cinemas were purchased in 1976, and restoration efforts began. Between the late 1970s and the early 1980s the adjacent theatres were extensively renovated and were reopened as the Empire and Regency theatres, returning stage performances to the site. In the late eighties, Theatre IV, a theatrical company, purchased the buildings, which now bear its name on the marquee. Specializing in family entertainment, Theatre IV continues to present live theatrical productions, maintaining this Broad Street location as one for the performing arts.

MONUMENT AVENUE, *View from east, 1930s.*

Appropriately named, Monument Avenue is one of the nation's most impressive boulevards. Prestigious residences skirted by tree-lined sidewalks face a wide median, bordered with trees, creating the effect from the air of four lines fading off into the distance. The tree lines are broken by six heroic monuments in remembrance of Civil War leaders J.E.B. Stuart, Robert E. Lee, Jefferson Davis, Thomas "Stonewall" Jackson, and Matthew Fontaine Maury, and tennis legend Arthur Ashe. The Monument Avenue concept derived from the placement of the Lee Monument in a field west of town. The statue was dedicated on May 29, 1890. The evolution was gradual, with the Stuart and Davis monuments following in 1907, the Jackson and Maury statues twelve and twenty-two years later, respectively, and the Ashe statue most recently in 1996.

Enhancing the beauty of the expansive avenue is the collection of residential designs from both locally and nationally prominent architects, including New Yorkers John Russell Pope, also the designer of Richmond's Broad Street Station, and William Lawrence Bottomley, the architect for several homes and an apartment building along the thoroughfare.

In the foreground of these views, the Stuart Monument, at Lombardy Street, is framed by Stuart Circle Hospital on the southeast, First English Evangelical Lutheran

MONUMENT AVENUE, *View from east, 1999.*

Church on the southwest, St. John's United Church of Christ on the northeast, and Bottomley's Stuart Court Apartments, designed in 1924, on the northwest. Immediately west of First English Evangelical Lutheran is Grace Covenant Presbyterian Church, built in 1922. Further west down the street, the Lee Medical Building, erected in 1950, faces the Lee Monument from the southwest. In May 1999 a plaque unveiling ceremony marked the 1997 designation of Monument Avenue Historic District as a National Historic Landmark, making the avenue the first such roadway in the nation to be so recognized by the National Park Service.

JACKSON WARD, *View from Top of Central National Bank Building, 219 East Broad Street, ca. 1931.*

Jackson Ward, as this century began, was one of America's most noteworthy seats of African-American business, politics, and culture. In this neighborhood lived and worked such famed leaders and celebrities as Maggie L. Walker, founder in 1903 of St. Luke's Penny Savings Bank (now Consolidated Bank and Trust) and the nation's first woman bank president; Giles B. Jackson, venerable attorney; John Mitchell, Jr., editor and publisher of the *Richmond Planet*; the Rev. John Jasper, Baptist minister and author and deliverer of the renowned sermon, "The Sun Do Move;" and the legendary entertainer Bill "Bojangles" Robinson, in whose honor a statue was erected in the 1970s at Adams and Leigh Streets. Fraternal organizations and churches, such as Reverend Jasper's Sixth Mount Zion, Ebenezer Baptist, and Third Street Bethel A.M.E., figured prominently in the life of this community.

The tall church steeple in the 1930s view is that of Hood Temple A.M.E. Zion

JACKSON WARD, *View from Top of Wachovia Bank Building, 219 East Broad Street, 1999.*

Church at the corner of West Clay and Adams. The building is the former Clay Street Methodist Church, built in 1859. The Hood Temple congregation acquired the church in the teens, and the spire, a later addition, was dismantled in 1945. Also noticeable in comparing the two photographic views, the Consolidated Bank and Trust now stands across 1st Street from its 1930s location.

In the 1970s Jackson Ward Historic District was awarded National Historic Landmark status, recognizing the area for its importance in 19th- and 20th-century African-American history and for its rich architectural heritage as well. The Maggie L. Walker National Historic Site, on Leigh Street, is presently administered by the National Park Service, and the district is home to the Black History Museum and Cultural Center of Virginia.

MEDICAL ARTS BUILDING, *2nd and Franklin Streets, mid-1920s*

LINDEN ROW, *100-114 East Franklin Street, 1937.*

LINDEN TOWERS, *2nd and Franklin Streets, 1999.*

Named for the linden trees that once occupied the site, Linden Row stands today much as it has since it was built in the mid-19th century. This Greek Revival row was constructed in two stages. Originally there were ten houses, the five easternmost ones built in 1847, and the western ones six years later, all being attributed to Richmond architect Otis Manson. The row has had many occupants over the years, notably Miss Virginia Randolph Ellett, who operated a girl's school in 112 East Franklin around the turn of the century. Miss Ellett's school was the antecedent of the present St. Catherine's School on Grove Avenue. In 1922 the two houses on the 2nd and Franklin corner were replaced by the Medical Arts Building, which included the Van Pelt & Brown pharmacy and the Baptist Book Store on the street level.

By the late 1930s the row was rental property, the site of small businesses and antique shops. Mary Wingfield Scott, eminent Richmond architectural historian, purchased the row to preserve it, giving it to the Historic Richmond Foundation in the 1980s. The entire block has now been revitalized. The Medical Arts Building has just been restored and reopened for apartments and offices as Linden Towers, and the row is now Linden Row Inn, a first-class hotel. In honor of Linden Row's rescuer, the cobblestone alley behind has been fittingly named, "Miss Scott's Alley."

CHAPTER 2

CHANGE AND GROWTH
Then and Now

When analyzing Richmond's changing scenes through the photographic archives at Dementi Studio, several sets of comparisons emerged. The first chapter explored past and present views from the same vantage point. This chapter will focus on the change and growth of a sampling of Richmond establishments, many of which outgrew their original surroundings as they prospered and chose to relocate either across the street or across town. The following photographs alone exemplify the evolution and success over the years of these institutions, businesses, and organizations.

HERMITAGE COUNTRY CLUB, *Hilliard and Brook Roads, 1940s.*

Early in the century, the Hermitage Golf Club opened on Broad Street near Davis Avenue, on the old State Fairgrounds site. By 1916, to make way for the new Broad Street Station, the club moved north, establishing a course at U.S. Route 1 and Hilliard Road on a former estate in Henrico County. The only major professional golf tournament to be held in Virginia, the 1949 PGA Championship was played on this course, and it was won by Virginian Sam Snead.

Membership to the club grew, and looking to expand its facilities, Hermitage Country Club again made a change, relocating in 1973 to outlying Goochland County. With the move, a new Hilliard Road club was opened to the public in 1976. Now known as Belmont Golf Course, the facility is part of the Henrico County park system.

The present Hermitage Country Club has been the site of amateur and professional golf tournaments alike, including eight Senior PGA tournaments in the 1980s featuring the likes of Arnold Palmer, Gary Player, and Chi Chi Rodriguez. The club hosted its second consecutive Trigon Champions senior tennis tournament in April 1999. This tour has come to Richmond for the past three years, bringing such talents as Jimmy Connors, John McEnroe, and Bjorn Borg.

HERMITAGE COUNTRY CLUB AND VIEW ACROSS LAKE, *Goochland County, 1999.*

VIRGINIA HISTORICAL SOCIETY, *Lee House, 707 East Franklin Street, 1930s.*

VIRGINIA HISTORICAL SOCIETY, *Battle Abbey, 428 North Boulevard, 1999.*

During the Civil War the Stewart family loaned their house, built in 1844, to the family of Gen. Robert E. Lee, and when he was in Richmond during the conflict, the General joined his family here. It was on the back porch of this residence that photographer Mathew Brady recorded his famous portrait series of General Lee in mid-April 1865, just days after Appomattox. Years later in the 1890s, the Stewart family donated the house to the Virginia Historical Society for its headquarters and as a repository for its collections. The Historical Society was established in 1831, with Chief Justice John Marshall serving as its first president.

The Battle Abbey was built ca. 1913 to house the collections of the Confederate Memorial Association, and it came into the possession of the Virginia Historical Society in 1946 through the merger of the two organizations. The Society vacated the Lee House in 1959, establishing headquarters on the Boulevard and passing the Lee House title to the Confederate Memorial Literary Society, the founding organization of the Museum of the Confederacy. In the past decade the Historical Society has renovated extensively, counting increased exhibition space, an expanded research library, and a new conservation lab among the improvements. More recently it welcomed to its facility the offices and collections of the Virginia Department of Historic Resources.

RYLAND HALL, *Richmond College campus, ca. 1900.*

Begun around 1830 as a small academy to educate ministers, the Virginia Baptist Seminary was incorporated in 1840 as Richmond College. Occupying the estate conveyed to the college by Mrs. Philip Haxall, the campus was bounded by Broad, Franklin, Ryland, and Lombardy, and it initially consisted only of Columbia, the old Haxall mansion, and its outbuildings. Its noted T.C. Williams School of Law opened in 1870. Ryland Hall, the massive structure depicted here, was built in the 1870s and was named for the school's first president, Dr. Robert Ryland.

In 1912 Westhampton College was founded. The same year Richmond College left the downtown campus, and both institutions settled in a parkland just west of the city. Westhampton College had evolved from the Richmond Female Institute established some sixty years earlier by the Baptists to educate young women. The two schools were joined in 1920 to form the University of Richmond, and graduate degrees were offered the following year. The E. Claiborne Robins School of Business was established in 1949, the School of Continuing Studies in 1962, the Jepson School of Leadership Studies in 1989, and the School of Arts and Sciences in 1990. Amenities of this private university include the Robins Center sports facility and the George M. Modlin Center for the Arts with its Jepson Theatre and Camp Concert Hall, which opened in 1996. Among the most picturesque of the Gothic buildings on the campus are the Cannon Memorial Chapel and the Boatwright Memorial Library, named for Dr. Frederic William Boatwright, the University's third president.

CANNON MEMORIAL CHAPEL AND BOATWRIGHT MEMORIAL LIBRARY, *University of Richmond, 1999.*

BLUES ARMORY, *6th and Marshall Streets, 1920s.*

The colossal Blues Armory was erected in 1909 as the meeting and drilling place for the Richmond Light Infantry Blues, a proud militia unit formed about 1790. From their inception, the Blues saw action in most major military conflicts, including World Wars I and II. The Blues were also a ceremonial unit, marching in parades, dedicating monuments, and representing the capital city both at home and abroad.

The Blues Armory was built on the site of the northern extension of the Sec-

SIXTH STREET MARKETPLACE, *Blues Armory, 1999.*

ond, or New, Market. The Second Market was first situated at the southeast corner of 6th and Marshall Streets in 1817, and in 1834 it expanded across Marshall. A street-level market was maintained in the armory, thereby retaining that corner as a component of the Second Market. The building also served as a sports arena. The structure accommodated the Richmond Blues until the mid-1960s. After renovations in 1985, Blues Armory again became a center of activity, forming the northern terminus of the Sixth Street Marketplace.

BYRD FIELD, *Henrico County, 1930s.*

The city of Richmond in 1927 moved to purchase a large tract of land to build a municipal air strip. The property had already been leased as a landing field by barnstorming ace Roscoe Turner, with financial assistance from a group of Richmond businessmen. After its acquisition by the city, the field became known as Richmond Air Junction. The name was short lived, however, for on October 15 of the same year, the site was officially dedicated as Byrd Field, named for the famed aviator, explorer, and Virginia native Richard Evelyn Byrd. The highlight of the

RICHMOND INTERNATIONAL AIRPORT, *Henrico County, 1999.*

ceremonies was the landing of another celebrated flyer, Col. Charles A. Lindbergh, who arrived in the "Spirit of St. Louis."

Pitcairn Aviation, from Philadelphia, a forerunner of Eastern Airlines, first administered the field. Temporary hangers and small buildings were utilized until the 1950 Byrd Field terminal was dedicated, with Rear Admiral Byrd as guest speaker. Since that time, numerous expansions and renovation campaigns have been undertaken at Richmond International Airport, as it is now known.

OLD FIRST BAPTIST CHURCH, *12th and Broad Streets, 1930s.*

FIRST BAPTIST CHURCH, *Monument Avenue and the Boulevard, ca. 1928.*

FIRST BAPTIST CHURCH, *Monument Avenue and the Boulevard, 1999.*

Prominent in Richmond's 19th-century skyline was the First Baptist Church, built in 1841 and designed by Philadelphian Thomas U. Walter. The First Baptist white members left their original 1802 church, one block east, to the mostly African-American congregation, and erected this striking Greek Revival temple-form structure. When built, the design included a short, wooden bell tower that is easily distinguishable in 19th-century Richmond photographs. Gradually, the building has been dwarfed by taller construction over the years.

During the Civil War, the call went out for churches to donate their bells to be melted down "for the cause." The First Baptist congregation voted to give their bell to the Confederate government, but James Thomas, a generous church member, stepped forward with an offer of gold in place of the bell. His offer was readily accepted.

After nearly eighty years in this location, in 1928 the congregation moved to the corner of Monument Avenue and the Boulevard, in the shadow of the Stonewall Jackson Monument. The bell tower was removed from the church the following year, and the original bell was taken to the Monument Avenue site, where it is presently displayed. Old First Baptist is now owned and used by the Medical College of Virginia.

A June 1927 groundbreaking ceremony marked the start of construction for the new church on Monument, and the design closely resembled the downtown church the members had just left. The first service was held in December 1928, and the church has been conducting services on this notable corner ever since.

**OLD FEDERAL RESERVE
BANK,** *100 North 9th Street,
early 1920s.*

**OLD FEDERAL RESERVE BANK, FOSTER STUDIO, AND ST. PAUL'S
CHURCH,** *North 9th Street, 1920s.*

FEDERAL RESERVE BUILDING, *701 East Byrd Street, 1999.*

A true feather in Richmond's cap was the 1914 selection of the city as the location for the Fifth District Federal Reserve Bank, which first established offices at 1109 East Main Street. Having outgrown this space, in 1919 the offices moved to a new building designed by the Baltimore architectural firm of Sill, Buckler & Fenhagen. The original block of the new structure was enlarged, and an annex was added within a few years by Richmond's Carneal and Johnston, Architects. Crowned by a band of lion heads, this stately edifice holds a commanding position opposite Capitol Square. The Virginia State Supreme Court now occupies the building.

The Federal Reserve's next move was a few blocks to the southwest, towards the James River. The architectural firm of Minoru Yamasaki and Associates, noted for Manhattan's World Trade Center, designed the new Fifth District headquarters built in 1978 near the site of the old Byrd Street Station. As seen in the photograph, the building is flanked by the west Riverfront Tower on the right and the Virginia Power building on the left.

Norfolk native Walter Washington Foster established Foster's Photographic Gallery in an adjacent building in 1890. It was his second attempt at opening a studio in Richmond, the first one being on Venable Street fourteen years earlier. In the interim, he worked for several photographic firms. Young Richmond photographer Anthony L. Dementi joined Foster in 1917, photographing in the field and developing prints outdoors on the side porch. Dementi stayed for several years before leaving and opening a new studio with partner William Faris. In 1928 Foster moved from the 9th Street address to 404 East Grace Street, where the studio operated long after Foster's death, until it merged with Dementi Studio in 1972.

PARKER FIELD, *North Boulevard, ca. 1965.*

Mooers Field, at Roseneath Road and Norfolk Street, was the home of the Richmond Colts baseball team from 1941 to 1953. In that year the team moved to Colonial Heights, and there was a move afoot to build a new facility to attract a Triple-A International Baseball League franchise. Parker Field, named for Richmond physician Dr. William H. Parker, locally renowned for his sports interests, was built on the old fairgrounds tract on the east side of the Boulevard and was opened April 8, 1954, as the home field for a farm team of the New York Yankees— the Virginians. The "Vees" played their parent club and lost 7-2 in the inaugural game, with the opposing bench including Yogi Berra, Mickey Mantle, and manager Casey Stengel. The Virginians spent eleven seasons at Parker Field, after which the New York farm team moved to Toledo. Parker Field was unoccupied for the 1965 baseball season, but the following year, a Triple-A team, the Richmond Braves, from the Atlanta organization took up residence.

THE DIAMOND, *North Boulevard, 1999.*

Aside from its use as a baseball park, Parker Field hosted other sporting events, including many a local high school Friday night football game. For years it was the site of the finale of the Tobacco Festival Parade. The 1960s interior photograph records the billboard advertisements of the many Richmond merchants who showed their support for the home team. In the background stands the Arena, which originally was an exhibition building for the State Fair. High school and university basketball games as well as craft and trade shows were held at the Arena, until its demolition in the 1990s.

After serving Richmond crowds for thirty years, Parker Field was showing its age. It was replaced in 1985 by a larger, sleeker ballpark, complete with corporate skyboxes, and appropriately named The Diamond. This site on the Boulevard, as it has for the past thirty-four seasons, continues to be the home of the Braves.

OLD HENRICO COUNTY COURTHOUSE, *22nd and Main Streets, 1930s.*

This ivy-covered structure resembles more a private residence than the third county courthouse to be built for Henrico County on or near the southwest corner of 22nd and Main. In 1752 Richmond was chosen as the site of the county seat, which had been in Varina, and the first courthouse predated by thirty years Richmond's incorporation as a city. A second courthouse superseded the first in 1825 and was damaged in the 1865 Evacuation Fire. Following repairs, it served its function until it was replaced in 1896 by the building depicted here.

HENRICO COUNTY COURTHOUSE COMPLEX, *Parham and Hungary Spring Roads, 1999.*

Included in the courthouse were the police headquarters and offices for the School Board, the Board of Supervisors, the Commissioner of Revenue, and the Health Department. The county sheriff's office stands to the right in the photograph, and despite the fact that these buildings were located in the City of Richmond, they continued to administer to Henrico until a new complex opened in the mid-1970s on Parham Road in the western part of the county.

JULIAN'S RESTAURANT, *926 East Main Street, mid-1930s.*

The striped awning and corner pilasters in this image mark the establishment of Guilio Moroni and Co., otherwise known as Julian's Restaurant. The restaurant was founded in 1929 in the hub of the financial district, in sight of Capitol Square. The Texaco gas station to the right is on the spot where the massive Times Building stood earlier in this century, at 10th and Bank. The structure rising over the rooftops to the left is Hotel Rueger at 9th and Bank.

Moroni was joined by his brother-in-law, Peter Poli, in the early 1940s. In 1947 Julian's moved to 2529 West Broad Street, across from Broad Street Station and

JULIAN'S RESTAURANT, *11129 Three Chopt Road, 1999.*

next door to the Capitol Theatre. For many Richmonders, a typical evening out would include dinner at Julian's before or after a show, dance, or sports event. The restaurant moved again, in 1987, just a few doors west to 2617 West Broad, where it remains today in the hands of Poli descendants.

Within the past year, Julian's has opened another location on Three Chopt Road, in the far west end, where, together with the West Broad operation, it continues the family tradition of serving Richmonders and visitors alike its Italian cuisine.

**CENTRAL NATIONAL
BANK BUILDING,**
219 East Broad Street, ca. 1969.

CENTRAL NATIONAL BANK, *3rd and Broad Streets, 1929.*

WACHOVIA BANK BUILDING, *James Center, 1021 East Cary Street, 1999.*

The hustle and bustle of a downtown lunch hour in the 1920s is evident in the 1929 image. The Central National Bank opened in September 1911 as a merchant-oriented bank at 307 East Broad, across the street and one block east from this scene. The bank was soon offering Saturday hours, and it flourished in this part of the city, several blocks northwest of the financial district. Within six years it had moved to the northwest corner of 3rd and Broad, amidst small locally owned businesses. As the bank progressed, more space was needed, and it found itself about to undertake a spectacular expansion project—the construction of Richmond's first modern skyscraper.

Despite the economic hardships of the day, the new Central National Bank opened across the street at 219 East Broad with a grand celebration in June 1930, a few months after the stock market crash. The towering 22-story Art Deco masterpiece by theatre-architect John Eberson, designer of Loew's Theatre a few years prior, changed the Richmond skyline forever. Central National merged with South Richmond's Mechanics and Merchants Bank in the mid-1950s, and in 1979 it began trading as Central Fidelity Bank. Within the past year the bank has been acquired by Wachovia.

In the 1960s the neon letters "CNB" were affixed on all four sides on the top of the building, and by their color, Richmonders could tell the weather of the day. Green letters meant it would be getting colder, red letters indicated a warming trend, and the letters blinked when it was about to rain.

DIETZ PRESS BUILDING,
109 East Cary Street, 1946 and 1999.

In 1890 August Dietz, Sr., a native of Germany, established the Dietz Press at 11th and Bank Streets in the old Goddin Hall. August Dietz, Jr., joined his father in the business in 1918, and soon the press concentrated on the publication of regional books, for which it has become so well known. Aside from publishing, Dietz has specialized in printing jobs, and it is credited with being the first press in the country to produce embossed printing on a letter press. For many years it has provided the Colonial Williamsburg Foundation with meticulously crafted reproductions of colorful prints popularized in the 18th century.

In 1923 Dietz Press located its printing operations on East Cary Street in a two-story building designed by Richmond architect Carl Lindner, noted for his small-scale commercial structures of the 1920s and 1930s. The press became a subsidiary of the William R. Smith Company, of Petersburg, in 1991, bringing with it the well-earned reputation for high quality printing and publishing for over a century. Although Dietz Press operations have left the East Cary Street site, the Dietz Printing Company name above the door is an integral part of the history of this city block, and the venerable press maintains a Richmond office managed by the great-grandson of its founder.

MARKOW FLORIST,
304 North 6th Street, 1933.

MARKOW FLORIST, *7th and Broad Streets, 1999.*

Polish-born Theodore and Alex Markow first sold flowers on the corner of 6th and Marshall Streets in 1922. Around 1930 they established a florist shop at 304 North 6th Street in a former barbershop. Within three years the business expanded by acquiring the adjacent building, shown in the photograph depicting Theodore Markow and perhaps his wife on a bright spring morning. The business maintained greenhouses just northeast of the city on North 19th Street, and gradually it expanded along North 6th Street, until it received orders from the City to vacate for the Project One convention center construction. In 1980, after more than fifty years at this location, Markow Florist moved to 817 East Broad, where it remained until the 1990s, when it moved to 700 East Broad Street. Markow Florist, still owned and run by the Markow family, now operates from four locations.

OLD STATE LIBRARY, *Finance Building, Capitol Square, 1940s.*

VIRGINIA STATE LIBRARY, *11th and Capitol Streets, 1940s.*

LIBRARY OF VIRGINIA, *800 East Broad Street, 1999.*

The Virginia State Library was founded in 1823, and its basic function was to serve the government of the Commonwealth. From its inception, it began collecting records and materials relevant to the state's rich history. In 1895 a Neoclassical structure designed by Richmonder William Poindexter was erected in Capitol Square to house the library collections. Presently known as the Finance Building, it served as the library for nearly forty years until a newer facility was built. The Finance Building is now used for state offices.

Facing Capitol Square and built in 1939 on the site of the 19th-century Ford's Hotel, the new Virginia State Library was one of a few key edifices constructed in Richmond by the Public Works Administration, under Franklin Delano Roosevelt's New Deal program. The efforts to clear the entire block before construction included moving a low-rise 1930s prefabricated office building, the Aluminum Building, by literally rolling it down Governor Street to a new location adjacent to Morson's Row. The new library was imposing, with an expansive, paneled lobby welcoming the visitor to the state's repository for books, archives, manuscripts, and artifacts chronicling the history of the Commonwealth. The building was shared with the Supreme Court of Virginia, whose entrance fronted on Broad Street, and it remained in constant use until the collections were moved to a new state-of-the-art facility three blocks west at 8th and Broad Streets, which opened in 1997. Now known as the Library of Virginia, the institution continues its efforts to maintain and preserve the historic records of Virginia, the premise on which it was founded more than 175 years ago.

RICHMOND MOTOR COMPANY, *9th and Marshall Streets, ca. 1930.*

RICHMOND MOTOR COMPANY, *Truck and Showroom, 10th and Broad Streets, early 1930s.*

RICHMOND FORD, *Richmond Motor Company, 4600 West Broad Street, 1999.*

The motorcar was becoming the popular mode of travel by the 1920s. Richmond Motor Company was established in 1916, and by the early twenties Waverly G. King, Sr., had built a Ford dealership in the middle of downtown, on the site of the present City Hall. Within a few years, as the 1930s photograph attests, a full automotive service station dominated the block, complete with a service area, gas pumps, a "lubritorium", a used-car lot, and a curious octagonal building. A show-room featuring the latest car models was at 10th and Broad Streets. In the photograph, over the rooftops can be seen the tip of the bell tower of First Baptist Church, the spire-less steeple of Broad Street Methodist Church, and then-City Hall, all on Broad Street. In 1960 Richmond Motor Company left the immediate area, moving to 4600 West Broad Street, where it remains today, still owned by the King family.

FIRST AFRICAN BAPTIST CHURCH, *301 College Street, ca. 1930s.*

FIRST AFRICAN BAPTIST CHURCH, *2700 Hanes Avenue, 1999.*

Richmond's original First Baptist Church was built on this College Street site in 1802. Within forty years the congregation had erected a new church edifice at 12th and Broad and sold the College Street building to the African-American members of the church. By law black congregations could only worship under the direction of a white minister, and Dr. Robert Ryland, Richmond College president, served this membership for twenty-five years. The 1802 structure was replaced by the present building, constructed in 1876 and originally covered with stucco and topped by a distinctive bell tower. The church remained in use until the late 1950s, when the First African Baptist congregation moved to the former Barton Heights Baptist Church building at 2700 Hanes Avenue, in Richmond's north side. The building on College Street is now owned and used by the Medical College of Virginia.

Through the years several African Baptist congregations have evolved from First African Baptist Church.

U.S. CUSTOMS HOUSE AND POST OFFICE, *1000 East Main Street, 1940.*

Over nearly a century and a half, the U. S. Customs House and Post Office has grown from its original 1858 three-story, three-bay design by Bostonian Ammi Young to the impressive four-story, 15-bay structure on the northeast corner of 10th and Main Streets. During the Civil War this building accommodated the Confederate Treasury offices, as well as that of President Jefferson Davis. In April 1865 photographs taken after the Evacuation Fire, it is the lone survivor standing amidst the rubble on Main Street. It was to this place that two years later Jefferson Davis was brought to be charged for treason but was subsequently released.

Architecturally, three major expansions occurred, including one around 1911

U.S. POST OFFICE, *Main Station, 1801 Brook Road, 1999.*

in which the interior was completely gutted. Sections of the original facades, however, were used in the rebuilding. Over the years the structure has served concurrently as a Federal Courthouse, fronting on Bank Street, and as Richmond's main Post Office, entering from Main Street. A new main Post Office designed by Marcellus Wright and Associates was built in the city's north side on Brook Road in 1970. The old building continued to house branch postal services until they were moved to the 700 block of Main Street within recent years. It remains, however, as the Federal Courthouse and stands symbolically for the resilience of a once-captured city.

ALBEMARLE PAPER MANUFACTURING CO., *North bank of James River, 1941.*

In 1918 a young Floyd D. Gottwald was hired as an office clerk at the Albemarle Paper Manufacturing Company, a Richmond firm established in 1887 and situated on the James River below Hollywood Cemetery. Within twenty-three years, Gottwald had worked his way up to the presidency of the company. He guided Albemarle Paper through some lean years, and in the mid-1950s he directed the company's purchases of several firms in the paper and paper products industry. By the late 1950s the company had acquired a prominent tract of city park land on Gamble's Hill overlooking the James, along with what remained of the Tredegar Iron Works, the famed Confederate foundry. Construction of corporate headquarters on Gamble's Hill was underway, when in 1962 the smaller Albemarle Paper purchased

ETHYL CORPORATION, *330 South 4th Street, 1999.*

the much larger Ethyl Corporation (Delaware), thereby forming the Ethyl Corporation of Virginia. In seven years Ethyl began selling its interests in paper manufacturing, with title to its Richmond paper holdings being passed to a new firm, James River Corporation, now Fort James Corporation. Ethyl had restored the Tredegar site by the 1970s and had sold its last remaining paper company to concentrate on chemicals and high technology. In the 1990s Ethyl Corporation strengthened its presence near the river by constructing a massive laboratory complex on the site of the old Virginia State Penitentiary. Over the years, philanthropically, it has given much to the community.

MAIN STREET STATION, *15th and East Main Streets, ca. 1905.*

Main Street Station had been opened less than two months when it witnessed its first of the many floods that for decades plagued the businesses lying in the James River flood plain. The French Beaux Arts-style train station was designed by the firm of Wilson, Harris, and Richards, of Philadelphia, and opened for service in 1901. Its construction was a combined effort between the Chesapeake and Ohio Railroad and Seaboard Air Line, both antecedents of the CSX Corporation. The station design, complete with its mammoth shed, incorporated an elevated track system to avoid damage from the frequent flooding. For years passenger trains stopped at Main Street Station, until the service terminated in the 1970s. In the mid-1980s, the train shed was transformed into a retail marketplace, which closed in 1988. The property was then acquired by the Commonwealth of Virginia and used for office space. Presently plans are being formulated for the City to purchase the station and for passenger rail service to run through the heart of downtown once again.

The ca. 1905 photograph captures the station from the west, looking down Main Street, showing the elevated track. The building is now wedged between the track on the west, a track on the east, and the ramp connecting I-195 to I-95. As seen from the east in 1999, its turn-of-the-century elegance stands in sharp contrast to the Commonwealth's Monroe Building to the rear.

MAIN STREET STATION, *15th and East Main Streets, 1999.*

PHILIP MORRIS, *Tobacco Row, East Cary Street, 1940s.*

Philip Morris USA is named for the London tobacconist who began producing cigarettes in the mid-19th century. Within twenty years of the venture, cigarettes were exported to the U.S, and in 1919 a group of investors brought Philip Morris and Co, Ltd., Inc., to Virginia. Marlboro cigarettes were first introduced in the mid-1920s, and by 1929 the company was producing cigarettes in this 20th Street facility.

In the photograph the famous marketing campaign of "Call for Philip Morris" is recalled on the upper story of the factory. In Manhattan in the 1930s, a diminutive Hotel New Yorker bellhop was asked by a company marketer to find "Mr. Philip Morris." Little Johnny obliged by calling for Mr. Morris throughout the

PHILIP MORRIS USA, *Commerce Road, 1999.*

lobby, and soon the renowned slogan reverberated across the nation. The 20th Street plant, now closed, is a major component in the revitalization of the historic Tobacco Row district, where the former tobacco factories and warehouses are being converted into luxury residential units, retail shops, restaurant, and commercial offices.

Richmond's Philip Morris manufacturing complex and headquarters are on Commerce Road, where they have been since the 1970s. Philip Morris remains a giant in the food and tobacco industries. The corporation has been generous in its sponsorships of sporting and cultural events and its contributions to various organizations and institutions both locally and nationally.

WARDS TV, *616 East Broad Street, 1958.*

Fifty years ago Richmonder Samuel S. Wurtzel opened a retail store at 705 West Broad Street to sell something new for the day—televisions. With this store, Wurtzel and his partner, Abraham L. Hecht, began a chain of television and appliance stores, Wards TV, that within a half century would evolve into a nationwide multi-billion-dollar corporation. The name Wards was formed from the first letters of the Wurtzel family's names, preceded by "W" for Wurtzel. By 1951 Wards TV had moved west to 1806 West Broad Street. Within six years there were three locations, two on Broad Street—one of which is the downtown store in this image—and one on Hull Street, and a fourth was added as the company celebrated its tenth year.

Company expansion started in the next decade, with the establishment of licensed departments in large discount stores. In 1965 Wards acquired the Carousel discount store, which sold appliances, toys, household supplies, and clothing, and a Delaware company with hardware-houseware sales departments in several Southeast stores. By 1970 the concern had opened its sixth store and its second Carousel store and, in addition to other acquisitions, had ventured into audio and hi-fidelity equipment sales. The same year, Abraham Hecht retired from the business, and Samuel Wurtzel turned over the presidency to his son Alan, with Samuel retaining the office of Chairman of the Board. The following year, two Sight 'N Sound stores

CIRCUIT CITY CORPORATE OFFICE, *9950 Mayland Drive, Henrico County, 1999.*

opened in town, followed by the 1974 Wards Loading Dock, a new concept in retail merchandising—a warehouse showroom—offering the consumer a large selection of products "all under one roof." By the end of the decade, the company had branched out to Washington D.C., North Carolina, and California, and a second Wards Loading Dock and the first of its Circuit City stores had come upon the scene.

In the 1980s a merger with Lafayette Radio Electronics Corporation brought business to the New York metropolitan area, the Loading Dock stores became Circuit City Superstores, and the company itself was renamed Circuit City Stores, Inc. The following year both Samuel Wurtzel and Abraham Hecht died. Under the leadership of chairman of the board Alan Wurtzel and chief executive officer Richard Sharp, Circuit City followed the savvy pattern of acquiring and releasing stores to focus on building larger, more consumer-serviceable operations. This pattern resulted in more Circuit City Superstores, and by the nineties, the corporation was pioneering the sales of previously owned cars with its new concept, CarMax, offering vehicles at set prices. In 1999 the electronics giant boasts, among other accomplishments, over five-hundred superstores, fifty express stores, and twenty-five CarMax operations.

BLOEMENDAAL FARM, *Grace Arents Garden, 1925.*

In the 1880s tobacconist and philanthropist Major Lewis Ginter purchased a Henrico County tract on which he built the Lakeside Wheel Club House and a zoological park. Years earlier, Ginter's widowed sister and her children had moved from New York to Richmond to be closer to him. Ginter's favorite among them was his niece, Grace, and it was she who inherited a sizeable part of his estate when he died in 1897. Grace Evelyn Arents followed in her uncle's footsteps in her philanthropic efforts. Among other charitable acts, for the Oregon Hill community she financed the building of St. Andrew's Episcopal Church, public baths, a library, a school, a housing project, and a playground.

Grace Arents did not inherit the Lakeside Wheel Club House property from her uncle, but she did purchase it and the almost-ten acres that surrounded it in 1913 from his Land and Improvement Company. Through extensive renovations, the clubhouse was soon remodeled into a facility for sick children. The project transformed the former one-story building into a two-story Dutch Colonial residence. The retreat served the children until 1917, when Miss Arents and her companion, Mary Garland Smith, moved into the house.

E. CLAIBORNE ROBINS VISITORS CENTER, *Lewis Ginter Botanical Garden, 1800 Lakeside Avenue, 1999.*

Gradually, Miss Arents had been acquiring acreage for the estate, and she chose the name Bloemendaal Farm, after the Ginter home place in the Netherlands. On the property she planted floral and vegetable gardens and a wide variety of trees and shrubs, reflecting her intense botanical interests. Grace Arents died in 1926, and her will stated that Mary Garland Smith had life rights to Bloemendaal and that at Miss Smith's death, the seventy-two-acre estate would pass to the City of Richmond to be used as a public park and botanical garden, the Lewis Ginter Botanical Garden, in memory of Miss Arents's beloved uncle. With Miss Smith's death in 1968, the property reverted to the City, however, it was not until sixteen years later that the Lewis Ginter Botanical Garden, Inc., a nonprofit foundation, was established to bring the undertaking to fruition.

The Lewis Ginter Botanical Garden, with its professional staff and educational outreach, has received widespread acclaim as a key horticultural center. In April 1999 the new, expansive E. Claiborne Robins Visitors Center opened to welcome patrons from all directions to this beautiful botanical sanctuary.

CHAPTER 3

A CENTURY OR MORE OF SERVICE
Then and Now

No celebration of Richmond would be complete without including a cross section of the Richmond community that has weathered the storms over the last one hundred years. The following images tell stories of survival, perseverance, and endurance of institutions and businesses that soon will experience their second turn of the century. Interestingly and understandably, many of the businesses included here remain family owned and operated, creating an unbroken chain of service, from then until now.

J. W. BLILEY FUNERAL HOME, *3rd and Marshall Streets, 1936.*

Joseph W. Bliley, Sr., established a funeral parlor in 1874 at the corner of 3rd and Marshall Streets, adjacent to the old St. Mary's Catholic Church. Over the past 125 years, the business has passed through a continuous line of family members, and it is now owned and operated by the third Bliley generation, Nicholas M. and Norbert M. Bliley. The funeral home had remained at the Marshall Street location for more than 120 years, when it relocated to the present West End site in 1995.

JOSEPH W. BLILEY FUNERAL HOME, *3801 Augusta Avenue, 1999.*

The firm maintains a strong interest in history, listing among its holdings an original turn-of-the-century carriage; the original steeple bell from St. Mary's Church, whose congregation moved to Gayton Road in the 1950s; and an extensive collection of original Civil War prints, permanently on display at the Central Chapel. The Joseph W. Bliley Funeral Home maintains two additional locations, the Chippenham Chapel and the Staples Mill Chapel.

JEFFERSON HOTEL, *101 West Franklin Street, early 1940s.*

Today the city continues to reap the benefits of the generosity, efforts, and talents of a young New Yorker who arrived in Richmond in the 1840s. As a businessman, financier, and tobacconist, Confederate veteran Lewis Ginter amassed his fortunes, and in the 1890s the longtime resident commissioned New York architects Carrère and Hastings to design a grand hotel for his beloved capital city. The result was the Jefferson Hotel, which Ginter built on the spot where Joseph Reid Anderson's stately residence had stood. The resplendent hotel opened in 1895. It was eclectic in design, inspired by the Italian Renaissance, with other European influences. The interior was spectacular, complete with a grand marble staircase leading to a palm court featuring a standing sculpture of Thomas Jefferson by Richmond's Edward V. Valentine.

A devastating fire nearly destroyed the entire structure in 1901, but the hotel was rebuilt and opened its doors again six years later. The rebuilding included the

JEFFERSON HOTEL, *101 West Franklin Street, 1999.*

addition of a ballroom to the east on the Main Street facade and the placement in the palm court of pools graced with live alligators. In its heyday the hotel was the site of many social events, such as balls and honorary banquets, and it counted among its guests Presidents McKinley, Wilson, Coolidge, Theodore Roosevelt, and Franklin D. Roosevelt, and a host of other celebrities including Charles Lindbergh, Charlie Chaplin, and Elvis Presley. The Jefferson suffered another fire during World War II, but, as before, it survived. Gradually in the last half of this century, its popularity and maintenance declined, leading to the hotel's closure in 1980. Purchased by a local investment group, the landmark was restored, and in 1986 it opened once again. This architectural gem continues to be a center of social activity. Not living to see the new century, Lewis Ginter died in 1897, yet his spirit remains alive and well in Richmond more than a century later.

PLANTERS NATIONAL BANK,
1200 East Main Street, ca. 1925.

**STATE AND CITY BANK
AND TRUST CO.,** *9th and
Main Streets, mid-1920s.*

After the Civil War had ended in April of 1865, Richmond quickly began to rebuild, and it was not long before banks were opened. One of the early banks was Planters National, established in December 1865. The new bank flourished, weathering the economic panics of 1873 and 1893, and it was successful enough to erect a new building during the latter crisis. Richmond architect Charles H. Read, Jr., de-

CRESTAR RIVERVIEW CENTER, *1001 Semmes Avenue, 1999.*

signed this stalwart structure in the Richardsonian Romanesque style, as introduced by H. H. Richardson in Boston two decades earlier. In the 1920s view Planters National's neighboring businesses include Southern Stamp and Stationery, behind its delivery truck to the right, marked by an oversized rubber stamp hanging above the entrance just under the fire escape. The old Planters National building was saved from demolition and restored in the 1980s for use by the Virginia Retirement System, its present occupant.

The State and City Bank and Trust Company was formed in 1922. The bank building at the northeast corner of 9th and Main Streets was constructed in 1923, and three years later a consolidation with Planters National Bank formed the State-Planters Bank and Trust Company. In the 1960s the bank joined with several state banks to create United Virginia Bankshares, soon trading as the United Virginia Bank. The company built an operations center on Parham Road in Henrico County, and in 1983 constructed its new headquarters at the southwest corner of 10th and Main Streets. In the late 1980s the bank became known as Crestar.

Aside from the Main Street location and the suburban Operations Center, Crestar recently erected its Mortgage Corporation complex on the south bank of the James River. Adjacent to the mortgage complex, the brand new Crestar Riverview Center opened in April 1998, giving the bank a strong presence on both sides of the James.

THE MUTUAL BUILDING, *909 East Main Street, 1920s.*

In 1794 Prussian immigrant Frederick William Ast chartered the "Mutual Assurance Society Against Fire on Buildings, of the State of Virginia," which soon was known as the Mutual Assurance Society of Virginia. The Society first met the following year, and by February 1796 the company began writing fire insurance policies, with Chief Justice John Marshall being among the first to insure his home.

THE MUTUAL ASSURANCE SOCIETY OF VIRGINIA, *4100 Fitzhugh Avenue, 1999.*

Four years later Thomas Jefferson insured Monticello. At the time, the Society's office was near Governor and Franklin Streets.

In 1900 the firm's offices were at 1014 East Main Street, adjacent to the Customs House. Within five years the Society relocated to the second floor of its new nine-story building, designed by New York architects Clinton and Russell, at the southeast corner of 9th and Main Streets. The remainder of the building was leased to other companies. Known as the Mutual Building, it was the tallest building constructed in Richmond up to that time, and by 1912 three stories were added, giving it the appearance it retains today.

Seventeen years ago the Society generously donated to the Library of Virginia its complete collection of original bound records for the years 1794-1966 as a rich source for research. In 1991 the firm moved to its new headquarters in Richmond's West End. It is the third oldest mutual fire insurance company in the country.

VIRGINIA ELECTRIC AND POWER CO., *702 East Franklin Street, ca. 1940.*

The evolution of today's Virginia Power began with an 18th-century company chartered to clear the Appomattox River to produce a serviceable transportation route to and from the western part of the state. By the mid-19th century, general interests were leaning towards street transportation.

The horse-drawn cars of the Richmond Union Passenger Railway Company had already been in operation, when, in 1888, New Yorker Frank Sprague was engaged to establish Richmond's electric streetcar system, the country's first successful such operation. Over the next twenty years, several railway companies served the city. In 1909 the Virginia Railway and Power Company was formed to purchase the more prominent street railway firms in Richmond.

Within four years the corporation established itself in a new home office at 7th and Franklin Streets. In the 1920s the company was renamed Virginia Electric and Power Company, or VEPCO, the name it kept until the mid-1980s, when it became Virginia Power. The building, as photographed around 1940, was crowned by a

VIRGINIA POWER, *1 James Plaza, 1999.*

series of lanterns supported by tiny electrical tower-like bases. In the view, to the right can be seen the building that a few years earlier had housed the Old Dutch Market, and to the left, north of the VEPCO building is C & P Telephone, now Bell Atlantic. The corporation has continued to grow through mergers and acquisitions, and over the last thirty years, it has been a leading force in nuclear energy production. In 1978 a new corporate headquarters was built on East Cary Street, north of the Federal Reserve Bank.

BROOKS TRANSFER AND STORAGE CO., INC.,
1224 West Broad Street, 1930s.

Brooks Transfer and Storage was founded in 1878 by Richmonder John W. Brooks and began its moving services with horses and wagons. Years later the company moving vans were Virginia tourism advertisements in themselves, richly painted with scenes of Virginia historic sites, such as Monticello, Mount Vernon, and the Wren Building at the College of William and Mary. When the vans traveled out of state, bystanders—especially school children—would marvel at them and the landmarks they displayed.

The firm acquired the building at 1224 West Broad Street from the National Pepsi Cola Corporation around 1931. Prior to that move the business had been at 8-12 South Linden Street. While Brooks Transfer conducted household moves, Brooks Transportation, its subsidiary with facilities in other states, handled freight, largely for the Great Atlantic and Pacific Tea Company, or A&P. Brooks Transportation, located at 1301 North Boulevard, was so successful that it was running more than nine hundred trucks on the road in the 1930s.

In 1947 Brooks Transfer entered a co-operative with seventeen moving companies, creating United Van Lines, with whom it continues today. Brooks Transportation was sold in 1959, and after the remodeling of the Boulevard site, the bulk of household operations relocated there. The Broad Street facility was maintained until about 1970, when all offices were consolidated at the Boulevard. In 1991 Brooks Transfer and Storage built a new headquarters in suburban Chesterfield County, where the enterprise continues after 127 years, under the ownership and direction of the Brooks family.

BROOKS TRANSFER AND STORAGE CO., INC.,
14200 Justice Road, Midlothian, 1999.

POLLARD & BAGBY REAL ESTATE, *Advertising Sign, 6th and Broad Streets, ca. 1915.*

POLLARD & BAGBY, INC., *2 South 5th Street, 1999.*

Henry R. Pollard, Jr., and John Bagby entered a partnership in 1894 to found the real estate firm of Pollard & Bagby, Inc., and the new company opened at 5-7 North 11th Street. Within eleven years James J. Pollard had joined the firm as a partner, and their offices moved around the corner to 1102 East Main Street. The business specialized in real estate sales for urban, suburban, and farm properties, including country estates, and conducted a successful rental operation as well. Another move, to 1009 East Main, occurred around 1920, and the firm remained at this address for more than half a century. Pollard & Bagby finally relocated to its present home at 2 South 5th Street, where it has been since 1975. Still prominent in the realty industry, Pollard & Bagby continues to be a family-owned-and-operated concern.

VIRGINIA UNION UNIVERSITY, *North Lombardy Street, 1930s.*

In 1865 a former jail in Shockoe Bottom served as the site of a school formed by the Freedmen's Bureau with the help of the American Baptist Mission Society to train African-American clergymen. The school soon became known as the Richmond Theological Institute, and five years later, it moved to the former Union Hotel, at 19th and East Main Streets. In 1899 the Institute merged with Wayland College and Seminary of Washington, D.C., emerging as Virginia Union University, and began construction on Lombardy Street. The 1930s aerial view exhibits the rural look of the campus and the Lombardy-Brook Road intersection at that time.

HARTSHORN MEMORIAL COLLEGE,
Lombardy Street, ca. 1930.

MAGGIE L. WALKER HIGH SCHOOL,
Lombardy Street, ca. 1938.

VIRGINIA UNION UNIVERSITY, *North Lombardy Street, 1999.*

In 1932 the Hartshorn Memorial College, established in 1883 by Providence, R.I., minister Rev. J. C. Hartshorn for the education of African-American women, joined Virginia Union, thus creating a co-educational institution. Hartshorn had been located on Lombardy, south of the University. The main building was torn down, and Virginia Union donated the land for the new African-American high school, shown under construction, named for Maggie L. Walker. The Maggie L. Walker High School served as a comprehensive high school and offered vocational training for nearly fifty years before closing in 1986.

A significant landmark on the present Virginia Union campus is the Belgian Building, with its lofty, rectangular tower. The structure was the Belgian Pavilion in the 1939 World's Fair and was brought to the campus and reconstructed in 1941. Virginia Union University is now a four-year private institution offering degrees from the School of Arts and Sciences, the Sydney Lewis School of Business, and the Graduate School of Theology. In the late 1990s the University dedicated the L. Douglas Wilder Library and Learning Resource Center, named for its famous alumnus, the former Governor of the Commonwealth.

C. F. SAUER CO.,
The Triangle Building,
West Broad Street, 1930s.

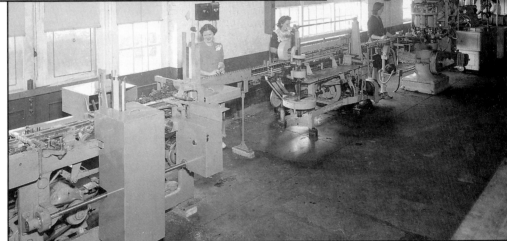

With the revolutionary concept of manufacturing and marketing prepackaged flavoring extracts, Conrad Frederick Sauer, a young, astute drug company salesman, launched his own enterprise in 1887 at 17th and Broad Streets. Making its extracts and spices readily available in packaged bottles and stressing the purity and quality of its products, the C. F. Sauer Company was successful from the start and soon outgrew its quarters. The company moved to 14th and Main Streets, then once more, to accommodate growth, before settling in 1911 at 2000 West Broad Street, its present site.

C. F. SAUER CO., *2000 West Broad Street, 1999.*

Aside from their products, the firm has been known internationally for their fanciful exhibits, inspired by Mrs. C. F. Sauer's blue-ribbon company display at the 1889 Virginia State Fair, and locally for the establishment of Italian and Japanese floral gardens featuring plants and statuary from the Sauers' excursions abroad. C. F. Sauer, Jr., took over the company in 1927, and soon other interests were acquired, leading to expansion into other product lines. In 1929 the Sauers bought Duke's Products Company, in Greenville, S.C., whose now-famous mayonnaise has been a favorite of several generations of consumers. From 1948 to 1951 the company sponsored the popular radio programs the Joan Brooks Show and the Sauer Show, broadcast over Richmond's WRVA and WRNL, respectively, and punctuated with advertisements for Sauer products. Since the 1950s, C. F. Sauer has continued to expand, purchasing a variety of manufacturers and businesses including a vegetable oil refinery, Dean Foods, Pleasants Hardware, and Highs Ice Cream. From its inception, 112 years ago, this company has been in the hands of the Sauer family, which continues to operate by its founder's ideals to provide products of quality.

The Broad Street plant with its animated lighted sign has been a memorable sight for years. Until the 1970s the "Vanilla" incandescent sign, containing over twelve-hundred bulbs, topped the administrative Triangle Building. To improve traffic flow at the congested intersection, the Triangle Building was razed, and the historic sign was moved to the top of a nearby building, where it now faces Downtown Richmond.

COMMONWEALTH CLUB, *401 West Franklin Street, 1920s.*

In the last third of the 19th century, three distinct private gentlemen's clubs were founded in Richmond. The Richmond Club had already been in existence, when the Westmoreland Club formed in 1877. Two years later, while located in the Lee House, the latter club purchased the forty-year-old Stanard House at the southeast corner of 6th and Grace. The third such social organization, the Commonwealth Club, was established ca. 1890 and settled at 401 West Franklin Street in an imposing structure designed by Jefferson Hotel architects Carrère and Hastings of

COMMONWEALTH CLUB, *401 West Franklin Street, 1999.*

New York. The building was erected on the site of the 1814 George S. Palmer House.

The Commonwealth Club had already absorbed the Richmond Club, when in 1937 it merged with the foundering Westmoreland Club, thereby acquiring an impressive collection of paintings of Civil War notables, which graces the club's interior today. The Commonwealth Club has occupied this Franklin Street corner for over a century—a testimony to the endurance of this distinguished organization.

BELL TELEPHONE BUILDING, *703 East Grace Street, ca. 1930.*

The South's first telephone exchange was inaugurated in Richmond in 1879 on the upper floor of 1219 East Main Street, and within a year Southern Bell Telephone and Telegraph was formed. Operations soon moved to 9th and Main Streets and subsequently were transferred in 1902 to a custom-designed facility, the Madison Building, at 711 East Grace. Since that time, for nearly a century, the tele-

BELL ATLANTIC BUILDING, *600 East Main Street, 1999.*

phone company has occupied the 700 block of East Grace. Southern Bell followed with the construction of the adjacent Randolph Central Office Building at 709 in 1906, seen far left in the ca. 1930s view.

Six years later the company became known as the Chesapeake and Potomac Telephone Company of Virginia, part of the nationwide Bell System, and the following year services were extended to the west with the Boulevard Central Office on Stuart Avenue, giving Richmond another exchange. Expansion continued, and in 1930 the new Art Deco building at 701 East Grace opened. By the next year Richmond was switched over to a dialing system, the equipment for which was installed at 701. The thirties photograph depicts the new building, with the Virginia Electric and Power Company building at 7th and Franklin to the right down 7th Street.

The success of the company is evident, as the 700 block site was continually built upon over the next several decades. With the divestiture of American Telephone and Telegraph in the 1980s, C & P Telephone of Virginia became a company within the new Bell Atlantic Corporation. Bell Atlantic-Virginia erected a new headquarters in the mid-1980s at 600 East Main Street, where along with its Grace Street operations, the company continues to be a leading force in the telecommunications industry.

OWENS & MINOR DRUG CO.,
1000-08 East Cary Street, ca. 1950.

Otho O. Owens and George Gilmer Minor, Jr., were wholesale drug salesmen employed by competitive firms in Richmond, when they formed their own company in 1882. Trading as Owens & Minor Drug Co., the fledgling concern first settled at 1007 Main Street, specializing in drugs, medicines, and sundries, both retail and wholesale. Through an 1887 reorganization, the company became a limited partnership, and included among its twenty-four investors was the noted Major Lewis Ginter.

OWENS & MINOR, INC., *4800 Cox Road, 1999.*

Owens & Minor relocated to 1000-08 East Cary in 1913, and within fifteen years it had become a corporation. Pharmaceutical research in the following decades yielded important discoveries, such as antibiotics and penicillin, that boosted the entire drug industry. In 1954 the company automated its order processing with a computer system. It then purchased Richmond's veteran Bodeker Drug Co. the following year, becoming Owens, Minor, & Bodeker, Inc. The corporation's next twenty years saw additional acquisitions.

With its centennial celebration in 1982, the firm reinstated its original name, and it was known once again as Owens & Minor. The rapid expansion of the previous decades accelerated in the 1980s, with steady growth in high technology and distribution systems. The company extended its holdings into the Midwest and then the West by the 1990s. Ten years after its centennial, Owens & Minor's wholesale drug division and pharmaceutical packaging subsidiaries were sold so the firm could concentrate on increasing customer services and strengthening communications through a nationwide network of distribution centers. Early in this decade Owens & Minor moved their corporate headquarters to 4100 Cox Road, in Henrico County's Innsbrook Corporate Center, where the firm, a technologically innovative and dynamic distributor for the healthcare industry, continues to build upon its 117 years of service.

NEWS LEADER SQUARE, *4th and Grace Streets, late 1920s.*

RICHMOND NEWS LEADER DELIVERY FLEET, *North 4th Street, late 1920s.*

The origins of today's Richmond Newspapers extend back to the *Dispatch*, begun by James A. Cowardin and W. H. Davis in 1850. Major Lewis Ginter, builder of the Jefferson Hotel, founded the *Times* in 1886, giving it to Joseph Bryan the following year. Around 1900 John L. Williams and Sons purchased the *Dispatch*, which Williams sold to Bryan in 1903, creating the *Richmond Times-Dispatch*. Concurrent with the birth of the *Times-Dispatch*, the Williams family obtained the *Evening Leader* from Joseph Bryan and adjoined it with their *News* to form the *News Leader*. Therefore, as of these mergers, in 1903 Richmond had a morning *Richmond Times-Dispatch*, owned by one family, and an evening *News Leader*, operated by another.

RICHMOND TIMES-DISPATCH BUILDING, *300 East Franklin Street, under construction, May 1999.*

Five years later Joseph Bryan bought the *News Leader*. He was succeeded by his son, John Stewart Bryan. The Bryans published both newspapers until they sold the *Times-Dispatch* in 1914. The next year Dr. Douglas Southall Freeman began as the *News Leader* editor, a post he would hold for nearly thirty-five years, during which he would become a celebrated biographer and Pulitzer Prize winner.

In the early 1920s the *News Leader* built a new facility on 4th Street between Grace and Franklin, and its substantial fleet of delivery trucks is shown in this 1920s image. The building was constructed in the middle of the block, and a strip of shops known as News Leader Square fronted on Grace Street. In between the two structures was the News Leader Bus Terminal. The paper changed names again in 1925 to the *Richmond News Leader*.

Fifteen years later through the repurchase of the morning paper, the Bryan family once again owned both newspapers, forming Richmond Newspapers, Inc. After fifty-two years of publishing both the morning and evening papers, in 1992 the publications were joined to form one morning paper, the *Richmond Times-Dispatch*.

For the past few years a vigorous building campaign has been conducted at 3rd and Franklin. In the spring of 1999 the construction of a new *Richmond Times-Dispatch* building, replacing the 1922 structure, nears completion across Franklin Street from the newly finished Media General corporate headquarters.

EGYPTIAN BUILDING, *College and East Marshall Streets, ca. 1940s.*

Hampden-Sydney College, in rural Prince Edward County, in 1838 situated its Medical Department in Richmond's Union Hotel, at 19th and Main Streets. The hotel building housed the school's classrooms as well as hospital facilities for seven years, after which the institution relocated to the newly completed Egyptian Building, a few blocks northeast of Capitol Square.

The Egyptian Building, now the South's oldest medical college structure, was the creation of Philadelphian Thomas S. Stewart, the architect responsible for Richmond's St. Paul's Episcopal Church. A classic example of the Egyptian Revival style of architecture utilized in America in the 1830s and 1840s, the edifice exhibits battered walls; columns with capitals of palm leaves; and symbolic medallions, each featuring a sun disc, wings, and a serpent. The structure is surrounded by a cast-iron fence complete with mummy-like posts. The interior, which originally included lecture and hospital rooms, was renovated in the 1930s, and additional remodeling occurred in the 1980s.

In 1854 the General Assembly chartered the school as the independent Medical College of Virginia. A rival school emerged in the capital city in 1893 with the establishment by Dr. Hunter Holmes McGuire of the University College of Medicine, and the two medical institutions led a competitive co-existence until their merger in 1913, maintaining the name Medical College of Virginia (MCV). After being directed by part-time presidents, in 1925 MCV welcomed its first full-time president Dr. William T. Sanger, who served in this capacity for thirty years.

Among the improvements Dr. Sanger began immediately after assuming the

VIRGINIA BIOTECHNOLOGY RESEARCH PARK, *800 East Leigh Street, 1999.*

college's presidency were the implementation of successful fundraising practices and the establishment of the School of Nursing. He also oversaw the construction of several key university buildings, among them the prominent Baskervill and Son 1930s hospital complex. The eighteen-story structure at 12th and Broad, funded through the Public Works Administration, opened in 1940. Since then the institution has continued to build within the surrounding blocks. Dr. R. Blackwell Smith succeeded Sanger, and in his twelve-year presidency, he furthered his predecessor's advancements in the institution's physical plant, faculty, and curriculum.

In 1968 Virginia Commonwealth University (VCU) was formed when MCV merged with Richmond Professional Institute. With this union, a new, modern urban university was created, melding the arts, business, and social work with medical life sciences.

Dr. Eugene Trani, VCU president since 1990, has set the university on a firm course to usher in the 21st century. Over the past decade Trani has spearheaded a dynamic expansion campaign involving both the medical and academic campuses. The most significant additions include the School of Engineering, which opened in 1996, and the recent Virginia Biotechnology Research Park, on East Leigh Street. Both facilities were established to work directly with private industries in advancing research in their respective fields. The Virginia Biotechnology Research Park furthers the concept by creating facilities and an environment for public and private concerns to collaborate in biotechnological exploration, quickly making VCU a leading national—and international—center for research.

RUFFIN & PAYNE, *1701 5th Avenue, ca. 1930.*

RUFFIN & PAYNE INC., *Laburnum Avenue, 1999.*

In the 1890s young Thomas C. Ruffin became a partner with Joseph P. Fourqurean in a small building materials supply company located at 1701 5th Avenue. The business flourished, and there was a change in partnership when Albert Payne, well acquainted with milling operations, joined the firm in 1916. The enterprise gradually channeled its interests towards millwork and lumber, and thirteen years later the name became Ruffin & Payne. The company sustained the Depression and expanded its inventory with residential construction supplies into the 1930s, only to lose much of it to fire in 1939. They quickly rebuilt and continued to expand on the site until the construction of a section of Interstate 64 made relocation necessary. Ruffin & Payne established itself on Laburnum Avenue in 1966, where it continues to serve Richmond as it has since its founding, as a major building material, lumber, and millwork provider.

CHAPTER 4

SPECIAL MOMENTS

Photographs have always had the unique ability to capture subjects at specific places and times. With the quick release of a shutter, a visual memory could be preserved of an automobile run, a store opening, an inauguration, a dedication, a sports match, and even a flood.

Some of the images that follow depict the war heroes, the explorer, the champion, and the entertainers—all celebrated guests for whom Richmond rolled out the red carpet. These glimpses are just a few of the many occurrences in Richmond during the century, yet they all capture and preserve special moments in the life of a city.

CONFEDERATE VETERANS REUNION, *600 Block East Grace Street, June 1-3, 1915.*

About 1885 Richmond's Confederate Soldiers' Home was built on the Boulevard, to house needy Confederate veterans. It is the present site of the Virginia Museum of Fine Arts. Nationally, the United Confederate Veterans organized in 1889, and Chattanooga was the site of their first reunion the following year. Altogether there were forty-two such reunions, with Richmond, the Confederate capital and location of Jefferson Davis's White House of the Confederacy, hosting five, including the last in 1932. One of the grandest of the Richmond reunions was in 1907, when monuments to both J. E. B. Stuart and Jefferson Davis were dedicated.

The twenty-fifth reunion was held in June 1915, and the group shown is lining up in front of Seventh Street Christian Church, on whose site the former Atlantic Life Building and parking garage now stand. The veterans reunions included parades, banquets, speeches, and entertainment, as well as opportunities for the old soldiers to renew friendships and share war stories.

VIRGINIA ENDURANCE RUN GROUP, *100 Block West Franklin Street, May 5-8, 1910.*

Beginning at 6:00 a.m. one May morning in 1910, twenty-three automobiles containing drivers and observers embarked from the corner of 10th and Main Streets for an unforgettable challenge through the Virginia countryside—the Virginia Endurance Run. Among the participants were eight women. Under the sponsorship of the *Richmond Times-Dispatch* and the American Automobile Association, the run entailed a three-day trek from Richmond to Washington to Harrisonburg, then back to the starting point. One of the main purposes for the event was to draw attention to the importance of having good roads in Virginia to facilitate visitation to the state's historic sites and attractions.

The vehicles were sent off at one-minute intervals, and the first day's itinerary took the contestants through Glen Allen, Louisa, Orange, and Manassas, then on to Washington, D.C. Citizens cheered the motorists as they rolled through the towns along the route. To prevent any car from getting lost, a pilot car ahead of the pack tossed confetti onto the roads to mark the way. The participating cars were divided into classes by model types, and the fastest speed permissible was a fleeting fifteen miles per hour. The second day began with a brief reception by President Taft in front of the White House, then the drivers were off towards Winchester to follow the Valley Pike to Harrisonburg. The final leg of the journey came through Staunton, Charlottesville, Goochland Court House, and back into Richmond.

The Endurance Run entrants were photographed on West Franklin Street in front of the Archer Anderson House and the Jefferson Hotel.

109

JACK DEMPSEY, *Broad Street Station, February 19, 1926.*

Outside of Broad Street Station, Richmond fans surrounded celebrated boxer Jack Dempsey, standing in center, who had held the heavyweight title since 1919. He was in town for a boxing exhibition at the Grays Armory at 7th and Marshall Streets. Seven months later in Philadelphia, Dempsey lost the title to Gene Tunney in ten rounds.

BASEBALL WORLD SERIES, *4th Street between Grace and Franklin Streets, October 2, 1926.*

It was the top of the seventh, Herb Pennock was on the mound for New York, and the crowd in Yankee Stadium was going wild, as their Bronx Bombers had just taken the field after going ahead 2 to 1 in the previous inning. Three hundred-fifty miles to the south in Richmond, 4th Street between Grace and Franklin was blocked off from traffic, and the pavement was packed with observers following the progress of the same event—the first game of the 1926 World Series between the St. Louis Cardinals and the New York Yankees. The *Richmond News Leader* set up a scoreboard featuring the lineup for each team, including Hornsby for St. Louis and Gehrig and Ruth for New York. In the center of the scoreboard was a diagram of a baseball diamond, on which markers representing base runners could be moved along when batters achieved base hits. The game was played on October 2nd, and New York went on to win 2-1.

There was a slight delay between the cheers at Yankee Stadium and those on 4th Street. Radio was in its infancy, and WRVA Radio, which had just started the year before, broadcast this game in conjunction with the *News Leader.* The City Editor's desk at the newspaper received the play-by-play by telegraph wires, and the details were relayed to WRVA. This procedure had been successful when the radio station, through the *Times-Dispatch* newsroom, had reported the Dempsey-Tunney fight the month before.

It was not for this game, but it was during this Series that Babe Ruth promised to hit a home run for Johnny Sylvester, hoping to boost the seriously ill boy's spirits. Ruth came through—he hit three! Despite The Babe's gallantry, the Cardinals took the Series four games to three.

CLEAN UP-PAINT UP WEEK, *East Broad Street, May 2-7, 1927.*

As observed from 7th and Broad Streets, a flurry of late twenties activity took place under a sign of civic pride, the hovering spring cleaning directive to "Make Richmond 'the City Beautiful.'" Captured here was a typical day on Broad Street, replete with cars, buses, trucks, and streetcars sporting signs "Baseball To-Day." The 600 and 700 blocks of East Broad were the focus of the retail district, with anchor department stores Miller and Rhoads, the white building in the center, and Thalhimers, to the left in the image.

GOV. HARRY F. BYRD WITH INDIAN TRIBUTE, *Capitol Square, late 1920s.*

In a tradition dating to a 17th-century treaty, two of Virginia's Native American tribes, the Mattaponi and Pamunkey, have presented gifts of game to the governor of Virginia, in payment for the use of their reservation lands. The fall custom continues to the present, with a ceremony in Capitol Square at Thanksgiving. Gov. Harry F. Byrd is shown receiving the tribute from a delegation including noted Pamunkey Chief George M. Cook, his wife, and his daughter.

GUBERNATORIAL INAUGURATIONS

Being the capital of the Commonwealth has afforded Richmond the great plea-sure of witnessing the change of the guard every four years in the form of the inauguration of the newest occupant of the Governor's mansion. As each quadren-nial event has approached, downtown has been abuzz with preparations for the inaugural festivities.

POLLARD INAUGURATION, *January 15, 1930.*

Williamsburg's John Garland Pollard assumed the governorship on a rainy day in January 1930. Despite the weather the ceremony drew a crowd to welcome the new state leader who would steer the Commonwealth through financially anxious times in the middle of the Depression.

DARDEN INAUGURATION, *January 21, 1942.*

On January 21, 1942, the month following the U.S. entry into World War II, Norfolk's Colgate W. Darden, Jr., took the gubernatorial oath. His address was delivered in less than fifteen minutes, and in deference to the events of the previous forty-five days, he canceled plans for a parade or ball.

John Stewart Battle, of Charlottesville, was inaugurated January 18, 1950, at the mid-mark of the century. He was the fourteenth in a long, unbroken line of Democratic governors elected since 1900. In the photograph, J. Lindsay Almond, Jr., Battle's Attorney General and a future Virginia governor, is seated to the extreme right.

BATTLE INAUGURATION, *January 18, 1950.*

STANLEY INAUGURATION, *January 20, 1954.*

Henry County Democrat Thomas B. Stanley followed John Battle to the Governor's mansion on January 20, 1954. The successful entrepreneur brought his business acumen to the Capitol. In a rare depiction, Stanley is captured with a host of Virginia dignitaries including six Virginia governors: (from left to right) former governors John S. Battle and William M. Tuck; U.S. Senator A. Willis Robertson; former governor Harry F. Byrd, Sr.; future governor Albertis S. Harrison, Jr.; Governor Stanley; and future governor J. Lindsay Almond, Jr., Stanley's Attorney General.

Almost eight months into the Depression, amidst rows of floral arrangements, Richmonders had good news to share with the formal opening of the new Central National Bank. The public was invited, and hundreds joined in the celebration. It was a social occasion not to be missed. Not only was a healthy financial institution observing nearly twenty years of serving the community, a city was welcoming a remarkable Art Deco skyscraper, its tallest building to date.

CENTRAL NATIONAL BANK BUILDING OPENING, *219 East Broad Street, June 5, 1930.*

Throngs waited on the sidewalk in anticipation of the Grand Opening of the Charles department store in May 1936, in the building that had previously been the Cohen dry goods store. The new establishment offered reasonably priced items and featured a revolving display window. Inside, the signs read, "Opening Special, Assorted Prints and Sheers 10¢/yd., Value to 29¢" and "Step Thru and Tie Fashionette Dresses $1.00," and after the doors opened, the crowd of bargain seekers spilled in and crammed the aisles. The Charles Store operated here for the next fifty years. During a renovation in 1987, the building was destroyed by fire.

CHARLES STORE OPENING, *13-17 East Broad Street, May 8, 1936.*

TATE FIELD, *Mayo Island, James River Flood, August 18, 1940.*

TATE FIELD, *Mayo Island.*

Richmond is no stranger to the flooding of the James River. Over the centuries, the James has left its banks numerous times, destroying businesses, homes, and even lives in its wake. In 1921 a ball park was built adjacent to the Virginia Boat Club on Mayo Island, in the middle of the James, connected to the north and south banks of the river by Mayo Bridge. The park was the site of football and baseball games, featuring teams from the major and minor leagues as well as area high schools and universities. The Richmond Colts played professional baseball there for twenty years, from 1921 to 1941. During that time, five years after opening, the park was named Tate Field for former Richmond major leaguer Edward Christopher Tate. Babe Ruth played at Tate Field in 1922, and although the Yankees lost to the Dodgers, The Babe homered. Ten years later Ruth and the Yankees were back at Tate, winning against the Colts.

It stands to reason that whenever the James flooded, Tate Field was immediately affected. Several floods during the baseball seasons in the thirties, and the one depicted here in 1940, took their toll on the stadium. After Tate was damaged by a fire in May 1941, Richmond Colts owner Eddie Mooers built Mooers Field in Scott's Addition, the area northwest of Boulevard and Broad, and moved the team to that location, their home until the 1950s. Presently outdoor concerts and events are held on Mayo Island not far from the spot where baseball legends once stepped up to home plate.

FRANK SINATRA AND ED SULLIVAN, *Mosque stage, December 16, 1945.*

During the first holiday season after the end of World War II, touring entertainment headliners played in Richmond. Count Basie and Les Brown and their orchestras performed at the Mosque in December of 1945, as did Frank Sinatra. Ed Sullivan, two-and-a-half years before his famed "Toast of the Town" hit the airwaves, was master of ceremonies for the December 16 Sinatra concert, a Victory Bond show jammed with squealing admirers of the popular singer. Sullivan and Sinatra received tokens of appreciation for their efforts towards the Richmond Victory Loan Campaign—a scroll and a set of golf clubs, respectively, presented by Robert V. Hatcher, the campaign chairman.

WINSTON CHURCHILL AND GEN. DWIGHT D. EISENHOWER, *Capitol Square, March 8, 1946.*

Several months after the close of World War II, two wartime heroes, Britain's then-former Prime Minister Winston Churchill and Gen. Dwight Eisenhower, visited Richmond on a victory tour. They arrived at Broad Street Station and were driven in the rain to Capitol Square, passing thousands who had lined the streets along the way. Churchill addressed the General Assembly in the Capitol, and at the urging of the audience, Eisenhower spoke as well. Williamsburg was the next stop for the touring party. This excursion was not the Prime Minister's first visit to Richmond. He had been hosted by Gov. Harry F. Byrd in 1929 during an earlier trip to the capital city.

LAST STREETCAR, *November 25, 1949.*

Richmond's successful electric streetcar operation was the country's first, begun in 1888. With the birth of the automobile industry and the eventual use of buses transporting Richmonders to the suburbs, the antiquated trolley system was no longer the choice mode of travel. In a bittersweet celebration, the last streetcars ceremoniously took their final run on an autumn day in 1949.

The only major Professional Golfers Association tournament to be held on Virginia soil took place in May of 1949 at Hermitage Country Club at Hilliard Road and Route 1. To the delight of the hometown crowd, Virginia-born Sam Snead took home the first place trophy and $3,500 of the total purse of $17,950. It was a banner year for the thirty-seven-year-old Snead, winning both the Masters and the PGA and being named the Player of the Year.

PGA AT HERMITAGE COUNTRY CLUB, *Hilliard Road, May 25-31, 1949.*

NIKE DOMINION OPEN, *The Dominion Club, May 13-16, 1999.*

Since 1993 the Dominion Club at Wyndham, northwest of Richmond in neighboring Henrico County, has been the home of the NIKE Dominion Open. The tournament is a minor-league PGA event that was first organized three years earlier as the Ben Hogan Tour. The year before coming to the Dominion Club, NIKE began sponsoring the competition. Noted golfers Tom Lehman, John Daly, and David DuVal have all played on the NIKE Tour. In 1999, as in past years, the tournament proceeds benefited local charities. The winner of the 1999 NIKE Dominion Open was Darron Stiles.

**NATIONAL TOBACCO
FESTIVAL SCENES,**
1950s-1960s.

An annual Richmond celebration of tobacco began in the fall of 1949 with the four-day-long Tobacco Festival. Events included a pageant, a spectacular parade, a collegiate football game (the inaugural Tobacco Bowl), fireworks, and a guest appearance by Frank Sinatra. Over the next thirty-five years, the Grand Illuminated Parade continued with regulars Philadelphia's Ferko's Wonder Bread String Band and the Motor Patrol of the Acca Temple; floats representing major tobacco companies and manufacturers, Richmond's banking and retail industries, and local organizations; and a variety of bands and military and marching units. A celebrity of

**NATIONAL TOBACCO
FESTIVAL SCENES,**
1950s-1960s.

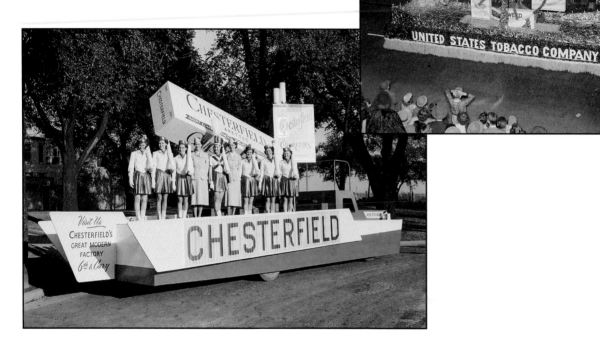

note was chosen each year as the Grand Marshal of the Illuminated Parade, and those serving in this capacity included actresses Eva Gabor and Edie Adams, entertainers Victor Borge and Susan Anton, television and screen actors Lloyd Nolan, Nick Adams, and James Arness, Peter Graves, John Forsythe, Raymond Burr, Greg Morris, and James MacArthur, and comedians Rowan and Martin. The parade moved down Broad Street and proceeded up the Boulevard to a grand finale at Parker Field. By the mid-1980s the Tobacco Festival's glory days had come to a close, and a once-great spectacle had become a memory.

REAR ADM. RICHARD E. BYRD PORTRAIT,
Unveiling, April 1, 1950.

Byrd Airport, now Richmond International Airport, was named for explorer-aviator Richard E. Byrd in 1927. It was not until 1950 that a permanent airport terminal was dedicated, and Admiral Byrd was the guest speaker at the ceremonies. The celebration included the unveiling by Harry F. Byrd III, the Admiral's great nephew, of a painted portrait of the polar explorer in his signature fur parka. The portrait still hangs in the airport terminal. Among the scores of guests participating in the festivities was television and radio personality Arthur Godfrey.

LT. COMMANDER RICHARD E. BYRD,
Academy of Music, 100 Block North 8th Street, 1920s.

TRIGON TENNIS TOURNAMENT, *Hermitage Country Club, April 28-May 2,*
1999.

The Trigon Champions Senior Tennis Tournament first came to Richmond in
1995 and was hosted by the Robious Racquet Club in Chesterfield County. The
next year the contest was moved to the Hermitage Country Club in Goochland
County, where it has remained ever since. Jimmy Connors won the tournament in
1999, earning his third consecutive tour win in Richmond.

RIVERFRONT AND CANAL WALK OPENING, *June 4, 1999.*

With Richmond having been founded on a falls, the benefits of a navigational system to connect the city and points eastward with westward destinations were soon evident. George Washington was an early proponent of the establishment of a canal system, and the James River Company was formed in the late-18th century to build it. Once intact, the canal stretched from Richmond to Buchanan in Botetourt County, with traffic carrying freight as well as passengers. Over the course of the 19th century, the canal ceased to be used for transportation, being eclipsed by the railroads.

Within the last thirty years, abandoned sections of the canal have been preserved, Reynolds Metals Company took the initiative in the 1970s to restore remnants of two of the stone Tidewater Connection Locks of the James River and Kanawha Canal adjacent to the Reynolds Wrap Distribution Center at the foot of 12th Street. When opened in 1854, the lock system of the Tidewater Connection, linking the Richmond dock to the Great Turning Basin, created a direct navigational route extending from the lower James to the western part of the state, thereby negotiating the rapids at Richmond.

The new Richmond Canal Walk has long been visualized by the city's business and civic leaders. Its opening is the culmination of years of research and planning to revitalize Richmond's historic riverfront. The ribbon-cutting ceremonies in June 1999 were just the beginning of an attraction planned to include retail, hotel, and real estate development and to become known for its present-day canal boats, reminiscent of the 18th- and 19th-century bateaux that once operated along this venerable waterway.

JAMES RIVER AND KANAWHA CANAL,
Tidewater Connection Locks, 1970s.

CHAPTER 5

MEMORIES

The remaining pages of this book create a visual tapestry of Richmond, through snippets of time recorded on film.

The photographs, like the threads of a tapestry, tell a grander story when woven together. Captured here are some places and events that exemplify everyday 20th-century life in an American city. By now, at the end of the century, most have long passed from existence; a few constitute very recent memories, but altogether these vignettes portray a city at work and at play.

As we cross the threshold to the new century, each new photograph of Richmond will further the visual tapestry.

ROBERT E. LEE BRIDGE, *James River, 1940s.*

The original Lee Bridge was constructed from 1933 to 1934, aided by the Public Works Administration. The structure connected the north bank of the James at Belvidere to Cowardin Avenue south of the river, cutting across Belle Isle. The span, with its graceful arches, was the design of the firm of Lee, Smith, and Van Dervoort, and it carried vehicles for over half a century until its closure in 1988. It was replaced with the new Robert E. Lee Bridge, which has been touted as the first bridge in the state to be cast in place and built via the balanced cantilever form of construction.

THE CLOVER ROOM, *4118 West Broad Street, ca. 1950.*

The Clover Room, a "safe" haven on a busy Broad Street, was the highlight of the day or evening—the place to meet—for several generations of Richmonders. Opened by Luck Dairy in the 1940s, the Clover Room was a family restaurant to visit in celebration of a birthday or a special event, after cotillion, or just to spend some quality time together over an ice cream sundae. The decor of the comfortable dining area included Frank Dementi photographs of Richmond and Virginia landmarks.

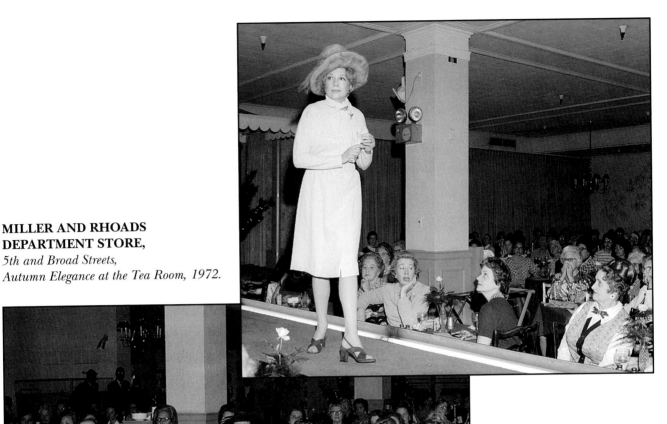

**MILLER AND RHOADS
DEPARTMENT STORE,**
5th and Broad Streets,
Autumn Elegance at the Tea Room, 1972.

Partners Linton O. Miller and Webster S. Rhoads started a dry goods business in 1885 at 117 East Broad Street. By the 1890s they had taken their store to the 500 block of East Broad. Over the ensuing years the store was enlarged gradually until it encompassed much of the block.

A favorite of generations for miles around was the Miller and Rhoads Tea Room. From fashion shows to special luncheons with the inimitable Eddie Weaver at the organ—and an occasional accompaniment by his daughter Jody—to breakfast with Santa, the Tea Room was an obligatory stop on shoppers' itineraries. Fashion events such as the Autumn Elegance exhibited the *crème de la crème* of the Miller and Rhoads selections for the season, including the exclusive Sara Sue hats. Above all, most memorable was Miller and Rhoads at Christmastime, with its enchanting holiday display windows and, of course, Santa.

For decades Miller and Rhoads and Thalhimers both rivaled and complemented each other, creating a firm foundation for the downtown retail district. In 1985 their 6th Street entrances opened into the enclosed mall of the Sixth Street Marketplace, as the stores were integral components of the new revitalization venture. After a combined 254 years of service, however, in the early 1990s, the two once-vibrant department stores ceased operations.

THALHIMERS DEPARTMENT STORE, *6th and Broad Streets, 1942.*

German native William Thalhimer first opened a dry goods store in Richmond's Shockoe Bottom in 1842 and moved the business to East Broad Street in the 1870s. In 1923 Thalhimers moved to a new five-story structure on Broad between 6th and 7th Streets, and the store continued to expand, ultimately to occupy three-quarters of the city block.

Despite the anxiety of the times during World War II, the company celebrated its one-hundredth anniversary with a "Centurama" fashion spectacular, including the appearance of an old Thalhimers delivery wagon for the occasion. The Thalhimers clock at 6th and Broad itself was a popular rendezvous point for downtown shoppers, and a shopping spree was incomplete without a visit to the store's bakery at the 7th Street corner, with its black-and-white-checked motif, for a piece of six-layer chocolate cake.

BYRD PARK, *Shields Lake 1930s.*

BYRD PARK, *Swan Lake, 1930s.*

Summertime fun in the middle of town was a splash in Shields Lake. Many Richmonders learned to swim and dive in this picturesque setting among the trees in Byrd Park. It was the site of picnics and gatherings for friends and families, and nearby Swan Lake was a great place to spend a lazy afternoon with the boys and the fishing poles.

TOM THUMB MINIATURE GOLF COURSE, *2301 West Broad Street, ca. 1931.*

Hot summer nights under the lights at the new miniature golf course on West Broad were a treat and a perfect diversion for Richmonders during the Depression. Located near Broad Street Station, the course was gone from the scene by 1932, but it brought its share of amusement to those who played there.

Another welcomed relief from the times were the feature presentations at the local movie houses. With a lilt in their step, many 1934 moviegoers left the Grand Theatre whistling "On the Good Ship Lollipop," after viewing America's little sweetheart, Shirley Temple, in "Bright Eyes."

GRAND THEATRE,
620 East Broad Street, 1934.

MARKET, *Northwest corner 6th and Marshall Streets, ca. 1935.*

The Second Market grew up around the intersection of 6th and Marshall Streets in the early to mid-19th century. With the 1909 construction of Blues Armory, a market operated under the armory's arcade. Across 6th Street from the armory an open-air market was still going strong in the 1930s, with sidewalk displays of fresh fruits and vegetables.

UKROP'S, *Short Pump, 1999.*

Ukrop's Super Markets opened modestly on Hull Street in the late 1930s. At the outset, Joe and Jacquelin Ukrop conducted business with respect for and full service to their customers. Expanding in the early 1940s, the establishment became a self-service grocery store. The family opened its second store in the early 1960s, and the ubiquitous Ukrop's stores have been popping up around Richmond ever since. For many Richmonders living with busy schedules, entertaining, tailgate parties, pot luck suppers, and simply weekly meals would be nothing without Ukrop's fried chicken or hand-tossed pizza or something from their delicatessens, bakeries, or salad bars. But the first memory of Ukrop's is service, with the friendly ritual of carrying groceries to customers' vehicles. It is a routine service, not one where compensation is expected. Long on family values, in a society where Sunday operating hours are the norm, Ukrop's stores are closed, reserving the day for worship and the family. The same is true for holidays. Whereas other grocery stores sell alcoholic beverages, Ukrop's sells none. All of this, and Ukrop's over the past decades has continued to drive the competition to distraction, even literally out of town. In addition, Ukrop's has been a major supporter of community projects and events.

WASHMOBILE AUTOMATIC CARWASH, *1908 Staples Mill Road, 1955.*

To this early fifties Chrysler, there was nothing better than a stop at the Washmobile Automatic Carwash at Staples Mill Road and Broad Street. Opened in 1955 by the Boisseau family, for nearly twenty years, within minutes, the carwash automatically restored that "like new" shine to road-weary vehicles.

GENERAL MILLS, INC., FARM SERVICE DIVISION, *Former Byrd Street Station, 701-705 East Canal Street, 1940s.*

The adaptive reuse of an old train station was evident in the 1940s, as the old Byrd Street Station served the farm division of General Mills. The depot was built in 1887 by the Richmond, Fredericksburg, and Potomac Railroad, and it operated passenger rail service for over thirty years, before being closed in 1919 at the opening of Broad Street Station. In its heyday the red-brick terminal saw much activity. The tracks extending west from the station led to a tunnel under Gamble's Hill, between 2nd and 5th Streets, and the neighborhood children delighted at the disappearances then reappearances of the trains taking that route. One of the station's final patriotic duties was to send off soldiers to World War I. The station had closed by the time the troops returned to Richmond from war. In the late 1950s the upper two stories were removed in a remodeling for occupation by the Atlantic Coast Line—the building's first railroad use for nearly forty years. The remains of the proud old station were demolished in 1973 to make way for the Manchester Bridge and the Downtown Expressway.

In a late 1930s Memorial Day parade, the John Marshall High School Corps of Cadets marched up Grace Street, passing the stone Seventh Street Christian Church, on whose site now stands the old Atlantic Life Building and parking garage. The Corps of Cadets was established in 1915 under the motto of "Duty, Honor, Country." This noted corps over the course of its existence participated in four presidential inaugural parades. Among its many honors, the unit received special notice from Winston Churchill during his brief Richmond tour in 1946.

On May 30, 1999, the John Marshall Cadet War Memorial was dedicated in Richmond's Hollywood Cemetery in memory of members of the corps who made the supreme sacrifice in World Wars I and II, the Korean War, and Vietnam.

JOHN MARSHALL HIGH SCHOOL CORPS OF CADETS, *East Grace Street, ca. 1938.*

On a November evening in 1954, onlookers at the Thalhimers Toy Parade gazed at the balloon of a lovable dragon, guided by a troop of Boy Scouts. The setting was a brick-paved section of East Broad Street across from the sponsoring Thalhimers department store. The Toy Parade, an annual event dating to just after World War II, had something for everyone, including marching bands, holiday floats, circus clowns, and upwards of forty balloons of all descriptions ranging from cartoon characters to sea monsters to pirate ships. Each year tens of thousands of parents and children packed the sidewalks along Broad Street for this pre-Thanksgiving extravaganza, which continued into the 1970s. The concept was revived in the 1980s by the Richmond Jaycees, and the annual Christmas parade is now held in December.

THALHIMERS CHRISTMAS TOY PARADE, *East Broad Street, 1954.*

U.S. ARMY RECRUITING STATION, *2nd and Broad Streets, ca. 1929.*

Between the wars the U.S. armed forces kept a high profile in Richmond with this prominently situated recruiting office at the corner of 2nd and East Broad Streets.

WAR BOND STREETCAR, *1943.*

The War effort was comprehensive—even VEPCO's Reddy Kilowatt joined in, announcing via this streetcar the launching of the second citywide bond drive in April 1943.

GROOME'S BUS SERVICE, *Howitzer's Armory, North 7th Street Addition, 1950.*

In 1934 H. V. Groome started a service that over the years has transported scores of Richmonders and visitors, both in and out of town. The firm, first known as Groome's Bus Service, incorporated in 1954 and changed its name to Groome Transportation, Inc. Known more commonly as just "Groome's," the name has for some time been synonymous with limousine service to and from Richmond International Airport. In 1950 it was not uncommon to see a long line of chartered Groome's motorcoaches in town, such as this one in front of the old Howitzers Armory.

MILITARY PARADE,
East Grace Street,
June 12, 1944.

Less than a week after D-Day, armored vehicles, military marching units, and women's corps made their way past the USO at 2nd and Grace Streets and towards Capitol Square in a parade to kick off Richmond's Fifth War Loan drive. The parade review stand filled with dignitaries was erected on 6th Street between Miller and Rhoads and Loew's Theatre, before a

billboard reading, "Back the Attack". The crowds were impressive along Grace, both at the street level and above at the open windows of the buildings along the route.

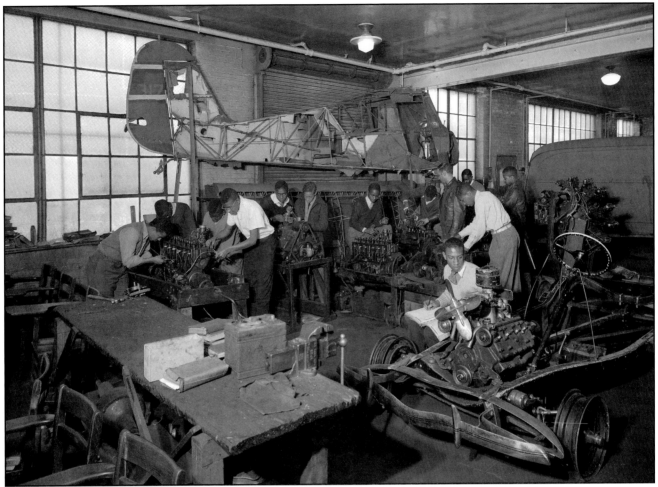

ARMSTRONG HIGH SCHOOL SHOP CLASS, *1946.*

A year after the close of World War II, when this shop class was photographed, Armstrong High School was located at 119 West Leigh Street, and W. W. Townsend was its principal. The school was built in the early 1920s and expanded around 1927. The origins of Armstrong date back to the late 19th century and the Richmond Normal and High School, whose noted alumni included Maggie L. Walker and John Mitchell. Armstrong High moved to its present location at 1611 North 31st Street in the early 1950s.

BROMM BAKING COMPANY, *516 East Marshall Street, 1940s.*

Long before Krispy Kreme™ and Dunkin' Donuts™ arrived in Richmond, doughnuts were available from Bromm Baking Company, founded in 1866. German-born Louis Bromm started the firm at 516 East Marshall Street, and it stayed in this location for nearly a century. The wholesale bakery was known for its breads and cakes, but its big sellers were Bromm's Old Virginia Fruit Cakes, in round tins. The business continued to distribute baked goods throughout town until the late 1950s.

CAPTAIN HERBERT'S SEAFOOD, *1701 Dock Street, 1940s.*

One could not find a more fitting setting in Richmond in which to purchase fresh fish than Captain Herbert's Seafood, which occupied a moored barge on the canal near the foot of 17th Street. Aside from fish sales there were limited dining accommodations as well. Captain Herbert's first opened in the early 1940s and weathered many James River floods, until the flood spawned by Hurricane Camille forced the business to close in 1969.

TRIPLE CROSSING, *Near 17th and Dock Streets, 1926.*

Believed to be the world's only triple-level train crossing, this trestle marked the junction of the Chesapeake and Ohio, the Seaboard Air Line, and the Southern railroads. The view of these mighty steam locomotives was taken from the south, a view now impossible to duplicate due to the placement of the 1990s floodwall.

ST. PHILIP AND DOOLEY HOSPITALS, *East Marshall Street, 1920s.*

The seven-storied St. Philip Hospital, built with community contributions, opened in 1920 as the nation's only general hospital for African-Americans and the first to house a nursing school for African-American women. In the early 1960s St. Philip's nursing program was incorporated into the Medical College of Virginia School of Nursing. For forty-five years St. Philip's provided medical care for African-Americans, until 1965, when it became MCV's East Hospital. In 1996 the Medical Sciences Building replaced the old hospital, yet it retains in its lobby the original portico inscribed, "Saint Philip Hospital," which was preserved from demolition.

Dooley Hospital, a contemporary of St. Philip's, was erected through the generosity of philanthropist Major James H. Dooley to be used as a hospital for children with infectious diseases. Over the years this building served MCV in various capacities. It too was razed during the Medical Sciences Building construction campaign, and its portal now stands as a monument on the courtyard between the new structure and MCV's Egyptian Building.

No Richmond parade seemed complete without the blue-and-white columns of the famed Richmond Light Infantry Blues. In this 1930 parade, the distinguished military unit passed by the ivy-covered facade of Centenary Methodist Church at 411 East Grace Street and its Sunday School addition, under construction.

RICHMOND LIGHT INFANTRY BLUES, *East Grace Street, 1930.*

RICHMOND HOWITZERS, *Howitzers Armory, 630 North 8th Street, 1920s.*

Much Howitzer training took place inside the confines of the armory on 8th Street. The Richmond Howitzers were established in 1859, and their first official assignment was in Harpers Ferry, following John Brown's uprising. The unit continued to represent Richmond militarily throughout the Civil War and in other military action through World War II, after which it became a unit of the Virginia National Guard. The vast armory was built in 1895 and utilized as such until it was razed and supplanted by the J. Sargeant Reynolds Community College downtown campus in 1981.

**ST. JOSEPH'S
CATHOLIC CHURCH
AND VAN DE VYVER
SCHOOL,** *700 Block
North 1st Street, 1940s.*

The first Catholic congregation formed for African-Americans in the South, St. Joseph's Church was established in the mid-1880s in Jackson Ward by Bishop John J. Keane of the Roman Catholic Diocese of Richmond. The church was constructed in the 700 block of North 1st Street, and a complex soon arose nearby, including a parish house; a Franciscan convent; and Van de Vyver Institute, the church school. The Institute, named for Bishop Keane's successor, offered courses in masonry, carpentry, business, and music, along with standard curriculum, and an estimated 3,500 or more African-American students matriculated there. Both St. Joseph's Church and Van de Vyver Institute closed in 1969. Demolition of the buildings followed, but the memories survive, evidenced by a late-1990s memorial, housing the old church bell, erected on the site by parish and school alumni.

FAMILY IN SLEIGH, *200 block East Grace Street, mid-1930s.*

A thirties "horseless carriage" and Walgreen Drug Store may not have been the perfect backdrop for this wintry family portrait, but a one-horse open sleigh after a Richmond snowfall—near 3rd and Grace Streets—alone is memorable.

CAPITOL BILLIARD PARLOR, *825 East Broad Street, 1927.*

By the late 1920s Peter Connella had opened a billiard parlor in a basement in the 800 block of East Broad. This view conjures up the typical image of a billiards establishment of the day—a crowded, almost claustrophobic, dimly lit, smoke-filled pool hall, with pipes suspended from a low ceiling. A short-lived venture, the parlor had closed by 1931.

Y.M.C.A.,
7th and Grace Streets, 1920s.

The Young Men's Christian Association, in Richmond since the mid-19th century, was located in the late 1880s at the corner of 6th and Main Streets. Around 1910 the organization constructed a new home at 7th and Grace Streets, where it served the city for thirty years, through World War I and the Depression. In the early 1940s the "Y" moved to a new facility at Foushee and East Franklin Streets. The building it vacated was subsequently torn down and replaced by a large addition to Thalhimers department store.

During World War II the Y.M.C.A. played an important role in caring for the troops by joining five other Richmond organizations to form the city's USO. The present "Y" has been at the same location for nearly sixty years, and in 1999 it is undergoing an expansion.

PRATT'S CASTLE, *324 South 4th Street, 1940s.*

William A. Pratt was barely a teenager when he came to America from England. He moved to Richmond in his late twenties and soon opened a daguerreian gallery on Main Street, which he ran from the mid-1840s to the late 1850s. In addition to photography, Pratt was a student of architecture and engineering, and in 1853, at the foot of 4th Street on Gamble's Hill, he built himself a whimsical, iron-clad, turreted residence that became known as Pratt's Castle. Alexander Gardner's well-known April 1865 panoramic photographs of Richmond from Gamble's Hill were taken from atop this castle. In 1865 Pratt sold the property and lived out his life near Waynesboro. What Pratt left behind in Richmond, however, aside from the fruits of his daguerreian artistry, was a conversation piece—a structure of which many have heard but have never seen, owing to its dismantling in 1957.

RICHMOND DAIRY,
*314-332 North Jefferson
Street, 1940s.*

The Richmond Dairy was established about 1890 and in the teens built a prime example of architecture reflecting the function of a building. The fanciful structure, sporting huge milk bottle replicas at three of its corners, housed the company and its home delivery service until the early 1970s. In 1999 the Jackson Ward landmark, through an extensive renovation, is being transformed into apartments.

VIRGINIA DAIRY, *1810-16 West Main Street, 1932.*

When home milk delivery was a way of life, glass milk bottles found their way to customers' doors first by horse-drawn wagons and later by motorized vehicles. Virginia Dairy began operations around 1920 and continued residential deliveries of dairy products in the Richmond area for nearly sixty years.

RICHMOND PROFESSIONAL INSTITUTE ART CLASS, *ca. 1938.*

Richmond Professional Institute grew out of the Richmond School of Social Work and Public Health, begun in 1917. Eight years later, in 1925, the school became a branch of the College of William and Mary and started to establish itself in the area of West Franklin and Shafer Streets. Within three years its famed School of Art began under the tutelage of Theresa Pollak, who would retire some forty years later. In the 1930s the institution opened the Costume and Interior Design schools, and other schools soon followed. In 1939 it officially became Richmond Professional Institute (RPI), although it remained a part of William and Mary for the next twenty-three years. RPI merged with the Medical College of Virginia in 1968 to form Virginia Commonwealth University.

Among the students sketching the model in this late 1930s image is a young Maurice Bonds, the future, longtime chairman of the Department of Art History.

VIRGINIA MUSEUM OF FINE ARTS ARTMOBILE, *Miller and Rhoads Department Store, 6th Street, 1967.*

The Virginia Museum of Fine Arts, founded in 1934, was built on the Boulevard at Grove Avenue, on the site of the Confederate Soldiers' Home, and has continued to expand there since that time. In 1953 it launched its first Artmobile, literally a museum on wheels traveling statewide to bring art and artifact exhibits to the people of the Commonwealth. As the program progressed, up to four Artmobiles were touring at the same time.

Artmobile III transported the "Treasures from the Guggenheim Museum" exhibit from September 1966 to January 1967 on the Collegiate Circuit, during which it visited Virginia college campuses. It made a stopover in downtown Richmond in front of Miller and Rhoads department store, the official exhibit sponsor. The Artmobiles ran until 1994, and they introduced the fine arts to thousands of Virginians for over four decades.

LIGHTHOUSE RESTAURANT,
1224 North Boulevard, ca. 1950.

Just down the Boulevard from Parker Field was the all-night Lighthouse Restaurant, specializing in hamburgers and ice cream. Opened around 1950 this Lighthouse Restaurant joined two others in Richmond, one on Hull Street and one downtown on 7th Street.

ESKIMO PIE TRUCK, *Lee Monument, 1950s.*

Eskimo Pie ice cream bars were produced first in the early 1920s in the Midwest, and they have since become the favorite frozen dessert of millions of consumers. Richard S. Reynolds, Sr.,'s U.S. Foil, precursor to Reynolds Metals Company, purchased the young midwestern company in 1924 and provided foil packaging for the new product. In the late 1930s Reynolds Metals headquarters transferred to Richmond from New York, and in 1954, Eskimo Pie Corporation came to town. For years the Eskimo Pie corporate offices were quartered in what became known as the Eskimo Pie Building at 6th and Main Streets, which was built around 1913 for the Richmond Chamber of Commerce and later occupied by the Atlantic Life Insurance Company. The corporate headquarters are now located in Chesterfield County's Moorefield Park office complex.

Lively decorated Eskimo Pie delivery trucks were a common sight on Richmond streets for years.

CIVIL WAR CENTENNIAL CENTER, *North 10th Street, 1960s.*

The Civil War Centennial Committee was established by Congress during President Dwight D. Eisenhower's administration, in preparation for the one-hundredth anniversary of the Civil War to be celebrated from 1961 to 1965. President Eisenhower selected the Committee members, and each state created their own commissions. Cities followed suit, and in 1959 Richmond Mayor A. Scott Anderson named the Richmond Civil War Centennial Committee, with J. Ambler Johnston as its chairman. A silver-domed visitor's center was constructed and conveniently located adjacent to Interstate 95, to assist in attracting visitors to Richmond's many Civil War historic sites. Among the accomplishments of the Richmond Committee were the organization of weekly tours of the various area Civil War landmarks, the presentation of a 19th-century ballet and a war-related historical drama, and the production of an impressive group of publications regarding Richmond during the war. After the centennial celebration the center was taken over by the Medical College of Virginia, and it now serves as a student cafeteria.

MOOERS MOTOR CAR COMPANY, *Showroom, 1114-1118 North Boulevard, ca. 1948.*

The large showroom sign said it all—enticing all to come to see the new 1948 Packards. Eddie Mooers, baseball player, manager, and later owner of the Richmond Colts, started Mooers Motors in the early 1920s, dealing in foreign cars and Packards. The Packard Motor Car Company traced its beginnings to 1899, and over the following six decades it produced some the most prestigious models in American automotive history. The familiar Packard slogan, "Ask the Man Who Owns One," became an integral part of Mooers Motors advertising ads. By the 1960s Packard production had ceased, but Mooers continued with their foreign car sales. Now known as Mooers Volvo, it is the oldest Volvo dealer in the state and serves Richmond from three locations.

RICHMOND BARBER SCHOOL, *721 West Broad Street, 1946.*

Anthony Seta opened the Richmond Barber School in 1946 on West Broad Street, and this portrait is undoubtedly of one of his first graduating classes. Low-priced haircuts were available from the student barbers, and the school operated at this site until the early 1960s.

SAUER GARDENS,
*Japanese Gardens,
1920s.*

**SAUER
GARDENS,**
*Monumental
Gardens, 1920s.*

They were places of beauty to go for a stroll, a high school graduation, or a wedding, and places to climb and scamper about for children. They were the Sauer gardens, planted in the 1920s by C. F. Sauer, Sr., the founder of the renowned spices and extracts company. As a means of giving back to his community, Sauer furnished these gardens with sculptures, plants, trees, flowers, and shrubbery that he had acquired during his global journeys. The Monumental Floral Gardens, laid out in the vicinity of Libbie Avenue and Broad Street, had an Italian flavor, with urns, statuary, and a reflecting pool, while the Japanese Gardens in Monument Avenue's 4300 block were a sanctuary resplendent with Japanese flora and ornamentation. As the years passed the gardens began to fade from existence. A condominium complex was constructed in the 1980s on the site of the Japanese Gardens, however many vivid memories of these fanciful grounds still linger.

AZALEA GARDENS, *Joseph Bryan Park, 1965.*

After the death of newspaper magnate Joseph Bryan in 1908, Isobel Stewart Bryan donated a large tract of land north of town to the City of Richmond in her husband's memory. This acreage became Joseph Bryan Park and has been used as a city park since that decade. A rite of spring for years was to visit the park when the azaleas bloomed. The breathtaking colorful array surrounding the fountained lake could only be outdone by the famous white azalea-formed Latin cross planted amidst a large bed of crimson azaleas.

FIRST DAILY PASSENGER FLIGHTS, *Byrd Airport, ca. 1930.*

The 1930s began with a boom in Richmond's air transportation. Within just a few years of the 1927 dedication of Byrd Airport, air passenger service became a daily occurrence via Eastern Air Transport, the forerunner of Eastern Airlines. Flights from Richmond to New York made four stopovers in between, including landings at Washington and Philadelphia. In tandem with the Richmond Greyhound Lines driver, the airliner crew welcomed the 1930s traveler with a smile and provided a full transportation service.

TANTILLA GARDEN AND TINY TOWN, *3817 West Broad Street, 1930s.*

Its list of headliners reads like a Who's Who from the annals of Big Band era history: Duke Ellington, the Dorseys, Fred Waring, Harry James, Glenn Miller, Benny Goodman, Guy Lombardo, Ozzie Nelson, and more. No less crowd pleasing were the hometown stars Bill Zickafoose and the Continentals, the bands of Babe Barnes and Jimmy Hamner, blind Charlie Wakefield at the piano, and tap dancer Pleasants "Snowball" Crump. All of this commuted to one word—Tantilla—and myriads of memories. Billed as "The South's Most Beautiful Ballroom," Tantilla Garden, approached from street level by a long staircase, opened in the early 1930s, with Tiny Town Bowling Alleys operating below. For more than three decades, through the Depression, World War II, and beyond, it was Richmond's hotspot of evening entertainment. In this noted nightclub, aside from the countless hours of nightly dancing that took place, many couples were engaged, many renditions of "Happy Birthday" were sung, scores of anniversaries were celebrated, and many long-lasting love stories were begun. The bands played to the delight of packed crowds, and before the days of air conditioning, a section of the roof curled back to provide dancing under the stars. The customary "Good Night, Sweetheart" signaled the last dance of the evening. Closing to the bittersweet melody of "Auld Lang Syne," the final dance at Tantilla Garden was held in March 1969.

**VIRGINIA STATE
FAIR MIDWAY,**
Strawberry Hill, 1960.

**VIRGINIA STATE
FAIR BOOTH,**
Old State Fairgrounds, 1939.

Exhibition buildings, livestock, competitions, entertainment, Deggeller mid-ways, circus acts, parades, equestrian events, car races, cotton candy, fried "Elephant Ears," sausage and peppers sandwiches—the Virginia State Fair has had it all over the years. State Fairs have been held in Richmond with relative regularity since the first organized exposition of 1854 at what is now Monroe Park. Five years later the fairgrounds removed west to Broad Street, where the Science Museum of Virginia (old Broad Street Station) now stands. For more than half a century, the fairs were held at this location, until 1906, when the Virginia State Fair Association was formed. For the annual event, the new organization leased from the city a more northerly tract of land between Hermitage Road and the Boulevard, the present location of the Diamond. On the new site a brick exhibition building, housing displays such as the A&P Coffee and T. W. Wood & Sons Seed exhibits depicted here in 1939, was

**VIRGINIA STATE
FAIR BOOTH,**
Old State Fairgrounds, 1939.

VIRGINIA STATE FAIR RACE TRACK, *Strawberry Hill, ca. 1960.*

erected initially along with a race track and grandstand, and additional structures were soon added. This exhibition building became known in the 1950s as the Arena, a venue for basketball games, trade shows, garden show, and even public roller skating.

State Fair activities were discontinued at wartime, but were resumed in 1946 at Strawberry Hill Farm, a new site north of town on Laburnum, under a new name and administration, the Atlantic Rural Exposition. The immense livestock building, Old Dominion Hall, designed by noted architect William Lawrence Bottomley, opened the following year. The Virginia State Fair has remained at this location since that time and now is also the site of the nationally acclaimed Richmond International Raceway.

finis coronat opus

VIRGINIA STATE FAIR PIGS, *Strawberry Hill, 1960.*

Our State Fair pigs have captured the moment...
We are at **the end** of the book!
We are at **the end** of the century!

After having had the privilege of
creating this book, we are more convinced
than ever that Richmond is
one of America's great cities —
and is well prepared for
the beginning
of the 21st century.

ACKNOWLEDGMENTS

The publication of a book is a group effort, and without the dedication, hard work, and assistance of many people, this volume would not have come to this point. Initially, we would like to thank our colleagues at Dementi Studio, who all had a hand in this publication: Laura Kinney, artist, for her help with subject identifications; Tayloe Moore, studio manager, for holding down the fort and assisting in every way possible along the way; Josefa Mulaire and Rich Nashette, our digital team, for their long hours of scanning and perfecting the images appearing in the book; Tracie Taylor, printer and artist, for producing prints of scores of images to help in the photograph selection process; Emory Waldrop, portrait photographer, for his encouragement throughout; and especially Erika Moore, studio assistant, for her enthusiastic and able research assistance. Our thanks also extends to those whose photography is included herein: Mark Mitchell, Hart Dementi, and Lanie O'Dell and to Beth Kronin of Graphics-3 for the cover design. We are thankful for the support of and excitement for the project shown by our publishers at The Dietz Press—Blackwell Smith, Wert Smith, and Robert Dietz—and their professional staff and for their tremendous help and faith in us to bring it all to fruition.

In the development of the book, Guy Swanson participated in initial discussions about the project, and his early input is greatly appreciated. A special thanks goes to Tucker Hill for his suggestions and guidance during the preparation of the manuscript. Bob Burchette and Marvin Heffner also rendered beneficial advice about the project. Ruth Ann Coski and Terri Hudgins generously gave of their time to read over the manuscript, offering extra sets of eyes and constructive enhancements, which we could not do without. We also wish to thank for their assistance and generosity in making available Foster and Dementi images from their collections: Dr. Charles F. Bryan, Jr., and Bryan Green from the Virginia Historical Society and William J. Martin from the Valentine Museum.

Research-wise, one cannot say enough about the helpfulness of the Reference Department of the Richmond Public Library and of Kathleen Albers of the *Richmond Times-Dispatch* research library. Other valuable assistance was received from Teresa Roane of the Valentine Museum, Terri Hudgins of the Museum of the Confederacy, Suzanne Durham and Jean McRae of the Virginia Department of Historic Resources, Doug Litts of the Virginia Museum of Fine Arts, and James R. Meier of *The Sporting News*. Dr. Francis Foster and Carmen Foster graciously shared time and information about the African-American experience in 20th-century Richmond, and L. Ray Ashworth assisted with some key photo subject identifications. Providing information about their institutions or companies were John Bagby III of Pollard and Bagby; C. Fair Brooks III of Brooks Transfer; Harold Groome of Groome Transportation; Florence Haskins, Virginia Aviation Museum volunteer; Jan Hathcock of the Library of Virginia; Roseann Hester of C. F. Sauer Co.; Skeeter Hickman of Julian's Restaurant; Nancy Jones of Bliley Funeral Homes; Bob King of Richmond Ford; Jeanne Lindholm of Circuit City; The Honorable Theodore J. Markow and Ted Markow of Markow Florist; Daniel Perkins of First African Baptist Church; Pat Ricketts of Owens and Minor; L. Gerald Roach of the Mutual Assurance Society of Virginia; Heather Smith of Ukrop's, along with Daniel Allen, Courtesy Clerk, and Carolyn, Matthew, and Andrew Elgin, Ukrop's customers; Bob Staples of Eskimo Pie; Dorothy Wagener of the University of Richmond; and James Walthall of First Baptist Church. For the assistance of all of these kind people, and of those whom we may have inadvertently omitted, we are most grateful.

Finally, our heartfelt gratitude extends to our families—our sounding boards—who have "eaten, lived, and breathed" this book with us every step of the way and who have endured more than their share of long work days, late nights, and microwaved dinners.

F. Wayne Dementi
M. Elisabeth Dementi
Corrine Pellegrin Hudgins

BIBLIOGRAPHY

*C*elebrate Richmond is a compilation of images from the photographic archives of Dementi Studio, and above all, it is a book of photographs—not a history book. The narratives have been written to give the reader more insight into the scenes depicted, but they are not, nor were they meant to be, comprehensive histories about the subjects they describe.

MAJOR SOURCES

The following general, reliable sources were used most extensively in the narrative research and preparations:

Antonelli, Lisa M. *Virginia: A Commonwealth Comes of Age*. Northridge, Ca.: Windsor Publications, Inc., 1988.

Dabney, Virginius. *Richmond: The Story of a City*. Garden City, N.Y.: Doubleday & Company, Inc., 1976.

Dulaney, Paul S. *The Architecture of Historic Richmond*. 2nd ed. Charlottesville, Va.: University Press of Virginia, 1976.

Loth, Calder, ed. *The Virginia Landmarks Register*. 3rd ed. Charlottesville, Va.: University Press of Virginia, 1986.

Lutz, Francis Earle. *Richmond In World War II*. Richmond: The Dietz Press, 1951.

Richmond City Directories, 1904-1999.

Scott, Mary Wingfield. *Houses of Old Richmond*. Richmond: The Valentine Museum,1941.

_____. *Old Richmond Neighborhoods*. Richmond: By the Author, 1950; 2nd reprint ed. Richmond: The Valentine Museum, 1984.

Tyler-McGraw, Marie. *At the Falls: Richmond, Virginia, and Its People*. Chapel Hill: The University of North Carolina Press, 1994.

Ward, Harry M. *Richmond: An Illustrated History*. Northridge, Ca.: Windsor Publications, Inc., 1985.

Winthrop, Robert P. *Architecture in Downtown Richmond*. Edited by Virginia Dabney. Richmond: Historic Richmond Foundation, 1982.

ADDITIONAL SOURCES

Bearss, Sara B. and Thompson, Patricia D. *Foster's Richmond*. Richmond: Virginia Historical Society, 1991.

Caravati, Charles M., M.D. *Major Dooley*. Richmond: [Published for the Maymont Foundation], 1978.

Carneal, Drew St.J. *Richmond's Fan District*. Richmond: Historic Richmond Foundation, 1996.

Chesson, Michael B. *Richmond After the War, 1865-1890*. Richmond: Virginia State Library, 1981.

"Circuit City Stores, Inc. Company History." 50th Anniversary News Release. Richmond, 1999.

"Circuit City 1949-1999: Celebrating Our 50th Anniversary." Anniversary timeline. Richmond, 1999.

Duke, Daniel L. *The School That Refused to Die: Continuity and Change at Thomas Jefferson High School*. Albany: State University of New York Press, 1995.

Edwards, Kathy; Howard, Esme; and Prawl, Toni. *Monument Avenue: History and Architecture*. Washington, D.C.: U.S. Dept. of the Interior, National Park Service, Historic American Buildings Survey, 1992.

"Empire Theatre Has Fourth Anniversary." Commemorative poster. Richmond, 1981.

Frassanito, William A. *Grant and Lee: The Virginia Campaigns 1864-1865*. New York: Charles Scribner's Sons, 1983; 2nd paperback printing, 1986.

Gallaher, Robin. "The 17th Street Farmers' Market." *Richmond Magazine*. August 1974, pp.32-45.

Ginsberg, Louis. *Photographers in Virginia 1839-1900*. Petersburg, Va.: By the Author, 1986.

Hale, Thomas F., and Manarin, Louis H. *Richmond: A Pictorial History from the Valentine Museum and Dementi Collections*. Richmond: Whittet and Shepperson, Printers, 1974.

"It Seems Like Only Yesterday". Special Commemorative Magazine. Richmond: *The Richmond News Leader*, May 30, 1992.

John Marshall High School: A Richmond Legend. Richmond: Dietz Press, 1985.

Kocher, A. Lawrence and Dearstyne, Howard. *Shadows in Silver*. New York: Charles Scribner's Sons, 1954.

Kollatz, Harry, Jr. "The Sauer Japanese Gardens." *Richmond Magazine*, January 1999, pp. 18-20.

Lee, Richard M. *General Lee's City: An Illustrated Guide to the Historic Sites of Confederate Richmond*. McLean, Va.: EPM Publications, Inc., 1987.

Lipscomb, Louise. "Jitterbugging Down Memory Lane—Tantilla Gardens Remembered." *Style*, August 4, 1987, p. 41.

Loth, Calder, ed. *Virginia Landmarks of Black History*. Charlottesville, Va.: University Press of Virginia, 1995.

Love, Richard. *Founded Upon Benevolence: A Bicentennial History of the Mutual Assurance Society of Virginia*. Anniversary publication. Richmond, 1994.

Manarin, Louis H. and Wallace, Lee A., Jr. *Richmond Volunteers, 1861-1865*. Richmond: Westover Press, 1969.

"Metro Richmond 1900-1999: A Century of Change." Commemorative section. *Richmond Times-Dispatch*, March 14, 1999, Section C.

O'Dell, Jeffrey M. *Inventory of Early Architecture and Historic and Archaeological Sites, County of Henrico, Virginia*. Richmond: Henrico County, Va., 1976.

100 Years: Pollard & Bagby, Inc., Realtors and Appraisers. Anniversary publication. Richmond, 1994.

Owens & Minor, Inc., 1882 and Beyond: A History of Service to the Healthcare Industry. Anniversary publication. Richmond, 1992.

Pepe, Phil. *The Yankees: An Authorized History of the New York Yankees.* Dallas: Taylor Publishing Company, 1995.

Pierce, Don. "The Great Canal Story: Richmond's Future May Be Locked in Her Past." *Richmond Surroundings,* April/May, 1990, pp 40-45.

Richmond News Leader. 1926-1989.

Richmond Times-Dispatch. 1910-1999.

Richmond, Va. Richmond Public Library. Newspaper Clippings Files.

Richmond, Va. The Valentine Museum. Vertical Files.

Richmond, Va. Virginia Department of Historic Resources. Architectural Survey Files.

Robert, Joseph C. *Ethyl: A History of the Corporation and the People Who Made It.* Charlottesville, Va.: University Press of Virginia, 1983.

Ryan, David D. with Rennie, Wayland W. *Lewis Ginter's Richmond.* 2nd printing. Richmond: By the Author, 1991.

Salmon, Emily J., and Edward D.C. Campbell, Jr., eds. *The Hornbook of Virginia History.* 4th ed. Richmond: Library of Virginia, 1994.

Sanford, James K., ed. *Richmond: Her Triumphs, Tragedies & Growth.* Richmond: Metropolitan Richmond Chamber of Commerce, 1975.

The C.F. Sauer Company: A Tradition of Quality Since 1887. Anniversary publication. Richmond, 1987.

Scott, Mary Wingfield and Catterall, Louise F. *Virginia's Capitol Square, Its Buildings and Its Monuments.* Richmond: The Valentine Museum, 1957.

Scott, Michael G. H. *Packard: The Complete Story.* Blue Ridge Summit, Pa.: Tab Books, Inc., 1985.

Seale, William. *Virginia's Executive Mansion: A History of the Governor's House.* Richmond: Virginia State Library and Archives, 1988.

"The United Virginia Bank Senior PGA." Official Program, September 8-14, 1986.

Utley, Arthur. "Slammin' Sam." *Virginia Golfer,* May/June 1999, pp. 12-15.

Valentine Museum. *Fifty years in Richmond 1898-1948, A Photographic Review.* Richmond: Miller & Rhoads, Inc. 1948.

Wallace, Lee A., Jr. *1st Virginia Infantry.* 3rd ed. Lynchburg, Va.: H. E. Howard, Inc., 1985.

Whiffen, Marcus. *American Architecture Since 1780: A Guide to the Styles.* Cambridge, Mass.: The M.I.T. Press, 1969.

WRVA: Serving You for 50 Years. Anniversary publication. Richmond, 1975.

INDEX

Booker-T Theatre, 26, 27
Borg, Bjorn, 36
Bottomley, William Lawrence, 28, 163
Boulevard, x, 39, 46, 47, 50, 51, 90, 154, 156, 162
Boys Shop, 5
Brady, Mathew, 8, 39
Braves, Richmond, 50
Broad Street, East, 12, 13, 18, 19, 30, 31, 46, 47, 56, 57, 59, 61, 62, 63, 64, 74, 91, 112, 116, 130, 131, 133, 138, 139, 149
Broad Street, West, 6, 7, 23, 26, 27, 40, 54, 55, 63, 74, 90, 94, 95, 129, 133, 136, 137, 157, 158, 161
Broad Street Methodist Church, 18, 19, 63
Broad Street Station, 6, 7, 24, 28, 36, 54, 110,119, 133, 137, 162
Brock, William, 23
Bromm Bakery, 143
Bromm, Louis, 143
Brook Road, xii, 36, 67, 92
Brookland Parkway, xi
Brooks Transfer and Storage Co., 90
Brooks, John W., 90
Brown, Les, 118
Brown's Island, 9
Bryan, John Stewart, 103
Bryan, Joseph, 102, 103; Park, 159
Byrd, Harry F., Sr., 113, 115, 119; Harry F. III, 124
Byrd, Richard E., 44, 45, 124
Byrd, William, Hotel, 7
Byrd Field/Airport, 44, 45, 124, 160 (see also Richmond International Airport)
Byrd Park, vii, 132 (see also Shields Lake, Swan Lake)
Byrd Street, 49
Byrd Street Station, 24, 49, 137
Byrd Theatre, vii

C

Canal (see Haxall Canal; James River and Kanawha Canal)
Canal Street, 24, 137
Cannon Memorial Chapel, University of Richmond, 40, 41
Capitol Billiard Parlor, 149
Capitol Square, xiv,13, 19, 49, 54, 60, 61,104, 113, 119
Capitol Street, 18, 60
Capitol Theatre, 55
Captain Herbert's Seafood, 143
Carneal & Johnston, 49
Carpenter, E. Rhodes and Leona B., 5
Carpenter Center for the Performing Arts, 5
Carrère & Hastings, 82, 96

Cary Street, vii; East, 15, 57, 58, 72, 73, 89, 100, 101
Central Fidelity Bank, 57
Central National Bank, 24, 30, 56,116
Chaplin, Charlie, 83
Charles Store, 116
Chesapeake & Ohio (C&O) R.R., 70, 144
Chesapeake & Potomac (C&P) Telephone, 89, 99
Chicken-in the Rough, vii
Churches [see Broad Street Methodist Church; Clay Street Methodist Church; Ebenezer Baptist Church; First African Baptist Church; First Baptist Church; First English Evangelical Lutheran Church; Grace Covenant Presbyterian Church; Hood Temple A.M.E. Zion Church; Seventh Street Christian Church (old); St. John's United Church of Christ; St. Joseph's Catholic Church; St. Paul's Episcopal Church]
Churchill, Winston, 119, 138
Circuit City Corporate Office, 75
City Hall (Old) (Courts Building) 13, 18, 19, 63; (new), 18, 24, 63
City Stadium, vii
Civil War Centennial Center, 155
Clay Street, West, 31
Clay Street Methodist Church, 31
Clean-up Paint-up Week, 112
Clinton & Russell, 87
Clover Room, vii, 129
Cohen Store, 116
College Street, 64, 65, 104
College of William & Mary, 152; Wren Building, 90
Colonial Studio, v
Colonial Theatre, 27
Colts, Richmond, 50, 117
Commerce Road, 73
Commonwealth Club, 96, 97
Commonwealth Park Suites Hotel, 17
Commonwealth of Virginia, 6, 13, 70
Confederate Memorial Association, 39
Confederate Memorial Literary Society, 39
Confederate Soldiers' Home, 108, 153
Confederate Veterans Reunion, 108
Connella, Peter, 149
Connors, Jimmy, 36, 125
Consolidated Bank & Trust (St. Luke's Penny Savings Bank), 30, 31
Continentals, The, 161
Cook, George M., 113
Coolidge, Calvin, 83
Cowardin, James A., 102
Cox Road, 101

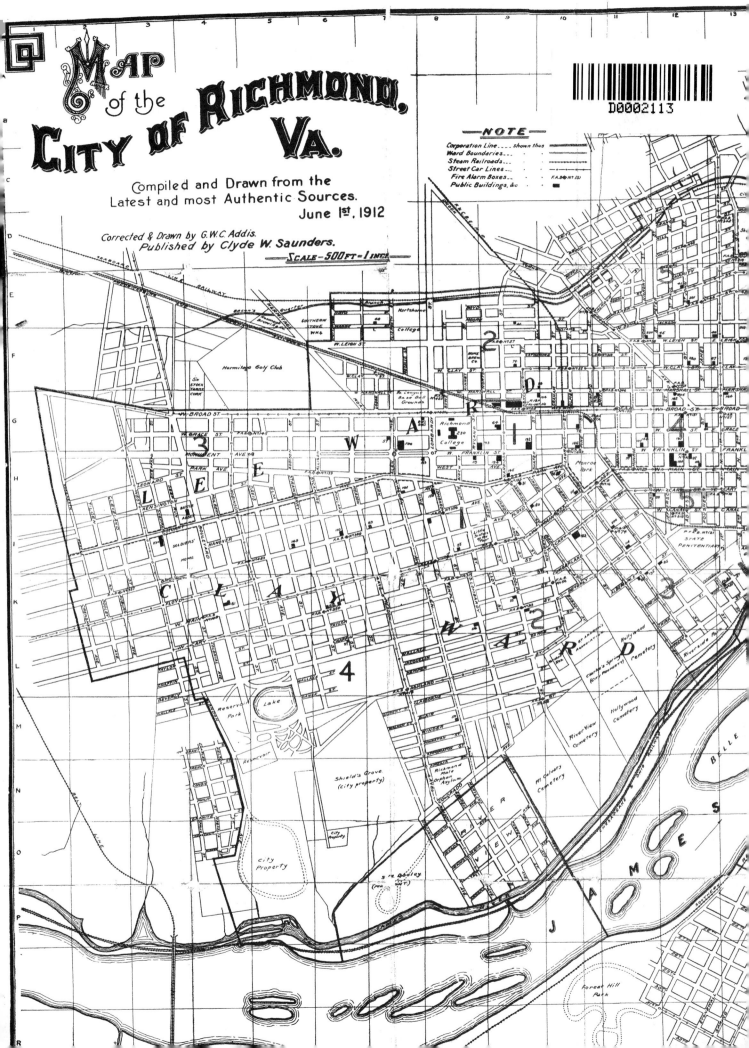

Map of the City of Richmond, VA.

Compiled and Drawn from the
Latest and most Authentic Sources.
June 1st, 1912.

Corrected & Drawn by G.W.C. Addis.
Published by Clyde W. Saunders.

SCALE—500 FT = 1 INCH

—NOTE—
Corporation Line .... shown thus
Ward Boundaries ...
Steam Railroads ...
Street Car Lines ...
Fire Alarm Boxes ... F.A.B. N° 151
Public Buildings, &c